Lesbian Choices

between men ~ between women
Lesbian and Gay Studies
Lillian Faderman and Larry Gross, Editors

between men ~ between women

lesbian and gay studies

Lillian Faderman and Larry Gross, editors

John Clum, *Acting Gay: Male Homosexuality in Modern Drama*

Gary David Comstock, *Violence Against Lesbians and Gay Men*

Laura Doan, ed., *The Lesbian Postmodern*

Allen Ellenzweig, *The Homoerotic Photograph: Male Images from Durieu/Delacroix to Mapplethorpe*

Lillian Faderman, *Odd Girls and Twilight Lovers: A History of Lesbian Life in Twentieth-Century America*

Linda Garnets and Doug Kimmel, eds., *Psychological Perspectives on Lesbian and Gay Male Experiences*

Richard D. Mohr, *Gays/Justice: A Study of Ethics, Society and Law*

Sally Munt, ed., *New Lesbian Criticism: Literary and Cultural Readings*

Timothy Murphy and Suzanne Poirier, eds., *Writing AIDS: Gay Literature, Language, and Analysis*

Noreen O'Conner and Joanna Ryan, *Wild Desires and Mistaken Identities: Lesbianism and Psychoanalysis*

Judith Roof, *A Lure of Knowledge: Lesbian Sexuality and Theory*

Alan Sinfield, *The Wilde Century: Effeminacy, Oscar Wilde and the Queer Moment*

Kath Weston, *Families We Choose: Lesbians, Gays, Kinship*

Lesbian Choices

claudia card

columbia university press

New York

columbia university press

new york   chichester, west sussex

Copyright © 1995 Columbia University Press
All Rights Reserved

Library of Congress Cataloging-in-Publication Data
Card, Claudia.
Lesbian Choices / Claudia Card.
p.   cm. — (Between Men ~ Between Women)
Includes bibliographical references and index.
ISBN 0–231–08008–5 (alk. paper)
1. Lesbianism.   2. Choice (Psychology)   I. Title   II. Series.
HQ75.5.C36   1995
305.48'9664—dc20   94-12527
CIP

Printed in the United States of America
c 10 9 8 7 6 5 4 3 2 1

between men ~ between women

lesbian and gay studies
Lillian Faderman and Larry Gross, Editors
Eugene F. Rice, Columbia University Adviser

Advisory Board of Editors

John Boswell, Yale University · History

Claudia Card, University of Wisconsin · Philosophy

Gilbert Herdt, University of Chicago · Anthropology, Sociology, Political Science

Barbara Johnson, Harvard University · Literature

Anne Peplau, University of Califorina, Los Angeles · Psychology

Rhonda R. Rivera, Ohio State University · Law

Between ~ Men Between Women is a forum for current lesbian and gay scholarship in the humanities and social sciences. The series includes both books that rest within specific traditional disciplines and are substantially about gay men, bisexuals, or lesbians and books that are interdisciplinary in ways that reveal new insights into gay, bisexual, or lesbian experience, transform traditional disciplinary methods in consequence of the perspectives that experience provides, or begin to establish lesbian and gay studies as a freestanding inquiry. Established to contribute to an increased understanding of lesbians, bisexuals, and gay men, the series also aims to provide through that understanding a wider comprehension of culture in general.

to the memory of my mother,

Achsah Susan Falconer Card, 1915–1972

and the futures of my nieces,

Melissa Jane Card

and

Ashley Susan Card

Contents

preface and acknowledgments   *xi*

Introduction: Finding My Voice—Reminiscence of an Outlaw   1

part one: constructing ourselves

  1. What is Lesbian Culture?   11

  2. Lesbian Attitudes and *The Second Sex*   36

  3. Choosing Lesbianism   47

  4. Lesbian Ethics   58

part two: lesbians in relationship: ups and downs

  5. Lesbian Friendship: Separations and Continua   83

  6. Horizontal Violence: Partner Battering and Lesbian Stalking   106

  7. Female Incest and Adult Lesbian Crises   131

part three: coming out: issues in a wider society

  8. Homophobia and Lesbian/Gay Pride   151

  9. The Military Ban and the ROTC: A Study in Closeting   169

10. Other People's Secrets: The Ethics of Outing   194
11. Sadomasochism: Charting the Issues   218

notes   239
selected bibliography   283
index   299

Preface & Acknowledgments

This book is the result of fifteen years' work in feminist and lesbian philosophy, fields that were very young when I began rethinking my life and my worlds in their contexts. From many in earlier worlds I gratefully acknowledge special gifts.

To my mother, Achsah Susan Falconer Card, who believed in me passionately from the moment of my conception and who taught me the power of words, and to my father, Walter Munro Card, who taught me to play and to argue, to my high school teacher and friend, Midge Pinkerton, who made all the difference at a critical moment in my education, and to the second home provided by my piano teacher, Emily Johnson, and then by her sisters, Adaline and Betty, I owe the feistiness, persistence, and basic optimism that have eventuated in this volume.

Treasured philosophical training and enthusiastic support came from my undergraduate teachers at the University of Wisconsin—Julius Weinberg (1908–1971), Gerald MacCallum (1925–1987), Robert Ammerman, William Hay, and especially, Marcus Singer. Together with my teachers at Harvard—John Rawls, Stanley Cavell, Willis Doney, Julius Moravcik, the late Henry Aiken—they became my models of philosophical style, creativity, discipline, and heresy. I have taken these gifts to heart.

To the Midwest Society of Women in Philosophy (SWIP) the essays in this volume are most directly and extensively indebted. SWIP provided welcoming forums and invaluable critical discussion for versions of chapter 2 and chapters 5 through 8. It has also enabled me to profit from vanguard work in progress by others. Most of all, SWIP has provided me colleagues in a field in which academic departments rarely have more than one philosopher. For years of sustaining friendship and for the example of their incalculably influential ovular work, I am deeply grateful to Marilyn Frye, María Lugones, Joyce Trebilcot, Sarah Hoagland, Jeffner Allen, Sandra Bartky, and Alison Jaggar. The collegiality of Chris Pierce (who flies to Midwest SWIP regularly from the East Coast), Lorraine Ironplow (who flies regularly from the West), Jacqueline Zita (on whose "male lesbians" essay Rush Limbaugh has recently fixated), Jacqueline Anderson, Naomi Scheman, and many more has also been invaluable.

Some contributions are more easily specified. An invitation from Joyce Trebilcot to review a book critical of lesbian sadomasochism helped break my writing block and produced a jump-start of chapter 11; an invitation from Peg Simons to do a joint session at the National Women's Studies Association convention stimulated an early version of chapter 1; another from Azizah al-Hibri to participate in a conference honoring Simone de Beauvoir yielded chapter 2; an invitation from Jeffner Allen to review a book on homophobia resulted in a preview of chapter 8, and a call for pieces on violence from Bat-Ami Bar On, a forerunner of part of chapter 6. Marilyn Frye brought me from New Zealand a book that I was unable to obtain in the United States, which also helped with chapter 6.

The University of Wisconsin Women's Studies Program provided me the special opportunity to teach a course on Lesbian Culture. It also provided a colloquium for chapter 9 and donated the use of the Women's Studies house for two SWIP conferences. I value support received over many years from colleagues Elaine Marks, Nellie McKay, Margarita Zamora, Virginia Sapiro, and former colleagues Evelyn Beck, Annis Pratt, and the late Ruth Bleier.

The Society for Lesbian and Gay Philosophy, initiated in 1989 by John Pugh and continuing with regular help from Richard Mohr, Noretta Koertge, Mark Chekola, and Lee Rice, has recently provided forums also for versions of chapters 3 and 11. Support in my home

Department of Philosophy—from the administrative services of John Moulton and Jim Anderson to the Aristotle and Plato citations supplied by Paula Gottlieb and Terry Penner—has facilitated my research, my teaching of lesbian feminist philosophy, and the hosting of two more SWIP conferences. Philosophy students, past and present, have added SWIP conferences to their already heavy course loads, and a new generation is preparing to carry SWIP into the twenty-first century. Generously sharing experiences, open to experimental pedagogy, ready with sympathetic criticism and warm support for work that does not always contribute much to fulfilling graduate and undergraduate program requirements, they have made my work rewarding. For such rewards, and more, I thank them, especially Lisa Badner, Chris Cuomo, Victoria Davion, Ruth Ginzberg, Amber Katherine, Ann Pooler, Jean Rumsey, Lorena Saxe, Lynne Tirrell, and a memorable class from the spring of 1979 at Dartmouth College.

I have also benefited from the scholarship and friendship of men working on issues variously analogous to issues discussed herein. I have learned from the diverse philosophical perspectives of Bernard Boxill, David Theo Goldberg, Howard McGary, Lucius Outlaw, and Lawrence Thomas, through their work on ethical issues and on meanings and forms of race, racism, ethnicity, and culture. The books in gay philosophy, *Gays/Justice* and *Gay Ideas*, by Richard Mohr—who has often shared with me his work in progress and has read and responded to my own faster than anyone—set an important context for work in part 3 as well as for some of the earlier chapters. While he was general editor of the series Between Men-Between Women, he mobilized me to write this book and was earlier a moving force behind what became chapters 3, 8, and 9. I have learned much also from the work of Jim Steakley, John Boswell, Randy Shilts, Michelangelo Signorile, and Edward Stein. Larry Gross generously shared with me a prepublication draft of his book, *Contested Closets: The Politics and Ethics of Outing*. Chapter 9 profited from Timothy Murphy's helpful questions and from his gifts of timely clippings from the *Windy City Times*, as well as from clippings sent by Richard Mohr and by Chris Pierce.

Chapters 1, 2, 8, and 10 benefited from friendly interaction with other audiences outside of Midwest SWIP at several universities, including first and foremost my own Department of Philosophy at the University of Wisconsin, and also audiences at the University of British Columbia, the University of Buenos Aires, Cornell University, the Free University in Amsterdam, Harvard, Humboldt State, Universities of Illinois at Urbana and Chicago, the University of Pittsburgh, Pennsylvania State, and SUNY-Buffalo.

A University of Wisconsin sabbatical in 1992–93 enabled me to complete several new chapters and revise others during what Wisconsin optimistically (or euphemistically) calls "the Spring semester." Portions of the manuscript were read and commented on during late stages by Jeffner Allen, Bat Ami Bar-On, Sandra Bartky, Lorna Benjamin, Chris Cuomo, Vicky Davion, Marilyn Frye, Ruth Ginzberg, Paula Gottlieb, Sarah Hoagland, María Lugones, Elaine Marks, Richard Mohr, Timothy Murphy, Nanci Newton, Annis Pratt, Janice Raymond, Ruthann Robson, Donna Shalala, Joyce Trebilcot, and Jacqueline Zita, for whose thoughtful responses and helpful research references I am most grateful.

For permission to reprint my previously published work, I am happy to acknowledge Garland Publishing, 717 5th Ave., New York, N.Y., for material used in chapter 4 from "Lesbian Ethics," *The Encyclopedia of Ethics*, ed. Lawrence C. Becker with Charlotte B. Becker, 1992; The Haworth Press, 21 East Broad Street, Hazleton, Pa., for material used in chapters 3 and 9, first published in *The Journal of Homosexuality* 23, no. 3 (Fall 1992), 39–51 and 27, nos. 3/4 (forthcoming); *The Journal of Social Philosophy*, Trinity University, San Antonio, Texas, for material used in chapter 11 from "Sadomasochism and Sexual Preference," Special Issue on Feminist Philosophy, ed. Joyce Trebilcot, 9, no. 2 (Summer 1984), 42–52; Oxford University Press, 200 Madison Ave., New York, N.Y., for material used in the Introduction from *Falling in Love with Wisdom: American Philosophers Talk about Their Calling*, ed. David D. Karnos and Robert G. Shoemaker, 1993, pp. 165–68; and the Pergamon Press, Maxwell House, Fairview Park, Elmsford, N.Y., for chapter 2, which first appeared in *Women's Studies International Forum* 8, no. 3 (1985), Special Issue featuring *Hypatia*, a Journal of Feminist Philosophy, 209–14.

In chapters 1, 5, 6, and 8, I have drawn freely on my earlier essays published as "Lesbian Culture before 1940: Search and Re/Search," *Feminist Collections: Women's Studies Library Resources in Wisconsin* 3, no. 3 (Spring 1982), 18–24; "Female Friendship: Separations and Continua," *Hypatia* 3, no. 2 (Summer 1988), 123–30; "Lesbian Battering," *APA Newsletter on Feminism and Philosophy*: Special Issue on Violence, ed. Bat Ami Bar-On, 88, no. 1 (November 1988), 3–7; "Defusing the Bomb: Lesbian Ethics and Horizontal Violence," *Lesbian Ethics* 3, no. 3 (Summer 1989), 91–100; and "Why Homophobia?" *Hypatia* 5, no. 3 (Fall 1990), 110–17.

Special thanks to Ann Miller and to Joan McQuary for their expert guidance, suggestions, and care in the editing of the manuscript. For companionship and nourishing conversation during the incubation of this work long ago, I thank Ellen Cronan Rose and Vivian Foss. For constant friendship and for advice and support at various stages in the writing of these chapters, I am especially grateful to Sharon Keller, Victoria Davion, and Joann Pritchett.

Lesbian Choices

Introduction

finding my voice: reminiscence of an outlaw

Often, when I am asked how I came to be who I am, the subject is my lesbianism. In 1990, however, I was asked to write about how I came to be a philosopher. What emerged was the story of my learning to integrate being a philosopher-teacher at a state university with being a lesbian-feminist and, finally, to write in a voice that I could call my own. As this book integrates some of my early philosophical research with more recent lesbian-feminist theorizing, an expansion of that tale seems a good way to begin.

Becoming a philosopher can be a lifelong process. This is a story of how I learned to speak with my own voice as a lesbian feminist philosopher with a certain set of histories. It is not about how I first chose philosophy—a tale, in my case, of adoration for teachers and texts—but about how I have been able to continue with it. I have had to find and help maintain communities of women to keep growing philosophically. The result has been intellectual development in directions I could not have foreseen.

In the early 1970s, I was in my early thirties. Soon after I was tenured at the University of Wisconsin, I developed a writing block, which was to last several years. I had taught and written through reflection on the written word, but not otherwise out of my life experience. During the late 1960s and early 1970s I taught an undergraduate course, "Crime and Punishment," which was popular and seemed highly successful. My students then were being arrested for crimes ranging from window-trashing on State Street to ripping the flag from the top of Bascom Hall in the heart of the liberal arts campus. A small "Stop 'n' Shop" grocery near campus was nicknamed "Stop 'n' Rob." When a large Kroger-chain grocery near campus went up in flames, a local counter-culture news sheet referred to the bystanders exchanging their "Kroger smiles." Some had graver encounters with crime. A woman student in my honors introductory philosophy class was found murdered in front of Sterling Hall in the spring of 1968, apparently interrupted on an early morning campus walk.[1] Two years later, a male student, also in my honors introductory class, made the FBI's Ten Most Wanted list in connection with the 1970 bombing of Sterling Hall—home of the Army Math Research Center—which killed physicist Robert Fassnacht.[2]

After writing an undergraduate thesis *and* a graduate dissertation on theories of punishment and then publishing an article defending mercy and another defending retributive justice in legal punishment, I had begun to wonder what it meant that I was mesmerized by such topics. I had never been inside a prison. I had never witnessed an execution. I had never even attended a criminal trial. Nor was I close to anyone who, so far as I knew, had. None of that deterred me. I had read many books and articles that taught me to identify with the perspectives of lawmakers who may never have had such experience, either. A combination of public events and events in my personal life soon led me to see that I did not yet have, or know, my own philosophical voice. I did not yet know how to speak or write from my position in the universe of space and time but only from my position in a universe of books.

My parents divorced after thirty-two years of marriage and four children and then died within eight months of each other in the early 1970s—first my mother, during the year that I was tenured. I began thinking in new ways about who I was, perhaps deciding who I wanted to be.

During the late 1960s and early 1970s, two things were sending young white middle-class U.S. citizens to prison, many of them students, for whom the experience proved a field trip to study the criminal justice system. They were mostly men who might otherwise have arrived at my point in their careers with no more firsthand knowledge of that system than I had. The two things for which they went to prison were marijuana and war resistance. Soon, my "Crime and Punishment" class was populated by students who had an intimate acquaintance with the workings of criminal justice and related institutions. This became evident when several voluntarily presented their papers to the class. I had asked the students to begin with the point of view of someone who might be accused of a crime or someone who might be victimized by a crime and to search for a solution acceptable from both points of view. A devoted student of John Rawls, I sought wisdom in the area of justice through the hypothetical reasonings of ideal legislators who would identify with both sorts of possibilities. At that time I assumed that since in reality anyone might either be accused of a crime or be victimized by one, everyone should be motivated to empathize with both perspectives.

The students' presentations were autobiographical, highly personal, and very moving. They were not typical philosophy textbook examples. Men spoke first. One had been sentenced to a drug rehabilitation center. Another was confined in a Navy brig for the crime of smoking grass. One was assigned guard duty at the Camp Pendleton prison. Others were arrested in war-related protest demonstrations. One was assigned alternative service as a Conscientious Objector. Encouraged by their classmates' frankness, women spoke up who might otherwise have kept silent. One, institutionalized at the age of thirteen by her father for being out of his control, had recently been released *in her mid-thirties* thanks to the efforts of a woman worker in the institution. Another, found "not guilty by reason of insanity" of the murder of her husband, had done time in an institution for persons so declared. The last speaker was a young man convicted of child abuse who had done time in both a regular penitentiary and an institution for the criminally insane, as required by the law of his state. Not claiming innocence and yet outraged at how he was judged and treated, he appeared little more than a child himself. The class, visibly disturbed, tried to engage him in thinking how to protect children from abuse.

The students tried, with amazing good will, to take up the perspectives of the assigned journal articles and textbooks. They tried to see crime and punishment through the eyes of the designers of penal institutions and to make that vision fit with those of people liable to suffer from such institutions. In doing so, they struggled with perspectives that did not fit their own well. I was struck by discrepancies between the results of their attempts and the assignment as I had originally envisaged it. Most of the philosophical literature that I had assigned seemed inadequate to get at the points of view of either those likely to be accused or those likely to be victimized (often, of course, the same people), much less to reconcile those points of view.[3] Instead, it offered the visions of men writing from the safety of not having to think much about *either* potentiality, overseers involved in neither the workings of penal systems nor the activities calling their machinery into action. Who *was* most liable to being accused of crimes or being victimized by crimes? Not (conventional, economically privileged, mostly over forty, white male) legislators, but, rather, the very young, the homeless, the poor, people of color (in this part of the world), women attempting to protect themselves or their children against battery and sexual abuse, rebellious women who refused the "protection" of men.

Take myself, for example—a young lesbian (thereby, an outlaw) from the rural village of Pardeeville (Wisconsin), catapulted by scholarships from village high school to state university and then by fellowships to Ivy League graduate school. I was living in one of the highest crime areas of the city in which I taught, without a car, with no more than the simple hardwon financial security of a monthly paycheck, in an abusive, closeted lesbian relationship. I knew firsthand the fear of murder. How did my philosophizing connect with the realities of my life outside the classroom and the library? Surely it was an escape. I began to suspect that much of philosophy as I had learned it served interests opposed to my own. A grant that I received to study the history of U.S. penitentiaries and other prisons helped me confirm that suspicion in detail. How could I avoid abandoning or compromising my truths while making "satisfactory progress" as a philosopher? I had reached a point in my life where I seemed unable to do either.

As my mother was dying, the University was deciding the fate of my employment, and I was stumbling through the crises of my first explicitly lesbian relationships, I also embarked on the first of two stages of feminist awareness. Both stages required intellectual interaction with women. I knew almost no other faculty women. There was no Women's Studies at Wisconsin (or most places) prior to 1975. A closeted lifestyle precluded my developing close friendships, even with the other nontenured woman in my department. My first intellectual community of women was a Conciousness Raising (CR) group that met weekly for three years, consisting of mostly graduate students in philosophy and in computer science. I was the only faculty member. The nonhierarchical structures, narrative style, and respect for emotion that characterized CR groups were things that many of us later tried to bring into our classrooms: we experimented with "rotating chair," encouraged autobiographical writing in philosophy papers, took responsibility for exploring anger and fear in the classroom.[4]

A second stage of feminist awareness began when I connected with the Midwest Society of Women in Philosophy (SWIP), two years after the CR group disintegrated. The SWIP connection precipitated my exit from the abusive relationship. I was able then to "come out" in my work and at my workplace, thereby also becoming less vulnerable to future abuse. I became less blocked in my writing as I began integrating my "life" with my work. I began finding answers to the question why I was spellbound for so many years by punishment and related topics, some of which will become evident in various chapters of this book. The CR group, SWIP, and, later, Women's Studies helped me heal and heard me into speech, enabling me to find and develop my voice as a philosopher who is, not incidentally, a semi-rural white-anglo woman, a woman-lover, and a survivor of domestic abuse—as well as the fortunate recipient of gifts enabling me to integrate these histories positively and put them to constructive use.

I found my (physical) speaking voice—a highly symbolic event—in delivering my "coming out" paper. On a warm day in May 1978, wearing a silver double-axe (the labrys, a symbol of ancient Amazons) that swung on its chain as I leaned over my paper, I presented my "Feminist Ethical Theory: A Lesbian Perspective" to an overflow crowd of philosophers, Women's Studies faculty, students, and community dykes in a Law School auditorium at the University of Minnesota. It was thanks to Kathy Addelson (then, Kathy Parsons) that I had the opportunity to do this. She was invited to present a paper on moral revolution, to which I had responded at an earlier conference, and she insisted, as a matter of feminist and anarchist principle (opposing hierarchies and heroes), that I be invited as well. The upshot was that each of us was invited to present a major paper and to comment on the other's major paper. Also, as a matter of feminist anarchist principle, we occupied the stage jointly for both presentations. That level of support gave me new courage.

My paper was excessively long. After years of silence, there was too much that I wanted to say. But the audience was so attentive that you could almost hear them breathing. At the beginning, I announced, as usual, that anyone in the back who could not hear me should wave a paper or call out, and that I would try to speak up. To my surprise, I began speaking from deep inside, without effort, in a large voice that I had not known was there. People later said they heard me in the hallways, even outside through open doors and windows. Anger fueled that voice, but also confidence (little inspires confidence like truth-speaking), despite some early anticipation of scorn ("what has that to do with *philosophy*?") from those I had been used to identifying as my audience. In fact, this audience received and discussed my presentation with more warmth and respect than I had observed elsewhere in professional philosophy colloquia.

I am no longer preoccupied with the perspectives of ideal legislators, nor with punishment, nor with the criminal justice system. Yet, in my current work, I draw freely upon what I learned in those studies. While supported by the grant to study prisons, I made a point to learn all I could about women's prisons and women in prisons, accepting invitations to give public lectures on the topic (one broadcast by a local radio station). Some of what I learned emerges in chapter 5 on friendship in the discussion of women prisoners' erotic bonding and the custom of "familying." In studying theories of punishment and autobiographies of prisoners while I was myself living through an abusive relationship, I began making connections between the way punishing works and the way battering works that emerge in chapter 6 in the discussions of battering and stalking.

The focus of my attention, however, has turned more to the goods and evils of interpersonal relationships and informal practices among those whose life situations are more like mine than like those of men who are apt to become legislators. My vision of philosophy has also evolved. I am no longer so absorbed in "eternal" or universal truths.[5] I seek wisdom not in relation to the abstraction of human life considered simply as human but in relation to lives fleshed out as gendered, as members of species, as having certain ethnic, economic, and religious backgrounds, even sexual orientations—things that vary, are *not* universal. A decade after affiliating with the Women's Studies Program, I began teaching environmental ethics and affiliated with the University's Institute for Environmental Studies. I still teach from books, but with more varied authors. I have even begun to write books. But I also teach from my life, and my writing flows from that life (with an awareness of its finitude) as well as from my reading (which is endless).

The audiences I now usually address in my work are no longer composed first of all of men who are oriented toward the men who have been conventionally selected as representative of humanity—many of whose works I nonetheless continue to read with profit. My primary audiences—those "in my head" as I write—now are composed of those who are in various ways more nearly my life-experience peers: mostly women, many lesbians, all with points of view shaped by surviving and resisting sexism, many shaped by surviving and resisting racism and other forms of oppression. They are my "juries" in the sense that their evaluations help keep me honest and growing. They enable me to write; they make me want to. I worry less how to make "satisfactory progress" as a philosopher. And I work productively, without fear of running out of things to say before time runs out in which I can say them.

Part One

constructing ourselves

Chapter 1

what is lesbian culture?

The 1970s was a decade of flourishing and experimentation for lesbian culture in the United States. Lesbian ingenuity created a kaleidoscope of alternative institutions, including music festivals, campgrounds, educational institutes, archives, small presses, periodicals, bookstores, coffeehouses, and more. Some were short-lived. Many survived. In October 1974, the Ambitious Amazons began mailing the *Lesbian Connection* newsletter (published by the *Elsie* Publishing Institute), from East Lansing, Michigan, "Free to Lesbians." Eventually, they requested modest donations, suggesting an amount but always adding "more if you can, less if you can't." In 1975, women in New York City issued a newsletter announcing the new Lesbian Herstory Archives (LHA), "to preserve for the future all expressions of our identity— written, spoken, drawn, filmed, photographed, recorded."[1] In June 1992, the LHA Newsletter announced the purchase of its long-awaited home, a magnificent building in Brooklyn.[2] The Michigan Music Festival, featuring the latest in lesbian music, held its first August camp session in 1976 and has continued every year, drawing as many as 9,000 by the early 1980s from many parts of the planet and by the

1990s, communicating by bumper sticker, "See you in August." In 1978, Liz Kennedy and Madeline Davis began their Buffalo Oral History project, resulting in 1993 in the book, *Boots of Leather, Slippers of Gold: The History of a Lesbian Community*.[3]

My files also contain a brochure from the Lesbian-Feminist Study Clearinghouse (LFSC), established in 1978 by Coralyn Fontaine at the University of Pittsburgh, on whose editorial board I served, with Becky Birtha, Peg Cruikshank, Madeline Davis, Karla Jay, Julia Penelope, and others. Lasting into the early 1980s, the LFSC was "an exchange mechanism for the sharing of Lesbian-Feminist vision, perspectives, and scholarship" through such materials as "descriptions and 'how-to' explanations of Lesbian-Feminist community projects, programs, political actions; speeches; course or workshop outlines; essays; drafts of articles; reprints from out-of-print or hard-to-get periodicals and newspapers; conference papers, etc."[4] Thirty-seven items, including unpublished articles and syllabi, could be ordered for a nominal fee.

The experimental Women's Learning Institute of the Maiden Rock Collective of Minneapolis held workshops in the summer of 1978 on its farm at Maiden Rock, Wisconsin.[5] A convention held March 17–19, 1978, in Los Angeles founded the National Lesbian Feminist Organization, that soon had branches in several states, including four in Wisconsin, two in Colorado, and one each in Arizona and Louisiana.[6] Like the LFSC, this organization did not survive. And yet, the spurt of cultural growth to which it belonged produced contacts among lesbians from coast to coast, even internationally. Lesbian life has not been the same since.

Culture vs. Cultures

I hear the question, "What is lesbian culture?" with the emphasis on *lesbian*. And I hear "culture" not necessarily as *a* culture, or culture*s*, but as lesbian developments within many cultures that would not usually be aptly described themselves as lesbian. "Culture" has many meanings. It is, for example, ambiguous between "the behaviors and beliefs characteristic of a particular social, ethnic, or age *group*," on the one hand and, on another, "the sum total of ways of living built up by a group of human beings and *transmitted from one generation to another*."[7] There has been little opportunity for lesbian culture in the second sense. Even with respect to the first sense, lesbians are not *a* social group but many social groups or, as I will suggest, a "family" of social groups. By studying lesbian culture as the behaviors and beliefs characteristic of many groups of lesbians, preserving and appreciating what we find and passing it on, we may contribute to the development of lesbian culture in the second sense.

Thus far, "lesbian culture" has consisted mostly of developments that are interesting as lesbian, although usually they have occurred in the midst of other cultures and are therefore usually also interesting from other points of view as well. When Ann Ferguson asked, "Is there a lesbian culture?" she apparently had in mind by "a culture" a social group distinguished by such things as a "common language, values, habits, rituals, arts, religion, philosophy, and so forth."[8] To judge by historical records, lesbians have seldom had such group cohesiveness or had it for long (even in recent decades), only a fraction of lesbians have belonged to such groups, and few such groups have been in mutual contact. Yet, lesbians have had a variety of social practices and relations, local customs, vocabularies, symbols, and so on. Individuals, couples, and neighborhoods have left writings, artifacts, and records reflecting their lives and insights as lesbians.[9] If, as Ann Ferguson notes, discontinuities between lesbian cultures make it misleading to speak of lesbian culture as though it referred to the culture of a unified social group, lesbian culture as developments within many cultures exhibits even further discontinuity in the contributions of those who never belonged to anything that could even be called *a* lesbian culture. The difficulties of establishing enduring lesbian social connections and preserving lesbian knowledge intergenerationally are salient in lesbian history (or, herstory).

Lesbian cultural developments—novels and poetry, autobiography, music and art, cuisine, artifacts, social networks and customs—have been routinely excluded from or rendered invisible in public education. They have been omitted entirely or included only under categories other than lesbian, leaving connections to lesbian life left unexplored, typically unmentioned. I first raised the question, "What is lesbian culture?" in creating a course on the subject, which I then taught for a decade, to begin to remedy this gap in public education. I continue to raise the question in thinking about the creation of lesbian studies programs in colleges and universities. For decades, when academic attention was paid to lesbians at all, it was from the points of view of hostile outsiders or, at best, of scholars who identified neither with nor as lesbians. What is needed for an empathetic study of lesbian culture is a willingness to enter into the points of view of those who live it, to study the literatures, the histories and the art created by lesbians (and by women for whom lesbian connections have been significant in their lives), to understand lesbian practices in what Oxford philosopher of law H. L. A. Hart called their "internal aspects."

In a justly famous book, *The Concept of Law,* H. L. A. Hart distinguished between "internal" and "external" aspects of rules.[10] The "external aspect" consists of "regular uniform behavior which an observer could record." This, he held, is something rules share with habits. The "internal aspect" consists of "a critical reflective attitude to certain patterns of behavior as a common standard" which displays itself "in criticism (including self-criticism), demands for conformity, and in acknowledgments that such criticism and demands are justified, all of which find their characteristic expression in the normative terminology of 'ought,' 'must,' and 'should,' 'right' and 'wrong.' " This, he held, differentiates rules from habits. To be more than reports on lesbian habits, or studies of lesbians as a curious species, studies of lesbian culture need to search out the internal aspects of lesbian life, its norms and values as experienced by those who have appealed to them. Although often reluctant to use the language of "ought," "must," and "should," lesbians have nevertheless frequently developed flexible norms and standards of evaluation, such as "more if you can, less if you can't." To appreciate their shaping of lesbian life, it is important to uncover writings, artifacts, and other records of lesbians and empathetic friends who take an "internal" point of view, who see themselves as making choices in accord with (or in violation of) norms and values.

Insiders *can*, of course, *adopt* a merely external point of view. Many do when they want to "pass." Thus, not every cultural production by lesbians is of interest to an empathetic study of lesbian culture. Nor is it absolutely necessary to be a lesbian to have access to "inside" views. However, since lesbians often have been compelled to hide, one may need to interact with lesbians in a fairly intimate (not necessarily sexual) way, to be trusted and received as a kind of "insider"—as, for example, children or siblings of lesbians—to have access to such views. What is required is less a lesbian identity than a willingness to identify with lesbians.

Teaching lesbian culture requires teaching detective work, which presupposes distinctions between how things appear and how they really are. Teaching detection includes teaching how to identify what has been deliberately censored or encoded as well as how to perceive ordinary things that others have missed. Both require the ability to take internal points of view on lesbian life.

As classroom exercises in detection, I have done the following. After showing an uncensored video of the 1931 German film *Mädchen in Uniform*, I have read to the class sections at one time cut by censors for U.S. viewers to remove evidence of the film's lesbian content.[11] I then asked students to consider, if they wanted to remake an obviously lesbian film into a heterosexual one, or disguise it so that it could "pass," what they would change and why, and also how they might leave clues for lesbian viewers. I have also read to the class a nineteenth-century poem written by an unhappy newly married woman to a dear woman friend.[12] The poem encodes a message opposite to its apparent message. At face value, it prattles on about the new bride's ecstasy. Decoded by reading every other line, the poem says she is miserable and her husband an alcoholic. We have then read aloud Gertrude Stein's short story, "Miss Furr and Miss Skeene," which sprinkles the word "gay" throughout at a time (the 1920s) when "gay" was a code term.[13] This story, like the poem, can be read as encoding a tale opposite in meaning to its surface tale. A well-known Stein critic interprets the story as the sad tale of a woman trying desperately to be "gay" after her friend has left. A footnote acknowledges that "gay" also sometimes means "homosexual" but ignores the implications for the point of the story.[14] This critic reads only from an external point of view, diagnosing, like a psychiatrist, the behavior of the characters, not considering what "gay" might mean *to* them or to lesbian readers. "Gay" can be heard not merely as descriptive but as a normative term, suggesting social constructions.

Lesbian Studies without caricature or distortion requires empathetic study of who lesbians have been, who our "ancestors" and "cousins" have been, what vocabularies we have used, how we have survived, how we have connected, how and why we have failed to connect. Such study takes seriously implications of suppression, censorship, self-censorship, and encoding. It recognizes societies that respected same-sex intimacy, acknowledging it in vocabularies that lack easy translation into languages of oppressive societies.

Ann Ferguson proposed an understanding of lesbian cultures as cultures of resistance (p. 138). This proposal excludes the lesbian culture of societies that respected lesbians, for example (as she notes), that of Sappho of Lesbos. It would exclude the same-sex primary relationships of women of many pre-Columbian Native American nations. To exclude such paradigmatically lesbian cultural material as Sappho's poetry would not fill the need my course was designed to meet. So narrow a conception suggests that lesbians distinguish themselves and develop social cohesiveness only around political insurgency or resistance. From the inside, however, we find the focus not exclusively, nor even primarily, on resistance to oppression, even when resistance is a prerequisite to much else. Lesbians' interests have often been primarily in women. The political consciousness we find is frequently disappointing. I would neither restrict lesbian culture to lesbian culture*s* nor restrict lesbian culture*s* to cultures of resistance. Lesbian culture is not only about past injustice. It is also about what lesbians know (and wonder) about the potentialities of society and about female relationships.

The Ethnicity of "Lesbian" and Respect for Diversity

Any word with a history—or herstory—has ethnic roots. "Lesbian" is no exception. Its roots are in the Aeolic Greek of Sappho of Lesbos, who was born (or flourished, by some accounts) about 612 BCE on the island of Lesbos in the Aegean Sea near present-day Turkey and in the city of Mitylene, which Diodorus Siculus said was founded by Libyan Amazon Queen Myrinna generations before the Trojan Wars. Many "lesbians" might find, with Audre Lorde, that an island in the Caribbean is more meaningful as a symbol for their identity than this island in the Aegean.[15] Paula Gunn Allen, Judy Grahn, and others have pointed out that words from Native American languages for women who were encouraged to dress like the men of their nations, fight in battles, and have wives seem to mean both more and less than "lesbian" has come to mean in English.[16] Judy Grahn has written of distortions introduced by Europeans who translated the Oglala Sioux "Winkte," the term for highly respected cross-dressing medicine men, as "berdache," a French word meaning "slave boy."[17] Some languages have no word that translates naturally as "lesbian" or "gay." Yet, the concept of "lesbian culture" delineated above seems to presuppose that we can abstract lesbian culture from many cultures. Is that supposition nonsensical? Arrogant? Culturally imperialistic? Is it disrespectfully assimilationist to identify as "lesbian" such non-Indo-European woman-loving women as the Mohave *Hwame*? I will argue that it need not be so, although these are dangers that call for sensitivity.

There appear to be two problems, a logical one and an ethical one. The logical problem is whether it makes *sense* to apply the term "lesbian" outside its cultural home. The ethical problem, presupposing the intelligibility of such usage, is whether doing so is disrespectful. Gay scholars, taking a sexual liberationist point of view, often focus on the logical question. Among feminist lesbians, I find more concern with the ethical question. At a certain point, the two become difficult to distinguish.

Consider the logical question first. Social constructionists in the history of sexuality sometimes resist cross-cultural or transhistorical applications of such terms as "lesbian" on the ground that such use is *essentialist*, pausing neither to clarify what "essentialist" means nor to defend the assumption that essentialism is bad.[18] "Essentialism," here, refers to the idea that there is a "lesbian essence," something objective that lesbians have in common that makes them lesbians. Such essentialism is popularly associated with a biologically genetic theory of the *origins* or *causes* of homosexuality, by contrast with a more voluntarist view. Yet, as critics have pointed out, these views need not be linked. Radical lesbians of the United States in the 1970s embraced identity politics, which some critics find "essentialist," together with the view that lesbianism is a choice for all women. Logically, cross-cultural and transhistorical uses of "lesbian" and "homosexuality" do not imply any theory of the origins or causes of lesbian or homosexual desire. In the last section of this chapter, I will argue that they do not commit one to essentialism, either, in the sense of a set of universally shared characteristics possessed by lesbians.

Diana Fuss helpfully analyzes "essence" as referring to a variety of things which it is often useful and important to separate, for example, universality, commonality, timelessness, permanence, irreducibility, immutability, and normativity.[19] It seldom refers to all of these at once. One may want to deny only some of these features while retaining others—to deny the immutability of the meaning of "lesbian," for example, but not that it picks out commonalities. It may not always pick out the same commonalities, and those it picks out at a given time may not be not universal. If Diana Fuss is right, the term "essentialism" is probably better discarded in favor of more specific concepts, such as normativity, immutability, or commonality. Some forms of what had been called "essentialism" may turn out to be compatible with social construction, which originally posed it as an opposite.

Recently, critics of the "social constructionist vs. essentialist" controversy have focused less on essences and more on the meanings of "social construction."[20] Constructionists regarding sexuality often begin with Michel Foucault. Since the English translation of the first volume of his *History of Sexuality*, many have taken the position that prior to the late nineteenth century, there were no sexual identities, no homosexual identity in particular, let alone lesbian or gay identity.[21] Foucault did not deny that there were homosexual *acts* (or desires), but only that *people* were classified into homosexual *kinds* on the basis of such acts (or desires). Homosexual acts, he held, were viewed as crimes or sins that *anyone* might commit. Homosexual identity was constructed in the late nineteenth century, on this view, by psychiatrists who medicalized the phenomena, much as witches were constructed as heretics, according to psychiatrist Thomas Szasz, by the Inquisition in the late Middle Ages.[22]

What does it mean to say that homosexuals, or homosexual identities, were *constructed*? It is one thing to claim that a certain *vocabulary*, such as "homosexual," "heterosexual," "lesbian," or "gay," has a recent history. It is something else to claim that only recently was it widely recognized that some people tend to be attracted to members of the same sex. Even were the vocabulary claim established, the recognition claim would not follow. The vocabulary claim may be difficult to establish, however. Vocabularies for forbidden subjects may be inaccessible to mainstream research. Shared vocabulary is also only one kind of evidence of recognition. We often recognize without being able to say how. As children, a sibling and I coined our own words for masturbation.[23] Although we could not talk about it with other children, we would surely have known what they were doing had we caught them at it.

If absence of recorded vocabulary is insufficient evidence of the impossibility of recognizing a hidden or oppressed group, such as lesbians, it is also insufficient evidence that individuals had no sense of themselves as having any special erotic orientation. As philosopher Richard Mohr asked recently, what are we to make of the fact that so many of us thought we were the only ones, even when we had no vocabulary to name whatever we thought we were?[24] As John Boswell points out in detail, for those tempted to maintain that homosexualities or homosexual identities have been recognized only since the late nineteenth century, there is substantial contrary evidence. An example well-known to philosophers is Aristophanes' speech in Plato's *Symposium*, which offers a myth to account not simply for same-sex *acts* but for the apparently widely recognized fact that some men prefer men and some women prefer women as partners in love, while other women and men prefer a partner of the other sex.[25] If the absence of a noun does not imply that the distinction it would mark is unrecognized, it certainly does not imply that the distinction is unreal, although it may tell us something about the values of those whose vocabulary is so impoverished.[26]

Foucault was not simply commenting on word histories, however, but was attentive to practice, and his concern with speech was more basically with underlying concepts. Yet neither was he offering a theory about *all* concepts, but only about *certain* ones that are politically interesting, such as those pertaining to "sexualities." This is not a radical cultural relativism. Rather, the point has been to distinguish sexualities (as for other constructionists, it has been to distinguish genders or races) from what is genuinely cross-cultural and transhistorical, such as certain facts of human biology (having two eyes, two ears, one nose, etc.).

But what is implied by the claim that *some* categories are "social constructions"? Are they bogus? Edward Stein distinguishes between "empty category" social constructionism, which maintains that, like "witch," the constructed categories do not really apply to anyone, and a more objective constructionism, according to which the categories really do apply, like "yuppie," but only at certain times and places.[27] However, I do not see two *processes* of construction, nor does Stein suggest different processes. Many feminists would prefer to say of the witches, to avoid erasing them and what *was* special about them, that *they* were real, although the conceptions many had of them were false, that witches were in fact really wise women, herbalists, midwives, abortionists.

A suggestion I find helpful is that of John Boswell that "construction" could be heard as derived from *"construe."*[28] If "construct" suggests "fabricate" (which suggests "lie"), "construe" suggests *"interpret."* "Construe" not only allows for sound and unsound construals but also fits with a straightforward, plausible way to understand "social construction," namely, as the development of *social institutions*, or *practices*. Institutions or practices are "constructed" through the elaboration of standards, rules, or norms defining offices and positions, powers and opportunities, which organize (thereby, construe) various activities and relationships.[29] Such construction may be either self-conscious and explicit or unself-conscious and implicit. Social institutions need not be universal, although some, such as wars and families, appear to have forms everywhere. To say that sexuality is *constructed*, in this sense, is to say that it is *institutionalized*, governed by elaborate sets of (presumably changeable) rules and expectations.

But what is "it" that is institutionalized? Is "it" intelligible independently of "its" institutionalization? It is and it isn't. And it depends—on what kind of institution is in question. Some activities or relationships might have existed more simply had they not been formalized. Had baseball not been formalized, perhaps something like it would be less uniform, more flexible, less detailed. Yet, because there can be no baseball without *some* rules, there is no baseball that might exist "unconstructed" (although baseball might have existed un-reconstructed). Baseball is constructed *throughout*—which does not mean that it is unreal. Such thorough construction is not true of all institutions, however.

Consider motherhood, as in Adrienne Rich's treatise *Of Woman Born: Motherhood as Experience and Institution*.[30] Institutionalizing motherhood imposes upon the activities of birthing and childrearing sets of expectations, rules, powers, liabilities, and so on. Can one understand birthing and childrearing cross-culturally and transhistorically? Insofar as these are activities involving choice-making, not just experiences undergone, the answer is less obvious than one might have thought. One may want to say, "yes, but the rules vary." But if the rules vary throughout, what makes it the same activity? A helpful answer may be Marilyn Frye's suggestion, responding to an analogous question regarding the many forms that women's oppression has taken, that there are *common patterns*.[31] There may be recognizable patterns in the rules, for example, in what they seem designed to accomplish or in what they in fact accomplish, even though the patterns are not everywhere the same and they do not affect everyone alike. Different terms for practices that share patterns in their rules may indicate an emphasis on different norms and values. At this point, the logical question may merge with the ethical question: is it *disrespectful* of diversity in woman-loving to apply the term "lesbian" cross-culturally or transhistorically? Sexual intimacy, for example, may not be *central*, from the internal view of its participants, to practices that include it; even woman-loving may not be central to practices that include it. One may want to acknowledge this by using quotation marks around "lesbian." On the other hand, extending a term beyond its cultural home can expand the term's meaning; its cultural homes may be enlarged. Whether the result is coherent and respectful of all concerned depends on the meanings, norms, and values of the cases at hand.

Such concerns are not restricted to cross-cultural and transhistorical usage. They also apply *within* a culture and time period. Consider, for example, terms used in the United States today by woman-loving women to refer to or describe themselves. Since at least the late nine-teenth century, speakers of Indo-European languages have used vari-ants of "lesbian" and "sapphic" for woman-loving women and erotic interaction between women. "Gay" has a longer history as a sexual term, although it is unknown when it was first used for same-sex lovers.[32] Since the 1970s in the United States, many feminists have pre-ferred "lesbian" to "gay," associating "gay" with forms of sexual libera-tion that are not always compatible with feminist goals. "Lesbian" and "gay" are not the only currently preferred terms, however. They have become the preferred *academic* terms, finding their way into literatures of the middle and upper classes. Working-class terms, such as "dyke" and "bulldagger," are preferred by many. They may convey a different image, a different cluster of norms and values.

Because "lesbian," shortened to "lezzie" by hostile observers, has been used as a term of ridicule, some older students in my lesbian cul-ture course were never able to use "lesbian" comfortably, although they had identified for decades as *dykes*. They react to "lesbian" in something like the way I react to "homosexual," which was also initially an insid-er's term.[33] Yet, even those who self-identify as "dykes" may not be comfortable being called "dykes" by outsiders. An advantage of "les-bian," for those who can use it comfortably, is that it now has a history of accepted respectful use by both insiders and outsiders.

If there are problems with "lesbian," analogous problems attach to other basic terms in feminist studies, such as "woman" and "feminist." "Woman" comes from the Anglo-Saxon "wifman," which has meant "wife."[34] Present usage stretches that meaning but also retains it, pre-senting (constructing—that is, construing) the adult female of the species as basically a wife (at least potentially) and thereby subtly prior-itizing in "Women's Studies" the study of woman's relationships to man. Women's Studies Programs, following patriarchal culture, use "woman" not only cross-culturally and transhistorically but as though it were a generic term for the adult female of the species. However, if some African American scholars identify as "womanist" rather than as "feminist," some lesbian philosophers refuse to identify as *women* at all. Monique Wittig, picking up on Simone de Beauvoir's observation that one is not born a woman, argued that lesbians are *not* "women."[35] Yet she (and, likewise, Sarah Hoagland, who follows her in this) seems to use "lesbian" as cross-culturally and transhistorically as others use "woman." She has coauthored a proto-dictionary of "lesbian peoples" encompassing "lesbians" from the ancient Amazons to the present.[36]

The issues these cases raise are not simply abstract but have to do with specific norms or values embedded in different "constructions." According to Sarah Hoagland and Monique Wittig, "lesbian" does not *mean* "homosexual woman," and the choice to be a lesbian rather than a woman is made on ethical and political grounds. (Still, if you use "lesbian" as though it meant "female homosexual," people generally know *whom* you mean, if not what you mean). When Alice Walker protested that "womanist is to feminist as purple to lavender," she thereby suggested that "womanist" is richer, has more depth, body, vibrance.[37] Similarly, "lesbian" may not mean quite the same as "dyke."

Then why speak of "lesbian culture"? Doesn't that treat "lesbian" as generic? Perhaps not. "Generic" suggests *kinds*. And yet adjectives like "lesbian" and "sapphic" do not obviously refer to *kinds*. These terms refer indirectly to the erotic content of the poetry of Sappho of Lesbos. Unlike "homosexual," they are not definable in terms of abstract properties, characteristics, or even rules, because they are derived from *proper names*. Adjectives based on proper names are like metaphors; perhaps they *are* metaphors. They suggest: reminiscent of Sappho, of what (may have) occurred on Lesbos, of Sappho's erotic poetry. "Lesbian" may be heard as a rich metaphor, very open-ended. Beyond her location on Lesbos and authorship of magnificent erotic poetry, almost every claim made about Sappho is controversial.[38] It is not clear whether she headed a school and if so, whether it was linked with a religious cult. Her poetry does not go into detail on how erotic passions of women and girls for one another may have been enacted. Sappho may have been married. One of her poems suggests that she was dark; another, that she had a golden-haired daughter, Cleis.[39] In addition to stories of Sappho and her poetry, many histories of the use of "lesbian" have further contributed to its meanings. It now suggests, among other things, sexual acts associated with the emotions described in Sappho's poetry, although the poetry does not describe sexual acts.

For relationships and careers as diverse as those of woman-loving women, a family of terms is needed. And that is just what we have. A well-chosen family member might be used to refer to the family as a whole, as long as we understand that this is "shorthand," expedient, even arbitrary. If the family is very extended, relationships among its members are not uniformly close, and the members will belong to other families as well. If a single term is to be used as a stand-in for such an extended family, a term that signifies in the way that metaphors do is advantageous.

Judy Grahn uses "gay" as her stand-in term, which allows her to refer at once to both females and males in discussing culture constructed around same-sex erotic bonding. "Gay" was long considered slang. Slang, like proper names, eludes definition, tending to be metaphorical, playful, and elliptical. "Gay" works the way "lesbian" works. Joyce Trebilcot prefers "dyke."[40] Like Sarah Hoagland, Julia Penelope, and Marilyn Frye, I use "lesbian" as my stand-in term, especially in addressing mixed audiences, although I also use "dyke" when I am among dykes, and I call man-loving men "gay." But when I speak of "lesbian culture," I mean to include dyke culture, to include bar culture, for example, as well as academic poetry.

A Course on Lesbian Culture

To elaborate the family metaphor in relation to "lesbian" and "lesbian culture," it is helpful first to look at what these terms have referred to, to make concrete some of the "lesbian" variety that stands as a background to the question, "What is lesbian culture?" And so, I here offer a brief overview of some of what I included in constructing a course on that topic.

Since there was no other course in the university on lesbian experience, deciding what to include was a challenge. My approach was both historical and cross-cultural. To extend students' acquaintance with materials beyond the lesbian shelf in the local feminist bookstore and beyond what the library now catalogues as "lesbian," at least half of the course emphasized materials prior to 1940. These materials came primarily from modern Europe and Europeanized North America and from the ancient Near East. The balance of the course emphasized materials since 1970—some of it looking back to earlier periods—from lesbians of color mostly in the United States as well as from Jewish lesbians, differently abled lesbians, and others writing explicitly from or about experiences and histories often imperceptible in earlier literatures.

Like Monique Wittig's proto-dictionary of "lesbian peoples," I offered a selective panorama from ancient Amazons to the present. A look just at materials prior to 1940 reveals enough variety to make vivid the difficulties of defining the subject, beginning with three ancient literatures from the Near East: the Amazon tales, the histories of Sappho and her school, and the biblical story of Ruth and Naomi. These turned out to provide useful models for lesbian diversity.

First in the popular mind, although not chronologically first, is Sappho. Her poetry was twice burned by Christian Churches—by the Eastern Church in the fourth century and by the Western Church in the eleventh century—and then twice rediscovered, first during the Renaissance in quotations by other writers, such as Aristotle, and then near the end of the nineteenth century in the sands of Egypt by German archeologists who unraveled papier-mâché coffins to find that they were strips cut from scrolls of Sappho's poetry.[41] Contemporary translators usually get Sappho's pronouns right, although some scholars still dispute whether Sappho herself was "homosexual."[42] Her poetry speaks for itself. Still, the autobiographical question is interesting, insofar as it appears that Sappho did not have to contend with social hatred of same-sex bonding. Her poetry gives no indication of social animosity toward woman-loving women, although it suggests that some pupils left her to marry.

Next most popular are the ancient Greek and Roman historians' and geographers' accounts of Amazons. Tales survive of two cultures of nomadic equestrian female warriors.[43] Helen Diner (pseudonym of Berthe Eckstein-Diener) refers to the earlier culture as "Libyan" (North African) and the later one as "Thermodontine" (after the Thermodon River in what is now Turkey, where they camped). Diodorus Siculus reports that both cultures included men by whom the Amazons had children and that the men were assigned domestic roles but not allowed to conduct war or govern. Others, such as Justin and Strabo, report that the later Amazons, possibly as late as the second millennium BCE, copulated annually with men of neighboring nations and reared only female children. Justin says the Amazons were overseen by two queens ("sisters," he also says), one for internal matters and the other for international ones. The Thermodontines (Black Sea Amazons) are immortalized in legends of Theseus' rape of their queen, Antiope (or Hippolyta), whom he carried to Athens (and by whom he begat a son, Hippolytus), thus provoking the Amazon seige of Athens led by co-queen Orithya.[44] This siege was a popular subject of Greek sculpture in the fifth century BCE, always showing Amazons with two breasts, usually one bared.[45] Second-century Greek geographer Pausanias described memorials to individual Amazons and Amazon battle sites in and near Athens, although evidence of these sites has since disappeared.[46]

The reality of both Amazon cultures is frequently denied by contemporary historians on the basis of allegedly insufficient evidence for their existence or on the basis of shallow arguments, some blatantly sexist, a tradition from historians and geographers of the first century BCE.[47] Diodorus reported that since the Amazons lost their strength after the seige of Athens, later historians claimed that stories about them were fictitious. Strabo, his skeptical contemporary, argued, "who could believe that an army of women, or a city, or a tribe, could ever be organized without men, and not only be organised, but even make inroads upon the territory of other people. . . . ? For this is the same as saying that the men of those times were women, and that the women were men."[48] Strabo also infers from the presence of mythical characters in the stories that the Amazons must be mythical, too—as though the presence of mythical characters were better at discrediting the historical reality of other characters than the presence of historical characters were at dissolving the mythical status of others. Finally, he throws in that reputable historians do not mention Amazons, an argument that would erase for future generations many people existing today. In his Marxian essay on the Amazons, Emmanuel Kanter reports the most preposterous denial, by historian John L. Myres, who, he says, argued that the so-called Amazons were probably *beardless men* of Scythia.[49] More popular today are psychological arguments, such as that of Abby Kleinbaum, that the invention of amazons served certain purposes for the Greeks—to flatter themselves or justify patriarchy. Were arguments from motives relevant, they would cut both ways. From such arguments nothing follows regarding the reality of the ancient Amazons. Nor have all modern investigators have found the tales implausible. Guy Rothery found evidence of amazons in every corner of the globe and in every historical period.[50]

Does it matter whether the ancient Amazons were real? We cannot say, as with Sappho, that their work speaks for itself. No work of theirs survives. I know of no evidence that they were even literate. The reality question takes on importance for women generally in view of sexist denials, such as Strabo's, however. Amazons have been models for women who would resist patriarchy in everything from pair bonding and daily tasks to government and war. For lesbians, traditions of coping with denials of our existence are themselves important to lesbian culture. I would put the burden of proof on those who deny what so many of the very earliest recorders—Herodotus, Homer, Lysias, Isocrates—evidently believed.[51] As with women burnt as witches in "Renaissance" Europe, however, it is worth remembering that all surviving early records are from men who identified with their mortal enemies.

A third ancient source is the biblical story of Ruth and Naomi. What is interesting here is not whether the events of the story actually occurred but how the story has been used, what abstract truths about women others may have perceived in it. In the story, Ruth, Naomi's widowed daughter-in-law, marries Boaz, Naomi's kinsman, through a ruse that Naomi devises. However, the passion celebrated in the story is not between Ruth and Boaz but the passion of Ruth for Naomi, to whom Ruth was "more than seven sons." Ruth's "whither thou goest" speech, declaring that she will go wherever Naomi goes and even be buried in the same place with her, is still included in Jewish wedding ceremonies, a fact that lesbians are eager to interpret as a recognition of the quality of the passion given voice by Ruth. The point is not necessarily that Ruth's passion for Naomi was erotic or sexual (although it may have been) but that it was a bonding of an *intensity* and coupled with *ideals* that today are encouraged in and associated with heterosexual marriage. Ruth's passion may not have been erotic or sexual; not all the passions of marriage are erotic or sexual, either, nor are such passions even prerequisite to marriage.

Engrossing tales survive of selected individual "amazons" from the fifteenth through the seventeenth centuries, cross-dressing adventurers, some "passing" as men, some—such as Joan of Arc—still not standardly recognized as lesbians or possible lesbians. French poet and horsewoman Louise Labé wrote love sonnets in the sixteenth century, dedicating them to her woman friend, Clemence de Bourges. The Spanish "Ensign Nun" Catalina de Erauso (contemporary of seventeenth-century philosopher René Descartes) went over the wall of her convent, reconstructed her habit into pants, and shipped off to South America where she fought fifteen years as a soldier, until she was wounded and unmasked. An engaging diary survives, although its authenticity has been questioned. Queen Christina of Sweden abdicated the throne in 1654 under pressure to marry, traveled Europe on horseback, and had affairs with women. A slightly older contemporary of Queen Christina from the other end of the social scale was London pickpocket Mary Frith, known as Moll Cutpurse, on whose life Thomas Dekker and Thomas Middleton based their 1611 play *The Roaring Girl*.[52]

Undisputed accounts from the pens of woman-loving women are more frequent from the eighteenth century on, as are tales of "cross-dressers" and observer accounts of women who chose to live with each other rather than marry. Among the latter are tales of North Atlantic pirates, Ann Bonny and Mary Reade, arrested for killing men and sentenced to hang in Jamaica in the eighteenth century.[53] Pleading pregnancy, they were pardoned. One died in prison; the other escaped. Another widely known adventurer was French opera singer Mlle de Maupin, who played male roles on stage and carried her adventures off stage. Théophile Gautier's novel, *Mademoiselle de Maupin*, was inspired by her life.[54] In early nineteenth-century Edinburgh, school teachers Jane Pirie and Marianne Woods successfully sued Dame Helen Cumming Gordon for slander when she started a whisper campaign that led parents to withdraw their children from the school. This case became the basis of Lillian Hellman's 1934 play, *The Children's Hour.*[55] Among the best-known first-person documents is the diary of Lady Sarah Ponsonby, who in 1779 eloped from Ireland to Llangollen (in Wales) with her niece, Eleanor Butler, and lived there with her for fifty years, during which time they were visited by many famous people and became known as The Ladies of Llangollen.[56] American Transcendentalist philosopher Margaret Fuller translated from German the early nineteenth-century correspondance between Karoline von Gunderode and her adolescent friend Bettina Brentano (novelist Bettina von Arnim). Their passionate friendship ended with Karoline Gunderode's insufficiently explained suicide on the bank of the Rhine, an event alluded to in later German lesbian fiction.[57] In nineteenth-century United States, Emily Dickinson wrote some of the best erotic poetry since Sappho, sometimes altering pronouns.[58] In England, volumes of poetry and drama were published by Edith Emma Cooper and Katherine Bradley jointly under the pseudonym "Michael Field."[59] The value of English composer Dame Ethel Smyth's Mass in D of 1891 has finally been recognized after one hundred years; it has finally been released on compact disc, with her "March of the Women" and an aria from her comic opera, "The Boatswain's Mate," in which a woman innkeeper refuses to trade her independence for marriage to "Mr. Wrong."[60]

American and English expatriates created a lesbian culture in Paris at the turn of the century and between the World Wars, leaving a wealth of material—erotic poems and stories by Renée Vivien (Pauline Tarn); biographical sketches of lesbians and gay men by Natalie Barney; paintings of well-known lesbians by Romaine Brooks; experimental writings by Gertrude Stein; overtly lesbian fiction by novelist Djuna Barnes, and more.[61] In the United States, Amy Lowell, who lived with Ada Russell for the last eleven years of her life, wrote volumes of poetry, some wildly erotic and without gendered pronouns.[62] The most full-blown lesbian culture in the United States before 1950, however, was probably the lesbian culture that belonged to the Harlem Renaissance and its analogue in Detroit, to which blues singers Ma Rainey, Bessie Jackson, and others contributed.[63]

The late nineteenth and early twentieth centuries also saw the birth of sexology and a homosexual rights movement in Germany.[64] Although the work of sexologists Richard von Krafft-Ebing, Havelock Ellis, and others is important background to Radclyffe Hall's 1928 novel *The Well of Loneliness*, the sexologists' writings about lesbians generally tell more about modern social hostilities toward woman-loving women than about lesbian culture.[65] The point of view taken in their published work is mostly what H. L. A. Hart would call "external." Except insofar as it became incorporated into works of lesbian culture, as in the case of Radclyffe Hall's novel, it is not very helpful for identifying and appreciating lesbian culture as developed by lesbians.

In considering what and whom to include in the course on lesbian culture, I drew at first unself-consciously on my undocumented accumulated fund of information, often second-, third-, or fourthhand, mixed promiscuously with gossip and mythology. I did not treat "lesbian" primarily as an identity. I took its adjectival use as basic—"lesbian" as applied to experience, fantasies, relationships, and desires—treating the noun as derivative, as indicating judgments about the importance of lesbian relationships in a life, and recently, as a political tool. Thus, I was less concerned with whether a contributor to lesbian culture was *a* lesbian than with whether she had lesbian experience and a lesbian imagination, whether she had contributed in an interesting way to the development of lesbian thought, art, social practices, and so on. To compose a course, however, one needs to face the question whether the selection and organization of such materials is coherent. And that takes us back to the meaning of "lesbian" and "lesbian culture" and to the metaphor of family connections.

Genealogy: Amazons, Sapphists, and Passionate Friends

It may seem that there is no lesbian consensus on who or what counts as "lesbian": is it basically a sexual concept? an erotic one? cultural? political? all of the above? how much of one's life need be lesbian for one to be *a* lesbian? can one (anyone?) choose it? is self-identification sufficient? is self-identification necessary? on what basis is it appropriate to so self-identify? must one have "done it" with another woman? what counts as "doing it"? Even where facts are clear, the question may remain whether "lesbian" applies. Yet, for all that, there *is* remarkable consensus among lesbians who identify as such on whom to include in lesbian anthologies, histories, and lists.[66] Admittedly, many use others as sources. Yet there is less argument with sources than one might expect.

Disputes have been less about *who* is lesbian than about what it *means* to say of anyone that she is. Consider, for example, the disputes running for more than a decade concerning what Janice Raymond and Adrienne Rich have referred to as a "lesbian continuum" of passionate connections among women.[67] The continuum idea rejects the task of deciding who is or is not really a lesbian in favor of appreciating many forms that lesbian connections have taken in women's lives. Some critics find the continuum problematic because it extends the concept "lesbian" through history and across cultures; others, because it does not mark the distinction between those who have taken substantial risks involved in lesbian commitments and those who have not, and still others, because it can politicize "lesbian," centering one's focus on resistance to patriarchy rather than on sexual behavior.[68] Contrary to the impressions of some critics, however, I do not find a hierarchy embedded in the idea of a lesbian continuum. Some lives are more lesbian than others, in that they are characterized by more lesbian activity or are more focused or organized around lesbian relationships. Yet from that nothing follows about their quality overall, even if "lesbian" is understood to imply political commitment, nor does anything follow about who has power over whom.

The continuum seems to me a positive step in the direction of acknowledging diversity. Yet, in that respect, it may not even be flexible *enough*. We may need related, or intertwined, continua. Consider the dispute related to the continuum dispute and running at least as long concerning what Lillian Faderman has called "romantic friendship" (which I tend to call "passionate friendship").[69] Many lesbians have found the term "romantic friendship" problematic because it can sound euphemistic, as though something physical needed to be covered over with a more spiritual-sounding term. Yet others prefer the emphasis upon friendship, because that makes *choices and values* central to the meaning of the relationship. Both points of view have something going for them. Yet they suggest different, perhaps overlapping, continua.

In trying to acknowledge and organize the insights of parties to these disputes, it struck me that the ancient tales might be seen as offering three branches of a genealogy of "the lesbian" as many of us know her today. Sappho, the Amazons, and such passionate friends as Ruth and Naomi might be seen as ancestors, who also serve as paradigms (offering salient patterns).[70] One need not regard this genealogy as comprehensive. An *essential* thing about genealogies is that they never are complete. Nor need one regard any particular starting point—or vocabulary—as basic. Any "lesbian" may start from where she is, with the vocabulary at her disposal. I took my cues from what I had been doing in identifying women worth studying in a course on lesbian culture, asking myself on what basis I—and the editors of various histories and anthologies—had selected for inclusion figures as diverse as Sappho, Queen Christina, Catalina de Erauso, the Ladies of Llangollen, Emily Dickinson, Ma Rainey, and Natalie Clifford Barney. What could it mean to say that all of these women are important to lesbian culture? Can lesbian culture be defined so as to make sense of the claim that it has an ancient history and a global scope, and at the same time so as to respect its discontinuities and diversity? The challenge was to make explicit what underlay my sense that this was possible.

My approach to lesbian culture presupposed neither that all lesbians have in common one thing (an "essence" in the sense of a *universal*) nor that they exist on the same continuum. It seemed to presuppose, rather, many limited continuities, commonalities, and relationships linking some "lesbians" with others, who are linked with yet others by other sets of commonalities and relationships. It seemed to presuppose different continua that have intersected and overlapped in history. Such connections may be all that enables one to use a single term, such as "lesbian," and the choice of "lesbian" as one's preferred blanket term probably has all the arbitrariness of the choice of a family name.

How it is possible to find unity in diversity is an ancient philosophical problem. Socrates thought that in order for many things to be rightly called by the same name, there had to be some shared characteristic in virtue of which they were so called: all just actions, for example, had to partake of the form, or universal, Justice itself. This theory was challenged by twentieth-century Viennese philosopher, Ludwig Wittgenstein (reputedly a man-lover), whose posthumously published *Philosophical Investigations* offer what is now commonly referred to by philosophers as the "family resemblance" conception of meaning.[71] Consider how we spontaneously recognize members of the same family. We do it even where there is no one characteristic, such as eye color or the shape of the face, that all family members have in common. Individual members share different commonalities: I have the same eye color, hair texture, and complexion as my father and as one of my brothers, but I have my mother's legs and sense of humor, and I was the only one in the family who was left-handed or had red hair. If you met one of my brothers, you might recognize his kinship to me when he smiled. Although we have the same surname and claim the same genealogy, we share "family resemblances," thanks in part to overlapping sets of genes, instead of an identical set of basic characteristics. As Marilyn Frye might put it, we recognize members of the family by way of shared and overlapping *patterns*—patterns of looks, gestures, speech, and so on.

The family resemblance idea seems to capture what I did—and what many others have done—in identifying contributors to lesbian culture.[72] In response to the challenge to produce something that lesbians share cross-culturally and through history, one can begin by pointing out, as Wittgenstein did, that a thing can hang together—a phenomenon, such as lesbian culture—even though its parts are not bound by a common thread, just as (to use another of his metaphors), a cable's strength does not depend on there being strands that run from beginning to end but relies, rather, on a multitude of shorter, overlapping strands. Both the family and cable metaphors accommodate discontinuity within something that nevertheless hangs together: the threads in one part of the cable may not touch any of those in other parts; some "lesbians" may not appear to have any characteristics in common with some other "lesbians" that are more significant than characteristics they share with many nonlesbians.

Applying this idea to the case at hand, I had found in Western histories three interconnected families of "lesbians": the amazonian, the sapphic, and passionate friends. Each suggests different, but also related, "social constructions," ways of institutionalizing practices of woman-loving women. Each might be considered as generating its own continua. Yet, like the strands of a cable, these threads have intertwined through history and across many cultures. Amazons, sapphists, and passionate friends have been drawn to each other, in every combination, in relationships ranging from brief erotic flings to lifetime commitments.

Ludwig Wittgenstein's idea of "family resemblance" may be understood as a time-slice of what Friedrich Nietzsche called a "genealogy." Or conversely, Nietzsche's "genealogy" may be understood as extending the family metaphor backward into history. A Nietzschean "genealogy" is a history of ancestors of present day concepts and practices. Like Wittgenstein's "family resemblance," a Nietzschean genealogy offers an

alternative to the Socratic search for a universal. It no more presupposes a common essence running back through history than a genealogy
presupposes a gene common to one's ancestors. Descendants arise by
combining a little from here with a little from there. In the second of
the three essays that comprise *On the Genealogy of Morals*, Friedrich
Nietzsche observed, "Only what has no history is definable," apparently meaning by "definable" what Socrates meant by it: having a common
characteristic.[73] What has a history has a genealogy *instead* of a definition—at least, in the Socratic sense of definition. In a larger sense of
definition—"to set limits to" or "identify the boundaries of"—it is
often possible, for practical purposes, to say what belongs and what does
not. Not every bit of matter that touches the cable is part of it; one can
still "define" it for practical purposes—recognize its boundaries well
enough to pick it up and move it to another location. What matters to
its integrity are the relationships among its strands. Strands not entwined
with others are not part of the cable (which does not preclude their
becoming interwoven in the future).

Applying the metaphors of family resemblance and genealogy to the
present concept "lesbian," we can go to work on the history of lesbian
culture, pursuing it strand by strand, a project that reveals meanings of
"lesbian" and at the same time involves empirical discovery of what
"lesbian culture" is and has been. In so doing, our understanding of
"lesbian identity" is enriched, as one's understanding of an ethnic
identity is enriched by appreciating its histories. This approach enables
one to explain what is coherent about lesbian culture. The histories and
connections pursued are not totally arbitrary. At the same time, there is
some arbitrariness in the choices of which relatives to recognize and to
honor, just as in a family genealogy, there are always lines not pursued—if only for lack of time and resources. There is room also for
choosing which norms and values to center.

To illustrate, a woman may be counted an *amazon* if, like Medusa of
the Gorgons in North Africa (a look at whose face was said by her
ancient Greek male enemies to turn male attackers to stone), she is
skilled in repelling male attackers. This is the basic kernel of truth
behind the myth that lesbians are *repulsive* and behind that patriarchal
reversal according to which lesbians are said to find men repulsive.[74]
Or, a woman may be counted an amazon if, like the Black Sea Amazons, she has equestrian skills, wears pants, is trained in the use of
weapons, or simply is an effective and persistent fighter. These practices
may go together, as with the ancient Amazons. But they can also inde-

pendently serve as bases of identification—as in the case of Natalie Barney, "the Amazon of letters," noted for her equestrian skills but not as a fighter, at least not one who uses weapons (during World War I, she was a pacifist), or Rosa Bonheur, who obtained legal permission from the French government in the nineteenth century to wear pants but was not, to my knowledge, particularly noted as a horsewoman or fighter nor for skill in the use of weapons. Amazons are ancestors of present-day dykes (for whom motor vehicles have replaced horses as symbols of independence and mobility), who tend to wear pants (though not necessarily or always) and to be, or appear, athletic, at least able to take care of themselves and others physically, and so on.

Passionate friendship's ancient model for lesbians is the story of Ruth and Naomi (as for men, it may be David and Jonathan). In modern times it is exemplified by the Ladies of Llangollen, by Katherine Bradley and Edith Emma Cooper ("Michael Field"), and by the "Boston marriages" of the late nineteenth and early twentieth century, such as that of Alice James and Katherine Loring, Miss Marks and Miss Woolley of Mt. Holyoke College, or M. Carey Thomas and Mary Gwinn at Bryn Mawr.[75]

In the case of amazons and passionate friendships, physical skills and emotional attachments are evident, but sexual activity is not. Yet this does not distinguish them from women commonly recognized as heterosexual. The orientation of attention, the flow of energies, the passionate connections—these may be basically what we note in our identifications.

In the sapphic model of the teacher, poet, or muse, erotic passions become a focus (not to suggest their absence elsewhere). Often they are aroused in an all-female environment, surrounded by a severely patriarchal one—a girls' school, a women's college, a convent, a women's prison, women's barracks. They may unite women far enough apart in age to be mother and daughter or close enough to be sisters. Sapphists may or may not form *couples*, as passionate friends do, and their passions may or may not endure. The attachment may or may not be reciprocal, circumstances may not cooperate, or triangles may complicate matters.

Many individuals exemplify more than one model. Natalie Barney and poet/horsewoman Louise Labé were at once amazons and sapphists, and Louise Labé may have had a passionate friendship with Clemence de Bourges (to whom she dedicated those love sonnets). If it appears that most women can find themselves on one or more of these continua, at least for parts of their lives, that should neither disquiet nor surprise. It neither negates nor exalts distinctions worth drawing between women whose lives are very lesbian and others whose are not.

Recently, Eve Sedgwick identified as one of two major "contradictions" in lesbian and gay theory a tension between *the minoritizing view* that homosexuality is something characteristic of, or of special interest to, only a minority of human populations and *the universalizing view* that homosexuality is characteristic of human behavior in general or of interest to human beings in general.[76] There is no contradiction, however, between granting, on the one hand, that lesbian connections are an ordinary part of female experience (which is not to say that all lesbian connections are ordinary) and insisting, on the other hand, that only some women make such connections central to their lives (and, in a patriarchal society, may then lead quite extraordinary lives). What distinguishes some as "lesbians" are such things as the importance one attaches to one's lesbian experience, one's attitudes toward it, the extent to which it characterizes or organizes one's life, and so on. To gauge such matters in another's life is greatly helped by the ability to take an internal point of view, to perceive her life as she does, in terms of values and norms that she prioritizes. Many of us do not identify as athletes, not because we have had no significant athletic experience but because we have not made athletics that important an aspect of our lives. Self-identification as lesbian, likewise, is not simply on the basis of significant lesbian experiences but usually indicates having made lesbian relationships central to one's life, having chosen to organize one's life around lesbian experience and possibilities, being committed to certain orientations of one's attention, energy flow, resources, etc.

The genealogical understanding of "lesbian" is useful not only for making sense of lesbian culture as a cross-cultural and transhistorical phenomenon but also for clarifying what it can mean to say that one has *chosen* to be or become a lesbian. Studying lesbian culture can reveal in a wealth of interesting detail what it means to say that there is room for choice here. The choices are many, not always liberating, and they reflect our value priorities by what we decide to make central and what peripheral.

The next chapter examines the views of a philosopher, Simone de Beauvoir, who anticipated, in certain respects, the current lesbian emphasis upon choice in becoming lesbian. She is the first philosopher, to my knowledge, explicitly to treat being lesbian as a topic worthy of extended philosophical reflection.[77] The remaining chapters explore the themes of choice and value in contemporary lesbian culture, their places in being and becoming lesbian, their places in lesbian ethics and politics.

Chapter 2

lesbian attitudes and **the second sex**

In the chapter on the lesbian in *The Second Sex* Simone de Beauvoir asserted that "homosexuality" is neither a deliberate perversion nor a physiologically, psychologically, or economically determined fate but, rather, "an attitude *chosen in a certain situation*—that is, at once motivated and freely adopted."[1] This choice, she maintained, must be evaluated according to its "authenticity"; it can be "a mode of flight" from one's situation or "a way of assuming it."[2]

What do these claims mean? What do they imply? How much truth do they contain? Is flight from reality, which sounds like failure to take responsibility for oneself, a likely danger for lesbians? How else might we evaluate lesbian attitudes and choices?

There is a lot of truth in Simone de Beauvoir's claims about what "homosexuality" is. Her proposal makes good sense of the radicalesbian position that one can take responsibility for one's sexual orientation. If she exaggerated about the choosing, she nevertheless opened up a fascinating topic for philosophical inquiry. Astonishingly, however, she failed to appreciate the implications of her claims about lesbians for what else she had to say about women in that book. Although it is unclear just what attitude "homosexuality" is (it may be several), the idea that it is *attitudinal* is clear enough that we can see a range of interesting implications regarding *heterosexuality* that Simone de Beauvoir apparently missed.

Flight from reality is not the most likely danger for lesbians, although there are realities from which lesbians do well to flee. If anything, it is probable that a woman who chooses to live as a lesbian has learned to take responsibility for herself. A more likely danger for lesbians than flight from reality is the temptation to exploit other women's conditioning to service and nurturance.

I may not be able to defend all these claims adequately in one chapter. But I will try to say something interesting about most of them, beginning with Simone de Beauvoir's fantastic failure to catch the implications of her own position.

Her views about lesbians were revolutionary in 1949, four years prior to the Kinsey Report on women. Since the American Psychiatric Association removed homosexuality from its list of mental disorders in 1973, her position seems less revolutionary to us. However, her claim that the lesbian "makes herself lesbian" remains a radical view.[3] Since the beginnings of gay activism in the Nineteenth century, sex researchers, mostly men, have quarreled over whether homosexuality has an inherited basis or is entirely acquired (and recently have challenged that dichotomy), but they have generally agreed that it is not something for which "homosexuals" are responsible. The "gay is good" slogan of the late 1960s paved the way for embracing responsibility here. It has not been "gays" who have gone that way, however. It has been radicalesbian feminists.

Simone de Beauvoir was no radicalesbian. She was an Existentialist dissatisfied with Marxian determinism. To acknowledge and affirm the implications of her views about lesbians for women in general, she would have to have written a far more radical book than *The Second Sex*. *The Second Sex* was not intended to rock the heterosexual boat but, on the contrary, to calm it. Her concern was to show that the "battle of the sexes" was not fated to go on forever and to consider what is required to substitute cooperation for battle between women and men. It appears almost incidentally, in applying the Existentialist concern with responsibility to the situation of lesbians, that she happened to formulate the position quoted above. She saw the implications and drew them out—for lesbians.

A great paradox of *The Second Sex* is its failure to draw the appro-

priately analogous conclusions about heterosexuality. Simone de Beauvoir seemed not to see that if homosexuality is a choice, heterosexuality is likewise a choice. To put it in her more specific language, it is an
attitude that is not physiologically, psychologically, or economically
determined and that can likewise be evaluated according to its authenticity. Except in the chapter on lesbians, *The Second Sex* does not treat
heterosexuality as a choice at all. Even in that chapter, it is treated only
as a choice rejected by lesbians, not as a choice embraced by heterosexual women. And what of heterosexual women? In the Introduction
to *The Second Sex* Simone de Beauvoir wrote:

> The division of the sexes is a biological fact, not an event in human his-
> tory. Male and Female stand opposed within a primordial [*original*] *Mit-
> sein*. . . . The couple is a fundamental unity with its two halves riveted
> together . . . [Woman] is the Other in a totality of which the two com-
> ponents are necessary to one another. (pp. xix–xx)

"The couple" in this context is clearly a heterosexual couple. Simone
de Beauvoir argued in Book One that women's *subordination* to men is
not necessitated by physiological, psychological, or economic conditions. However, she appears to have assumed at the outset that the *opposition* of the sexes is a straightforward consequence of the biological *division* of the sexes, given the nature of human consciousness, on which
she refers us to Hegel:

> Following Hegel, we find in consciousness itself a fundamental hostili-
> ty toward every other consciousness; the subject can be posed only in
> being opposed—he [*sic*] sets himself up as the essential, as opposed to the
> other, the inessential, the object. (p. xvii)

Thus we are presented with the primordial soil in which the "battle of
the sexes" can grow.

Only in the chapter on lesbians does it appear to strike her that the
requirement of two sexes for human reproduction does not entail an
attitude of heterosexuality on the part of the animal. More specifically, it
does not entail that we structure our significant or on-going relationships to others around heterosexual attitudes, that we be *heterosexually
oriented*. Even in that chapter, however, she takes the negative heterosexual attitudes (or presumably attitudes of heterosexual indifference)
of lesbians—to whom she refers, significantly, as "inverts"—to need
special explanation: "What must be explained in the female invert [*l'in-*

vertie] is not the positive aspect of her choice, it is the negative" (pp. 407–8). The heterosexual woman's negative or indifferent homosexual attitudes are not acknowledged, much less thought in need of explanation: "[The lesbian] is distinguished not by her taste for women but by the exclusive character of this taste" (p. 408). Granted that "women have always loved women," heterosexual women frequently manage not to let their lesbian attitudes determine their sexual orientation in a major way, and Simone de Beauvoir did not pause to ask why not.[4] Throughout the rest of *The Second Sex* her focus is on women whose heterosexual orientation is utterly taken for granted. Thus the chapters on sexual initiation and on mothers do not discuss lesbian sexual initiation or lesbian motherhood, and the chapter on married women does not discuss lesbians who marry men.

The positions of *The Second Sex* on lesbians and heterosexual women contradict each other doubly. First, the position that the lesbian "makes herself lesbian" seems to imply that any woman *can* choose a lesbian orientation, although only some are moved to do so. This implies, however, that any woman *can* reject a heterosexual orientation, although only some are moved to do so. That sounds incompatible with the claim that the heterosexual couple is a "fundamental unity with its two halves riveted together." Second, if a lesbian orientation is sometimes chosen *authentically*, how could it be that Woman is part of a primordial heterosexual *Mitsein* and that Man is necessary to her? Choosing a lesbian orientation sounds like denying, rather than assuming, her situation as a member of such a couple. One way out is to deny that lesbians are women. According to Marilyn Frye, that is just what phallocratic culture has done, and Monique Wittig has embraced this implication.[5] In the terms adopted by Simone de Beauvoir, however, one would have to say that lesbians *choose* not to be women. Against the background of a heterosexual primordial dualism, that sounds like saying the lesbian's attitude is not authentic, that it is a "flight from her situation" rather than "a way of assuming it." But Simone de Beauvoir asserted in the chapter on lesbians that it was a great mistake of psychoanalysts to regard the lesbian attitude as always inauthentic (p. 406).

Had she noticed these contradictions, Simone de Beauvoir might have questioned Jean-Paul Sartre's pessimism about human relationships in a very different way from the way she did in *The Second Sex*.[6] Instead of identifying *human* relationships with *heterosexual* relationships and assuming that the significant Other for any consciousness is probably an Other of the "opposite" sex, she might have challenged Hegel's assumption of an original hostility in human consciousness toward others and raised the question how the sexes ever *came to be* "opposites." Following up her own observations about the consequences of the "special circumstances" of lesbian liaisons, she might have considered whether the tendency of any consciousness to regard another *a priori* as an object of hostility is not rather a *consequence* of oppressive institutions than among the conditions giving rise to them. The "special circumstances" of lesbian relationships on which she comments consist in the absence of social institutions and conventions sanctioning and regulating the relationship:

> [Lesbian liaisons] are not sanctioned by an institution or by the mores, nor are they regulated by conventions; hence they are marked by especial sincerity. Man and woman—even husband and wife—are in some degree playing a part before one another, and in particular woman, upon whom the male always imposes some requirement.
>
> (pp. 419–20)

The same institutions and conventions responsible for the absence of such sincerity in heterosexual relationships may be responsible for the "oppositeness" of the sexes as well.

Acknowledging that institutions and mores present obstacles to the development of sincerity in heterosexual relationships should raise the question whether a woman's heterosexual orientation can be authentic in such a context. Simone de Beauvoir does more than acknowledge such obstacles. Her long chapter "The Woman in Love" (with a man) documents copiously the contradictions involved in a woman's attempt to be a subject and at the same time attract and keep a male lover under the rules of femininity. Yet she did not raise the question whether the choice to persist in heterosexuality under such conditions is an authentic choice. It seemed not to occur to her at that level that any choice was involved.

It might briefly appear natural for a feminist theorist to take the position that although lesbians freely choose to be lesbian, heterosexual women do not freely choose to be heterosexual, because heterosexuality is compulsory—as Adrienne Rich and others have amply documented—and lesbianism surely is not. Both choices, however, confront the same woman. Is she free, or is she not? The lesbian's freedom may be more readily apparent because her choice is a defiance of convention; the heterosexual woman's freedom less apparent, because her choice can easily appear determined by convention. The compulsoriness of heterosexuality does not, however, imply that women are forced to choose it. Heterosexuality is compulsory in the sense that severe penalties are attached to its rejection. One can choose to live with many of those penalties, however. Lesbians are not free from them. The question is whether they are so severe as to render only the heterosexual option tolerable, in which case the lesbian's "freedom" is simply the "freedom" to be irrational—or perhaps heroic.

The complicated truth may be that lesbians are *choosing to be free* of convention, to be relatively autonomous, self-determining (Simone de Beauvoir: the lesbian makes herself lesbian), whereas heterosexual women are *choosing to be determined* by convention, relatively less autonomous. Whether the latter choice is inauthentic, however, may not be determinable independently of a consideration of the nature of the conventions by which she is choosing to be determined.

The idea of choosing to be or not to be determined by conventions or institutional requirements is relatively unproblematic. That is, most people would probably feel that they understood what that means. Choosing a lesbian or heterosexual orientation does not seem that simple. Many people are not at all sure they understand what that means. If Simone de Beauvoir was right in her assertion that "homosexuality" is "an attitude chosen in a certain situation," the attitude does not seem to be simply an attitude toward conventions or institutions. But then, what attitude is it? And what does it mean to say that it is chosen?

Some of the puzzlement one may feel about Simone de Beauvoir's position on lesbian choice may be alleviated by distinguishing between "choice" as an *option* (of which one may or may not be aware) and "choice" as the *act* of choosing from among options (which presupposes one's awareness of them). Gay Rights activists and heterosexual feminists are no doubt often right in their insistence that they *did not choose* their sexual orientations but, rather, discovered that they already had them. That admission, of course, does not touch the claim that other options exist, that there are still (possible) choices. Simone de Beauvoir appeared to have in mind the *act* of choosing, not simply the existence of an option. This may account for her failure to see relevant analogies between lesbian and heterosexual women. Since it is easy for women not to appreciate the existence of a lesbian option in a severely heterosexist society but impossible to be ignorant of heterosexuality, it is more likely the lesbian than the heterosexual woman who has *actually exercised* choice at the level of her sexual orientation. It is, however, also possible for lesbians not to have chosen the lesbian *orientations* that they have developed as a result of their more specific choices. Being committed to a lesbian orientation, positively embracing it, goes beyond simply having one.

A different sort of uneasiness about the position of Simone de Beauvoir may be due to unclarity about whether sexual orientation is the kind of thing that *can be* an object of choice. One may be able to take various attitudes *toward* one's sexual orientation—for example, be proud of it or ashamed of it—but can one choose the orientation itself? A popular view of sexual orientation is that it is simply a matter of taste and that there is no accounting for tastes, and *a fortiori*, no accounting for them in terms of one's choices. Another version of the sexual mystique likens sexual orientation to right- and left-handedness, calling attention to the alleged 10 percent incidence of both left-handedness and homosexuality and the difficulty of changing either kind of habit. Who knows what this suggestion means? There is no consensus regarding the origins of right- and left-handedness either. Simone de Beauvoir's approach is more interesting. She suggests an answer that makes good sense of various sides of the controversy: the object of choice, as she presents it, is an *attitude*. If being lesbian (and, similarly, being heterosexual) is a matter of attitude, it is easy to see why there is no consensus on the question of choice. It is also possible to argue that those who maintain that there is a choice are closer to the truth than those who hold that there is not.

To describe adequately the processes by which a woman's sexual orientation becomes either lesbian or heterosexual, a more generous vocabulary is needed than is provided by the dichotomy of "freely chosen" on the one hand and "fated" or "determined" on the other. As Aristotle saw, not everything that is voluntary is chosen, and not everything that is not voluntary is *in*voluntary.[7] Choice, for Aristotle, is desire that is the product of deliberation. The voluntary is action that is neither compelled nor done because of ignorance. Much conduct that is neither compelled nor done because of ignorance is not the product of deliberation, either (and thus, is voluntary although not chosen). The area of conduct for which one can be responsible includes the voluntary in general as well as the chosen in particular and can also include conduct that was, apparently, not voluntary—because of the ignorance factor—but that could have been voluntary had one reflected or paid attention. Attitudes often seem to fall within the latter areas. Often, our attitudes emerge as a product of many specific acts, and we are not aware of them as attitudes unless we make a point of attending to them reflectively.

What is an attitude? An attitude can be a pose, a position, a stance, a disposition. Originally a technical term from the Arts of Design (according to the O.E.D.), "attitude" has come to be a psychological term referring to dispositions, complexes of behavior and valuation.[8] Like emotions, attitudes have objects: they are held *toward* things (or people, situations, etc.). They also tend to have valences, that is, to be positive or negative, favorable or unfavorable, pro or con. And they tend to have foundations, bases, which can be either reasoned or unreasoned judgments or valuations together with relevant perceptions and beliefs. Because of the epistemological content of the bases of attitudes, attitudes are often modifiable through insight and understanding. Because of the behavioral aspect of attitudes, attitudes, like habits, can outlive the judgments upon which they were originally based. Both of these possibilities are claimed for sexual orientation in the experiences people report. Attitudes sometimes dissolve with the ignorance or misinformation upon which they were based, and at other times are remarkably stubborn.

Can an attitude be chosen? We speak of cultivating attitudes, getting over them, refusing to get over them, encouraging and discouraging them, falling or lapsing into them, snapping out of them, persisting in them, adopting or striking them, and so on. Most of this is the language of agency. Clearly, there are things we can do that contribute to the production, modification and elimination of an attitude, and thereby to the production, modification, and elimination of tastes as well. If attitudes are not directly the objects of choice, choices are among their fairly proximate causes, including such choices as the choice to acquire certain attitudes.

Even if attitudes are not objects of choice, much about them is voluntary. Behavior that manifests an attitude is typically voluntary, even if exhibiting the attitude was not (say, because one was unaware of having the attitude). As Elizabeth Telfer has observed about friendship, however, one is not really committed to it unless one has *acknowledged* or *affirmed the pattern* exhibited by the particular acts that one has chosen.[9] Frequently we discover our attitudes rather than choose them. Yet we tend to hold ourselves responsible for them anyhow. Probably we judge people as often by their attitudes as by their specific acts. We expect people to take responsibility for their attitudes. If sexual orientation is an attitude, then the idea of taking responsibility for one's sexuality belongs to that general expectation.[10] Taking such responsibility requires developing habits of noticing things about oneself, identify-

ing one's attitudes and determining whether they are well-founded or
not. One can choose to do or not to do these things. Once some of
these choices have been made, one's resulting beliefs may no longer be
subject to one's control. To the extent that one's attitudes are based
upon beliefs not—or no longer—within one's control, the attitudes
themselves seem involuntary.

Even if attitudes are not chosen, they can still be evaluated as authentic or inauthentic. They can be honest or dishonest, responsible or irresponsible. What is required for such evaluations is that *like* choices, attitudes be capable of being based upon beliefs and judgments, not that
they be themselves direct objects of choice. What matters is that we can
be responsible for them.

Is "homosexuality" an attitude (or set of attitudes)? If so, what attitude, or attitudes, is it? Are there attitudes that distinguish lesbians from
other women? The answer to the latter question seems to me, fairly
obviously, yes. Lesbian attitudes toward women tend to be distinctive.
And yet, according to Simone de Beauvoir, what distinguishes lesbians
is a certain *heterosexual* attitude, namely, a negative attitude toward men.
It was on this that she fixated when she came to assess the authenticity of some lesbian choices. Thus she reviewed in relatively favorable
terms lesbians like Gertrude Stein ("rather rare," she noted) who are so
assured of their virile powers that they want only men as friends and
companions. (This is hardly fair to Gertrude Stein, whose closest friend
and companion was Alice Toklas.) And she looked askance, even with
horror, upon those who form their own clubs, rejecting men socially
as well as sexually (pp. 422–24). The only way I can make sense of her
judgments in these cases is by supposing that she assumed that the dyke
separatist, unlike Gertrude Stein, bases her attitude toward women *upon*
a negative attitude toward men, rather than the other way around. So
understood, the separatist is reduced to a case of Nietzschean *ressenti-
ment*: sour grapes. Simone de Beauvoir offered no reason, however, for
thinking that this is the separatists' motivation. She did not consider
separatists' attitudes toward women at all. What about the lesbian's *lesbian* attitudes? What about her attitudes toward women?

In pursuing the claim that it is not the lesbian's "taste for women"
that distinguishes her from other women, Simone de Beauvoir mentioned a kind of case that suggests to me a good example of inauthenticity in lesbian behavior. "Disappointed in man," she tells us, a woman
"may seek in woman a lover to replace the male who has betrayed her.
Colette indicated in her *Vagabonde* this consoling role that forbidden

pleasures may frequently play in woman's existence: some women spend . . . their whole lives in being thus consoled" (p. 418).

Others use women lovers for regeneration until they are able to deal with men again. The kind of "inauthenticity" that may characterize such cases as these is not what Simone de Beauvoir thinks of as "inauthenticity," not the kind involved in *self*-deception and failing to take responsibility *for oneself*. It is possible that such failures are also involved.[11] It seems more likely that the woman in these cases, who would probably describe herself as "bisexual," has her situation very well in hand, from the point of view of taking charge of her own life.

The "inauthenticity" apt to characterize these cases is a kind that can be easily involved in what Aristotle distinguished as friendships of utility and friendships of pleasure, by contrast with true friendship.[12] In true friendship, we care for our friends for their own sakes; in friendships of utility or friendships of pleasure, we care for the sake of the utility or pleasure. A friend of the latter sort who is not up front about it is guilty of a kind of inauthenticity. Friendships of utility and friendships of pleasure are not necessarily inauthentic; they need not pretend to be what they are not. Still, they are not "*true* friendships." Anticipating Ludwig Wittgenstein's idea of a "family resemblance" among things rightly called by the same term but which do not possess any one characteristic in common, Aristotle said of friendships of utility and friendships of pleasure that they were both called "friendship" only because of their resemblances (different in each case) to true friendship, which is also normally both useful and pleasant.[13] Something similar is true of the lesbian liaisons formed by women who are still in important ways basically heterosexually oriented: their attitudes are "lesbian" insofar as they resemble true lesbian attitudes, which also normally include receptivity to regeneration and nurturance from women.

In the consolation and regeneration cases, if there is inauthenticity, it is not just that the *woman* may be being inauthentic: her *lesbianism* may be inauthentic. What was it that Simone de Beauvoir intended in saying that "the choice of the lesbian" must be evaluated according to its authenticity? Which choice? The choice of a particular relationship? The choice of *women* as lovers? At times she seems to mean no more than that lesbians are subject to *exactly* the same sorts of inauthenticity as other folk:

The association of two women, like that of a man and a woman, assumes many different forms; it may be based upon sentiment, material interest, or habit; it may be conjugal or romantic; it has room for sadism, masochism, generosity, fidelity, devotion, capriciousness, egotism, betrayal: among lesbians there are prostitutes and also great lovers.

(p. 419)

And

Like all human behavior, homosexuality leads to make-believe, disequilibrium, frustration, lies, or, on the contrary it becomes the source of rewarding experiences, in accordance with its manner of expression in actual living—whether in bad faith, laziness, and falsity, or in lucidity, generosity, and freedom.

(p. 424)

These comments assess lesbian relationships simply as human relationships, not specifically as lesbian. What is being commented upon is not a lesbian attitude *as such*, not the choice to be lesbian. All that need have been chosen for these evaluations to be appropriate is a particular lover or relationship, not a sexual orientation. As close as Simone de Beauvoir comes to assessing what really looks like a choice to be lesbian is in her comments on the dyke separatists, and there she simply *assumes* inauthenticity rather than seeing the possibility of amazon creativity and playfulness.

The historical models discussed in the previous chapter suggest some fairly distinctive and characteristic lesbian attitudes, which are interesting to examine in terms of the temptations they present and the possibilities they offer: those of amazons (who tend to be physically skilled and economically independent), those of sapphists (poetic and sensual, often significantly older or younger than their lovers), and those of passionate friends (often highly erotic, like sapphic attitudes, but also remarkably enduring and not necessarily sensual). Studies of woman-loving women in other cultures are bound to reveal further patterns. Understanding such attitudes as these in terms of Wittgensteinian "family resemblances" suggests the complexity of the question what lesbian attitudes are, and, like Adrienne Rich's suggestion of the "lesbian continuum," can recognize lesbian attitudes among women whose general sexual orientation is not particularly lesbian.[14]

One of the implications of the view that being lesbian is a matter of attitude is that lesbians do not form a natural kind. And for the same reasons, neither do heterosexuals. That insight about lesbians may be Simone de Beauvoir's most important contribution to the subject.

Chapter 3

choosing lesbianism

What Is the Problem? Ever since Alix Dobkin sang, "any woman *can* be a *les*-bi-*an*," there have been women who felt oppressed by such optimism.[1] Although they sleep with men, they spend their days working with and for women. Deploring the feminine masochism inculcated by heterosexist institutions in misogynist society, they sometimes express a wistful envy of those of us able to live lesbian lives, hinting that they would also if they could. Some find the idea of the song cruel in its apparent "voluntarism" regarding the malleability of sexual desire.[2]

In this chapter I take up the assumption implicit in that response that lesbians are, somehow, luckier than other feminists in being free to lead lesbian lives. I look at what it means to make lesbian choices in this society. Actual choosing, in advance of being able to know much about the meanings of the choice, is required in order eventually to make lesbian choices both more widely possible and more rewarding. There is luck, here, to be sure, but the luck is both good and bad. How lucky *I* am in my choice to be lesbian may depend in part on what *others* choose, as may the meaning of the choice itself. In other chapters

I have more to say about the values of lesbian choices. Here my strategy is not to defend the choice but to focus on what it can *mean* to choose to be lesbian, thereby extending the task, begun in chapter 1, of exploring how the meanings of "lesbian" are constructed. As for the view that "*any* woman can," that may be literally true of nothing whatever. The point is that many who think they can't could, and the intriguing question is, under what conditions?

Does it really matter whether a woman "can"? This is a question to which I continually return, from a variety of angles. Even if there is more truth than falsity in the song (as I think), what matters politically, first of all, is what "lesbian" means. Our erotic options matter when our choosings can affect the meanings of such concepts as "lesbian," even though lesbian choices may not enhance our freedom much (in the sense of expanding our options) during the process of revolution. I find "lesbian" (the adjective as it applies to women, desires, fantasies, relationships) defined to a great extent by interaction between individuals and institutions. But I do not find *lesbians* (referents of the noun "lesbian") to be entirely constructed by social interaction. The concept of oppression presupposes beings who are not *totally* constructed by the institutions that nurture or oppress them.

It is also important to bear in mind the ambiguity of "choice." As argued in chapter 2, "choice" is ambiguous between "option" and "(intentional) act of choosing." These two meanings suggest different questions: (1) whether an *option exists*, and (2) whether someone (intentionally) *exercised choice* (i.e., chose). In a patriarchal society, lesbians are more likely to have *exercised* choice in becoming lesbian than heterosexual women are to have exercised choice in becoming heterosexual. The initially more interesting question, I think, is what kinds of options exist for both. Yet, because choosing can itself expand or contract the range of one's future options, both senses of "choice" remain interesting.

Exercising choice presupposes belief by the chooser in the existence of an option at the time of choosing, although it does not necessarily presuppose belief in the continuing existence of that option—some choices are irrevocable. One can, of course, mistakenly believe that an option exists—as in believing one can go through either doorway when in fact one door is locked. The existence of genuine options, real alternatives, however, does not entail intentional acts of choosing. Options can be ignored. One can be unaware of them.

Although it can be misleading to say that an option exists for someone who is unaware of it, there are contexts in which this can be a sensible position to take, as where both doors were *un*locked although one noticed only one door or discovered only of one that it was unlocked. A woman unaware of lesbian options may not *feel* there was any choice (and in one sense, there wasn't: no choosing occurred). In another sense, however, perhaps there was: there may have been unrealized, even unrecognized, options. Kathleen Barry relied upon such distinctions in arguing that prostitutes who are unable to escape from "the life" are subject to involuntary servitude, regardless how they got there: even if they chose to get in, they may have no option to leave—a point that can be generalized to battered intimates in many situations.[3] Consciousness-raisers appeal to such distinctions to make the point in combating sexism, racism, and hostilities toward gay men and lesbians that the *option* to unlearn such attitudes does not presuppose that one ever *chose* to develop such attitudes in the first place.

Why has it mattered whether women have lesbian options? In gay history, the absence of options regarding sexual orientation has mattered to reformers who wished to persuade legislators that punishment for homosexual behavior was useless, unjust, or both. A hard lesson learned from the Nazi regime is that belief in the absence of such options is no guarantee of toleration. For feminists, the concerns have been more complex. According to feminists, whether women have lesbian options matters also because heterosexual practices in misogynist patriarchy subordinate women and protect men who abuse women. This makes heterosexual bonding in such a context at least potentially masochistic for women. The power to abuse can easily become part of the turn-on, hooking us into supporting the very practices that subordinate us, putting our lives at war with feminist politics, creating self-estrangement.[4] By contrast, lesbian intimacy appears to offer more feminist integrity insofar as women who can choose to be lesbian can thereby develop sounder relationships (an assumption not to be embraced too quickly, however; see chapters 6 and 7). Still, the potentiality at present for divisiveness among feminists over whether any woman "can" should be apparent: if lesbian options often do promise more feminist integrity, and if such options commonly exist for women now leading heterosexual lives, how are women who currently lead such lives to suppose that lesbians feel about them as companions in feminist struggle? How are they to feel about themselves?

Thus, clarity regarding lesbian options matters to possibilities of community and solidarity among feminists. Lesbian options are morally and politically worth having insofar as they promise a certain integrity of emotional response with political belief and thus facilitate political commitment. Part of the value of this integrity, however, rides on the supposition that lesbian emotional responses are liberating, a supposition encouraged by feelings of liberation in acting on such emotions in societies that do everything under the sun to discourage it. Yet it is one thing to escape others' domination and another to develop the positive potentialities that domination had closed off. It may be false that lesbian emotional responses in patriarchy are as yet very liberating for many in the latter sense. They may manifest freedom *from* psychological domination. But what do they manifest freedom to *do*? Acting on them is for many of us morally irreversible. Such choices thereby *eliminate* for us options we previously had without necessarily creating new ones that comparably extend our range of freedom or offer compensating privileges. Let us consider an example,

The Situation of Renée

Renée ("reborn," in French), a so-called "born-again" lesbian feminist, is a political lesbian in the best sense. She is lesbian in much the way that she is a vegetarian.[5] Both identities involve basic passions with far-reaching effects upon her life—where she lives and works, who her friends are, etc. Although she loved girls and disliked eating animals from early childhood, these passions did not receive familial or other social encouragement (an understatement, of course). Regarding both "girls" and gourmandism, she eventually made choices that were morally and politically informed. Because her original inclinations and passions had been stigmatized as immature, however, she had worked to develop tastes and passions that were considered more mature. She had learned to eat most of the animals conventionally consumed around her and to *enjoy* it. She learned gourmet carnivore cooking. She dated men, *enjoyed* pleasing them, fell in love with a few, dreamed of having children, and nearly married—but her career plans intervened. There were times when she could have gone either way—heterosexual or lesbian, omnivore or vegetarian—without self-estrangement and without disrupting lifetime commitments or risking anything as drastic as being separated from children (she had none). The ways she ultimately chose felt like "coming home" in that they went with fantasies and habits dating from her childhood. Yet, although that may have made it easier for her to make those choices, it was not her reason for the choices. Her morals and politics added dimensions to both vegetarian-

ism and lesbianism that were absent from her childhood. These led her
to reject as oppressive and supportive of cruelty the very practices that
a larger society had taught her were mature. They led her also to form
relationships of trust and confidence with like-minded others. It is no
longer *morally* an option *for Renée* to choose omnivorousness or heterosexuality; *she* could not now do so without self-estrangement. Nor
is she tempted, despite residual susceptibility to relevant nostalgia.

Renée is not everywoman. But, then, no one is. She is not an
uncommon creature, however. And while she has always remembered
vividly her passions for women, even from childhood, many others
who are otherwise very much like her have, for one reason or another,
in one way or another, forgotten theirs.

It does not follow that heterosexual feminists are generally moral or
political hypocrites, or that they are any more hypocritical than lesbians. Owing to extensive commitments and responsibilities undertak-
en early in life, heterosexual feminists' lives can be complicated in ways
that Renée's was not. The best any of us can do in oppressive environments is to strike balances regarding the conflicts we can live with and
those we cannot, and these are not the same for everyone. Nevertheless, I find the situation of Renée metaphysically suggestive about what
is possible, and morally interesting as well.

Some will interject: but, Renée was *bisexual*! However, as an option,
bisexuality was a choice Renée rejected, for some of the same reasons
she rejected heterosexuality. As an option it never attracted her much.
But, the interjector may insist, *that's* not what "bisexuality" means; a
"bisexual" is just someone who *can* go either way, not who necessarily
does "swing both ways." Yet the idea that one who (intentionally) rejects
lesbianism or heterosexuality *must really* be bisexual, unlike those who
(intentionally) reject nothing, begs the question what options exist for
those who reject nothing. If the point is simply that all of those for whom
both heterosexuality and lesbianism are in some sense options are really
bisexual, that could be granted as a matter of metaphysics. But there
remain moral and political problems with the language of bisexuality.
For it seems disrespectful of the values and choices of someone like
Renée. One who rejects an option on moral grounds may no longer
have, *morally speaking*, what once presented itself as an option. For
Renée, heterosexuality eventually remained an "option" only in the sense
that one can still choose to do what one finds morally objectionable.

Still others may want to say that the fact that what Renée chose felt
like "coming home" indicates that she was *really* a lesbian all along, that

those passions from childhood are critical. Though she is tempted to say that herself, she also finds it misleading. For, she could take up smoking cigarettes again, and if she did so, that, too, would feel like "coming home." She was an enthusiastic chain-smoker for most of two decades, her parents were lifelong smokers (unfortunately, not long-lived smokers), and she has significant positive associations with smoking (not surprising, having smoked through every significant event of her life for nearly twenty years). Is she then "really" addicted to nicotine even now? I find it less misleading to acknowledge both that she *broke* the dependency and that she could (perhaps easily) *recreate* it. The feeling of "coming home" can reinforce or tempt one to choices. But that does not negate the reality of choice. Equally, the feeling of "coming home" may not offer a good reason for a particular choice. Some homes are not, morally, places where one can finally live well.

In neither the vegetarian nor the lesbian case can Renée imagine wanting to make the previously rejected choices *now* (which is not to say that she cannot imagine what it would be like if she did). Certain options are no longer "live" for her, not morally or politically viable. She knows what it would take for her to separate her passions from her ethics and politics: the tactics that quiet an inconvenient conscience. Anglican Bishop Joseph Butler (1692–1752) described them well in his philosophical sermon on self-deceit: ignore the troubling sides of an issue, attend only to certain facets, ask *not whether but how* one is justified, rationalize.[6] She would have to learn to ignore factory farming and heterosexual privilege, or to rationalize them. For her to think that she could not would probably be arrogant. No doubt most of us do it with respect to many of the products we consume, for example. Ignorance is not, strictly speaking, absence of knowledge; it is absence of attention, producing absence of knowledge or blocking access to knowledge.[7] Renée could doubtless produce "ignorance" enabling her to return to old ways but cannot imagine what would justify her doing it now, given her history.

Does this mean that feminists whose passions are at war with their politics are necessarily able to change those passions if they just try hard enough? Not necessarily. The damage of spirit-binding may become, like that of foot-binding, irreversible. Thus Sandra Bartky has claimed, "One of the evils of a system of oppression is that it may damage people in ways that cannot always be undone. Patriarchy invades the intimate recesses of personality where it may maim and cripple the spirit forever."[8] In other cases, ties that bind may indicate a certain moral honor. Nor is it clear what enables some to succeed in changing—in terms of environments, communities, luck regarding unpredictable stress, etc. Not all who try succeed in becoming vegetarian, or in quitting smoking or alcohol, either. And there are degrees of success.

Renée's difficulties and challenges in implementing her choices included such things as loosening ties with old communities and friends, putting down new roots, developing new habits of attention, breaking entrenched habits of dependency, being creative. Her sense that she was losing some things of value in making such choices does not imply that she was not really making choices. Also, she needed to have deep concern for herself in order to break old ties. Because women in misogynist societies commonly lack deep self-love, a circle may trap many in heterorelations: developing deep self-love may require emotional responses from other women, and these responses may fail to be forthcoming or fail to touch the women who need them because of misogyny and histories of misogyny. Lesbian love for another may nurture that other's deep self-love only if it can reach through the layers of misogyny that devalue that love because of its object and its source.

Why Insist on Lesbianism as a Choice?

If creating lesbian options can be so difficult, and can furthermore present women with morally irreversible choices, then why insist on lesbianism as a choice? It is important to insist on lesbianism as a choice because such choices potentially shape future institutions that, in turn, help define future choices. Here I return to the idea of social construction as useful and enlightening. It is important to insist upon the very widespread existence of lesbian options in oppressive patriarchal societies that are ripe for revolution, even though some such options may not be *morally* open to everyone to take and some may not be *emotionally* open to everyone at every stage of their lives. I am not referring to *legal* options or the legality of options, though that is also an important topic. I am referring to what I believe Williams James meant when he spoke of options that can be "live" or "dead," and I want to suggest that social construction can enter into both their meaning and vitality.[9]

Social construction introduces complexities into questions about choice. Of the "symbolic interactionists" and their forerunners, I have found particularly clear and helpful the posthumously published lectures of George Herbert Mead and Edwin M. Schur's version of "labelling theory," which does not take labels to be everything (i.e., does not hold that what is labeled need be constructed throughout, or entirely, by its labels).[10] In Schur's view, there are many levels of social construction. The aspect of social construction that particularly interests me here is the interaction of individuals with institutions. Institutions are activities structured by often elaborate rules that define, as philosopher John Rawls tends to put it, offices and positions, opportunities and immunities, benefits and burdens, thereby creating and distributing various advantages and disadvantages.[11] Punishment is an example of an institution; marriage is another. Institutions create and restrict options for individuals. Yet the interaction of individuals with institutions is a two-way phenomenon. This is a clue that social "construction" is also a two-way phenomenon: institutions partially "construct" the lives of those they govern, and they are in turn "constructed" by human behavior.

Richard Mohr has suggested that "construct" is ambiguous between "cause" and "define."[12] As indicated in chapter 1, I prefer something closer to the "define" interpretation, agreeing with the suggestion of John Boswell that we hear the word "construe" in the background of "construction." If individuals sometimes explicitly define the meanings of institutions, say, through legislative choices, institutional rules can also determine the meanings of individual choice and behavior, and, in some cases, thereby, of our social identities: we are sometimes identified in terms of the options that are open to us or foreclosed to us. (Consider "resident alien," for example: someone who is allowed to reside, although not granted many of the options of citizens).

What does one choose in taking up a (way of) life? Becoming a lesbian, like becoming a philosopher, is the product of many choices as well as of many bits of fortune—"product" not in the sense of "causal result" but in the sense of something *so constituted*. Yet one can affirm or disown this product, as one can affirm or disown one's relationship with another as a relationship of friendship. And certain choices going into the product are salient—going to graduate school, accepting certain jobs; pursuing women, making love with them. Often one wants to know what made *those* choices attractive. But let us put that on hold while we look more closely at what makes them *salient*.

In marrying, those who say "I do"—at least the first time—often know little of what they have chosen until afterward. They may encounter the relevant laws only at the stage of divorce. The step taken with the marriage ceremony, like a guilty verdict in the courtroom, initiates an unfolding of options and events that can now come into play, depending upon various contingencies. This is an instructive example of choices significantly defined by institutions or practices. An implication is that the meaning of some choices can actually change *after* one has made them, because rules defining later stages of the process can be altered or abolished and new ones can even be instituted between the time of one's choice and the time for them to come into play in one's own case. Another example of a choice the meaning of which can change after one has made it is becoming a "naturalized" citizen; the political constitution can change with consequences for one's rights but without undoing one's citizenship. The idea that the meaning of one's choice can change *after* one has made it sounds bizarre at first: what was one doing at the moment of choice? Yet upon reflection, one sees that of course such change would be possible for choices the meanings of which were significantly defined by rules of complex institutions, rules that come into play *over time* and under various contingencies. Marriage shows the phenomenon to be ordinary. Not only can marriage legislation change without undoing one's marriage, but marriages from other jurisdictions are respected (one is even *held* to them), although a different set of laws and customs now governs them. Consider, for example, the case of Betty Mahmoody, married in the United States to an Iranian man with whom she returned in 1984 to Iran for what he had led her to believe was to be a brief visit. Once there she found she was trapped because as the wife of an Iranian man in Iran, she lacked mobility rights that she had in the United States when she married him. Lesbian choices, although circumscribed more by custom than by law, can be at least as open-ended as the commitments of those who marry.[13]

The fact that one's choices are salient determiners of social identity, then, does not in itself indicate that the individual chooser has a high degree of *autonomy* or *control* over her identity. It does not preclude *discovery* about what one's choices mean. I may choose to be lesbian, but how much do I choose about what that *means*? Were I to go to leather bars I might discover that my choice to wear keys on my belt on a certain side has a set of meanings that I never dreamed of.

The questioner I left behind wanted to know what made lesbian choices attractive. I want to change the question to: what makes the attractions one experiences "lesbian"? Usually the view that one has little if any control over one's so-called sexual orientation is upheld by reference to the "nature" of one's passions. Yet, institutions with which we interact enter into the "construction" (not causation) of even our passions. We discover what our "lesbian" passions mean, what they "are," not only by introspecting their intentions and engaging in reverie but also in part by acting them out interpersonally and discovering what responses we get, not only what satisfies us but also what we arouse in others. The meanings of our passions—their qualitative "natures," their characters—are at least partly discoverable only in interaction. Although these meanings are not simply a function of our intentions, even the meanings of our *intentions* are partly determined by options created or foreclosed by institutions. (It follows from the observations above, for example, that this is true of the intention to marry.)

In elaborating the idea of compulsory heterosexuality more than a decade ago, Adrienne Rich presented a view that makes sense of the claim that lesbian existence is a very widespread option in patriarchal society (perhaps, better, that it is at least as many options as there are locations on a "lesbian continuum").[14] She did so by suggesting an unconventional understanding of "lesbian" in terms of women's choices to foster many forms of primary intensity with other women. She offered no *causal* explanations, however, of either heterosexual or lesbian existence. A difficulty for attempts to read her account as though it did offer a causal explanation of heterosexuality has been how to explain why there are as many unambiguous lesbians or gay men as there are, given the severity of the penalties for deviation from heterosexual norms. Adrienne Rich's idea of compulsory heterosexuality offers, rather, certain *rationales* for women's rejections of women as lovers (in terms of prices, penalties), presuming that there is no need of a rationale for why women do not reject women when we do not. Lesbians in patriarchy, on this analysis, are rebels; we refuse to play by certain patriarchal rules. This analysis offers no causal account of either lesbian rebellion or heterosexual submission, why lesbians rebel, why others do not. What it suggests is a political reconstruction of the meanings of "lesbian" and "heterosexual."

If exercising lesbian options does not give a woman enhanced control over her life, why is it important whether she has them? To answer, we need to distinguish different levels of the exercise of choice.[15] The level of picking from among options already defined by existing practice is one thing. The levels of creating new options through new social practices defined by new rules, or through changed understandings of social practices, is another. The latter levels have the *potentiality* to offer us enhanced control over our lives, but only indirectly, through positively redefining (at the level of the rules) the meanings of our (lower

level) choices. The situation is analogous for one's choices to be vegetarian or even a nonsmoker. Both can be regarded as basically nega-
tively defined choices, at present, telling us mostly what the agent *does-
n't* do, what practices the agent rejects. (What *do* vegetarians eat? Some
of us are not frankly that crazy about many vegetables. What do non-
smokers inhale? Unfortunately, too often, environmental smoke. What
do lesbians *do*?) Such choices tend to become morally irreversible for
those who make them, narrowing the range of ("live") options. The
power of such choices to improve life lies mainly in their potential *positive* meanings. And these are realizable through innovative social practice only in community with others.

Chapter 4

lesbian ethics

This chapter reflects on literatures of lesbian ethics, past and present. My aim is not to propose a new lesbian ethic but to suggest ways of thinking about lesbian ethics and to consider it in relation to other recent ethics with which it shares concerns, such as gay and feminist ethics. I also take up the question posed recently by Marilyn Frye, and raised in the nineteenth century by Nietzsche's speculations concerning morality: why *ethics*?

Prolegomena to Lesbian Ethics

For more than a decade I have taught a history of philosophy course called "Classics in Feminist Theory," examining selected works from Mary Wollstonecraft through Virginia Woolf. Although I have seldom chosen texts for their lesbian connections, I have kept an eye out for the positive influence of lesbian experience or awareness and for material whose paradigms may have come from lesbian relationships or fantasy. There is, of course, a wealth of overtly lesbian material in novels, poetry, and literary essays from Left Bank Paris in the early twentieth century and between the World Wars. Renée Vivien's novel, for example, *A Woman Appeared to Me*, explores androgyny and infidelity. Colette's essays in *The Pure and the Impure* reflect on ethical values concerning a variety of sexual relationships, including lesbian ones. There is also material from counterculture periodicals of the early homosexual rights movement in late nineteenth and early twentieth century Germany. In more explicitly philosophical works, however, I have not found lesbian material presented as such prior to Simone de Beauvoir's chapter in *The Second Sex*.[1]

What I did find was that many authors had significant experience or attachments that were recognizably lesbian under one or more of the passionate friendship, amazonian, or sapphic paradigms, and that some of them had expressed unmistakable interest in or had actually defended someone or a relationship that was recognizably lesbian under one or more of those paradigms. This should not surprise. Perhaps all that surprises is that the possible significance of such data goes largely unrecognized and unexplored. Knowing these histories suggests layers of lesbian meaning implicit in the work of these authors. Where the work reflects upon ethical norms and values, material so influenced might be considered "prolegomena to lesbian ethics." For those interested in pursuing such layers of meaning, I offer a brief look at five such authors: Mary Wollstonecraft, Margaret Fuller, Charlotte Perkins Gilman, Emma Goldman, and Virginia Woolf.

To identify such prolegomena to lesbian ethics, people thinking about this subject for the first time may need to discard the assumption that married women or mothers are heterosexually oriented with respect to erotic and other passions—that their emotional bonds and political commitments are defined by their legal ones. Many women have had little choice about marriage; their socially sanctioned choices have been limited to spinsterhood, religious orders, or marriage. Spinsterhood and nunneries can easily camouflage lesbian liaisons. So can marriage. Runaways in earlier times, as now, landed in prostitution or a series of affairs. Lesbian liaisons are also found among prostitutes. If extramarital heterosexual affairs made a woman notorious (as they did for Mary Wollstonecraft and Emma Goldman), lesbian affairs have been literally unmentionable, rendering them all but imperceptible to later generations.

Each of my five feminist thinkers married. Some did so reluctantly, and some marriages were brief. For none does marriage appear a dominant force in her life, even though for some, heterosexual liaisons were major forces. Although when they discuss relationships, it is often as an ideal of "marriage," the focus is not usually on law. At least three did not believe in monogamy. Of three who birthed children, two did not live to raise their children; a third was happy for her daughter to live with her first husband and her best friend (his second wife). One, unable to conceive children, refused "corrective" surgery. All had keen senses of humor.

In eighteenth-century England, not long before the French Revolution, the young Mary Wollstonecraft had a passionate friendship and a brief teaching partnership with Fanny Blood, who then married and soon after, died in childbirth in Portugal—attended by Mary. Mary named her first daughter (conceived with Gilbert Imlay out of wedlock) Fanny. The friendship of Mary Wollstonecraft and Fanny Blood may have provided a model against which Mary Wollstonecraft measured marriage relationships in her critique of the status of women and of ideals of virtue for both sexes in her *Vindication of the Rights of Woman* (first published 1792).[2] Just before birthing her second daughter (to become Mary Wollstonecraft Shelley, author of *Frankenstein*), Mary Wollstonecraft married her anarchist lover, William Godwin, for the sake of their child to be. They did not, however, believe in marriage as a legal institution, nor in the double standard of character associated with it.[3]

Also compromising Godwin's earlier professed beliefs, they eventually shared a residence. But each had their own work, their own friends, and they lived to a great extent independently of one another. This is also how lesbian lovers ordinarily lived (as many do today), although usually it was not economically an option for them to share a residence.[4]

Second, consider (Sarah) Margaret Fuller, born in New England in 1810, educated by her father (who had wanted a son) with an intensity that has been compared to John Stuart Mill's early education and on subjects then usually reserved for boys. Her famous essay, "The Great Lawsuit: Man vs. Men. Woman vs. Women," appeared in 1843 in the *Dial*, an American Transcendentalist journal that she edited for a year and to which she contributed a great deal. The essay questions the correlation of femininity and masculinity with women and men. Expanded and published in 1845 as *Woman in the Nineteenth Century*, it maintains that an individual soul exhibits both femininity *and* masculinity in proportions that vary from soul to soul, treating this as ordinary, not unusual.[5] The year before "The Great Lawsuit," Margaret Fuller published her translation of the passionate erotic correspondence of 1905–6 between a young German poet (whom she calls a "Canoness"), Karoline von Gunderode, and Karoline's younger friend, Bettina Brentano (later, the novelist Bettina von Arnim).[6] An undated excerpt from Margaret Fuller's journal (omitted by Ralph Waldo Emerson but restored by her biographer Mason Wade, in 1940) observes, reflecting on the intimacy between Mme Recamier and Mme de Staël, that "It is so true that a woman may be in love with a woman, and a man with a man."[7] Other entries record her own passionate attachment at the age of thirteen to an unnamed English woman.

Much of Margaret Fuller's social criticism has been related to her early education and the social and intellectual aspirations it fostered. However, her critique of social expectations of women may have roots also in her passions for women and in her admiration of women who had similar passions. If falling in love with women is "masculine," for example, masculinity exists in women, too, and if female masculinity is not unusual, perhaps neither are women's passions for women. Her ideal of marriage in *Woman in the Nineteenth Century* is of a multidimensioned partnership between friends, a mutual support system to which gender and roles seem basically unimportant.[8] There is no apparent reason why her ideal of "marriage" could not be fulfilled equally well by same-sex partners.

Margaret Fuller appears to have been one of the first whose urging survives in print that women who wish to challenge oppressive social expectations of women should turn to other women for help in this endeavor and not rely upon men. She wrote, "I believe that, at present, women are the best helpers of one another," "Men, as at present instructed, will not help in this work," "Once I thought that men would help to forward this state of things more than I do now," and (about men on women), "Their encomiums, indeed, are always, in some sense, mortifying; they show too much surprise."[9] Yet, even John Stuart Mill, more than a decade later, still held that "Women cannot be expected to devote themselves to the emancipation of women, until men in considerable number are prepared to join with them in the undertaking."[10]

Margaret Fuller seems also one of the first whose complaint survives in print that "Too much is said of women being better educated, that they may become better companions and mothers *for men*."[11] A long passage praises "old maids," mentioning that such a woman may be, among other possibilities, "a canoness, bound by an inward vow" (no doubt recalling Karoline von Gunderode).[12]

Like Mary Wollstonecraft, and unlike Margaret Fuller, Charlotte Perkins Gilman (1860–1935) was mostly self-educated, except for her study at the Rhode Island School of Design. In her autobiography, in a chapter entitled "Girlhood—If Any," she wrote of having four years' "perfect happiness" in her friendship with Martha Luther, beginning when she was seventeen and Martha sixteen.[13] She contrasts her feelings about young men unfavorably with her feelings for Martha, noting in regard to losing one of these "princes" that it was nothing compared to losing Martha.[14] All her life she had intense friendships with women. During the 1890s, between marriages, she lived three years with her close friend Adeline E. Knapp.

After the birth of her daughter, Katherine, a little more than a year after she married Charles Walter Stetson (which, her autobiography reveals, she had talked herself into doing), she suffered what my mother would have called "a nervous breakdown," spent a disastrous month trying the "rest cure" at the sanatorium of Philadelphia "nerve specialist" Dr. S. Weir Mitchell, and then found that she recovered when visiting friends in California away from her husband and child, only to relapse when she returned to them.[15] She divorced Stetson, led a fairly nomadic life of lecturing for several years, and in 1900 married George Houghton Gilman, her cousin. These facts, and the misogyny of Weir Mitchell's "rest cure" (often a follow-up to ovariotomies he is reported to have performed on "disorderly women") are now well-known, thanks to the rediscovery of Charlotte Gilman's powerful short story, "The Yellow Wallpaper" (which was apparently not appreciated as feminist by decades of male critics) and its republication, with a historical afterword by Elaine Hedges, by the Feminist Press.[16] Less well-known today, although at the time it made her notorious, is her agreement to young Katherine's living with Stetson and his second wife, Grace Ellery Channing (also Charlotte Gilman's best friend). This was hardly the abandonment that a hostile public perceived, as the three friends participated jointly in Katherine's up-bringing.

Charlotte Gilman's treatise *Women and Economics*, a college text in the 1920s, translated into seven languages, presents as ideal a home geared to amazonian rather than domestic life. It does not presume that lovers cohabit (although it finds this a good idea) nor that one's residence is ordinarily a site of childcare, cooking, or housework by its occupants (none of which it finds a good idea): no kitchens, for example (or sewing rooms, etc), except for those who enjoy cooking (or sewing) as a hobby. Cooking would be done by professional cooks at communal eating halls, cleaning by professional housecleaners going from house to house, and so on.[17]

Her 1915 novel, *Herland*, portrays a society of women who value nonviolence but are competent at self-defense, as at everything else.[18] Featuring reproduction by parthenogenesis and yet not mentioning lesbian intimacy, this work may be unique in the history of feminist utopias in being devoid of sexuality. Yet a relatively nomadic life brightened, stabilized, and energized as much by passionate female friendship as by her second marriage appears to underlie ideals that emerge even in this work.

Emma Goldman (1869–1940), an immigrant from Russia in 1885, became the first U.S. public speaker known to defend homosexual rights, according to Magnus Hirshfeld, founder of the Berlin Institute for Sexual Science.[19] She spoke out in defense of Oscar Wilde when he was imprisoned in England at a time when, she later wrote, "my sole acquaintance with homosexuals was limited to a few women I had met in prison (where I was held because of my political convictions)."[20] She continued publicly defending homosexual rights, despite colleagues' objections, reporting in her autobiography that in their view, "anarchism was already enough misunderstood, and anarchists considered depraved; it was inadvisable to add to the misconceptions by taking up perverted sex-forms," and that her response was, "Censorship from comrades had the same effect on me as police persecution; it made me surer of myself, more determined to plead for every victim, be it one of social wrong or of moral prejudice."[21]

This position fits Emma Goldman's sexual libertarianism and anarchism. However, her continuing commitment seems based not just on abstract principles but also on events in her life. Jonathan Katz has published exerpts of passionate love letters to Emma Goldman from Almeda Sperry, with whom Emma Goldman spent at least a week in the country.[22] The correspondence suggests that Emma Goldman returned Almeda Sperry's affection, although not so desperately or intensely. It would have been consistent with Emma Goldman's character to have publicly announced her "Uranianism" (as she and others then sometimes called homosexuality), or her bisexuality, if she thought either truly applied to her.[23] In any case, her continuing ethical stances on homosexuality, like her stances on such other issues as prostitution, appear grounded in direct knowledge of those involved—not necessarily (although possibly) in her own activity, but at least in having been the object of Almeda Sperry's passions and as an acquaintance of lesbians in prison (and possibly of lesbians among prostitutes).[24]

Emma Goldman also opposed marriage, in part because she opposed monogamy. In "The Tragedy of Woman's Emancipation," she took feminist career women to task for accepting the "either/or" of "career or family," complaining that it was not enough to get rid of "external tyrants" as long as the "internal tyrants" of puritan mores condemned the most educated and economically successful women to loveless lives.[25] Had she lived more with lesbians outside prison, she might have noted that unmarried women whose intimate relationships were less open than her own extramarital heterosexual ones are often far from loveless. Nevertheless, her point is well-taken. She could have extended her rejection of puritan mores and her advocacy of "free love" to support lesbianism as warmly as she supported extramarital heterosexual companionship and motherhood. The potentiality, perhaps the implication, is there; but it is not explicit. Her explicit defense of homosexuality was in terms of noninterference, toleration, and respect, whereas she positively advocated extramarital heterosexual partnership and motherhood.

Finally, there is Virginia Woolf (1882–1941), whose late and most radical feminist work, *Three Guineas*, takes a highly separatist stance, advocating that women create separate educational institutions with their own practices designed to foster noncompetitiveness and nonviolence and that women withdraw from supporting men who support violence, refusing even to witness their parades, mend their socks, or nurse their battle wounds.[26] Such separatism sets a stage for positive lesbian engagements. It is also most apt to be generated against a background of such engagements. In this work, addressed to a man who was soliciting her antiwar support, Virginia Woolf does not mention such possibilities. However, a decade earlier, a year before the publication of *A Room of One's Own*, she had published *Orlando: A Biography* (actually, a novel), dedicating it to Vita Sackville-West, who was in love with her and whose attachment she apparently reciprocated.[27] She illustrated Orlando throughout with photographs of Vita in many costumes. *Orlando*, a delightful fantasy as well as social and literary criticism, is about someone born male (Orlando) who lives through several centuries and wakes up one morning (halfway through the novel) to find himself in a female body (which stays female for the rest of the novel). Quentin Bell, Virginia Woolf's nephew and biographer, wrote of the relationship between Virginia Woolf and Vita Sackville-West, "There may have been—on balance I think that there probably was—some caressing, some bedding together. But whatever may have occurred between them of this nature, I doubt very much whether it was of a kind to excite Virginia or to satisfy Vita."[28] He recognizes throughout the biography that Virginia Woolf was in love with many women and that many were in love with her, also, including composer Dame Ethel Smyth.

Commentators have called attention to possible effects on Virginia Woolf's work of childhood sexual abuse by her stepbrothers.[29] To stop there, however, attending only to negative experiences in childhood, is to ignore her positive adult experiences with women and a certain progression in the development of her feminist ideas. Her thinking about values and sexual politics moves from exploring androgyny in *Orlando* and *A Room of One's Own* to *Three Guineas'* focus on exploiting positively values women have learned in surviving oppression, rejecting the values of masculinity. The timing of this progression, as well as details of her observations, suggest as much adult appreciation of women as childhood trauma from boys.

It is unclear how much or what kinds of lesbian experience entered the lives of these theorists. Yet they were clearly aware of lesbian possibilities, had generally positive attitudes toward them, found them interesting and occasionally worth defending. Perhaps only the label "lesbian" was missing. Still, lack of explicitness regarding the data of lesbian lives constrains philosophical reflection. Even Simone de Beauvoir, writing openly about lesbianism less than a decade after Virginia Woolf's death, was not open about her own passions for girls and women.[30] For openly self-reflective ethical thinking based on an explicit and rich body of lesbian data, we need to turn to the decades since 1970.

Ethics and Politics: Why Ethics?

To grasp lesbian and feminist ethics, it is important to study works that identify themselves as political—such as Sara Ruddick's *Maternal Thinking: Toward a Politics of Peace*—as well as those identifying themselves as ethical or moral.[31] In recent history, the focus on politics came first.

In an essay reflecting on Sarah Hoagland's *Lesbian Ethics: Toward New Value*, Marilyn Frye raises the question whether lesbians need ethics, wondering whether "instead of seeking to create a Lesbian Ethics, many of us who are attracted by a book titled *Lesbian Ethics* might consider learning to do without ethics entirely."[32] She suggests that what Sarah Hoagland's book offers may not really be ethics but perhaps a better alternative, namely, a theory of agency as the creation and maintenance of meaning and value.[33] This "alternative" also sounds like Marilyn Frye's understanding of *politics*, which she presents in another essay as concerned with forces that create forms of agency, "engaging will in the making of value."[34] Her skepticism about the value of ethics is not totally maverick. Among feminist lesbians and other political insurgents, the view circulates—although it is not often explicitly defended—that although politics is essential, ethics may be dispensable. Using Marilyn Frye's queries as a springboard and exploiting insights from her more recent essay, "Getting It Right," I want to take up the question, Why ethics? as requesting an answer, rather than as rhetorical rejection, and consider some of the relations between politics and ethics.[35]

In "Getting it Right," Marilyn Frye laments the political right's cooptation, and the consequent degeneration in meaning, of the term "political correctness." She defends political understanding as having the objective of engaging "wills and resources in movement that enhances and furthers the well-beings of individuals, of groups, and of social-historic processes that it is good to enhance and further," observing in an endnote that "there is not agreement about what *is* good to enhance and further."[36] This objective of politics stated in terms of well-being sounds to me inclusive of ethics. What counts as well-being and what is good to enhance and further are customary preoccupations of ethics. Ethics is commonly understood as a study of norms and values, the right and the good, as these enter into or support human well-being, norms that political arrangements can respect (or disregard) and values that politics can promote (or hinder).

What is politics? Marilyn Frye offers a metaphor that captures well a postmodernist understanding of political power (such as that of Michel Foucault): "the politics of a situation," she suggests, is like "climate and weather, topology and soil: a multidimensional, multileveled, temporally extended, constantly changing, moving medium," a "highly structured and fluid play of powers, which both sustains and threatens all the vital processes of human community existence; a sum of forces and pressures, current, turbulences and calms, variations of density," the conditions of which at particular times and places "determine what can be done and by whom."[37] On this view, politics does not simply restrain preexisting agents; it creates new forms of agency.

The weather metaphor also brings *variability* to the fore. Weather can change rapidly from day to day, week to week, month to month, and it tends to go in cycles. These features, on which Marilyn Frye does not comment, make the weather metaphor especially appropriate for politics. They also suggest a difference between ethics and politics. Ethics is relatively resistant to local change. If political values are like the winds, ethical ones tend to be more like bedrock: ethics can change, and it does over time, but usually slowly. This difference is easily missed if one is doing revolutionary ethics, which Sarah Hoagland means to be doing. In times of upheaval, both ethics and politics can be scenes of profound and relatively rapid change. However, variability tends to be the order of the day with politics even in nonrevolutionary times. Such variability is uncharacteristic of ethics.

Noting limits of the weather metaphor, Marilyn Frye acknowledges that the *forces* in question, unlike physical elements of the weather, are *socially constructed* and, accordingly, subject to disagreements regarding what is worth constructing. And if they are not physical, what are these political "forces" if not *norms*, *standards*, sometimes even *rules*? Some are explicit, others implicit. They define forms of behavior, practices (such as rotating chair or check-in as group processes) that are shared among members of social groups, action in accord with which has social consequences.

I find no sharp line between ethics and politics, but, rather, overlap and mutual conditioning, especially when ethics is understood to include morality. Etymologically, "ethics" refers to habits, not mindless repetition but habits of choice, of noticing (or ignoring), habitual attitudes, dispositions. "Ethics" (from ancient Greek) suggests character and agency. "Morality" (from the Latin "*mores*") suggests social custom and tradition. Contemporary philosophers often use "ethics" and "morality" interchangeably (ignoring a popular usage that associates "ethics offenses" with financial transgressions and "morals offenses" with sexual ones), taking the field to include reflection on both character and customs. So understood, ethical values are often used to evaluate political power and its uses by reference to such concepts as human well-being, dignity, integrity, fidelity, fairness, honesty, and so on. Political norms that embody ethical values thus become ethical as well. However, politics does not necessarily embody ethical values (even when it should). Nor is ethics exhausted by political norms. Individual agency and interpersonal relationships are highly *underdefined* by the politics of their environments. Ethics is also about attitudes toward oneself and others, fate, the universe, even when these attitudes have no political consequences, are neither aligned nor disaligned with social forces, neither contribute to nor detract from them. "Forces" (bringing about movement, consequences) are not always the subject of ethics. If politics is basically about socially produced power, ethics is also about vitality and well-being that are not entirely the product of social construction. If ethics totally abstracted from politics is naive, politics without ethics can be frightening, or worse.

The questions whether we need ethics, and why many evidently want it, are reminiscent of Nietzsche's project of revaluing moral values.[38] Nietzsche hypothesized that the moral concept of "evil"—designating what deserves to be hated—originated self-deceptively among the weak to stigmatize the powerful whom in reality they envied. "Good," he argued (citing philological evidence), was first used narcissistically by the powerful and lucky who considered themselves noble, contrasting themselves with the "bad" ("low," "common," "ordinary"), whom they found pitiable (not worthy of hatred) and toward whom they were sometimes benevolent. But when goodness is opposed to *evil*, it is turned upsidedown in that it now exalts weakness (rather than power), hardly a promising value. "Good," after the inversion, means "not evil"—safe, harmless, perhaps even *useful*—whereas formerly, it had meant "noble." Thus, Nietzsche's speculations pose the questions whether the moral mode of valuation, insofar as it involves the opposition of good and evil, is based on self-deception and whether morality deserves to be transcended.

Nietzsche's hypotheses concerning the "genealogy of morals" are insightful regarding the meanings of "goodness" but also flawed by his often apparently uncritical assumption of the honesty and goodwill of his hypothetical powerful elites. He often seems unaware that the powerful are as easily self-deceptive as the weak and that the hatred in judgments of evil is as at home in the standpoints of the powerful as in those of common folk. In particular, the powerful hate mockery from common folk, who, far from envying them, often do not find them so wonderful as they find themselves. The powerful often consider those they hate to be "traitors," "ingrates," undeserving of the goodwill of their "protectors." Paradigmatically evil, from the perspective of the powerful, are rebels among those whom the powerful trust to serve them (women, children, servants, slaves). The greater the trust, the greater the potentiality for "evil." As Mary Daly saw, Eve was "evil" not because she was powerful but because she was *insubordinate*.[39]

A political view of history suggests a more straightforward, more plausible hypothesis than Nietzsche's, namely, that the powerful "originated" *both* conceptions of goodness: one, a nonutilitarian conception (the "nobility" conception), applied to *themselves* and their peers; the other, a highly utilitarian conception, applied to *others* whom they used freely and found, at best, faithful and, at worst, treacherous. What Nietzsche called "the slave mode of valuation" sounds like a development—perhaps an internalization—of values that powerful oppressors applied to their slaves. Good slaves, women, children, servants, are loyal and grateful; they do not rebel; they do not challenge dominance orders. It would not be surprising if many born into chattel slavery or other forms of servitude internalized such values. If democracy results in the elevation of those values, this is not an inversion of the values of the powerful so much as the oppressors' own utilitarian attitudes toward others returning to haunt them.

Insofar as judgments of "evil" are grounded simply in fear of power or of challenges to dominance, however, there is nothing specifically moral or ethical about them, regardless whose perspectives they embody. "Evil" becomes a moral, or ethical concept, when what is threatened is not simply power or dominance but such values as integrity, humanity, respect, justice. The Nazi Holocaust and American slavery are paradigmatic moral evils not because they manifested extreme power or challenged dominance orders but because of the values they failed to respect, because of *what* they destroyed, what they aimed to destroy.[40]

If Nietzsche's "slave values" are basically utilitarian, they are not obviously moral, even if embedded in the mores of populations and even if they discourage many of the same actions that moral values discourage. Transcending such values is thus not obviously transcending morality. However, neither is it obvious that a slave society, its descendants, or its reflective thinkers, have believed predominantly in utilitarian values. Many surviving sources on what slaves have believed are highly contaminated, as most slaves have been illiterate, their words filtered through others, often others from classes who have had power over them. Even freed slaves have said what they believed interviewers wanted to hear. It would be rash to conclude that utility is the interviewee's highest value. Utility and self-interest are often *contrasted* with morality because they do not make adequately intelligible such important values as dignity, self-respect, and integrity. Recognizing oppression arguably presupposes a nonutilitarian conception of the value of agents. Oppression rides roughshod over such things as self-respect, pride, integrity. Yet, many slaves unquestionably recognized their oppression. Harriet Jacobs, for example, narrating her years as an American slave, wrote, "When I lay down beside my child, I felt how much easier it would be to see her die than to see her master beat her about, as I daily saw him beat other little ones," and later observed, "Hot weather brings out snakes and slaveholders, and I like one class of the venomous creatures as little as I do the other. What a comfort it is, to be free to *say* so!"[41] Harriet Jacobs refused permission to a Northern white woman who wanted to buy her out of slavery, on the ground that she did not consider herself an article of property and that "being sold from one owner to another seemed too much like slavery."[42] This is not a utilitarian perspective. To the extent that Nietzsche relied on self-deceptive perspectives of powerful oppressors for his understanding of slaves and other servants, his hypotheses gravely underestimate the wisdom and the values of common folk.

Marilyn Frye's hypothesis differs from Nietzsche's in that she suspects that the currently popular desire for ethics among lesbians may come from a background of having learned to *identify with those who have power over us*, applying to ourselves the values they apply to themselves (an improvement, surely, over internalizing the values they apply to us). She suggests that needing to be "in the right" may be specific to those who assume that it is their business to oversee the behavior of others and to be judges of their behavior, illustrating by quoting Minnie Bruce Pratt's account of how she was raised to be "a *martyr*, to take all responsibility for change *and* the glory, to expect others to do nothing . . . to be a *peacemaker*, to mediate, negotiate, between opposing sides because *I* knew the right way . . . to be a *preacher*, to point out wrongs and tell others what to do."[43] Minnie Bruce Pratt's account reminds me, in part, of a standpoint I have called in another context—characterizing the preoccupation with social control of contractarian and utilitarian modern moral philosophy—"the administrative point of view."[44] Administrators often coordinate others' behavior, telling them what to do and determining whether they have done as they ought. Administrators can get into deep trouble if they do not "get it right." As Marilyn Frye argues regarding "political correctness," however, the concern to "get it right" is not restricted to such standpoints.

An administrative standpoint suggests one kind of investment in the need to know right from wrong. Women eligible for "token" positions of power may come to identify with such a standpoint. However, many who insist on distinguishing right from wrong are not eligible for tokenism—many dykes, for example, especially separatist dykes, and women whose social backgrounds are "wrong." I would not describe my *moral training*, as distinct from my training as a moral *philosopher*, the way Minnie Bruce Pratt described her moral training. Her account may apply to many whose works have become classics of moral philosophy, works basic to my training as a moral philosopher. But I was not raised at home or school to tell others what to do, nor to point out their errors. If anything, I was *raised* not to judge, "lest I be judged." I had to learn the hard way that without making judgments, I had no way to protest abuse, nor to recognize the justifiability of protecting myself (or anyone else) against abuse—no way even to *distinguish* between abuse and a mere conflict of wills. The latter understanding of domestic battering—perceiving it as simply a conflict of wills—has given rise to the concept of "mutual battering," just because it has no way to distinguish between abuse and mere clash.[45] Making judgments, here, does not mean imposing sentences. It means *evaluating*. The standards of evaluation are used to judge the uses of power and remain meaningful even where power is unavailable.

Thus, I resist the temptation to collapse ethics into politics. We need ethics to evaluate powers by reference to values they enact, promote or protect. I doubt that Marilyn Frye would take issue with the substance of this idea; in rejecting ethics, it is not clear that she means to reject justice, decency, integrity, respect, and so on, as values by which to assess political arrangements. Yet, to me, these are paradigm ethical values. However, Marilyn Frye is right to suggest that Sarah Hoagland's *Lesbian Ethics* offers more than ethics. I have never been clear on what it means to "create value"—which Sarah Hoagland's *Lesbian Ethics* professes to be about—unless it means to embody values in, or attach value to, options that we create. The creation of options, or practices, can be very political, however ethical the values they embody. Sarah Hoagland's work has the explicit political aim of identifying ways to introduce stability into lesbian community, to work through conflicts without destroying the organizations we create. Her vision of lesbian ethics is centered on conflict resolution and problem solving that draw upon care and respect. Such a vision integrates politics with ethical values.

What Is Lesbian About Lesbian Ethics?

Lesbian ethics is a relatively new field of philosophical inquiry with a growing body of literature. At present at least one quarterly journal in the United States is devoted to the field, and many are receptive to contributions in the area.[46] Activity in this direction was underway at least fifteen years ago. I have in my files a two-page letter from Toni McNaron, professor of English at the University of Minnesota, accompanying a flyer for the 1978 Summer Program of a Women's Learning Institute on their farm at Maiden Rock, Wisconsin, which lists a workshop, "Ethics for Feminists and Lesbian-Feminists," with Sarah Hoagland as a facilitator. I first heard the term "lesbian ethics" that year when Sarah Hoagland read her essay, "Lesbian Ethics," in Chicago to a semiannual conference of the Midwest Society of Women in Philosophy. Over the next decade that essay developed into the book, *Lesbian Ethics: Toward New Value*, which remains, at the present writing, the most extended and influential philosophical inquiry on the subject. Other roots of contemporary lesbian ethics are Adrienne Rich's "Women and Honor: Some Notes on Lying," exploring women's bringing to relationships with women values learned in oppressive relationships to men, and Marilyn Frye's "Some Thoughts on Separatism and Power," discussing not only power but values promoted by separation, a theme that so many have found "so exciting and so repellent."[47] Both essays circulated as pamphlets in 1978, serving as texts for CR groups and workshops from coast to coast. Also from this period is *For Lesbians Only: A Separatist Anthology*, edited by Sarah Hoagland and Julia Penelope, begun in the early 1980s and published in the same year as *Lesbian Ethics: Toward New Value*.[48]

Other contributors to and influences on the literature of lesbian ethics include philosophy professors Jeffner Allen, Bat-Ami Bar On, and Chris Cuomo; archivist Joan Nestle; novelist Joanna Russ; poets Gloria Anzaldúa, Judy Grahn, Susan Griffin, and the late Audre Lorde and Pat Parker; theologian and philosophy professor Mary Daly; women's studies professor and former nun Janice Raymond; environmentalist and former nun H. Patricia Hynes; philosophy professor and former beatnik Joyce Trebilcot; philosopher, women's studies professor and film critic Jacqueline Zita; and philosophy professor and political organizer Maria Lugones.[49] Sociological studies by Susan Cavin and cultural histories by Lillian Faderman and Judy Grahn have also been invaluable.[50]

A possible misunderstanding of lesbian ethics is to suppose that it is simply *applied* ethics, an application of preexisting standards to issues facing lesbians. Such an understanding would be embodied in a conception of lesbian ethics as focused on political correctness. "Politically correct," originally used by Leftists as a semi-mocking term of self-criticism, sounds mocking and trivializing because "correct" suggests only accuracy or skill in applying a standard, leaving open both the value of the standard and the question whether its wielder appreciates its value. "Ethically correct" is equally mocking and trivializing. In ethics, as in politics, reducing rightness to to correctness makes the relevant agency appear superficial.

Lesbian ethics, as engaged in by thinkers named above, is not "applied ethics." It is not the application of theories or principles defined by others to issues encountered by lesbians. Like feminist ethics (which, Julia Penelope maintains, has branched off from it), lesbian ethics includes thinking and theorizing at all levels, from such immediately practical matters as how to run a lesbian restaurant to such abstract matters as which concepts are central to resolving ethical problems from the perspectives of lesbian living.

What makes lesbian ethics lesbian are, first of all, its backgrounds, its sources, the histories out of which it has grown, and its paradigms, the data on which it draws. Lesbian ethics is self-reflective ethical inquiry carried out on the basis of lesbian experience, imagination, relationships, and so on. This, of course, gives it the potentiality for great diversity.

As a historical phenomenon, lesbian ethics has had the aim of being revolutionary in relation to philosophical traditions of Western European thought. Much interesting work in women's ethics and feminist ethics, as in lesbian ethics and in the likewise relatively new field of environmental ethics, is characterized by the theme of rejecting Western traditions that devalue the physical, the material, the transitory, concrete particulars.[51] Advocates of these new ethics often move toward holism, stressing the importance of relationships, although they work with varying paradigms of relationship. Lesbian ethics, like contemporary feminist philosophy generally, is often skeptical of rules and rights, institutions, hierarchies, dualisms, and competition, as well as curious about such things as anarchy, personal relationships, the erotic, sexuality, self-development, agency, and creativity. Sarah Hoagland questions not only the primacy but the value of the concept of justice for contemporary lesbian communities. There is no consensus on such things, however. These are themes; even as themes, they do not characterize all of lesbian ethics.[52]

Lesbian ethics is not only, or even primarily, about erotic or sexual liaisons. A common complaint from lesbians has been that sex and the erotic receive too little attention in many of the writings of lesbian ethics. Lesbian ethics has a comprehensiveness comparable to that of older traditions in philosophical ethics, although it tends to be more self-conscious about limitations that may stem from its sources, leaving open whether others besides lesbians may also find it useful or enlightening. Lesbian ethics aims to address all aspects of lesbian living—economic and political issues, education and moral development, emotional and physical well-being, violence and abuse, spirituality, racial and ethnic differences, physical disabilities and illness, and such matters as the significance of age and body size for ethical interaction. The fact that its contributors write for a lesbian audience does not make it more parochial than other ethics. It is not true, for example, that it lacks concern for global issues, such as the physical environment, poverty, or racism. Ethical theory by white male philosophers has also been based on selected, less-than-universal paradigms, and lesbians are among those left out of those paradigms. Historically, such theories have drawn simply on the interactions of white men with other white men, assuming an audience of educated white men, usually with wealth or power that might be threatened by other men. It is commonly assumed without argument that ethics elaborated on such paradigms is universal and eternal. In lesbian ethics, that assumption is replaced by leaving open questions of wider applicability for others to answer for themselves.

Even in *feminist* ethics, many writers presume heterosexuality in their paradigms, often taking the experience of heterosexual mothers as a basis for articulating norms and values.[53] Lesbian ethics shifts the focus by shifting to lesbian paradigms. As to the differences this makes, it is early to say with much confidence or clarity, although themes, patterns, and hypotheses, such as those mentioned above, can be identified in the literature. However, it is possible to comment on the approaches to ethical thinking that lesbian ethics has so far exhibited.

In being self-consciously grounded in history, lesbian ethics is "particularist," rather than "universalist." By "particularist," I do not mean "relativist." Relativism denies the existence of universally (cross-culturally or transhistorically) valid norms or values. Particularist ethics need not deny such possibilities, but neither does it take as its objective the articulation of ethical norms or values in abstraction from the kinds of particulars that differentiate some groups of people from others. Like universalist ethics, it aims for truth, or, better, for truths. But its model of truth is more like that of the potluck, as suggested by Joyce Trebilcot, or perhaps a patchwork quilt, than like that of the bullseye on a target or the top rung of a ladder.[54] Target and bullseye models suggest a picture of everyone aiming for the same truth, possibly even competing to get there. The models of a potluck or patchwork suggest a picture of different contributors bringing stories from their various histories to establish parts of a truth that outruns the efforts of any individual and only parts of which are even of interest or relevance to individual contributors. On the potluck or patchwork models, coherence plays a large role, but it is not everything. Not all dishes are digestible nor all patches usable. Yet, with ingenuity, many contributions can find a place. Patchworks and potlucks come closer to Wittgenstein's metaphor of the cable, hanging together as one thing, though no strand runs throughout.

Universalist approaches to ethics are apt to appear, from the perspectives of lesbian ethics, like the attempt to construct an ideal diet or meal without making use of dishes that have a cultural history. Perhaps it can be done. Even so, it is hardly the only way to eat well. Universalist ethics presumes to abstract from the differences among us and to articulate norms and values for human beings considered simply as such. Universalists are apt to use "we" as though it referred to all humanity. Particularists tend to use a more limited "we." Feminist ethics, like lesbian ethics, has tended to be particularist.

Although lesbians are not necessarily feminist, the standpoints that lesbian ethics has developed have been, historically, feminist. The histories out of which lesbian ethics has grown have been histories of homophobia, misogyny, and violence against lesbians (and against women generally), on the one hand, and histories of individual and communal resistance to the oppressiveness of those things, on the other. Homophobia, misogyny, and violence have enforced lesbian invisibility and female economic dependence on men, making women until recent times nearly inaccessible to one another for sexual relationships and intimate life partnerships. Consequently, a fundamental concern of lesbian ethics has been to discover what promotes the establishment and thriving of good and strong lesbian connections, what promotes lesbian community and basic lesbian safety. Against this background, lesbian ethics has had the objective of defining conditions of well-being for woman-loving women.

Lesbian Ethics vs. Gay, Women's, and Feminist Ethics

One reason it is difficult to characterize lesbian ethics generally is that the experience out of which it grows exhibits the variety of the paradigms delineated in chapter 1—amazonian, sapphic, and passionate friendship paradigms—which overlap but are also occasionally in tension. Nevertheless, it is possible to make some general observations distinguishing lesbian ethics, as a complex historical phenomenon, from other recent ethics that share some of its concerns.

Lesbian ethics is not the same as gay ethics, for example, although there is overlap. The phrase "lesbians and gays" uses "gays" to refer only to men. This is confusing because some lesbians identify as "gay." "Gay" is preferred by many whose political concerns are with legal reform or whose chosen communities include a mixed-gender counterculture.[55] Gay ethics has not yet aimed for the theoretical autonomy of lesbian ethics. It works with gay paradigms of moral *issues*, but so far conceives itself as applied ethics, extending ethical theories, principles, or ideas originally defined by others (who worked with other paradigms). Unlike lesbian ethics, it has not yet aimed to be revolutionary in relation to Western philosophical traditions in ethical theory, although its conclusions regarding particular issues contest received wisdom. The newer phenomenon of Queer Ethics, however, with roots in gay culture, seems revolutionary in aim.[56] The "queer" of Queer Ethics encompasses many varieties of sexual heresy, not only gay and lesbian ones.

Gay ethics and Queer Ethics have focused more on sexuality than lesbian ethics (at least of the amazonian and friendship varieties). "Gay" suggests a counterculture that has not always been sensitive to feminist concerns.[57] In the past decade, however, gay culture has become increasingly sensitive not only to gender issues but to issues of race, class, and disability. The gay organization, Black and White Men Together, has now been active for many years. The Society for Lesbian and Gay Philosophy, founded in 1988 as a satellite of the American Philosophical Association, has begun to facilitate intellectual contact between lesbian and gay philosophers. If philosophical gay ethics develops more theoretical autonomy, it can be expected to reflect differences between lesbian histories and histories of men's same-sex relationships (differences, for example, in histories of the relationships of gay men and lesbians to male privilege in a misogynist society).

Nor is lesbian ethics identical with "women's ethics." Nor is it just another term for feminist ethics. *Women's* ethics has leading advocates in professors of education Carol Gilligan, a psychologist at Harvard, and Nel Noddings, a philosopher at Stanford. Carol Gilligan describes a women's voice in ethics, articulating an "ethic of care," by contrast with the "ethic of justice" she finds oftener among men.[58] A central concern

of the care ethic is nurturing in close relationships that are not voluntary, or not entirely voluntary. Nel Noddings explores philosophically
the idea of a care ethic, likewise taking as paradigms relationships that
are not, or not entirely, voluntary, especially those of adult care-takers
to children.[59] Recently, she has examined major evils—poverty, illness,
war, and terrorism—from the standpoints of women's experiences,
analyzing evil in terms of pain, separation, and helplessness.[60] Unlike
Nel Noddings, Carol Gilligan does not devalue justice in defending
care. Carol Gilligan's earlier view was that care ethics and justice ethics
were complementary; more recently she has perceived them as incompatible gestalts that most people can entertain although not simultane-
ously, finding that most also prefer one to the other.[61] Nel Noddings,
however, defends care as superior to justice, finding justice a poor substitute for caring. This may make her work appear closer than Carol
Gilligan's to the outlaw element in lesbian ethics, which also is often
skeptical of the value of justice for amazons.

Proponents of lesbian ethics have been skeptical of the care ethics of
both Carol Gilligan and Nel Noddings as femin*ine* rather than femin*ist*,
as not revolutionary but, on the contrary, politically conservative for
women.[62] The basic criticism, voiced by Sarah Hoagland, has been that
such care ethics takes as its paradigm of caring—explicitly or implicitly—the role of mother as defined under patriarchy, a role that feminists
find oppressive.[63] Also problematic is the valorization of togetherness,
especially heterosexual togetherness in a misogynist society. In lesbian
ethics, separation from men and from institutions of heteropatriarchy
has been a strong positive theme. Care has been as central to lesbian
ethics as to "women's ethics." But lesbian paradigms of caring have been
those of openly lesbian consensual relationships, subversive of patriarchy, and between parties more nearly equal in power than parents and
young children. Although significant political power differences are
hardly absent from multicultural lesbian communities, paradigms of
caring in lesbian ethics have not been defined so as to *valorize* power
differences or their consequences. It is important, however, for lesbian
ethics also to acknowledge the importance of relationships that are not
entirely voluntary. In choosing lesbian community, one may acquire
neighbors with whom one would not otherwise have chosen to interact. Even in choosing a lesbian lover, one may acquire a proximity to
her friends or family that one would not otherwise have chosen.

Although one popular misconception of feminist ethics is that it is
the same as "women's voice" ethics, feminist ethics (like lesbian ethics)

has in fact been critical of the women's voices valorized by Carol Gilligan and Nel Noddings. However, feminist ethics, like "women's voice" ethics, tends to presume a wider range of relationships with men as potentially ethically acceptable within even a patriarchal society than lesbian ethics does. Sara Ruddick's "maternal thinking" retains heterosexual motherhood as a basic paradigm of caring, attempting to distinguish what is valuable from what is oppressive in that paradigm. Nonviolence, a major theme of her work, has been more a characteristic theme of feminist ethics than of lesbian ethics.

In contrast to the discussions of violence in much feminist ethics, Jeffner Allen offers a nonpacifist lesbian response in her reflections on being raped.[64] Like many lesbians in discussing violence, she draws attention to violence women suffer from men, often private rather than public, often in domestic settings. Feminist ethics has tended to take as its paradigms of violence *public* activities, commonly with men as both agents and victims—violence of war, street crime, corporal or capital punishment—and has often advocated a pacifist response.[65]

When lesbian ethics is based on amazon paradigms, it is apt to be skeptical of philosophies of nonviolence coming from mothers in a patriarchal context. Amazonian ethics, sometimes also called daughter ethics, is more filial than maternal, as all amazons are daughters but only some are mothers. Amazonian ethics not only does not presume that all women should or ideally will birth children but also does not presume that all women should or ideally will share childcare, nor that all who do will be or should be disposed toward nonviolence. Amazon society is sometimes inaccurately characterized as matriarchal, although in Amazon society, public affairs were defined and constituted by the activities of women who were bonded with women, not by mothers as such. Amazons were historically warriors and nomads. Amazonian ethics suggests contexts of mobility, rather than domesticity, where women make and execute major social decisions, including decisions about defense.

Lesbian ethics need not be amazonian, however. It can be based on sapphic paradigms or paradigms of passionate friendship, such as that of Ruth for Naomi. If amazons tend to be nomadic and physically skilled, sapphic paradigms often suggest confinement in or retreat to an all-female institution surrounded by a male-dominated society—a girls' school or women's college, a women's prison, women's barracks, a convent. Sapphic paradigms focus on the erotic. They sometimes suggest involvements with the arts, relationships between artist and muse, teacher–student relationships. Sapphic paradigms also include teacher–teacher and student–student attachments, often relatively ephemeral and not always reciprocal. Any of these relationships can embody a power imbalance, and the imbalance can become part of the attraction. Yet, there need not be an *overall* power imbalance, even in teacher–student relationships, and when there is, it may not be obvious where the advantage lies. Still, sapphic ethics often has attended to issues presented by power imbalances. It has reflected, for example, on norms and values involved in such issues as butch and femme roles, sadomasochism, pornography, and what for lack of a better term is commonly called "non-monogamy."[66] Sapphic ethics also overlaps with amazonian ethics, at least where butch paradigms overlap with amazonian ones.

Sapphic ethics also overlaps with the ethics of passionate friendship. Lesbian ethics based on paradigms of passionate friendship tends to be concerned with long-term relationships that may or may not have an erotic focus, or that may have it only at some stages. Economics comes more to the fore in long-term relationships, both in the current sense of concern with resources and in the ancient sense of homemaking.[67] Long-term relationships suggest a concern with one's environment, both one's domicile and the larger environment of communities and the physical world. A natural connection of lesbian ethics with environmental ethics is through the paradigm of passionate friendship.

Lesbian ethics as sketched here is not simply ethics theorized and practiced *by* lesbians. Lesbians help construct many kinds of ethics, including gay ethics, queer ethics, feminist ethics, and women's voice ethics, as well as older traditions that have been labeled in accord with their contents or after their male creators. However, lesbian ethics *is* the creation, primarily, of lesbians who prioritize their relationships with lesbians, who make lesbian identity central to their lives.

Although the aim of lesbian ethics has not been to educate others, and lesbian ethics may not suit the needs of just anyone, many can learn from it, if only by learning to empathize with lesbian perspectives as fully as with those whose values have informed classical ethical theories.

Part Two

lesbians in relationship: ups and downs

Chapter 5

lesbian friendship: separations and continua

In recent years, feminist reflections on friendship have given special attention to issues of bonding across racial, class, and other socially constructed boundaries. Sarah Hoagland examines friendship across many kinds of boundaries among lesbians in community with lesbians.[1] María Lugones and Vicky Spelman have written about cross-cultural bonding in ways that apply equally to nonlesbian friendships.[2] In this chapter, I take up issues that arise among lesbians when the boundaries between intimate and nonintimate friendships are thrown into question, or, perhaps, into chaos. The way such issues used to be posed was in terms of "friends vs. lovers." And that is how the writer with whom I begin tends to delineate the problems. However, by "lesbian friendship" I mean friendship between lesbians, regardless whether they are, or have been, each other's lovers.

Can Lesbians Be Friends?

Nearly twenty years ago, two letters signed "Margy" were printed in the *Lesbian Connection* (LC) newsletter, under the heading, "Can Lesbians

Be Friends?"[3] Margy posed a number of questions about friendship from a lesbian perspective, including why it is often easier for lesbians to find lovers than to find good friends, how to deal with sexual aspects of friendships so as to preserve the friendship, how to "draw the line" between affection and sex, what can be done to prevent isolation in lesbian couples, and what to do with the difficulties of becoming friends with a lesbian who is "monogamously" coupled. The letters were unusual in their frankness and their refusal to glorify lesbian friendships. Readers who responded in subsequent issues of LC tended to agree with Margy on the difficulties.

Margy began by recalling that through her childhood and youth, female friends were the most important people in her life but that in college, men began coming between them. Initially, she thought lesbian friendships would be ideal because men would not come between lesbians. Then came the disillusionment of finding a greater obstacle: sex. Setting aside complications introduced by other lesbians in the life of either, Margy's first letter explored ways that sex seems to become an obstacle to friendship between lesbians. Understanding "coupled" as "monogamous" and "lovers" as sexually involved, she set out the consequences for noncoupled lesbians of having been socialized in heterosexual society to prioritize lovers over others, of seeing every lesbian primarily as a potential lover, and of not having learned how to develop friendships with potential lovers. She described both the damage to the possibility of a future friendship after a lover relationship between lesbians who had not already established a friendship and the damage to established friendships between lesbians who then become lovers but whose lover relationship did not last. Recalling the complaint that in friendships with nonlesbian women, lesbians have felt as though they had to take second place to some man, Margy concluded her first letter, "Well, I'm tired of taking second place to sex."

Margy's second letter took up obstacles posed by sex to friendship between lesbians at least one of whom is coupled with someone else, this time focusing on complications introduced by the lover and by members of a lesbian community that does not acknowledge butch-femme roles. Here, the tendency to see any lesbian primarily as a potential lover created jealousies in present lovers and gossip in the community regarding any two lesbians who begin spending time together. A common upshot is the isolation of lesbians in couples, reinforced by tendencies of many noncoupled lesbians to see coupled ones as "already taken" and thereby a waste of one's time. A lesbian who becomes interested in forming a friendship with a lesbian who is already coupled may have to pass a trial period in which she proves her "trustworthiness." She may have to like and be liked by the friend's lover. She may find it difficult to get to know her friend independently of the lover. Because of all this, some lesbians get together only in groups of couples. While doing so may circumvent gossip and jealousy, it multiplies other difficulties. Not only is it more difficult for many to get to know each other well in this way but, also, as couples break up, friendships formed in groups undergo upheavals.

Part of what makes the jeopardizing of friendship regrettable is, as Margy noted, that lover relationships, as such, tend to be relatively unstable, whereas good friendships tend to last and have a greater impact on one's life.[4] She looked forward to the day when lesbians would appreciate and validate the importance of nonsexual friendships. The issues are not just personal. They have political consequences. She raised the question whether we were not getting ahead of ourselves in trying to form lesbian communities and organizations, observing that a lesbian community composed of lovers, ex-lovers, and potential lovers may be missing "a very critical and necessary element—friends."

As Margy noted, lesbians who embrace butch and femme roles may have fewer such problems, because at least butches seem able to become friends with butches and femmes with femmes without creating jealousy and gossip. Roles may facilitate friendship by setting bounds to sexual involvement. In heterosexual society, family structures with prohibitions against boundary violations among kin may do the same. Aristotle included kinship relations among affiliations he counted as friendships. An absence of all these things—roles, kinship structure, and boundary prohibitions—leaves lesbians in the position of not being able to presume that any relationship formed with another lesbian will not become sexual. This situation presents problems of trust and confidence with respect to seeking support and advice from anyone who is not one's lover, not only advice regarding existing relationships but support in general. For, the possibility of underlying sexual agendas in all transactions raises questions about motives.

Experiences of women prisoners who have almost no opportunity for sexual activity suggest that the problems Margy described are not necessarily tied to the possibility of sexual activity but can arise where there is simply erotic bonding. Some women prisoners seem to have met the difficulties by reproducing elaborate kinship networks among themselves, a practice referred to by sociologist Sister Esther Heffernan as "familying."[5] In "familying," women who bond erotically with each other may adopt one another's friends as "mothers," "fathers," "brothers," "sisters," "uncles," "aunts," and so on, complete with kinship boundary prohibitions against erotic intimacy. These "families" provide counsel and support to members during crises or hard times, socialize new inmates to prison society, and offer a stability that the couple relationships tend to lack. Couples come and go, but the families remain. Since, unlike birth families, these families are largely chosen, they may be even more likely than birth kin to generate friendships.

Rose Giallombardo, who was perhaps the first to do an extended study of such kinship networks in a women's prison (Alderson Federal Penitentiary), reported a similar practice recorded by Ju-K'ang T'ien in a 1940 study of women in cotton mills in China who worked in same-sex settings and lived away from home in dormitories.[6] She quotes T'ien's description of one such family of female cotton mill workers: "Of the seven 'sons' four have left and entered other 'families' as 'sons-in-law' (according to the matrilocal pattern). One of the remaining 'sons' (worker named Chang) 'married' a worker named Chow. Another 'married' a worker named Ho. The third one is not yet 'married' but is in love with a 'girl.'"[7]

She concluded, however, that "by forming exclusive family groups and by relating all meaningful interactions and functions to those inmates who are linked by kinship bonds, the Alderson inmates have in effect created a social structure which deters the possibility of a leadership emerging that could unite many prison families."[8] Although she saw the problem as one of hindered leadership, it may be, more basically, that conflicts between individuals that are mediated by "families" reappeared as conflicts between families themselves with the result that families became rivals instead of allies. This may suggest a need for mediating social structures that do not depend totally on personal loyalties, perhaps something serving the functions of law.

The practices reproduced in women's prisons and among women of the Chinese cotton mills—sex roles and family structure—have taken highly oppressive forms in society at large. Yet, perhaps kinship networks need not distribute power oppressively. At least one kinship relation, sisterhood, has been adopted as a feminist ideal. Even though kinship networks in women's prisons and other same-sex total institutions have reproduced male-dominant distributions of authority, they may be relatively unoppressive in prison contexts because so little real power is possessed by any of their members. Yet, the problem remains that if the kinship structure itself becomes a source of difficulty, there is no procedure to modify it or address the difficulty.

It may be tempting to blame "monogamy" for the problems Margy described.[9] Without monogamy, where would be the grounds for jealousy or gossip? Yet, I find it unclear to what extent tensions between erotic bonding and friendship result simply from practices, such as monogamy, that have been oppressive to women in a heterosexist, male-dominant society and to what extent conflicts or tensions would arise anyway because of differences having to do with the nature of friendship and erotic bonding themselves. Lovers, for example, require a certain privacy that necessarily excludes others (including friends), even if they are not monogamous, whereas friendship is relatively public, a matter to which I will return. Margy's letters did not challenge monogamy. The assumptions she questioned were that lover relationships are the most important ones and that one needs a lover for closeness, affection, and companionship. These assumptions are easily seen as carryovers from the heterosexist mandate that a woman find a male lover and structure her life around him. Yet, what about her questions concerning obstacles to future friendship presented by becoming lovers without having first established a friendship? or concerning risk to existing friendship between friends who become lovers? or how to deal with the sexual aspects of friendships and where, or how, to "draw a line" between affection and sex? Nonmonogamy might multiply rather than alleviate such difficulties as these.

The way Margy put the question about getting ahead of ourselves in attempting to form lesbian organizations and communities may suggest a psychologizing of the difficulties of lesbian friendship, as though the solution were to work on ourselves and our assumptions about each other. Alternatively, at least some of the difficulties we face might be alleviated by friendlier background institutions, that is, by the establishment of social practices with friendlier conventions. Perhaps it is a case of the chicken-or-the-egg: do we need first to learn how to establish good lesbian friendships before we can build good lesbian community? or do we first need the background of lesbian community to make possible good lesbian friendships? Not knowing how better to resolve this one, I work with the hypothesis that we need to go back and forth in a manner suggested by what John Rawls called "reflective equilibrium" in writing about how to evaluate theories of justice.[10] That is, we might try attending now to the context of social institutions or practices and now to the nature of friendship itself, shifting back and forth, aiming, ultimately, for a good fit between them.

By "institutions" I mean (as in chapters 1 and 3) social practices defined by rules, or conventions, that create such things as roles and positions and through them distribute benefits and burdens of social cooperation. The hypothesis that backgrounds set by social institutions define contexts that encourage or discourage friendships of various kinds, and the idea that friendship itself may be institutionalized, are explored by Janice Raymond in her genealogy of female friendship. I turn to explore some of her ideas next. Identifying supportive background institutions and considering possibilities of institutionalizing friendship inevitably also require attending to kinds and values of friendship. Accordingly, the final section of this chapter takes up the most extended philosophical discussions of that topic prior to the twentieth century, namely, those of Aristotle. Building on pragmatic aspects of his approach, I offer a somewhat Aristotelian approach to evaluating the difficulties of lesbian friendship noted by Margy.

Jan Raymond and "Gyn/Affection"

A decade after Margy's letters, Jan Raymond devoted about a fifth of her treatise, *A Passion for Friends: Toward a Philosophy of Female Friendship*, to obstacles to friendship between women.[11] Although elsewhere, Jan Raymond has taken up lesbian ethics, *A Passion for Friends* does not focus specifically on *lesbian* friendships, nor does it treat sex as an obstacle to friendship.[12] However, its discussion of obstacles created by a social environment oppressive to women is helpful for understanding how sex can be socially constructed so as to become an obstacle to lesbian friendship. *A Passion for Friends* focuses on friendship among women, introducing the term "Gyn/affection" to encompass the varieties of female friendship, taking the "affection" of "Gyn/affection" to include both the bonds of passionate friendship and the impacts of friends on each other, including "influencing, acting upon, moving, and impressing" as well as "being influenced, acted upon, moved, and impressed."[13]

Feminist literature on female friendships has tended to focus on exceptional individual relationships, from Ruth and Naomi to Helen Keller and Annie Sullivan. Jan Raymond argues that without background institutional support, passionate female friendships in a misogynist environment are likely to remain exceptional. She also points out that female friendship does not have the widespread history that male friendship has of being itself an institution. She finds not only that obstacles to female friendship are presently supported by background institutions that may need to be resisted or dismantled, but also that positive furtherance of Gyn/affection may require creating alternative background institutions and institutionalizing female friendship itself.

Thus, she challenges, at least implicitly, the skepticism popular in much current lesbian ethics regarding rules, institutions, and disciplines, arguing that such things need not be oppressive. This is a view with which I sympathize. Institutions do not necessarily concentrate power; they can also *block* concentrations of power. Nor do they only impose restrictions on previously defined forms of agency. Often, they define new forms of interaction, create forms of agency, provide a friendly background setting that can reduce needs for individual initiative-taking to create such a background, freeing up individual energy for creative projects. Just as heteropatriarchal institutions have characteristically supported male bonding, some exceptional institutions have encouraged bonding among women. Writing partly out of her twelve years as a nun, Jan Raymond notes that religious convents fostered such bonding so effectively that the Catholic Church found it necessary to forbid "particular friendships" among nuns.[14] If we understand our capacities for organization and discipline as positive, as things we can use to further our own interests, rather than seeing them only as externally imposed hindrances or restraints, the questions arise: what *kinds* of institutions foster the development of female friendships, and to what kinds of institutions do empowering female friendships give rise?

In a society in which friendship among women is made generally difficult, the difficulties of lesbian friendship may be due at least in part to more general obstacles to Gyn/affection. In a more supportive social context, sexuality might not be the threat to lesbian friendship that it often is. Were women commonly jointly engaged in interesting, creative, and politically significant work in the world, sexuality might not have the kind of importance that it acquires in a society where for many women, social options are more domestic than worldly, where women's work—domestic or not—tends to be more routine than innovative and, consequently, women's lives often revolve around little as absorbing as the dramas of sexual involvement. Where less is invested in sexuality, its relative instability may be of less consequence. Our attractions to one another might be based on interest and admiration of many sorts. Bonds between lesbians might become multifaceted, tougher, more resilient. An irony of recent fears over lifting the ban on lesbians in the military is that lesbians have been drawn to the military because it offers precisely such an environment, one in which lesbians can work together at jobs that are interesting, challenging, even exciting, thereby forming bonds that are not based simply on sexual attraction.[15]

To begin to answer the questions what kinds of background institutions would support Gyn/affection, Jan Raymond initiates a genealogy of female friendship, working on the hypothesis that where women's development is supported, women will naturally be drawn to each other. She has in mind developing our capacities for constructive discipline and for "the rigors of discernment" (a phrase borrowed from Alice Walker) without destroying our wildness as "loose women" (not bound to men) and without domesticating or taming us. Central chapters of *A Passion for Friends* are case studies of two institutions that fostered such discipline and discernment: the medieval European convent prior to the thirteenth-century rule of enclosure (and similar institutions, such as those of the Beguines), and the vegetarian houses and spinsters' houses created by "marriage resisters" in nineteenth- and early twentieth-century China.[16] In these historical settings, women developed bonds through working together in the world in ways that furthered their moral and political beliefs and aims. They created institutions within which women could take for granted the possibilities of female friendship, as men have been able to take for granted male bonding in heteropatriarchy.

In the case of nuns, vows of chastity might be thought to have "solved" the problems Margy described. However, just as women prisoners have commonly formed erotic bonds (not always thinking of them as sexual), and just as many lesbians elsewhere are not deterred by heterosexist prohibitions, neither are many lesbians in convents deterred by vows of chastity from forming intense couple relationships.

Jan Raymond's general hypothesis concerning obstacles to female friendship is that, historically, *women have suffered from worldlessness* and that "worldlessness produces friendlessness."[17] The early medieval convents and the Chinese vegetarian and spinsters' houses are presented as exceptions to this general situation. They provided contexts enabling women to live and act directly in the world, constructively developing their capacities for discipline and discernment, making them admirable and attractive to one another, successful in working together, and, in general, mutually supportive. The Chinese "marriage resisters" seem to have included many lesbian couples who worked together (p. 133).

Jan Raymond notes that such institutions as heterosexual marriage have been responsible, historically, for many women's lack of direct access to the world. However, she takes up in detail three stances enjoying (some) contemporary feminist advocacy that have also resulted in "worldlessness" for women. She refers to these stances as *dissociation* from the world, *assimilation* to the world, and *victimism* in the world. I will explore the first of these stances, dissociation from the world, as it raises controversial issues regarding separatism that have been much discussed in the literature of lesbian ethics.

"Worldlessness" is a concept borrowed from Hannah Arendt, who contrasted "the world" as the public sphere, or "what lies between people," with the private sphere (hearing "privacy" as "privative"), that sphere to which one gets to deprive others of access.[18] "The world" refers not to the physical planet, earth, but to a social construction, the realm of public artifacts, culture, and politics. The world is also, importantly, the source of other perspectives that we need to evaluate our own conduct and that of others.

Jan Raymond's "worldliness," posed as opposite to Hannah Arendt's "worldlessness," includes having access to the world, being *in* it although not necessarily *of* it (being in it the way that Hannah Arendt's "conscious pariah" or Virginia Woolf's "inside outsider" is in it), and *acting* in it rather than being simply acted *on* by it.[19] Worldly knowledge is important because we need to understand our places in the world or our relationships to it when it contains forces dangerous to us. Hannah Arendt argued that separatism kept European Jews unnecessarily ignorant of forces in the world and of Jewish positions in those forces, leaving many highly vulnerable. Jan Raymond's references to Hannah Arendt's arguments suggest that women might be in an analogous position. We might fail to appreciate our power positions in the world (economic power positions, for example) or in relation to it, thereby failing to anticipate hostile responses of others and becoming vulnerable to hostilities that we lacked the perspectives to appreciate.

But how is worldlessness an obstacle to *female friendship*? Jan Raymond does not address this question directly, apart from the general dangers to one's existence posed by worldlessness. However, the following line of reasoning might fill out a relevant argument, in relation to women's historical domesticity and relegation to menial labor. Like the housewives in soap operas, who have no very direct access to the money, power, and action of the world, relationships among worldless women easily degenerate into a series of emotional dramas, developing our worst potentialities rather than our best, perhaps producing scenarios like those drawn in Margy's letters. Were lesbian friendship a casualty of such decadence, feminist communities offering culture and politics might provide solutions by creating environments more likely to develop our better selves than our worse ones.

Thus, if worldlessness aggravates obstacles to female friendship, one might expect radical lesbian separatist communities to be a viable solution, because they create lesbian *worlds* and get lesbians "out of the closet" if not "into the streets." And, indeed, separatism has been a major issue in lesbian feminist politics for nearly two decades. Sarah Hoagland made the option of withdrawal from heterosexualism central to her lesbian ethics.[20] She addressed her work to members of lesbian community, understood as "the loose network—both imagined and existing now—of those who identify basically as lesbians," "not a specific entity: but "a ground of our be-ing" which "exists because we are here and move on it now."[21] A decade earlier, Marilyn Frye presented separatism as a denial of male access to females, arguing that since "access is one of the faces of Power," such a denial has "the form and full portent of assumption of power."[22]

In examining "dissociation from the world," however, Jan Raymond mentioned as examples "some feminist separatists" who have made dissociation a political ideal, foregoing access to power, money, and interaction, "the most basic conditions of worldliness," risking philosophical narrowness in vision and political vulnerability for the sake of "the freedom and untouchability of outcasts."[23] Neither Marilyn Frye nor Sarah Hoagland has advocated foregoing access to power or money, although Sarah Hoagland does advocate a lesbian ethic that is not centered on control. Their visions have been of lesbians putting resources into alternative communities and practices that may be located geographically in the midst of the misogynist world from which they withdraw. Still, depending on what separatists are willing to attend to, the risks of "philosophical narrowness of vision" and a vulnerability analogous to that discussed by Hannah Arendt may be real. I will return to this after sketching ways in which having *a* world (which others may want to contrast with *the* world) seems to offer a supportive context for female friendship.

"Worldless" sounds like an overstatement when applied to separatist communities that create worlds of their own. Such communities are, in part, a response to having outlaw status in a larger world that does not acknowledge lesbian relationships nor, in general, honor female friendships except insofar as they provide support networks for men. The creation of separate communities has made it possible for many lesbians to live far more honest lives than "*the* world" has been willing to countenance. Such honesty is no small consideration with respect to the quality and stability of lesbian relationships—friends, lovers, or both. It makes one less manipulable by others, protects against common forms of extortion. Living in a closet is much closer to being worldless than living in lesbian community. A closet, unlike a community, is not a world; one peers out at the world from a closet. Closeted, one is cut off from community, immobilized, impotent. Lesbian community offers a world in which to act, a forum for politics, perspectives to balance against one's own. Even the language of "*a* world" as opposed to "*the* world" can sound question-begging with respect to values that matter. For, like *the* (larger) world, *a* (smaller) world can be characterized by artifacts, culture, and politics. To members of the latter world, that may *be the* world, that is, the one that really matters.

Jan Raymond mentions "rootedness" as a consideration, pointing out that "in contrast to other oppressed groups, women do not possess the past of a cohesive and self-conscious community with its own political traditions, philosophical vitality, and history."[24] Rootlessness, she says, is responsible also for the lack of female friendship. "Gyn/affection cannot be sustained where women have 'the great privilege of being unburdened by care for the world.' "[25] To the extent that separatists create an alternative world for members who do assume the responsibilities of caring for it, it should *be* a place where its members can put down roots, grounding Gyn/affection.

How inclusive a world is necessary to ground gyn/affection? The friendship of the Ladies of Llangollen lasted fifty years, as long as they both lived.[26] Yet, they saw little of the world. Famous people are said to have visited *them*. But the diary left by one does not discuss the French or the American Revolution, major events of their time.[27] They did not even have a lesbian community (so far as we know). Natalie Barney and Romaine Brooks had a comparably lengthy relationship, buttressed by Left Bank lesbian communities in Paris that were materially well-off although hardly as politically conscious as one could wish.[28] That relationship was eventually broken not by attacks from outside but by Natalie's unceasing "infidelities." (The life and loves of Natalie Barney, by the way, interestingly exemplify difficulties that Margy described.) Perhaps, however, these relationships were able to endure as long as they did only as exceptions.

More than one kind of consideration is at stake in worldliness. Insofar as worldliness is a matter of engaging with money, power, and politics, separatist communities can be and often are very worldly. Privacy and publicity are matters of degree. Distinctions between private and public can exist *within* such communities. However, insofar as worldliness is a matter of engaging with outsiders who have the power to impact on one's community, even such otherwise worldly separatist communities may be in danger.

Both Sarah Hoagland and Marilyn Frye support a redirection of lesbian *attention* and a redirection of interactive engagement by lesbians. Although neither advocates totally ignoring what outsiders do, a major redirection of attention, if not explicitly qualified, could put at risk one's knowledge of the larger world.[29] In view of the danger of vulnerability to external attack, even otherwise worldly separatisms raise the question how it is possible to withdraw from what Sarah Hoagland calls "heterosexualism" (in Jan Raymond's terms, "heteroreality") without withdrawing from the world that is dominated by it. To put it in terms from Marilyn Frye's analysis, how is it possible to *deny* male access to females without *losing* female access to the world and thereby to perspectives on ourselves that we may need to understand in order to defend or protect ourselves?

A key distinction for both Malcolm X, in his analysis of Black separatism, and Marilyn Frye, in her analysis of feminist separatism, has been the distinction between *separation* and *segregation*.[30] Segregation, as in Jane and Jim Crow practices in the United States, is done at the initiative of oppressors to serve their interests. Separation, by contrast, as in Black nationalism and lesbian or feminist separatism, is initiated or maintained by the oppressed for their own eventual empowerment. Hannah Arendt's reflections on being a pariah enable us to raise the question whether lesbian separatists might not become in effect segregated in the sense that their separations facilitate the goals of segregation, serving the interests of oppressors and acquiring for lesbians the dubious "freedom and untouchability of outcasts." Just as lesbian and feminist separatists have had to compromise separatism to gain access to material resources and do outreach to women who need separatist alternatives most but are least able to find them unaided, separatists may also need to compromise with respect to attention and the flow of information.[31] Striking a balance between attending to one another and not ignoring one's position in relation to hostile oppressors is a general problem for any oppressed group. What Jan Raymond's work suggests to me in this context is that woman-friendly institutionalizations of female friendship might free up female energy in ways that could make it easier to strike such balances.

Perhaps María Lugones' conception of "world"-travel, of moving back and forth among many "worlds," can be sufficiently worldly without invoking a concept of *the* world at all. As a woman of color and a native speaker of Spanish, María Lugones has had to " 'world'-travel" daily in the United States to white anglo worlds. The "world"-traveling that she recommends as an antidote to arrogance is, as she puts it, a "willful exercise" of an acquired flexibility in shifting from one construction of life, in which many are understood as outsiders, to other constructions of life, in which some of these (former) outsiders are at home, or more nearly at home, and in which one may figure oneself as an outsider.[32] Sarah Hoagland advocates "world"-travel *within* lesbian communities that are multicultural, intergenerational, and include lesbians of varying physical abilities. Whether that is possible may depend on how historically one understands "worlds." For María Lugones, "world"-travel involves encounters with others on *their* terms and on their *turf*, for which one needs a certain psychological preparedness, such as a readiness to play the fool and not take oneself too seriously. Marilyn Frye conceived separating as an alternative to assimilating. María Lugones's "world"-travel may be an alternative to both. The "worlds" of "world"-travel remain distinct. But the traveler grows in experience, understanding, and, ideally, in political wisdom, acquiring and maintaining access to the perspectives that Hannah Arendt found so important for evaluating and maintaining a realistic assessment of one's own positions in a hostile world.

Jan Raymond's objections to separatisms that involve *dissociation* from the world sound like objections to *isolationism*. "World"-travel might be one answer to isolationism. Another, however, might be to identify nonisolationist separations.[33] If we think of feminist separations as severing certain kinds of relationships, that leaves open the possibility of retaining or substituting other kinds of relationships to some of the same parties. In divorce, one of Marilyn Frye's examples of separation, one set of relationships between parties to a marriage is substituted for another, a formal set for an intimate set. Where the idea of separation is to deny intimate access to us, except on our terms and at our initiative, this tends to mean, as in divorce, a retreat from affective and intimate relationships to formal relationships, from closeness to something more distant. "Distance" here is a spatial metaphor; it stands in no easy correlation with real spatial distance. Retreating from affective to formal relations need imply neither losing access nor giving up one's ability to act. Formality does not preclude communication; it structures communication. Putting relationships with men on a formal basis, as in business relationships, rather than an intimate basis can be a step forward in putting women in a better position to insist upon access to resources. It enables us to appeal to rights, for example. A significant cost of intimacy is often a foregoing of the appeal to rights, leaving one at the mercy of others' goodwill.[34]

Are formal connections with outsiders sufficient to protect separatist contexts that support lesbian friendship? Formality is an interesting concept in this context in that it both links and separates. I suspect that protecting lesbian friendship may also require respect for formal relationships *within* lesbian community. In two brief discussions in *The Human Condition*, Hannah Arendt maintained that love is essentially private, unlike friendship.[35] This leaves the possibility, although strictly does not imply it, that friendship needs a public. Strictly, all it implies is that friendship is *not* essentially private, not that it *is* essentially public. In discussing forgiveness, however, Hannah Arendt maintained that respect is "a kind of 'friendship' without intimacy and without closeness," "a regard for the person from the distance which the space of the world puts between us" (p. 243). In other words, respect, on this view, is a kind of "friendship" for others that requires a public. From this, an argument may be derived for the conclusion that friendship generally requires a public. The argument needs simply the plausible premise that respect is necessary to any good friendship. Fostering lesbian friendship, then, would require creating and maintaining conditions of respect, that distance which the space of the world puts between us, even within lesbian community.

Aristotelian Pragmatism and Lesbian Friendship

Men writing on friendship have not focused on obstacles to male bonding. As Jan Raymond observed, social institutions have supported male bonding to such an extent that men take it for granted. Men have written about dangers to existing friendships, about what loyalty requires, about how to resolve conflicts of loyalty, when to break off friendship, and how to treat former friends. Often, they have been moved to write about friendship on the occasion of a friend's death, as a way of grieving the loss.[36] Despite the differences in perspective between men's philosophical writings on friendship and the situations of lesbians, I have found it worthwhile to examine the best of those philosophical writings for insights that might be extended or developed in other directions.[37]

The most-developed, systematic, and insightful classical philosophical discussions of friendship are Aristotle's discussions of *philia*, a term that encompassed a variety of affiliations, including those of kin, companionship, intimacy, and citizenship.[38] The *philia* that interested him most, however, would today also be recognized as paradigms of friendship. Aristotle began by defining friendship as mutually recognized reciprocal goodwill in a relationship that endures over time and through various trials. He noted that while the *wish* for friendship arises quickly, friendship itself does not. His further accounts make clear why not and also suggest that Margy's observation that it is often much easier for lesbians to find lovers than to find good friends should not be surprising, that *this* fact does not distinguish the situations of lesbians from those of others. A supportive set of background institutions, then, should provide contexts in which potential friends are able not only to meet and have fun but also to come to know each other over time and to observe each other and interact in a variety of situations. Bars, for example, have obvious limitations in these respects, but so do even coffeehouses and private house parties.

Aristotle then asked whether there is only one kind of friendship or many, and if many, how they are interrelated. He answered that there are basically three kinds of friendship, distinguished by the bases of goodwill: friendships of pleasure, friendships of utility, and friendships of excellence. In friendships of utility and friendships of pleasure, the bases of well-wishing are utility and pleasure, respectively, whereas in friendships of excellence, the basis is the friend's character. Anticipating Ludwig Wittgenstein's "family resemblance" idea, Aristotle maintained that friendships of utility and of pleasure are called "friendships" because of their resemblances to friendships of excellence, which are also, ordinarily, useful and pleasant. Friendships of excellence give his interpretation of "true friendship." He finds it unambiguously the best kind of friendship and the most stable, although he allows that the others are valuable, too, as far as they go. When he speaks without qualification of friendship, he usually means friendship of excellence, to which I will usually refer, hereafter, as "true friendship."

Aristotle also offers further classifications of friendships as between equals or unequals and as having mixed or the same motives, noting that special difficulties arise for unequal friendships and those involving mixed motives. The tripartite classification on the basis of motivation, however, remains basic, and he appeals to these differences time and again in answering questions commonly raised about friendship, such as how many good friends one can have at once, how long a good friendship should last, and whether only good people can be friends. He engages in more casuistry (examination of cases) regarding the ethics of friendship than regarding any other topic in his writings on ethics.

Lover relationships, as such, for Aristotle, exemplify friendships of pleasure. The relative instability of lover relationships is thereby explained: where pleasure is the basis of a relationship, one can expect the relationship to last only as long as the pleasure.[39] There is no need, in the nature of the case, for lovers to admire each other's characters, although they may. The pleasure uniting them as lovers does not require deep acquaintance, even if it gives rise to illusions here.

Others of Margy's concerns require more consideration of the nature of true friendships. Recall that her letters to LC raised the questions how to deal with the sexual aspects of friendships, how to become friends with potential lovers and remain friends with former lovers, how to keep sex from ruining already established friendships, how to prevent lesbian isolation in couples, and how to become friends with lesbians who are already coupled with others. An approach I find suggestive for responding to these questions is to consider what friends do that makes them friends, and then consider what being able to do this well requires and what is required for being able to continue doing it well—not simply what character traits are required but also what background institutions support the development of the relevant traits.

Insofar as Aristotle saw politics as providing this kind of background to ethics, and insofar as what good friendship requires is the development of excellences of character, understood as habits of choice and of voluntary emotional response, this approach may be considered Aristotelian. However, Aristotle did not develop the implications for friendship systematically in writings of his that survive. Here, the genealogical analyses of Jan Raymond, exploring European medieval convents prior to enclosure and Chinese marriage resisters and vegetarian houses, are highly suggestive and helpful.

In the case of friendships of pleasure and friendships of utility, there is no special mystery about what the friends do. They do whatever is the source of the relevant pleasure or utility. But what do *true* friends do? Aristotle's views here often seem excessively vague: true friends live together and exercise their excellences toward each other; that is, they display in their conduct toward one another their virtues (excellences) of character, which are discussed elsewhere in Aristotle's ethics—such things as courage, temperance, liberality, and so on. But in what kinds of behavior does their conduct toward one another consist? In his casuistry of friendship, Aristotle mentioned reciprocal favors. Elsewhere he mentioned receiving help in times of trouble and sharing joys in times of prosperity. He referred to a variety of shared activities, noting that these vary from friend to friend—some are bodily, some artistic, others philosophical. However, he did not relate the activities of friends systematically to virtues *specific to* friendship, even though some of his observations about how friends respond to one another seem to imply such virtues. He noted, for example, that "the friend wants, if possible, not merely to feel pain along with his friend, but to feel the same pain."[40] This alludes to a capacity to empathize, which is mentioned nowhere explicitly as a virtue. One might conclude that he did not think friendship required any *special* excellences of character. Such a view would be surprising. For, there are good people who seem to lack true friendships, and they are often naive with respect to certain forms of practical wisdom. Yet, such a view would make sense of Aristotle's difficulties in explaining why a virtuous person should also need friends in order to be happy.

Aristotle's general approach to ethics inspired the pragmatism of my question, "What do (true) friends *do?*" For Aristotle, a life is the history of an ensouled being, and different kinds of ensouled (living) beings are defined by the different kinds of *doings* of which they are capable. A good one performs its characteristic doings well. It develops through exercise traits that consist in dispositions to perform well the activities that make that soul the kind of soul that it is (in this case, human). Well developed, these traits are one's virtues (excellences). We can look at the *Nicomachean Ethics'* catalog of virtues—for which Aristotle does not claim completeness—as a list of ways of performing well the kinds of activities that Aristotle takes to define a life as human: courage is being good in battle, temperance is being good in the activities of eating, drinking, and sexuality, liberality is being good in spending, magnificence is being good in spending huge sums, pride is being good in self-assessment when one is also otherwise a good person, and so on.

A survey of these activities reveals, actually, that the life that most interested Aristotle was not simply human but male, free, and fairly "well born." His list of virtues reflects that perspective, both in what it includes and in what it omits. It includes virtues with respect to consumption, fighting in war, and spending money, for example, but not virtues with respect to *producing* material necessities or engaging in basic *care-taking* or *maintenance*. Thus, it does not represent well the doings of women and other laborers of ancient Greece, those not so free or "well-born," a matter over which Aristotle stumbled briefly in Bk I of his *Politics* and then moved on.[41]

Justice, which the *Nicomachean Ethics* treats in a book to itself, does not fit well the model of the other virtues. Not only does it have only one opposite, injustice, whereas the other virtues have two (for example, rashness and cowardice, in the case of courage), but also it applies to *relationships* between persons, not simply to the dispositions of individuals. Justice applies to the way shares are distributed among men governed by law or common practices. Nevertheless, in developing the idea of justice as a virtue, we can inquire with what kinds of human activities justice is associated and what it means to do well in relation to those activities. Thus, John Rawls defines the sense of justice by reference to principles for evaluating social institutions according to how well they distribute the benefits and burdens of social cooperation.[42] Agency here is, first of all, that of institutions, and then, of individuals within contexts those institutions define.

Friendship does not fit Aristotle's model of the other virtues, either, because it is a *relationship* between two or more parties. It occupies something like the position of justice. Sometimes, Aristotle seems even to consider it another way of getting at the topic of justice, observing that "to inquire . . . how to behave to a friend is to look for a particular kind of justice, for generally all justice is in relation to a friend" and "justice involves a number of individuals who are partners, and the friend is a partner."[43] As with justice, we can ask what activities define friendship, what friends do *as such*, and then consider what it means to do those things well and what doing them well requires.

Aristotle's list in *Rhetoric* II:4 of characteristics by which observers recognize people as friends or enemies comes closer to addressing such questions than the accounts in his more theoretical ethical works. In the *Rhetoric* he notes, for example, that friends are not too ready to show us our mistakes, are not cantankerous or quarrelsome, that they have the tact to make and take a joke, that they praise such good qualities as we possess, especially the ones that we are not too sure that we *do* possess, and that they do kindnesses unasked and without proclaiming the fact

that they have done them.[44] A natural place to pick up the thread in the
Nicomachean Ethics is with Aristotle's mutually recognized reciprocal
goodwill: through what activities is goodwill expressed in friendship?
Answers might yield an approach to friendship that is "Aristotelian,"
that is, in the spirit of Aristotle, even if it is not what Aristotle said
(although perhaps it is what he should have said).

Like a life, a friendship has a history: a beginning, a middle, and an
end (if only because eventually death intervenes). Different activities
may be more characteristic at different points in this history, although
some continue throughout. Consider, for example, the "getting to
know you" stage. Characteristic activities here are exposure and exploration, activities with potentialities for developing trust—provided
nothing terribly untoward occurs during trial exposures and explorations. These are activities that may continue throughout the history
of a friendship. The friendship may become boring if they do not.
Goodwill here is communicated by (perhaps, means) friendly interest
and receptivity.

Other activities that evidence growing friendship are seeking each
other out (sometimes for no special purpose) when fate happens not to
conjoin you and manifesting joy at mutual encounters when it does
(tail-wagging in dogs; people smile).

A natural next stage is defining one's spaces, setting boundaries and
gaining recognition of them. This may take trials and a few skirmishes.
It also sets limits to (at least to the timing of) exposures and explorations
begun earlier and to the aggressiveness and nature of contact-seeking.
We might think of this stage as one of gaining, and then maintaining,
respect.

Once boundaries have gained respect, friends may move on more
comfortably to mutual "grooming" or "stroking" rituals—pleasantries
and small services beyond what utility requires. At least part of what
feels good about the "grooming" or "stroking" is that it is done by the
other person, not by just anyone, and that she chose you, not just anyone, to receive it. Like exposure and exploration, nurturing and grooming activities also ordinarily continue through a friendship. If boundaries have not been worked out, however, this activity risks being construed as, and might easily become, sexual. One response to the
question how to "draw the line" between expressions of affection and
sexual behavior is that without friendly background institutions, that is,
rule-defined social practices, to define the social meanings of "grooming" or "stroking" rituals, individual understandings need to be reached

at the stage of defining spaces in friendships between lesbians who could potentially become lovers. Here is a place where friendly background institutions can be useful in reducing troublesome ambiguity and needs for taking initiatives. Here is a place where lesbians are apt to feel the lack of what Adrienne Rich called "a common language."[45]

Probably the most discussed mutual activity of friendship is sharing. As Elizabeth Telfer has pointed out, sharing takes many forms.[46] One form is offering something to be appreciated, as my cat once brought me a mouse. Sharing joys and sorrows, which Aristotle mentions, may fall under this kind of sharing. Appreciation ordinarily requires a basis in shared values, although one may appreciate the intent in any case. A different kind of sharing is pooling resources. Yet another, which Aristotle also mentions, is doing together things, such as eating, sleeping, working, or playing, that one could have done alone or with someone else.

Perhaps the next most discussed range of activities of friends is one that includes giving gifts and performing services, doing and accepting favors, offering to come to each other's aid or defense and at least sometimes accepting such offers, nursing each other's wounds, providing mutual support.

Finally, when friends have been engaged in such activities over a long period of time, if one dies or disappears, the other grieves.

This list is not exhaustive. When a friendship breaks up or is challenged, other activities enter. However, this is enough to respond to Margy's remaining questions concerning lesbian friendship. This model allows for degrees of closeness in a relationship, according to how intimate activities become. And it allows for friendships of varying degrees of comprehensiveness and depth, according to how comprehensively and how fully and well the patterns of interaction are developed. Elizabeth Telfer finds it also important that friends acknowledge and affirm the pattern, thereby exhibiting a commitment to the relationship.[47] People can discover that they have developed a friendship without having committed themselves to it, although at the point of discovery, continued friendship may require such affirmation, as a failure to affirm it then might tacitly communicate rejection.

By the way, friendship—like eating, drinking, and sex—appears not to be an exclusively human phenomenon, although it has specifically human forms. The activities of friendship, abstractly considered, appear also to be found in dogs and monkeys, for example. Aristotle thought the ability to perceive another's choice made only humans capable of true friendship, although he recognized friendships of pleasure and utility among other animals.[48] His understanding of "choice," however, includes *deliberation*.[49] It may be more basically the capacity for human *language* that distinguishes human friendship. Language makes possible more kinds of space to define, explore, and share. If "choice" is not understood to require deliberation but is understood more simply as uncoerced, intentional acceptance or rejection, many nonhuman animals may be capable of choice and at least sometimes of telling the difference between the presence and absence of choice in others.

The virtues Aristotle discusses in Books II and IV of the *Nicomachean Ethics*—courage, temperance, liberality, magnificence, pride, good temper, friendliness (not to be confused with friendship), truthfulness, and ready wit—are clearly an aid to friendship (pp. 63–105). Yet, friendship requires in addition more *responsiveness and receptivity* than that list exemplifies—such things as trust, respect, empathy, and sympathy (some of which Aristotle's observations on friendship imply). Had he included among his paradigms of friendship the cooperative activities required by production and maintenance and the relationships of caretakers to those whose well-being they nurture, his list might have been more comprehensive in these respects. Friendship requires different kinds of initiative-taking than are exemplified in Aristotle's earlier lists, for example, showing interest, what Marilyn Frye and Sarah Hoagland, following Simone Weil, have called "attending."[50] These things are also subject to *choice* and thus count as doings in the relevant sense, and they may have their own associated virtues. The answer to the question what friendship contributes to a good life should be, first of all, that it develops the virtues of friendship, as justice develops the civic virtues. Exercising the virtues of friendship is as definitive of a good life as is exercising the virtues Aristotle cites elsewhere.

In terms of this Aristotelian model, lesbian lovers can also be true friends. What began as a friendship of pleasure or utility may deepen into true friendship. Without time and trials, one may have no way to tell whether a friendship is "true." However, those who become lovers before becoming friends may find it difficult or painful to go back and gain respect for defining their spaces differently, which they may want to do to become better acquainted. The more promising route seems to be to ground the friendship nonsexually, first. However, Margy also noted that friends who then became sexually involved sometimes found that they were unable to continue as friends when the sexual involvement ended. Again, it may be difficult to gain mutual respect for retreating to an earlier understanding of boundaries. However, in this case, the reason for wanting to retreat is different. Here, one may want to retreat if the level of sexual feeling on both sides *does not wane at the same rate.* If retreat proves impossible, it may be necessary to withdraw from active friendship. If the problem of nonreciprocal waning of sexual feeling does not arise, boundary may issues may not arise, provided the friendship has been true. Many lesbians who have been lovers find that they are able to continue as the best of friends for the rest of their lives. However, in relationships known to me, where this has been true, they were usually friends already before they became lovers. (Some who became lovers first may, of course, be lucky.)

The Aristotelian analysis of friendship implies that if one's true friends (those whose relationships to oneself are characterized by the *virtues* of friendship) and one's lovers are not the same, one does better to live with the friends. It supports Margy's values. The publicity required for respect in friendship seems also to require that true friends not be too isolated in couples. With regard to the difficulties of becoming friends with someone who is living with a lover, I have two suggestions, both supported by Aristotle's understanding of the conditions of true friendship and by Jan Raymond's genealogy of female friendship. One suggestion is to support the background practice of lovers *not* sharing a domicile unless they are also true friends. The reason is that the privacy a lover requires tends otherwise to envelope the life of the beloved, cutting her off from true friendships, and doing other sorts of mischief.[51] Challenging the practice of lovers' *cohabitation* may be thought of as an alternative to challenging monogamy, which is more usual. Without challenging a monogamous focus of sexual or erotic energies during a given period, one may advocate cohabitation with friends, even with many friends. Individuals may still benefit from this suggestion even if it is not generally adopted as social practice. Yet the benefits would be multiplied if it became social practice.

The second suggestion is that we think of *cohabitation* with friends as basically sharing a habitat, an environment, that emphasizes work and play *in the world*, a world larger than the domicile to which one may return periodically for rest and sleep, rather than thinking of cohabitation primarily as sharing private sleeping quarters. Thus, Jan Raymond's examples of the medieval convents, prior to the rule of enclosure, and of the vegetarian and spinsters' houses in China, illustrate cohabitation of friends (some of whom may also have been lovers) whose lives seem to have been more worldly than domestic. Such a social world of female friendship sounds amazonian, in a sense that would no doubt have appealed to Charlotte Perkins Gilman.

When someone is already living with a true friend or friends, the Aristotelian approach suggests that getting to know her with a view to true friendship does require including her true friends as well. This is not quite the same as the situation lamented by Margy. For, if the friend's relationships really are true friendships, although the expenditure of effort to join the circle may be high, so presumably would be the rewards, including a stability that lover relationships frequently lack. The difficulty of being able to spend the requisite time and resources to make friendship true with many people was one of the things that led Aristotle to the conclusion that one should not expect to have many such friendships. (The other was the rarity of individuals with high character.) This still leaves room for many more limited ones, friendships of pleasure and of utility, which have their own value.[52] Perhaps, however, Aristotle should also have acknowledged the possibility of many friendships that are *true* even though not based on *extensive* mutual knowledge.[53] If what distinguishes friendship as true is its basis in character, one may be able to ground a friendship of excellence despite knowing relatively little of the other's history, likes and dislikes, and so on. Character can sometimes be revealed in significant choices in a relationship that is limited in its extensiveness. A friendship may be true as far as it goes and yet, because of circumstances, be unable to go as far as the friends might otherwise have chosen to take it. Such relationships might be very important to the viability of lesbian community (perhaps, to the viability of any community).

To return to Margy's concern about founding a lesbian community based on lover relationships, it seems important to acknowledge at least these two things. First, true friends are not necessarily intimate friends. And second, when lovers *are* also true friends (which they need not be), a community founded on their relationships would seem to have as solid a beginning as one could imagine. To endure over time, however, and to grow to any great size, lesbian communities may need to foster friendships that are in an important sense "true" among lesbians who have never been and may never be lovers and who may never even know many details of each other's lives.

Chapter 6

horizontal violence: partner battering and lesbian stalking

Prologue On Friday the 13th of January 1989, Catherine, former manager of Lysistrata—the celebrated feminist restaurant that existed for five years (1977–1982) in Madison, Wisconsin—took a gun purchased a few days before, drove to the house of her ex-lover, Joan, who had recently ended their relationship, and shot her three times, dead. She had warned Joan days before of her intentions, had practiced shooting in the country. She did not find Joan's new lover. She then drove home, answered the phone. It was her sister, a university dean of students who, worried, had set up emergency counseling for her. Catherine said, "Thank you very much," did not mention having shot Joan, hung up the phone, and shot herself, dead. Thus concluded a life begun as an abused child and marked by both violent lesbian relationships and lesbian-feminist activism.[1]

Two-and-a-half months earlier, the day before Halloween, Annette Green—who later appeared on Geraldo's TV talk show—shot and killed Ivonne Julio, her lover of eleven years, at their home in Palm

Beach County, Florida. She pleaded self-defense. After only two-and-a-half hours, a jury convicted her of second degree murder (the prosecutor had charged first degree), in spite of the prosecutor's acknowledgment that she had been battered, had been shot at before by Ivonne, had a broken nose, broken ribs. Annette was the first lesbian to use the battered woman defense.[2] Lesbian attorney Ruthann Robson, who has extensive experience advocating for battered women, finds that, "To successfully use a defense based on being battered, a woman must be the stereotypically good wife," and comments, wryly, "Given that many heterosexual women are insufficiently wifely to sustain the defense, it is perhaps not surprising that Annette Green could not do so."[3]

Communities of lesbians raised in a patriarchy are time-bombs of Catherines and Ivonnes. We need ways to defuse the bombs—or, better yet, to use the energy constructively. This chapter takes up horizontal violence among lesbians, that is, violence of lesbians against lesbians (and violence against lesbians fueled by lesbian passions), with a focus on stalking and partner battering. It ends with questions, invitations to the reader to think of creative responses that we can live with.

Published materials responding to same-sex partner battering are, to date, limited, but what exists is highly valuable. The past decade has produced three books (two on lesbians, one on gay men), brief discussions within other books, many conference workshops, counseling manuals, and a change of consciousness in urban lesbian and gay communities.[4] Of great practical value are *Men Who Beat the Men Who Love Them* by David Island and Patrick Letellier (a survivor whose riveting narratives introduce each chapter), with outstanding chapters on getting out, staying out, and helping friends who are trying to get out and stay out, and *Naming the Violence: Speaking Out About Lesbian Battering*, edited by Kerry Lobel, which includes survivor narratives, theoretical essays, and workshop suggestions.[5] *Violent Betrayal: Partner Abuse in Lesbian Relationships* is a study by self-identified heterosexual sociologist Claire Renzetti who, with the Philadelphia Working Group on Lesbian Battering (including many survivors), designed survivor questionnaires, from which she concluded that a major source of stress is one partner's greater dependence on the other, that batterers may use substance abuse and family violence histories as "excuses," and that although battered lesbians are even less successful than other women in receiving legal help, mediation—as an alternative to criminal justice—is problematic, because it implies mutual responsibility and fails to hold batterers accountable.[6]

These materials prioritize the plight of the battered partner.[7] In contrast, Melanie Kaye/Kantrowitz, longtime activist in the movement against violence against women, identifies with lesbians who hit as well as with lesbians who are hit and urges reclaiming the power of violent lesbians.[8] Still, all share the beliefs that battering is an unnecessitated choice, that it is always wrong, and that batterers should be accountable for the harm they do. This chapter shares those beliefs.

Batterers may face difficult obstacles. Alice Miller maintains that often desperately violent adults are influenced by histories of childhood abuse inaccessible to them in ordinary consciousness.[9] Several contributors to *Naming the Violence* said that they were not abused as children but that their batterers were. *Violent Betrayal* found more abusers than abused partners from violent families, but as many abusers from nonviolent homes as from violent ones.[10] Even though histories of childhood abuse may become accessible to adult consciousness, survivors and counselors are not optimistic about batterer reform and take a dim view of "couple counseling," focusing instead on how battered partners can disengage and heal. However, Melanie Kaye/Kantrowitz argues that because lesbian battering is horizontal (internal to an oppressed group), it may be easier get the batterer to redirect her anger against systems oppressive to both partners.[11]

In *terminology*, lesbian work on lesbian battering does mean to call attention to the battering partner. "Lesbian" in "lesbian battery" could be ambiguous between batterer and battered, but "battering" names activity in the active voice, resolving any such ambiguity.[12] Thus it contrasts with the term "battered woman," commonly used to describe women battered by men, which directs attention to the battered partner, as though she were a certain kind of woman, amd deflects it from the batterer. This lesbian/heterosexual asymmetry in usage is unfortunate insofar as it highlights lesbian assailants but allows male assailants to remain invisible. Still, "lesbian battering" is the term preferred by lesbians to emphasize that battering *is* activity, the result of agency, choice, not an event (like a tornado) that just "happens."

Batterers do not always confine their hostilities to intimates. I begin, however, in the next section, with intimate partner battery, abuse in relationships between lesbians who are or have been lovers. This is the context presumed in the works mentioned above. Battering here is commonly called "domestic battery" in the popular press, which avoids pointing the finger at anyone and directs attention to the usual site of episodes.

In the section following that, I take up batterers who stalk in relatively public settings, seeking or pretending an intimacy either lost or never granted. Stalking is beginning to receive legal recognition as having potentialities as lethal as those of domestic battering and as capable of dominating the lives of survivors.

Partner Battering

Those unfamiliar with the realities of lesbian battering may wonder what behavior is identified by lesbians as abusive or as instances of battering. Patterns described in *Naming the Violence* include being thrown against walls, hit with and without weapons, choked, burned, stabbed, confined physically, and being robbed of sleep and necessary physical aids such as eyeglasses. Some patterns included violent property damage, threats with guns, threats to significant third parties including animal companions, threats to reveal a partner's lesbianism to homophobic employers and kin, economic control, humiliation, violent accusations, and character assassination. One set of guidelines for counselors adds "driving recklessly" to its list of physically aggressive forms of abuse; "*terrorist* driving" might be an even better term.[13] The guidelines break down further examples under sexual abuse, emotional abuse, and psychological abuse, defining the latter as emotional abuse where there is also a background of physical abuse, since the threat of violence, once present, "constitutes a threat forever in the relationship," producing "psychological erosion" in the battered partner.[14] *Violent Betrayal* found among the most common abuses "being forced to sever ties or contacts with relatives."[15] It also notes batterers' inventiveness in tailoring abuses to partners' specific vulnerabilities: one abuser forced a diabetic partner to eat sugar; two respondents who were physically disabled "reported that their partners would leave them in dangerous situations (e.g., an isolated wooded area) without assistance or transportation" (p. 21). Whatever the nature of the abuse, what sustained the naming of *battering* was not isolated incidents of hitting but ongoing patterns, often including a variety of abuses, which enabled the batterer to dominate the relationship.

A controversial issue in contemporary lesbian communities is whether lesbian sadomasochism constitutes partner abuse. The term "sadomasochism" has been applied to so many different activities that it is important to make distinctions. I postpone that general discussion to chapter 11. Here I note briefly that issues raised by sadomasochism can overlap with those raised by battering in that sadomasochistic sex plays with dominance, not just with power. Even feigned hostility can produce real harm, and there may be a danger of its passing over into real hostility. If either partner should become truly hostile, what began as consensual play can become abusive. If the activity is genuinely consensual, dominance is not thoroughgoing. On a fundamental level, the will of each is respected throughout. (Again, see chapter 11 on higher order and lower order desire and choice for elaboration of how this is possible). In a battering relationship, fundamental mutual respect is absent.

Many lesbians have been reluctant to acknowledge themselves as battered because they are told that they, too, batter since they verbally provoked assault, hit back, or engaged in other violent self-defense. Ironically, the main difference between lesbian and heterosexual battery appears to be that battered lesbians fight back oftener, thanks to feminist consciousness of assertiveness, self-defense training against sexual assault, and a lesser physical power differential between partners.[16] Batterers whose partners fight back and lesbian communities wary of moral hierarchies, as well as outsiders who do not take seriously lesbians' potential for dominance, have sometimes promoted the concept of "mutual battering." The idea that partners are "battering" each other avoids fingering one party as the batterer and stigmatizing the other as submitting, suggesting instead that no one is a victim, that responsibility is mutual, and that what we have is "just fighting" between lovers. Many who have worked in shelters or as counselors argue that "mutual battering" is a myth.[17]

Melanie Kaye/Kantrowitz again stands out as something of a dissenter. She argues that we should be sensitive to other sources of physical fighting in relationships than the attempt to control and dominate—for example, inadequate controls on the expression of anger, "being 'able' to express violence against an intimate for the first time, because of relative equality of size and power," and she notes that "Sometimes two women in love have radically different tolerances for shouting, for physical gesture; what seems normal to one is terrifying to another."[18] These observations are well-taken. Ethnic and other differences in manner can be misread, cause tension, strain, and fear. Not all violent lesbian relationships are cut from the same cloth. Melanie Kaye/Kantrowitz follows up with a candid narrative of a relationship in which she might have been identified as the battered partner, even though she hit, too. And yet she felt that although she and her partner needed intervention, what she did not need was for anyone to decide that her partner was a batterer and exclude her for that reason from the lesbian community (pp. 38–39).

Insisting on distinctions between battering and self-defense is an urgent practical issue, however, to lesbians seeking shelter or restraining orders. Mutual *abuse*, mutual *combat*, and mutual *control* are all possible. These activities can be engaged in from either a dominant or a subordinate position. But mutual (that is, simultaneous) *domination* is not possible. This is a conceptual point about "domination." If a battered partner is understood to be not only abused but dominated, "mutual battering" is an incoherent concept. Although "mutual *combat*" may accurately describe some cases, the perception of "mutual combat" appears also a too convenient way out for judges who are unable or unwilling to determine which lesbian, if either, is a batterer. Unfortunately, as Ruthann Robson notes, judicial perception of "mutual combat" can lead to *mutual restraining orders*, with the result that activities of self-defense are as likely to be in violation as assaults.[19] Perhaps some kinds of role alternation are possible. Batterers who were battered as children have been in both roles—but not in the same relationship or during the same life-stage.

The important point regarding so-called "mutual combat" is that fighting back in self-defense implies neither reciprocal abuse nor reciprocal domination. Self-defense can be abusive if its measures are excessive, but it need not be. It may *damage* a partner's *dominance* without being abusive. Ideally, a partner who fights back will escape her partner's dominance. It does not follow that she thereby becomes dominant herself. Just as abuse is insufficient for dominance, neither is the effective thwarting of another's attempts to dominate sufficient to establish a new order of dominance.

Based on her years of service to battered women, Barbara Hart offers an analysis of "battering" designed to be helpful in this regard.[20] She rejects "mutual combat" as a myth, along with such other myths as that batterers must be larger, stronger, or personally more powerful or that batterers are more likely to be from certain ethnic groups or social classes. She also offers a list of commonly identified "violent and coercive behaviors utilized in lesbian battering," which helpfully exposes their variety. Any such list of behaviors, however, is also liable to mislead, for many of the same behaviors may also be used in self-defense. For example, battering lesbians frequently claim to be abused by partners who *withdraw*.[24] Withdrawal and deception are common defenses, often the only ones, or the most justifiable ones, available. Yet, lying and withdrawal appear on Barbara Hart's list of "coercive and abusive behaviors characteristic of lesbian battering" under "psychological or emotional abuse."[22] To determine who, if anyone, is battered, it is necessary to look not just at specific actions but at *patterns* of behavior over time and their consequences for overall distributions of power and control in the relationship, as well as for the partners' overall well-being. Barbara Hart's frequently quoted definition offers a good beginning:

> Lesbian battering is that pattern of violent and coercive behaviors whereby a lesbian seeks to control the thoughts, beliefs or conduct of her intimate partner or to punish the intimate for resisting the perpetrator's control over her. Individual acts of physical violence, by this definition, do not constitute lesbian battering. Physical violence is not battering unless it results in the enhanced control of the batterer over the recipient. (p. 173)

The focus on *patterns* and *relationships* rather than simply on individual acts is helpful. I will return to that. The reference to control, however, is not sufficient. Domination is more to the point. Controls can be exercised by both dominators and subordinates, as in lying and withdrawal. Self-defense can require checking the partner or shielding oneself; both are controls. The aim of self-defense, however, need not be domination.

In drawing attention to the context of an ongoing intimate relationship, Barbara Hart's definition improves significantly on the legal understanding of battery. To focus on relationships is not to suggest that the partners are co-responsible. Rather, the idea is that it is not possible to characterize adequately what domestic batterers do apart from the contexts in which they do it. In relationships of voluntary intimacy, we rely on goodwill, rather than enforcement of rights, to resolve differences. When goodwill is replaced by sustained hostility, the relationship becomes dangerous. A systematically hostile intimate is in a position to do severe damage before outside help is possible. Under such circumstances, it can be fatal to wait until a specific attack is in progress, or even until a specific threat has been issued, before mobilizing defenses. Yet, by the criminal definitions, there is no battery except during specific physical attacks, nor assault without an explicit threat or willful attempt to injure.

Black's Law Dictionary defines battery, first, as "intentional and wrongful physical contact with a person without his or her consent that entails some injury or offensive touching," and criminal battery as "the unlawful application of force to the person of another."[23] These definitions are generally understood as having four elements (as does Barbara Hart's definition): (1) the "defendant's" conduct (act or omission), (2) the "defendant's" "mental state," (3) harm to the victim, and (4) a causal connection. They are more specific than the ordinary understanding of battering as "beating persistently or hard" or "pounding repeatedly," which could, however, be understood to encompass verbal and emotional battering.[24] The definition in *Black's* seems both narrower and wider than Barbara Hart's. First, it seems narrower in requiring *physical contact*. (Even a surgical operation would be, legally, "technical battery," regardless of its result, were it not for the patient's consent). It thus excludes psychological and verbal attacks, such as ridicule, mockery, threats, and warnings (some of which may, however, count legally as assaults).[25] Second, the definition in *Black's* is wider in recognizing *isolated acts* as battering even when they do not produce dominance patterns. It defines datable actions, not ongoing relationships. *Black's* has entries for "battered child" and "battered child syndrome" but none for "*domestic* battery," "battered spouse" (or partner, intimate, woman, wife), nor for "battered partner syndrome."

By its conception of "battery," the criminal law thus catches within its net battered partners who strike back at the only times when they have much chance of success, namely, when the dominant partner is not at that moment embarked upon an act of *criminal* battery against them, and it lets slip many abusers who terrorize without engaging in frequent physical abuse.[26] A hostile dominator may not even need the explicit conventional language of verbal threats or warnings but can often control, threaten, and warn by gesture, facial expression, tone of voice, a "language" well-enough understood by intimates although opaque to others. Domestic partner battering, like battering under American slavery, has often relied in its daily workings on psychological harm, specifically, on incapacitating fears of physical harm based on past beatings, which need not have been frequent to be effective.[27] As British philosopher J. D. Mabbott pointed out more than fifty years ago in his famous essay on the theory of punishment, it is the *threat*, not actual punishment, that does most of the work of deterrence; actual punishments often indicate failures of the threat.[28] Likewise, in battering relationships (domestic and otherwise), credible threats can do most of the work of domination.

Thus, being battered is not *reducible to* having been hit physically, although the state of being battered is a common consequence of it. That state is not only a matter of being in pain or suffering gross bodily injury; it is a matter of *being robbed of one's agency* in being held captive through fear by a partner whose infliction of bodily harm has created an ever-present threat of more and worse. Attorney Joyce McConnell argues persuasively that when a battered partner is held to the services of a wife, although she is not literally enslaved (she cannot be legally sold, for example), it should be recognized that she is being held to *involuntary servitude* in the sense of the Thirteenth Amendment, regardless how voluntary the relationship may have been initially.[29]

According to psychologist Lenore Walker's widely received "cycle theory" of domestic violence, acute physical battering is the culmination of a long tension-building period that includes many forms of coerciveness and abuse.[30] She analyses the cycle of violence into three phases: (1) the *build-up of tension* (the longest phase, sometimes years), including progressively more serious battering incidents often of less than life-endangering severity, (2) the *acute battering phase* (usually from two to twenty-four hours, sometimes as long as a week), often the only phase gaining publicity, and only then because of needs for medical help or other intervention, and (3) the *"honeymoon phase,"* (shorter than the tension-building phase), immediately following the acute battering. Because in the "honeymoon phase" the batterer may become charming, extravagantly nurturing, apologetic, resolve never to do it again, Lenore Walker has referred to this phase as the "hook" that retains battered women when they would otherwise have the greatest motivation to leave. Many other factors, however—money, fear for her own or her children's lives, lack of confidence in her ability to succeed or in others' responding with needed help—can be sufficient to deter leaving. Many batterers escalate violence when a partner tries to leave, and the danger of killing may be greatest at this point.[31] Without adequate help, not leaving may be a partner's best survival strategy. Some report, also, that the honeymoon phase drops out after a while and the cycle simply alternates between periods of escalating hostilities and crises.

Lenore Walker found a woman battered only if the cycle of violence is played out at least twice. She saw a woman who left after one cycle as having successfully resisted battery. The partner may be guilty of criminal battery, the woman severely beaten, even hospitalized. Yet, because she *broke the cycle*, Lenore Walker did not find her *a battered woman*.

On Barbara Hart's account, as on Lenore Walker's, a batterer may control largely by credible *threats*. *Black's Law Dictionary*, however, contrasts threats as "assaults" with "battery" as their physical enactments (hence the combination "assault and battery").[32] A threat not enacted is not battery, however damaging. It may constitute harassment. An abuser who does no *bodily* harm may be held responsible for causing some harm by way of threats or harrassment. But this can easily also be an unclear situation. If there is a history of battering, the causal relationship between threats or harrassment and subsequent harm is complex, in that the threats may do the harm they do only *because of* that history. Thus, there is a need for a concept that takes into account the ways in which what the law distinguishes as battery and assault work together over time in an ongoing relationship, which is not the same as the way that assault and battery are commonly associated in a barroom fight. In law, battery includes assault, which is presumed to have preceded it; assault that stops short of battering is thus considered less serious than the combination of assault *and* battering. In domestic battering, however, the effectiveness of what may appear "mere" assaults (threats or attempts) are due to *past* battering (in the legal sense). In this way, they do far more damage than assaults that lack such a history. The concepts of "partner battering" and "domestic battering" are meant to capture this complexity. Perhaps the term "relationship battering" would get the point across better.

In law, the reason classically given for not punishing threats and other attempts as seriously as successful enactments has been to give the perpetrator a motive not to carry out the threat or a motive to cut short an attempt while there is still time to prevent harm.[33] The effectiveness of threats in terrorizing a battered *partner*, however, give the perpetrator encouragement and the opportunity to do *more* harm rather than less. The classical rationale for leniency with "mere" threats does not apply here.

Reflection on the concept of *violence* is also helpful for elucidating the fears of partners who are battered and for showing how threats work in a battering relationship. A significant aspect of violence is its *suddenness*.[34] Violence is distinguished from other injury or abuse in being characterized by sudden gross movement or change, tending to produce shock as well as damage to a system or thing. In a state of shock, one's responses are frozen; one is caught off-guard and may not understand what is coming down. To think of "violence" simply as "violating" is to miss the suddenness and shock, for violations need be neither shocking nor sudden. A loose sense of "violence," as in "doing violence to," does sometimes seem to mean only "violate." But paradigms of violence tend to incorporate suddenness and shock, even some paradigms that lack a clearly pejorative meaning (as in "the violence of the storm").

Battering relationships are violent in this sense, although not each act of abuse is so violent. Such relationships are characterized by episodes of recurring sudden, shocking harm. On Lenore Walker's cycle theory, the acute battering stage is clearly violent. Yet, even steady verbal battering can produce a violent eruption of consequences when the victim's breaking point is finally reached and she says or does something that elicits a sudden escalation of violence from her assailant. Part of the terror in the plight of the battered is due to the suddenness of violence. The *onset* of battering attacks is often sudden. They can seem to come "out of the blue" (or out of a calm, like a tornado). Even though it becomes predictable *that* they will occur, the timing is often unpredictable.[35] Attacks themselves often consist of sudden, gross movements or brutal communications. And acute battering characteristically produces sudden gross pain or injury. Suddenness facilitates control for the batterer by taking the partner off guard, not giving her time to realize what is happening, to get braced, to think what to do, to respond in a prudent, let alone wise, manner. Sudden gross pain distracts the injured person's attention from the agency of the batterer, focusing it instead on how to make the pain stop or on how to repair damage or prevent the situation from becoming worse. It can thus make "battering incidents" appear *happenings* rather than *acts*, masking abusiveness, allowing the disaster to appear the result of one's misfortunes, inadequacies, whatever one did not foresee or do that might have prevented it. Thus, battering, utilizing shock, immobilizes, resulting in impotence. Fear of violence is greatly fear of impotence. And fear of impotence is as incapacitating as self-confidence is empowering.

A batterer's experience of sudden power may be exhilarating, exciting. Claire Renzetti hypothesizes, on the basis of discovering the extent to which violence in her study was correlated with batterer dependence on a partner, that battering alleviates the batterer's feelings of dependency. "Batterers," she suggests, "are individuals who feel powerless and use violence as a means to achieve power and dominance in their intimate relationships."[36] To the extent that she is right, the appearance of batterer anger against partners may often be misleading. A batterer, although emotionally agitated, may be no angrier with an intimate than predators are angry with prey. There is a sense in which a predator is *hostile* to its prey simply in being a predator: its interests are *opposed to* (incompatible with) those of its prey. But "hostility" in this sense does not imply attitudes of anger, hatred, resentment, or the like. Batterers addicted to the exhilaration of sudden power may be more desperate than angry, even when angry because desperate.

Stories in *Naming the Violence* reveal domestic battering as desperate, violent, predatory domination of intimates. If violence helps explain the victim's terror, predation helps explain batterer tenacity and, thereby, the longevity of the intimacy. "Why do battered partners stay?" is the wrong question. The questions should be *"why are batterers so tenacious?"* and *"why is batterer tenacity so successful?"* The predator model clarifies batterer tenacity.[37] Predators are highly invested in stalking and studying prey, the better to capture it. They may put more thought, energy, and resources into capturing prey than those who do not think of themselves as prey put into protection. There are predators who mesmerize prey. In a relationship dominated by a batterer, the batterer's needs, more than those of her partner, determine the longevity (as nearly every other significant aspect) of the relationship.

Lesbian Stalking

If battering is understood as a pattern of domination that includes many abuses not falling under the legal conceptions of "battery," it should be recognized to apply not only to domestic partner abuse but also to abuse inflicted by stalkers, often in relatively public contexts. To my knowledge, lesbian stalking has not been addressed in the literature of contemporary lesbian culture. Like lesbian domestic battering and female-female incest, the subject is sensitive in a society where many who have been taught to hate lesbians would be only too eager to exploit such images in the service of antilesbian hostility. Yet, if lesbians do not address it, others will, and they are less likely to do so in ways helpful to lesbians. The film, *Windows* (1980), for example, offered an extremely homophobic fictional portrayal of a psychotic lesbian stalking a heterosexual woman, terrorizing her by such measures as breaking into her apartment and shutting her cat into the freezer.[38] In reality, a lesbian stalker, like heterosexual male stalkers, is apt to be a batterer whose partner has escaped or is trying to escape. Such stalking has ordinarily not been treated as distinct from domestic or partner battering. However, like heterosexual stalkers, lesbian stalkers can also be fans, clients, patients, students, and others who become attached to relatively public figures in their lives (or in their fantasies), such as entertainers, social service providers, doctors, teachers, and so on, relatively public figures who may not even know the stalker or may know her only professionally. Stalking should be considered a form of battering—not *domestic* battering and not necessarily *partner* battering, but perhaps *relationship* battering, even if the relationship is created by the stalker. It fits the sense described by Barbara Hart when it is persistent, oppressively harassing, and facilitates, or is intended to facilitate, the the goal of domination. It may have many of the same consequences as domestic or partner battering, not uncommonly ending in death for one or both parties and occasionally for others as well.[39]

Stalking by private individuals has only recently been acknowledged as a crime. Between 1990 and 1992, twenty-one states passed anti-stalking laws. As of May 1993, the number had risen to forty states, with similar laws pending in the other ten and the District of Columbia.[40] Between 1989 and 1992, at least thirteen articles on stalking appeared in popular magazines. The TV news show "48 Hours" devoted a program to it.[41] Of the instances described in the articles, two involved a woman stalking a woman, and they received publicity probably only because the woman stalked was, in each case, a celebrity.[42] Stalkings receiving the most publicity are of celebrities stalked by fans who are strangers to them. Most individual stalkers, however, appear to be either would-be or former intimate partners, whether the person stalked is a celebrity or not, adult or child, male or female, of the same sex or not. Commenting on a study of "inappropriate letters" to Hollywood celebrities in 1989, psychiatrist Park Dietz (who directed the study, sponsored by the National Institute of Justice) found that most of the letter-writers acted like spouses or suitors. He said, "If you didn't know who the two people were, you would think it was a normal love letter."[43] Even Robert Coker, a grown man who stalked Crystal Peterson for four years beginning when she was *seven years old*, wrote from jail after seeing her in the courtroom, "When I saw her, I wanted to drop to my knees and ask her to marry me."[44]

Stalkers, in these reports, not only physically follow on foot or by car but also send letters and gifts, deposit them at residences or workplaces, make phone calls (often asking for contact, sometimes making threats), intercept mail, monitor communications, observe through telescopes, and seek information (sometimes pretending to be someone else or using a fictional identity) from the stalked person's friends, relatives, acquaintances, even from the Department of Motor Vehicles. Like battering partners, a stalker with few scruples may be expert at manipulating others by way of their scruples to get into positions of physical proximity that appear to third parties (and may be, legally) quite legitimate.

The stalkers in these magazine articles, the kind of stalker against whom recent legislation is directed, were motivated by personal interest, usually, apparently, erotic.[45] They did not do it for hire, say, as contract killers or intelligence agents. Stalkings of the latter sorts may be actually commoner. Stalking by intelligence agents has the potential for battering.[46] Randy Shilts' recent research reveals that military intelligence has stalked gay and lesbian enlistees for decades, often with the sanction of law.[47] Wiretaps and intercepted mail are means of stalking, whether in violation of law or with government sanction. Lesbians have probably been more often targets than perpetrators of stalking, when stalking for hire and by perpetrators of hate crimes are included. On May 13, 1988, Claudia Brenner, 31, and her lover, Rebecca Wight, 28, were shot by an apparent perpetrator of such a hate crime. Rebecca was killed and Claudia wounded by Stephen Roy Carr, 28, who followed them while they were backpacking on the Appalachian Trail in south central Pennsylvania; he fired eight bullets at them.[48]

Stalking for political purposes even by lesbians may also be a greater danger to lesbians than lesbian stalking out of passion. In military contexts, for example, lesbians have participated in hunting down other lesbians. (For more on this topic, see chapter 9.) Horizontal stalking done in service to an oppressor has long been recognized as a problem.[49] The point is not that lesbians stalkers of passion are the greatest danger to lesbians. Clearly, they are not. Rather, such stalkings, like other lesbian battering and like female-female incest, present some of the greatest challenges to lesbian ethics.

Recently publicized cases make no longer tenable the notion that stalkers of passion are simply annoying but relatively harmless or that tolerating such harassment is a price one must pay for a free society. The case bringing the issue to public attention was the killing of Rebecca Schaeffer, 21, by Robert John Bordo, then 19, a fan who walked up to her apartment door and shot her when she opened it.[50] It is now recognized that when stalkers are former or would-be lovers, murder and suicide are real dangers—as in Catherine's stalking of Joan.

Commenting on individual stalkers of passion, a psychiatrist quoted in *Good Housekeeping* estimates that one in forty persons may be stalked at some time in their lives and stresses the possibility of violence "especially when the stalker feels rejected."[51] A study mentioned in *U.S.*

News and World Report puts the estimate much higher, at one in twenty.[52] Linda Farstein, chief of the Sex Crimes Unit of the Manhattan District Attorney's office reportedly said that she sees about ten cases annually and suspects they are grossly underreported.[53] With regard to what makes a stalker violent, several of the published stories suggest that it may be enough that the stalker *disapproves* of behavior in those in whose lives he, or she, has invested so much passion; stalkers may become violent to "*punish*" disapproved behavior. A common pattern in communications from a stalker is alternation between passionate declarations of love or adoration and hostile accusations, sometimes accompanied by threats.

Lesbian stalking, like its heterosexual counterpart, may be done by passionately engaged strangers or by professional acquaintances (clients, patients, students, for example). The "lesbian" of "lesbian stalking" may apply only to the motivating passions of the stalker, but not to a general orientation or identity acknowledged and embraced by the stalker herself. Similarly, the target of such "lesbian stalking" may or may not embrace a lesbian orientation. In the cases I will mention, however, the women who were stalked, or similarly harassed, are lesbian (mostly openly lesbian), and so were most of the stalkers.

Consider the position of openly lesbian teachers. An openly lesbian teacher is in the limelight for lesbian students as celebrities are for fans. Students can become passionately attached to teachers in the classroom and can want to carry the attachment outside the classroom. They may try to learn where the teacher spends time, who her friends are, where she lives, where she shops. They may send letters, bring gifts, leave notes, phone, make frequent unnecessary appointments, try to make appointments at inappropriate times or places, linger excessively after class or at one's office, and so on. When such conduct persists despite discouragement and without purposes related to learning, when it begins to establish a relationship in which domination is a goal, it has become stalking.

In my experience, women students' attachments are usually benevolent and respectful, even when enthusiastic. Yet, instances are known to me—some reported to me in confidence by lesbian professors and others from my own experience—which indicate that such attachments are not all benign and that some are seriously ambivalent. The objective in some cases appears to be domination and less than friendly manipulation, and for that reason, I view them as belonging to the family of stalking behaviors. I have no reason to think there was anything unusual about the professors in these cases (including myself) that might make us more likely than other openly lesbian professors to be targeted. I omit obscene and amorous messages scrawled in the dust on my car, anonymous notes left at my office, vandalism, crank phone calls and messages, and other isolated incidents. In the following instances, the perpetrators were persistent. They were known to us. Generally, they wanted to be known to us.

The first instance reported to me is the most complex. A formerly devoted but later disappointed and resentful lesbian student apparently intercepted a lesbian professor's mail several times, gained illegal access to her office by deceiving office staff on at least one occasion, went through the professor's files, removed things and, possibly most disruptive of all, spread false stories about the professor among other students and among faculty. As members of an unpopular minority, lesbian and gay professors are especially vulnerable to libel. Fortunately, this professor already had tenure. Although the harassing behavior went on for years, she never took the case to court, whether for lack of hard evidence or as a matter of feminist scruple. As a result the student managed to corral her attention for years, to be a recurring source of anxiety by apparently innocuous behavior—repeatedly finding excuses for "professional" contact, forever turning up in the same public places (where she had a legal right to be), sitting one or two seats behind or watching from a corner of the room.

A second case, from my own experience, is of a lesbian student who was disappointed that after two appointments I refused further meetings with her outside my office hours. She then began badgering me in and after class in the presence of students who were unaware of the background, irreparably damaging the classroom atmosphere, turning what had been a favorite class for many of us into a daytime nightmare. As she protested my stinginess to other students, she was meanwhile writing me privately with an affectionate and intimate tone, still seeking contact. The goal seemed clearly to dominate. She withdrew into stony silence when I wrote back suggesting that we meet with another professor and with someone of her choosing to work things out.

Patterns from these first two instances are repeated in yet another instance, reported to me, of a formerly devoted student whose demands of time and energy became excessive and who, upon the professor's setting limits and eventually withdrawing, turned hostile and spread false stories about her among other students and among faculty. Again, the aim seemed clearly to gain power over the professor.

Another kind of case, probably just as common although less dramatic, has the potentiality for stalking. It incorporates some stalking patterns but has not clearly manifested the aim of domination. This one is from my own experience and that of a lesbian colleague at my home institution. Each of us has been for years the recipient of occasionally intense and periodically frequent letters from the same former student. As my student, the author of these letters once brought to class extravagant treats for my birthday but on another occasion was harshly and openly critical of me in the classroom. The letters, in my case, alternate between lavish praise and sternly taking me to task; they have an air of intimacy, as though we were old friends engaged in a continuing conversation (although I do not answer the letters). On one occasion, in written communication to someone else, she falsely attributed to me derogatory remarks about others. No intervention has seemed indicated. Yet, given the potentialities, we file the letters.

There are other examples of students less persistently engaging in some of these potentially harmful activities. Two in my case are students who did not regard themselves as lesbian but spread tales, one of a fantasy relationship with me, which almost brought a pair of irate parents to my office door, and the other—a student who kept asking me to phone her—of a fantasy pursuit by me, apparently the product of deep homophobia. In these cases, the objective was not obviously domination or manipulation. I learned of them only thanks to the alertness of other students. And yet each incorporates salient patterns of stalking, suggesting the need for alertness to the potentiality for development in that direction.

From such examples regarding lesbian teachers, and from what has been reported regarding heterosexual celebrities and doctors stalked by patients, one can guess what the experience of lesbian therapists and other lesbian social service providers may be. The point is not that lesbians are *frequent* targets of stalking by lesbians. For fairly obvious reasons, we do not know the frequency. On the whole, lesbian students have been a major support of my work. Before I taught as an openly lesbian professor, I was harassed by male students (who in the 1960s were often overtly hostile) with a frequency and intensity far greater than anything perpetrated by female students. Regardless of frequency, however, lesbian stalking and related abuses are a trial for lesbian ethics.

Horizontal Violence and Lesbian Ethics

Many lesbians do not wish to use courts of law, at least when a situation is not life-threatening. Because of the courts' history of hostility toward women in general and toward lesbians in particular, it seems a betrayal to turn to them. Yet, without alternative responses, stalked and otherwise battered lesbians may be left in the position of succumbing to domination.

Thinking of Catherine and Joan, whose story opened this chapter, I turned once again to Sarah Hoagland's *Lesbian Ethics: Toward New Value*, the most sustained and influential work in lesbian ethics to date.[54] This time, I approached the book reflecting for the first time on possible implications for horizontal violence. *Lesbian Ethics* has as its agenda to develop an ethic for horizontal interaction among lesbians, that is, interaction of lesbians in community with lesbians, as opposed to the vertical interactions of lesbians in a power hierarchy with men or with nonlesbian women. Although the language of "horizontal" and "vertical" is mine, not that of *Lesbian Ethics*, the book argues, in effect, that the survival ethics that we have learned in vertical interaction with oppressors can be self-defeating when we apply it to horizontal difficulties in lesbian community.[55] And this survival ethic, it argues, is an ethic based on social *control*. *Lesbian Ethics* works with the hypothesis that if we can develop our agency without such a focus on *control*, we might even become resistant to oppression by becoming dishabituated to domination and subordination.[56]

Paradigms of horizontal difficulties that initially inspired *Lesbian Ethics* came from relatively *public* settings, lesbian community organizations that collapsed during the late 1970's under pressure of internal disputes.[57] Most of the illustrations throughout the book, however, are from personal interaction. Although this is also the setting of intimate partner battering, the book says little about that. Lesbian battering turns up briefly among the examples in *Lesbian Ethics* but is not treated as though it raised special issues.[58] The solution suggested here, as for other intractable difficulties, is withdrawal, at least, withdrawal of attention. Yet, the impossibility of withdrawal from batterers has been part of the problem. Withdrawing attention when one is unable to withdraw physically can, of course, be fatal.[59]

Lesbian Ethics treats the issue of safety in lesbian community as an overly dramatic way to describe desires to be free from criticism, disagreement, or insensitivity, a usage of "safety" not uncommon among those who have not experienced frequent physical danger. "The issue of safety among lesbians in community mostly involves not being laughed at, put down, ignored, out-shouted, or in general taken for granted" (pp. 194–95). This explains the otherwise puzzling claim that "not only is safety an illusion under patriarchy, it is not a useful goal among ourselves—for attempts to guarantee safety involve attempts to control" (p. 194). But in contexts of hostile intimacy, safety is an urgent objective, and it refers not to freedom from insensitivity but to such things as freedom from bodily battering and from malicious assaults on one's self-concept.

Battering raises issues different from those arising in contexts where general goodwill can be presumed. And yet, the lesbians involved often claim to love each other and to see themselves as basically wishing each other well. Lesbian batterers are not, as such, more politically powerful than their partners. However, the goal of battering is domination. Being battered by a partner can be extremely oppressive. Thus, lesbian battering presents a mixture of contexts. The violence is horizontal insofar as it comes from one who does not occupy a political position of superiority (or inferiority), and yet it also gives rise to a dominance order, reproducing structures of oppression. Thus, interaction with a lesbian batterer seems horizontal in some respects but vertical in others.

As Sarah Hoagland points out, those who have suffered domination, such as slaves, have responded with sabotage, often masked as subordination and deference, sometimes as incompetence or laziness (pp. 39–49). A problem with *feigning* deference is that it can serve the same ends as genuine deference. The Sambo personality under American slavery, as portrayed by Stanley M. Elkins, may be interpreted as feigned deference; the behavior of prisoners who became kapos in Nazi concentration camps, as reported by Bruno Bettelheim, may be interpreted as feigned subordination.[60] Although slaves or camp kapos may have extended their lives, their strategies did not disrupt domination scripts. Although they enable one to survive and even salvage self-respect, such pretenses neither alter power structures nor empower saboteurs to achieve goals of their own. Thus, Sarah Hoagland argues, although feminine "incompetence" may be sabotage by which dominated women have salvaged self-respect in situations of near impotence, it is not otherwise constructive or empowering, and it feeds oppressive images of women. A saboteur may prove that dominators cannot control her motives, feelings, or the attitude with which she obeys. She may get "one up" by anticipating orders and carrying them out with her own agenda. But when we turn such strategies *on one another* to resolve horizontal disputes, the result may be that we alienate and control each other, serving our oppressors.

Speculating that ethics based on social control fosters domination and subordination, Sarah Hoagland proposed to substitute in lesbian community an ethic of agency and integrity in which the activity of *attending* is a major strategy of empowerment (pp. 120–43). She presents attending as basically a way of being there to and for others without attempting to control them. Referring to the example of a friend in pain, she observes that "if, instead of trying to control things, we attend her, our action empowers her in that it enables her to gather and focus her own strength," and "when I attend you, I stretch toward you, I am present to you, I engage with you. I focus my energy on you, my rhythms"; "I become a witness" (p. 127). She notes that attending was central to ancient midwifery. The midwife did not control birth; rather, by attending, she helped steady the birthing woman, "acting as a beacon or a magnet," creating between them an enabling power (p. 127). Enabling power, the eliciting of "power from within," by contrast with controlling power, or "power over," is central to Sarah Hoagland's valuing of attending (pp. 117–18, 126). Thus, she suggests, in effect, that in horizontal interaction, we do better to become each other's "midwives," enabling each other, than to try to get each other to do the right thing.

"Midwife" was also, according to Plato, the metaphor invoked by Socrates to describe his profession as a philosopher. Socrates, claiming to follow the profession of his mother, a midwife, rather than that of his father, a carpenter, denied that he was a builder and maintained that he only assisted at others' creations, at the birth of ideas, noting also that only those past childbearing age were allowed to be midwives.[61] There is disingenuousness, of course, in his disclaimer of creativity. Still, the midwife metaphor enabled him to distinguish between system-building and helping others think for themselves. Analogously, Sarah Hoagland seeks an ethic that does not aim to get other lesbians to do what is right, or even to determine what that is, but seeks, rather, to elicit and enhance agency and integrity. Unlike Socrates, she does not present attenders as no longer capable of creativity. Her vision is of lesbians creating new value together, eliciting the best in each other instead of provoking the worst.

On whether this lesbian ethic is only for lesbian contexts, she hesitates:

> What I am calling Lesbian Ethics are meant to be used in lesbian community, among ourselves. . . . Whether these values can be developed from a different angle as part of a political strategy to confront patriarchy is an open question. . . . I once felt these values were meaningless in patriarchy. I am no longer sure. (p. 22)

The hesitation is interesting. An ethic helpful for dealing with intimate batterers might be helpful in vertical interaction with external oppressors. By the same token, a lesbian ethic not helpful for dealing with batterers needs qualification and supplementation even for lesbian community.

What is "attending"? As "stretching," attending can mean turning the mind to, serving, waiting upon, escorting, accompanying. If "attend*ing*" suggests service, which sounds friendly, "atten*tion*" suggests absorption, which may or may not be friendly. "Turning the mind to," *paying* attention, suggests epistemic activity—noticing—as well as care and discrimination, which may be but need not be ethical. *Attendance* can be just *being there.* The military command, "Attention!" calls forth a rigid posture. We have just traveled from stretching to rigidity, an interesting set of potentialities. (I have the image of a woman shouting, "Attention!" and everyone stretching in response.) The spectrum of ethical potentialities may be equally rich.

For both Socrates and Sarah Hoagland, attending is not without effects; its intention is *benign influence*, eliciting positive development. As a fundamental ethical stance, however, attending is problematic, because it need not be friendly. It can be harmful if it does not respect boundaries, even if its intention is friendly. Even among lesbians who say they wish each other well, attending can be the problem rather than the solution. Domestic battering and stalking are two such contexts.[62]

Where erotic passions are activated, attending can become intrusive. When those passions are frustrated, it can turn hostile. If friendly attending suggests readiness to serve, hostile attention suggests watchfulness that can escalate into monitoring, policing, readiness to criticize, accuse, to demand an accounting, to punish. If friendly attention empowers, hostile attention debilitates. Hostile attention is a weapon of control and domination.

I am wary of a possible slide from rejecting an ethic *based* on social control to rejecting controls that we may need for self-defense. Perhaps a goal of *Lesbian Ethics* is to prevent such crises from arising. Still, although Sarah Hoagland does not claim to reject all forms of control—and her endorsement of withdrawal implies an endorsement of the control implicit in that strategy—there seems to be an underlying supposition in *Lesbian Ethics* that among lesbians who find themselves doing each other in, despite intentions to be mutually helpful, the need does not arise to defend ourselves against deep hostility that refuses even to respect withdrawal. That has not been my experience. *Denial of deep hostility* by batterers and stalkers is an element of the problem. In ambivalence, deep hostility coexists with goodwill. Where lesbians are raised in a society in which female caretakers are often each other's instruments of torture, it should not surprise if lesbians are often deeply ambivalent toward lesbians.[63]

What place *should* control have? Control is not in itself bad. It does not necessarily imply domination. It need not even be conflict-oriented; when it is, it can repel rather than invite domination. Control can be a source of well-placed pride. I cannot imagine *creativity*, for example, without it. Control brings order out of chaos, guides development with intelligence. Controls I value are *shape-giving*—not particularly conflict-oriented (for example, tone control, ideally effortless, in playing a musical instrument)—and being able effectively to *repel* unwanted intervention (definitely conflict-oriented). I have learned slowly to shape my life and protect it against assaults, repelling as well as withdrawing. I like the T'ai Chi concept of deflecting and redirecting hostile power.[64]

To control is to check or to regulate. Both have degrees. To check is to stop or to scrutinize. Domination checks from all directions, leaving no leeway, nothing unmonitored, plays God (*Dominus*)—literally, "lords" it over someone. To exercise controls is not necessarily to be "*in* control," for controls can also be exercised by subordinates. Controlling activities include monitoring, restraining, intimidating, preventing, and policing; the point of these activities is not so much to determine *what* another does as to remove certain options. However, controlling activities also include directing, commanding, seducing, manipulating, all of which sound more like Sarah Hoagland's idea of "bending others to our will."[65] These forms of regulation sound more like determining or shaping what others do. Yet even such bendings need not dominate. If command suggests hierarchy, it also gives us imperatives with which to check aggression: *basta!* stop! go away! Manipulation is devious control. Yet, even manipulation can be valuable in the service of connection or disconnection among the oppressed.

Control, like money, is valuable for what it gets us. One thing it gets us is attention. When attention is valuable, that is often *not* for what it gets us but *for itself.* We bask in it; it warms like the sun, makes us feel valued, important, affects how we value ourselves. Attention is to the soul what air, water, and food are to the body—they keep it vital. I have found lesbians relatively good at attending lesbians—not always exercising good judgment about it and not equally good at attending all lesbians but often the best appreciators of lesbians, good at perceiving what lesbians like, want, do well, enjoy—no mean achievement in a world rendering us invisible.[66]

Loss of attention may be more demoralizing than loss of control. If invisibility raises the spectre of attention starvation, perhaps we should think about how we deal with needs for attention, how we solicit attention. One means is abuse of attention itself.

Impertinence can be an abuse of attention. Impertinence is manipulative. Men are routinely impertinent to women, pointedly noticing what is irrelevant (usually anatomical) to purposes for which we have consented to interact (say, job interviews). When lesbians do it, the pointed noticing is as apt to be of some irrelevant idiosyncrasy of manner or style as of anatomy or apparel. By pointed noticing we get another to attend to the fact that we are noticing, engineer an attention shift from the ostensible matter at hand to produce interaction on a different level. We learn such maneuvers to become visible to each other where overt lesbian approaches are unsafe. If we sense danger, an adjustment of attention allows us to pretend that nothing was happening. Manipulative behavior can be constructive, imaginative, fun, playful. Flirting may be impertinence *par excellence*, walking a thin line between respectful play and disrespectful intrusion.

If isolated impertinence is not a major concern, constant impertinence is crazy-making. More dangerous, however, is concentrated hostile attending. I find obsessions with control at the heart of lesbian violence. But I find attending there also. Battered and stalked lesbians are targets of focused, hostile attention, of monitoring. The perpetrators focus inordinately, often in ludicrous detail, on their targets. Disengaging from hostile monitors can be dangerous, require skills. Refusal to engage can also be dangerous. Hostile monitoring, even more than acute battering incidents, is the batterer's great source of control. *It is a form of control available even to those who are otherwise relatively impotent.*

In Sarah Hoagland's paradigm of oppression, to which *Lesbian Ethics* was a response, we lack control as lesbians over situations that we can neither abandon nor significantly alter but within which we can still *respond* and "make a difference."[67] Another paradigm of oppression, however, is to have "learned" helplessness within situations that we could actually learn to avoid, or within which we could *learn to make* significant alterations, were we not already so engaged. We need skills for *disengaging*, even within lesbian community. I doubt that Sarah Hoagland would disagree with that, as it fits with her insistence upon retaining the option of withdrawal. However, it also calls for further qualifications concerning the value of mutual attendance.

A hypothesis to add to Sarah Hoagland's hypotheses about obstacles to lesbian community is that patriarchy gives us good reason to fear each other's *hatreds* because, as lesbians, we have more *access* to each other than to those with power over us and because the social penalties for harming each other have not been high. In his essay "Why Blacks Kill Blacks," Alvin Poussaint argued that black men in the United States who kill are more likely to kill black than white women and men because it costs so much less and it is so much easier to gain access.[68] Likewise, lesbians who kill are probably more likely to kill lesbians than to kill anyone else.[69]

Solutions?

How might we empower each other to respond effectively and well to threats of violence among us? Counselling withdrawal is unhelpful when battering prevents withdrawal and when batterers stalk. Some attempts to withdraw escalate the violence. Withdrawal of *outsiders* from batterers—ostracizing them—facilitates battering. Domestic battering is often a highly private affair; some who would not dream of violence in the presence of outsiders will do incredible things to intimates in private. For such cases, *attendance* of *outsiders* may be an exploitable strategy. We may need emergency outside attendance in relationship crises to interrupt scripts, disengage, even intimidate, thereby controlling—i.e., checking—without punishments and without domination. In this way, transforming a private context into a public one, or a less private one, may be effective against some domestic battering.

Something similar to this strategy, applied to heterosexual battering, is described by Melanie Kaye/Kantrowitz in the first of her "War Stories, 197-," a tale entitled "The Day We Didn't Declare War," included in *My Jewish Face and Other Stories*.[70] In this tale, rape crisis volunteer counselors form a group, The Godmothers, who go in pairs to stay with women who are being battered but who do not want to or are unable to go to a shelter.[71] The Godmothers do not just attend, however; they go not only with sleeping bags but with nightsticks and a new lock for the front door. They believe in "modest weapons." And they insist that the woman go to a shelter if she was threatened with a gun or a knife. But where a batterer simply gets drunk and punches a woman around,

which most of them do, the Godmothers put up a sign on the door saying, "This house is under the protection of a restraining order and THE
GODMOTHERS."[72] It is effective. Major problems? Not *enough*
Godmothers to go around. And many women under attack not at
home but by stalkers in parks or at shopping malls. And so, Melanie
Kaye/Kantrowitz imagined a second "war story" ("The Day We Did"),
another response, in which crisis counselors, after receiving calls from
women raped at knifepoint in the park and being unable to arouse effective help from police, meet in a nameless group and prepare to take
more aggressive measures, as anonymous women, to stop the violence.[73]

Melanie Kaye/Kantrowitz wrote these stories about male violence
against women, not about horizontal violence among lesbians. Homophobic films notwithstanding, lesbians do not have a history of raping
lesbians (or anyone else) at knifepoint in the park (or anywhere else).
Violence has not been *institutionalized* among us as it has been institutionalized among heterosexual men. Still, individual lesbians are as
capable of violent behavior as anyone. Some lesbian batterers and stalkers may not be amenable to rechanneling their hostilities against
oppressive institutions. If lesbian communities are not prepared to use
the force of law for protection against horizontal violence, do we need
Godmothers, too? If midwives are not enough, where *does* that leave
us? Where does it leave lesbian ethics?

Chapter 7

female incest and adult lesbian crises

Prologue Fifteen years ago, mention of "incest" among lesbians in my town evoked smiles at the idea that everyone in the lesbian community eventually became intimately connected with everyone else or their lover, producing highly "incestuous" political organizations. That is not the "incest" of this chapter. The term evokes no humor today. "Incest" among lesbians then referred to boundary blurring between sexual and nonsexual *adult* friendships, conjuring up issues discussed in chapter 5. Such blurring is not always good or even funny. Widespread, it creates possibilities for abuse in any organization that gives power to some over others (most organizations). But such abuses are not often so traumatizing as to produce amnesia. Their damage to health does not commonly last decades. They can be resisted by choices adults have to move in and out of organizations and relationships. By contrast, children have little choice about their environments and relationships, especially intimate ones with adults. *Incest in this chapter is child abuse.* Its traumas commonly produce amnesia. Its effects often last decades. Its manifestations often go unrecognized.

The child abused in female incest is paradigmatically a prepubescent girl bonded to a woman, such as Mother, who holds a position of trust or authority in relation to her. Abusers may also be other trusted relatives, older sisters, babysitters, neighbors, family friends, service providers.[1] In this chapter I consider some forms of female incest—what it means, where it has been found, how to recognize it, what has been written on it—with the aim of encouraging speculation about its possible significance for (adult) female interaction and lesbian relationships, especially crises internal to lesbian relationships and to feminist groups, organizations, and classrooms, including intergenerational crises among feminists. If heterosexual incest has significant implications for adult relationships, it would be astonishing if same-sex incest had none. My approach is from the point of view of the adult lesbian survivor.

Originally, I had called the topic of this chapter "lesbian incest." That term provoked overwhelming outcries from lesbians distressed that it would reinforce stereotypes of homosexuals as child abusers. Many also resisted conceiving such abuse as lesbian. Hence, I have retreated to the title "female incest" (short for and less cumbersome than "female-female incest"). However, much of the objection to the language of "lesbian incest" stems from current fixations on the *noun* use of "lesbian," which allows "lesbian incest" to suggest "incest *by lesbians*." That was *not* the sense that I intended. I intended "lesbian" as an adjective applying to the *abuse*, leaving unspecified the abuser's sexual orientation, although I also had in mind, primarily, survivors who identify as lesbian. I have known many lesbian-identified women and children of lesbian-identified women but have not found lesbian-*identified* women who were *sexual* abusers of children.

The incest perpetrators of this chapter did *not* identify themselves as lesbians. Nor did they live lives that others would identify as lesbian. They may never have had adult peer lesbian relationships. Most were wives and mothers and were presumed heterosexual. Yet, in their erotic and sexual interactions with children, they acted to satisfy their own desires; they were not simply functioning as agents of others (such as husbands or pornographers). Even if "lesbian" does not well describe such abusers, reflection on female incest is important in the context of lesbian ethics because some of us have survived it, some of our lovers have survived it, some of us teach students who have survived it, or we have other friends and coworkers with such histories. Like lesbian battering, female incest, viewed from the perspective of female oppression, is horizontal abuse, although it also has vertical aspects in that the abuser is more powerful and uses her power to dominate. Understanding female incest may be yet another avenue to insight into how things can go wrong among us.

My reflections on horizontal violence grow in part out of attempts to understand my own experiences of surviving female horizontal hostility, first, as the child of a mother who both celebrated and abused me; then, as a young lesbian with a passionately attached partner who did the same; and, more recently, as a survivor of painful political battles with close feminist coworkers and as a teacher who occasionally encounters puzzling hostilities or deep ambivalences from a female student in the classroom. Long-range, my goals bear a kinship to those of Sarah Hoagland in *Lesbian Ethics: Toward New Value*, although perhaps less close a kinship than I once thought.[2] As indicated in the previous chapter, that book seeks a remedy against the collapse of lesbian community organizations such as its author witnessed in Chicago in the late '70s and early '80s, collapses due less to external pressures than to internal relationships gone wrong among lesbians with shared feminist aims. Speculating that the control ethic we learned for survival in patriarchy was backfiring, *Lesbian Ethics* proposed an ethic intended not to be social control-oriented but meant as an alternative to a justice-orientation. At first, I read that book as addressing horizontal abuse.[3] I no longer see it that way, although it is clearly concerned with often painful horizontal interactions.[4] *Histories* of horizontal abuse, however, may be among the sources of the difficulties that the book does address, especially, the damaging internal stress to which feminist lesbian relationships have been liable. It may also be among the sources of difficulties that initially inspired the book, the internal stresses that have so often led to the collapse of lesbian feminist organizations.

All of the academic feminist organizations to which I have belonged for more than fifteen years have endured recent rounds of major internal stress. Some of the stress seems to have been triggered by restructuring proposals as the organizations face generational changings of the guard. Sarah Hoagland's concern seems to apply here, at least abstractly, insofar as committed feminists find themselves interacting in ways that jeopardize their own common interests. In proposing new values as a remedy, *Lesbian Ethics* seems to presuppose that our motivational dynamics are open to inspection, if we but reflect. Ordinarily, we assume such openness. Where there has been incest, however, the roots of our motivational dynamics may be too deeply buried to be readily accessible to introspection. Reassessing our *values* may not be enough. We may need also to reassess our early bonds with women. And some classic values, such as justice, may be useful in assessing and reassessing our positions in those relationships.

What Is Incestuous About It?

Because of its histories in law, medicine, and anthropology, "incest" is a misleading term for abuse. Anthropologists have meant by "incest" sexual relationships (including consensual ones) between genetically related kin. In political contexts, this use is morally objectionable because it assimilates the rape of children by adults or older children to consensual adult sex, such as between first cousins who sometimes marry. Some feminists reserve the term "incest" exclusively for rape and other sexual abuse of children. Perhaps most of what is called "incest" *is* child-rape. So, why not call it that, instead of "incest"?

Some do. Yet not all child-rape is incestuous. There is not always a relationship of trust or authority. Incest is often *ongoing* abuse which the child cannot escape. Incestuous or not, sexual abuse can devastate a child more than it would an adult. Credibility problems are compounded for a victim who is both female and a child. The child Maya Angelou was unable to speak for months after she was raped.[5] Abusers with *continuing access* compound the abuse by intense patterns of control and manipulation. In this respect, adult-child incest can resemble partner battering. Battering can accompany the incest. Because it marks continuing stress and long-lasting adaptations that mold children subjected to ongoing control by a sexual abuser in the house, I retain the term "incest," despite its difficulties.

To identify incest at home, it is useful to reflect upon and reassess some seemingly mundane matters that one may have been raised to keep "all in the family." Female incest, like heterosexual rape and pornography, need be neither dramatic nor extraordinary. Examples in the "mother-daughter incest" chapter of Susan Forward and Craig Buck, *Betrayal of Innocents*, like some examples reported to me informally, are easily recognizable as incest because they report mothers engaging in clitoral stimulation of daughters, sometimes encouraging daughters to reciprocate, during tickling, bathing, or sharing beds.[6] Everyday female incest, however, need not be defined by, nor understood as restricted to, clitoral stimulation any more than heterosexual rape need be understood as restricted to vaginal penetration. Perhaps even more readily than heterosexual abuse, female incest may "pass" for something else, such as care-taking, punishment, or affection. It is difficult enough for well-socialized members of patriarchy to conceive "what lesbians do," let alone to conceive what would count as "female *incest.*" Elsewhere, I have argued that lesbian love-making is not well-described as "sexual."[7] What is at stake in the sexual abuse of children, however, is not well-described as love-making. I here defer to common usage in calling it "sexual."

Spanking (ostensibly as punishment) and enemas (ostensibly for reasons of health) can be sexually arousing and can be carried out with varying degrees of publicity and ritual, which, in turn, can become part of the arousal. Both activities are common in consensual sexual sado-masochism. Punishment is an easy outlet for sadistic sexuality; it can easily become a domestic ritual. But, also, rituals as ordinary as dressing, undressing, bathing, and health monitoring can become sexualized occasions for abuse. Other examples may be less ordinary. As with battering, perpetrators have ingeniously tailored their abuses to available resources. The examples from the following queries are not fanciful. My sources, which are many, include my own experience, reports by my mother of what her mother did, reports from acquaintances and colleagues of what their mothers did, and published survivor narratives. All are from homes passing as normal or even exemplary.

Were you forced as a child under threat of punishment to pose nude for photographs after you were well past infancy? (Were the photographs shared or sold? How would you know? And, did your home have a photographic darkroom?) Did you ever discover that a bedroom mirror was also a window covered by a hanging decoration in the adjacent room? (Who were the voyeurs? Did any pay for the privilege? How would you know? Was this a bedroom in which a child was spanked? or given enemas?) Did Mother put you down as "prudish" for complaining of sexual harassment by a sibling, whom she excused or exonerated, although she forbade you to tell? Did she, or any other caretaker, tell you that you were a very special child, different from other children who would not understand special things that you and she did together, which you must never reveal? Did some of those special things occur when you slept naked together? Did she often stroke or squeeze your body parts? Did she talk to you a lot about sex, or about sexual variations, while you were prepubescent? Were you forced to kiss her friends or guests when it was clear that you did not want to? Were you forced to kiss her right after she punished you? Did she yell at you if you ceased struggling and let your body go limp when she was spanking you? Did she enjoy humiliating you when she caught you

disobeying? Did she put you through elaborate apologizing ceremonies? Did she expect from you adult sensitivity to her feelings when
you were, say, five? Was she jealous when you became attached to other
women? (Did she also encourage it?) Did she (or any woman) ever ask
you to examine her "down there" (for any reason whatever)? or to give
her an enema? Did she force you to take unnecessary laxatives? to sit
on the toilet for what seemed hours until she gave you permission to
get up? deny you bodily privacy in the bath or on the toilet? (If you
remember, you were probably old enough for bathroom autonomy.)

Obviously, such treatment exhibits poor childrearing. Isolated
instances may mean nothing more. However, persistent patterns, especially those involving several such behaviors, suggest reexamining one's
early relationship with the relevant caretaker. The bathroom examples
seem to illustrate obsessions with control. It is not surprising if house-
wife-mothers are excessively controlling of children, given how
responsible they are held for children. Obsession with control, however, is also frequently characteristic of sexual abuse. In fostering obsessive
control of children, especially of daughters, patriarchal housewife-
motherhood may be conducive to incestuous attachments of mothers
to rebellious daughters whose rebellions they at once punish, envy,
and encourage. If so, that "different" socialization of girls documented
by Nancy Chodorow and recently valorized by many feminists may be
a source of more trouble than is often suspected.[8]

Mother usually turns up in sociologists' writings on incest as the
"silent partner" in heterosexual abuse, blamed for failing to protect
Daughter from Daddy. If "silent partner" analysis is harsh on mothers
battered by men who terrorize daughters, it also ignores mothers who
are willing participants, masterminds or voyeurs, perceiving only
stereotypes of passivity instead of taking seriously our real positions and
possibilities. In correcting this bias, there is, of course, a risk of misogynist mother-blaming. The child-raising responsibilities imposed on
individual, often isolated mothers are awesome, and conditions of
mothering, often impossible. While they do not excuse abuse, neither
are abusive mothers responsible for those conditions. Apart from such
conditions, many mothers might never have become abusive.[9]

Thus, just as I am not entirely satisfied with the term "incest" for
sexual abuse of children by trusted caretakers, neither am I happy
about the terms "perpetrator," "abuser," and "victim," although I find
them ineliminable. I use "abuser" to indicate a locus of responsibility,
although not all abusers are malicious. Some seem to convince them-

selves that they do no harm. Yet, they are wrong. They can ordinarily be held responsible even if they claim not to know this. And they can be wrong on a number of counts, ranging from exploitation of trust and of vulnerability to cruelty and sadism. Putting these abuses into one category, "incest," ignores distinctions that would be morally relevant from the points of view of perpetrators. From the points of view of victims and survivors, such distinctions make less difference. After years of not describing women as "victims," I now sometimes use "victim" or "target" in preference to "survivor" out of respect for those who did *not* survive, to avoid suggesting that not surviving implies any deficiency of character or resourcefulness on the victim's part. For the past decade and a half feminists have avoided the term "victim" in writing about violence against women because the term suggests passivity, reinforcing feminine stereotypes. Stereotypes of passivity need to be resisted by new appreciations of what "victim" means—it does *not* mean "passive," for example—and new appreciations of what "survivor" means—that our agency is often a function of luck, for example. When I use the term "survivor," say, to emphasize that an assault was life-threatening, I do not mean it as a term of commendation.

What Has Been Written?

At first there appears very little written about female incest. Academic studies of child abuse scarcely mention mother-daughter incest, although maternal violence is well-documented.[10] However, there is more than one might think, although most of it is not labeled "incest." My sources, in addition to personal experience and confidential infor mal reports from others, are first, published narratives and studies of women, such as the woman well-known as Sybil, who have regained memories of childhood sexual abuse and torture, and second, recent studies of cult ritual abuse (primarily although not exclusively in satanic cults).[11] Many women recovering memories in therapy of childhood abuse at home or in cults have identified themselves as multiple personalities.[12] Other survivors experience dissociations less drastic than amnestic "splitting," ranging from hearing named voices carrying on dialogues "in one's head," and isolated episodes of amnesia, to the ordinary experience of daydreaming. Even the American Psychiatric Association's *Diagnostic and Statistical Manual of Mental Disorders* now acknowledges in its relatively recent entry on "Multiple Personality Disorder" that "Several studies indicate that in nearly all cases, the disorder has been preceded by abuse (often sexual) or another form of severe emotional trauma in childhood."[13]

Since the mid-1980s literature on multiple personality with roots in childhood abuse has been growing.[14] There are periodicals devoted to multiple personality and dissociation, and self-help organizations exist for survivors who identify as multiple.[15] Other materials, unpublished, have been assembled by and for counselors and survivors.[16] Until the past decade, most published discussions of multiple personality seem ignorant of its connections with childhood abuse, and some who are now not ignorant nevertheless continue mostly to disregard those connections. Stephen Braude, for example, who recently published what may be the first philosophical book devoted to multiple personality, does note the roots in childhood abuse, but then ignores them in his subsequent treatment of the subject.[17]

Adam Crabtree's *Multiple Man* treats the occult and the psychological as two theoretical approaches to many of the same phenomena.[18] In occult tradition, the relevant theoretical concept is "possession," rather than "multiple personality." In relation to childhood abuse, a discussion both fascinating and horrifying in which religion and psychology come together occurs in Freud's letters to Fliess, in which he refers to the witches of Renaissance Europe. Possible histories of childhood abuse as a source of many of the witches'"possession" adds a new layer of appreciation to the reexaminations by Andrea Dworkin and Mary Daly of the witch trials and of the Church's fifteenth-century Inquisition manual, the *Malleus Maleficarum* ("hammer of witches"), detailing how to recognize witches.[19]

Freud commented to Fliess on the similarity between the confessions of those witches and the stories of childhood sexual abuse that he was hearing from his middle-class female patients.[20] Thus it appears that the witches of Renaissance Europe may have been first sexually abused as children and then later burned (perhaps by some of their assailants) for dissociative skills they developed to survive. In letter #56, Freud wrote, "Do you remember my always saying that the mediaeval theory of possession, that held by the ecclesiastical courts, was identical with our theory of . . . the splitting of consciousness? But why did the devil who took possession of the poor victims invariably commit misconduct with them?" (pp. 187–88). In letter #57, he writes "to this very day there is a class of persons who tell stories similar to those of witches and my patients; nobody believes them, though that does not shake their belief in them. As you will have guessed, I refer to paranoiacs, whose complaints that excrement is put in their food, that they are abominably maltreated at night, sexually, etc. are pure memory-content" (p. 190). And in the same letter, "I am toying with the idea that in the perversions . . . we may have the remnants of a primitive sexual cult, which . . . may once have been a religion (Moloch, Astarte)" (p. 189).

In fairly direct partial confirmation of something like Freud's latter hypothesis, memories of some contemporary multiple personalities are of ritual abuse, including child murder, in clandestine religious cults.[21] Because female guardians sometimes subject children to and participate in sexual initiations in "cults that kill" (as one author calls them), the literature on such cults is among the sources on female incest.[22]

Where Has It Been Found?

In published narratives by women who have recovered memories of abuse there are two major contexts of female incest: the first is home or a homelike setting, relatively private; the second is ritual cult meetings, less private but nevertheless clandestine. These contexts need not be mutually exclusive. They may be linked intergenerationally. A woman who was ritually abused in a cult may abuse a daughter at home, for example. From Sybil's accounts, it seems likely that her mother was also multiple; it is possible that her mother was a survivor of cult ritual abuse.

At home, where incest tends to be one on one by a parent, older sibling, relative, neighbor, family friend, and so on, the abuser may rationalize her behavior to the child as caretaking, either justified correction (punishment) or "medicine." In cults, a child may have no way to understand what is occurring or why, for lack of both sexual and religious (or occult) concepts.

Cult ritual abuse is not restricted to sex; it includes many forms of torture and murder. The task force of the Los Angeles County Commission for Women defines ritual abuse as "a brutal form of abuse of children, adolescents, and adults, consisting of physical, sexual, and psychological abuse, and involving the use of rituals," pointing out that, "ritual does not necessarily mean satanic," but noting that, "most survivors state that they were ritually abused as part of satanic worship" and that "ritual abuse rarely consists of a single episode" but "usually involves repeated abuse over an extended period of time."[23]

Survivor Elizabeth Rose (pseud.), who recently revealed in *Ms* magazine that she witnessed the cult murder of her baby sister, maintains that perpetrators can be "family members or strangers, men or women, rich or poor, educated or uneducated people."[24] She writes that her mother's "otherwise ordinary middle-class family participated in a generational satanic cult" into which she was indoctrinated when she was four or five years old. She was reprieved when her mother had to leave the locale where the cult was based to join her husband when he returned from the war in Vietnam. She recalls abuse, including forcible impregnation and sodomy, aimed at women and children but recalls witnessing no abuse of adult men.

Anne, another survivor, reports that her experience as a victim of cult ritual abuse included "electroshock, cutting, burning, needling, hanging, confinement, sleep and food and water deprivation, cannibalism, drugs, spending time with body parts, animal and human sacrifices, suicide games, constant exposure to life-threatening situations, incest, rape, sodomy, gang rape, gang sodomy, prostitution."[25]

In both domestic and cultic contexts, sexual abuse of children can be fatal for the child. Kate Millett's *The Basement* reports on the 1965 sexual torture murder of Sylvia Likens by a gang of teenagers led by Gertrude Baniszewski of Indiana in whose care Sylvia and her younger sister Jenny were left while their parents worked Midwest state fairs.[26] Miraculously, police were alerted by Jenny Likens, and the perpetrators were convicted. Sylvia's torture was incest in the sense of abuse of trust and authority; Sylvia and Jenny were neither kin to nor emotionally bonded to their abusers. A 1991 Afterword to the reprint of *The Basement* reports that Paula Baniszewski, a convicted perpetrator and daughter of Gertrude, has been released and "is married and the mother of two" (p. 342).

How many Gertrude Baniszewskis and Paula Baniszewskis are raising daughters? How many Sylvia Likens have disappeared? Introducing their anthology on child abuse, psychiatrist Gloria Powell and clinical psychologist Gail Wyatt report that in 1984, according to the American Humane Association, 200,000 new child abuse cases were *reported* to child protective services in 19 states (although "only" 100,000 were substantiated, 78% involving a female child).[27] Nothing is said of murders, nor of children who disappear. Because fewer victims may escape the control and the monitoring of cults, domestic incest is probably more easily exposed. This may create the impression that domestic incest is commoner, which could be false. Cults have more resources than the average family for self-protection. To date, however, I know of no formal investigations undertaken to determine the extent of cult ritual abuse of women and children in this country nor how widespread it has been in the past.

For survivors of cult ritual abuse, speaking out is dangerous. Thus, most publicly available information so far has been written by (ostensible) outsiders, such as investigative journalists and therapists. Robert Mayer, New Jersey professor and therapist, writes about a patient he calls Ned, who as a child may have been programmed to kill himself to avoid betraying cult secrets.[28] Ned did kill himself shortly after regaining, under hypnosis in therapy, memories of childhood ritual abuse. Such stories raise unsettling questions about the creation of personalities to carry out specific tasks, such as murder or self-destruction, to prevent betrayal of cult secrets. Most survivors who have been willing to publish their experiences have used pseudonyms or withheld surnames. One survivor acknowledges that although talking is dangerous for her, so is not talking.[29]

More than a decade ago, the Canadian woman known as Michelle Smith, and more recently, Jenny Walters Harris of the southeastern United States, remembered as adults physical abuse, including sexual abuse, that they suffered as children in religious cults to which female caretakers introduced them.[30] Like Ned, both Michelle Smith and Jenny Harris report being tortured, drugged, and compelled to participate in ritually murdering other children. As criminalization follows the "seasoning" (torturing to break the will) of a newly abducted prostitute so that she can have no confidence of enlisting outside help and as an outlaw is in no position to betray others to legal authorities, likewise "seasoning" and criminalization are recognizable in patterns of induction into clandestine cults that engage in ritual murder and sexual torture.[31]

Ritual abuse referred to in all of these sources appears to have Christian or pagan backgrounds. It is not to be confused with the Blood Libel, which began with case of Hugh of Lincoln in twelfth-century England and which falsely accuses Jews of killing Christian children for blood to make Passover matzos—a fabrication on the basis of which anti-Semitic Christians have slaughtered entire Jewish villages.[32] An interesting question is whether ritual abuse practiced by esoteric Christians inspired the Blood Libel against Jews—which would make that Libel, in Mary Daly's terms, a reversal.[33]

The above contexts of female incest contrast sharply also with the lesbophobic mythology of incest in such novels as Diderot's *The Nun* and Winifred Ashton's *Regiment of Women*, which present girls' schools and convents as sites of sexual abuse.[34] Although serious questions have been raised about the infiltration of *daycare* centers and *pre*schools by abusive cults, I have not found religious convents or schools for older girls to be among the contexts of sexual abuse in the published memories of women recovering from long-term effects of female incest.[35] With respect to the body of erotic lesbian-authored or lesbian sympathetic fiction—novels and films, such as *Mädchen in Uniform*—with the theme of pupil-teacher crushes that end in major suffering or suicide, it is worth remembering that suicide endings were nearly "obligatory" to get lesbian pulp novels of the 1930s and 1940s past censors.[36] In the lesbian literature of girls' school erotics, the suffering portrayed is generally that of *unrequited* love (or its perception), or of ostracism, not the result of sexual relations between teachers or nuns and girls.

More Questions Than Answers

What significance, if any, have histories of female incest for battles among feminists, such as academics in Women's Studies Programs, in the National Women's Studies Association, or in the various Societies of Women in Philosophy? For classroom hostility between female instructors and female students, perhaps especially where the generation gap is sizable? For lesbian battering and other lesbian partnership difficulties? How likely is it that our early caretakers (not only mothers but also grandmothers or babysitters), or the caretakers of our friends, lovers, students, or teachers were victims of ritual abuse, as Sybil's mother may have been? Or that they participated in other abusive or murderous activities, as did Paula Baniszewski (recall, now mother of two)?

One may wonder whether survivors of cult ritual abuse or sexual abuse at home would be able to become relatively independent professional or businesswomen or turn up in academic feminist communities. And yet, Sybil, whose incest was severe, was an artist. To most people, she has "passed" most of her life. Michelle Smith's psychiatrist, Lawrence Pazder, found that cult participants in British Columbia included *highly respected physicians and businessmen*. In recent years, more than one of my students has identified herself as a survivor of cult ritual abuse, and two female university professors have identified themselves to me as survivors of incest by their mothers. This is not, of course, a helpful indication of frequency, but it does indicate that such histories need not preclude professional achievement.

Sexually abusive initiations have been reported of some campus fraternities, according to Peggy Sanday.[37] Who knows how many other secret societies in mainstream culture engage in such initiations or other such rituals? How would outsiders know? *Insiders* may have amnesia for decades (even without developing multiple personalities). Those who experience atrocities as adults may also lose the memories. As Andrea Dworkin put it in her recent novel *Mercy*, "No one remembers the worst. . . . It's the only thing God did right in everything I seen on earth: made the mind like scorched earth. The mind shows you mercy."[38] Amnesia may enable one to function, to most appearances, as normally as anyone. Michelle Smith (who does not present herself as "multiple") appears to have been leading an ordinary life before satanic holidays triggered memories and dissociations. Her book leaves the impression that she returned to ordinary living after she concluded tape-recording memories with her therapist (whom she then married). And yet, the absence of memory does not mean that we are unaffected or that our interactions with others are unaffected.

Epistemological challenges to answering questions about cult ritual abuse and other childhood sexual abuse can appear overwhelming. Some philosophers and psychologists dismiss multiple personality as a hoax by clever patients, created to please therapists or in response to therapists' suggestions, or, as in the more sophisticated hypothesis of philosopher Ian Hacking, as an apparently arbitrary social construction.[39] Like victims who are still children, psychiatric patients remembering abuse face well-known credibility issues. If multiple personality is presented as a construction in the sense of a *construal*, however, we can look at what is being so construed and thereby reach back to relevant histories of abuse. (On meanings of "social construction," see chapter 1.)

Protesting the insensitivity of believers who nevertheless use the adjectives "incredible" and "unimaginable" to describe survivors' accounts, (survivor) Anne maintains that what is incredible is the level of general ignorance of these practices.[40] Professionals in law enforcement and health care now take ritual abuse seriously enough that they have special police task forces and workshops on it.[41] Although professionals are more ready today to take seriously ritual abuse as a fact, individual survivors still have difficulty gaining credence. What would make a survivor credible? She either is, or was at the time, a child. Assuming for argument's sake that she is as honest as the day is long, children still often cannot recognize when adults are lying. They may lack concepts to understand adult behavior. Many are unable to interpret their memories. Survivors may have been programmed to silence (or worse). In a survivor who is multiple, different personalities may tell different and conflicting tales. Different rules of evidence seem needed than those designed for adults in courtroom trials.

Such epistemological challenges to women's history are not new. The European witches left us only so-called "confessions" extorted under torture. Who knows what they would have said freely? The ancient Amazons were illiterate nomads. Our sources on them are from ancient Greek men, their avowed enemies. Descendants of those enemies have denied the Amazons' reality without much argument. Both cases are instructive. Historians taking up the standpoint of the vanquished search, where possible, for similarity of detail and patterns in the testimony of authors who are ignorant of each other's reports. Similar methods are used by Holocaust historians in setting out for future generations evidence discrediting revisionists who deny the murder of millions.[42] Egyptologist Margaret Murray used this method to examine the European witches' trial transcripts and to develop her theory of the "witch cult in Western Europe."[43] Freud was busy noting patterns of similarity before he discovered that such hypotheses were unacceptable to the medical establishment. Investigators of ritual child abuse note similarities of detail in reports from children who lack contact with one another. This method, although limited, yields clues and renders credible that certain kinds and patterns of events are real.

In her philosophical essay on ritual abuse, Chris Cuomo cautions against attending only to the most extreme or dramatic examples of ritual abuse, ignoring continuities with ordinary socially sanctioned activities embedded in mainstream culture, such as widely respected religious rites, white supremacist groups, and the rites of publicly respected fraternal orders.[44] Likewise, in thinking about domestic mother-daughter incest, we might do well to attend to continuities between the more and the less obvious instances of sexual or sexualized behavior and relationships, as suggested by the queries listed earlier in this chapter. Perhaps incestuous mother-daughter attachments or interactions of varying degrees of severity and duration are more ordinary than one might have thought at first. They may be as ordinary, or nearly as ordinary, as abusive punishments.

It seems possible that the intensity and deep ambivalence of attachment of a daughter to a sexually abusive caretaker may be unknowingly replayed, in varying degrees and forms, in conflicts within feminist organizations, conferences, and classrooms. Lesbian stalking, which characteristically exhibits profound emotional ambivalence, might also have roots in childhood female incest. A phenomenon that I have observed is that women (lesbian or not) sometimes feel rejected or neglected by openly lesbian women who simply treat them with respect, where there has been no history between them to account for an expectation of intimacy. Among those who feel thus rejected but do not identify as lesbian, the grievance often turns into the complaint that the lesbians are taking over, dominating, that the organization is turning into a lesbian one, answering to the interests primarily of lesbians.

A similar phenomenon sometimes occurs with respect to complaints by younger feminists against older feminists who refuse "mothering" roles. The younger feminists may complain that the older feminists are dominating. In the classroom, a student who feels rejected by a teacher who refuses to treat her differently from the other students may act up, complain that the teacher is biased against her or rude to her. There may be many plausible explanations of such behaviors. But perhaps one factor worth thinking about is a history of incestuous childhood abuse that might partly explain otherwise puzzling perceptions, expectations, ambivalences, and attachments that give rise to surprising emotionally intense disappointments.

Incestuous childhood abuse may also be a factor in the recent "sex wars" among feminists over pornography, sadomasochism, and prostitution. Much consensual sadomasochism even among lesbians may be a playful reenactment of childhood abuse. In an essay in the journal, *Lesbian Ethics*, Ardel Thomas reflects on her experience both as the masochist in lesbian sadomasochism and as a survivor of mother-daughter incest, arguing that the two are interconnected.[45] She compares Kathy Evert's descriptions of abuse by her mother with passages from the lesbian sadomasochist novel *Macho Sluts* by Pat Califia of Samois, a lesbian sadomasochist liberation group.[46]

Consensual sadomasochism is sometimes defended in a way that suggests a recognition of the continuing influence of histories of sexual abuse, as, for example, in the theory that playful sadomasochism is a catharsis. (For more on this theory, see chapter 11.) Turning daytime nightmares of childhood abuse into sadomasochistic adult games may be intended to defuse the harmful potential of such a history. And yet, as Lori Saxe has asked recently, what if it quiets the terror *without* defusing the potential for damage?[47] Even if lesbian sadomasochistic activities are not themselves directly harmful, what are their implications for participants' recognition and evaluations of real abuse? Or for their motivations to expose and resist real abuse? Do they not threaten to "justify," or vindicate, childhood abuse by extracting "good" (pleasure) from it in erotic replays?

Nearly a decade ago, Sarah Hoagland criticized sadomasochistic "exchanges of power" among lesbians as a poor substitute for real political power.[48] By eroticizing control of each other, sadomasochism may divert our energies from genuine empowerment. Like sadomasochism, internal battles among feminists and among lesbians may also exhibit our obsessions with control. If our relationships and organizations undergo major stress because of attempts to manipulate each other, this may be the legacy not only of an *ethic* focused on control (as Sarah Hoagland argues persuasively that it is), but it may also be the legacy of *hidden histories* of abuse, including mother–daughter incest.[49] Such histories may be an overlooked aspect of the reproduction of patriarchy, routinely undermining attempts at feminist revolution.

What, then, should we do? Many contemporary lesbians and other feminists reject ethics based on justice, rights, and law, in favor of ethics based on other values that have proven helpful in women's experience.[50] I am drawn to the idea of ethics based on values from women's experience, and yet, I remain skeptical of rejecting justice while injustice is so prevalent in our interactions with one another. If justice has not helped us, that may be because we have been excluded from its institutions, discouraged from using them, and discouraged from learning to perceive injustice against ourselves. Injustice suggests *wrongful boundary crossing*. Incest, like rape in general, is a paradigm of wrongful boundary crossing. For caretakers, wrongful boundary crossing is a major risk. This risk is one that lesbians who have been mothered by women (or older girls) in a misogynist society should take seriously.

Instead of hastening to abandon the idea of justice, we might appreciate more fully how little justice we have known. We might use our caretaking skills to listen better to each other and to ourselves with what Theodor Reik called a "third ear"—that is, listening to our dialogues with others as though we were third parties, observers.[51] This is a technique that multiples seem to have perfected. Perhaps all female survivors of patriarchy could benefit from developing such skills. They might help us to recognize injustices we have suffered not only from men empowered by patriarchy but also from female caretakers in whose lives misogynist injustice was the order of the day. We might learn to hear when it is not just a present party who is being addressed and to identify convoluted but intelligent emotional responses, surprisingly intense for the current situation, as clues to early histories. We might learn to think back through our mothers without the needs of a child, without romance, without matriarchal fantasies.

Part Three

coming out: issues in a wider society

Chapter 8

homophobia and lesbian/gay pride

Contexts   The *New York Times* ran an article a few summers ago head-ed "Studies Discover Clues to the Roots of Homophobia."[1] It began, "Gay men and women in America face a hatred that is often more intense, open and intractable than that directed at any other minority group." It went on to claim that antigay self-righteousness is more bla-tantly institutionalized today than other hatreds, that for the largest group of antigay haters "homosexuals stand as a proxy for all that is evil," and that blatant antigay hostility is so acceptable that overwhelm-ing majorities of children and teenagers interviewed say freely that it would be bad to have a gay neighbor.

My interest is not in the question who is most hated but in the fact that the article is about hatred, socially sanctioned hatred, not about fear, and yet the term used is "homo*phobia*," which highlights fear, not hatred. What is popularly called "homophobia" is antilesbian or antigay *hostility*—hatred, scorn, or contempt, too frequently untempered by fear. This usage may be too well-established to alter. Yet, its assimilation of fear and hatred is both unwarrantedly generous to those who hate us and unjustly harsh regarding the real fears of lesbians and gay men. I resist the assimilation to lesbian-hating of terrors that I felt from the age of eleven until two and a half decades ago, fears I find rightly enough identified as homophobic. Such an assimilation is not only unfair to facts, but also increases our vulnerability to manipulation by way of our shame at being considered "homophobic."

Many fears and hostilities travel under the umbrella of "homophobia," most—fears of harassment, rape, and child abuse—based on false stereotypes. However, one basic fear, often grounded in truth, is commonly *mis*read as hostile. That is the fear of *being* or *becoming* lesbian or gay, the fear of one's own actual or suspected homosexuality. In this chapter I want to *vindicate* this form of homophobia, at least somewhat.

Fear of becoming lesbian may be the most basic form of homophobia. It has the merit of being genuinely a fear. Yet, it is of a "higher order," more abstract, than the term "homophobia" may suggest. By that I mean that it is not *simply* a fear of being or becoming homosexual, although referring to it that way is natural. It is, more precisely, the fear of being the pariah that homosexuals have been, of having the status (or, nonstatus) that homosexuals have had in societies that support hatred of same-sex sexual or erotic bonding. The more direct objects of the fear are the hatreds of others. Being homosexual (the object of the feared hatreds) is at most an indirect object of one's own fear. We tend to individuate emotions by reference to their objects. When the object of one emotion is another emotion with its own object, the two are easily conflated and both identified by one object. Thus, it is easy to refer to both others' hatreds of homosexuality and one's own fear of being the object of such hatred as though the object of each were, simply, homosexuality. And, in fact, the fear of others' attitudes may be *transferred* to the object of those attitudes, in this case, being or becoming homosexual. Still, it is important to recognize that the *basis* of the fear, in such a case, is not homosexuality as such. Because of this, such homophobia may be an important precursor of lesbian and gay pride, rather than the enemy it is commonly taken for.

Because this emotional response to one's own actual or suspected homosexuality is truly a fear and because the social facts on which it is based are true and uncontroverted, I refer to it as genuine homophobia. I do not know whether there are other forms of homophobia of which the same can be said. Although what I have to say about genuine homophobia applies to any who may suffer it—lesbian, gay, or neither—I focus here on homophobia as experienced by lesbians and thus do not always reiterate "lesbian or gay" where one could.

Not all lesbians have known homophobia as intimately as I have. The millionaire Natalie Clifford Barney, for example, seems never to have experienced it, unlike the majority of lesbians my age and older whom I have known. Such exceptions are what one would expect if homophobia is basically a response to others' hatreds. Millionaires may have relatively little to fear from others, at least after their inheritances are secure.

Fear of being or becoming homosexual is commonly referred to in lesbian and gay circles as "internalized homophobia," where the "internalization" refers to a nonrational process of identifying with the attitudes of others. Fear is, of course, "internal" (an emotional state). Its alleged object in this case may also be regarded as somewhat internal (one's own homosexuality). But the fear itself need not have been "internal*ized*." It need not reproduce others' fears. Rather, it can be a rational reaction, self-originating and self-protective in intent, to antilesbian and antigay hatreds that are socially tolerated and even institutionally sanctioned.

The position that I develop here treats genuine homophobia as a *response* to oppression and questions the popular view that it is a *basic cause* of oppression (although it may have the potentiality to aggravate oppression). In calling it "rational," I mean to distinguish it from irrational and nonrational reactions as an intelligible response, that is, one with a rationale that is not bizarre. I do not mean to beg the question whether the fear is *justifiable*, all things considered. But I do mean to encourage a certain respect for it as a manifestation of self-care, compatible with a positive valuing of one's homosexuality, and I mean to discourage the popular contempt for it as a manifestation of self-hatred. Respecting a fear does not mean yielding to it. It means such things as attending to what it can tell us, taking it seriously, even letting it have a certain space.

Even if genuine homophobia has an intelligible rationale and is worthy of (some) respect, the same is not true of hostile emotions surrounding homosexuality in general. Some are based on bizarre beliefs. Others are probably disconnected from any very specific rationale at all. Not all emotions are so disconnected, however. Philosophers have a long history of portraying emotions as irrational, as stumbling blocks to knowledge and right conduct. Against the background of that history, recent philosophy of emotions has rightly stressed the cognitive aspects of emotional response, criticizing especially the Emotive Theory of the Logical Positivists, an extreme form of noncognitivism.[2] Holistic thinkers have also rightly criticized the hierarchical dualisms of man/nature, mind/matter, and reason/feeling, which have lain at the heart of so much modern ethical thinking.[3] And yet, powerful emotions *can* become detached from cognitions that would (and perhaps originally did) explain them in the sense of giving an intelligible rationale. Socially sanctioned *hatreds* often exhibit such disconnection, and not only in the mob situations of Freud's group psychology.[4]

To evaluate emotional responses to socially sanctioned hatreds, we may need to appreciate, on the one hand, that our own fears often do have intelligible rationales and on the other, how *tenuously* emotional communication and interaction can be connected with perceptions and beliefs initially grounding emotional response. Genuine homophobia may respond to disfiguring hatreds that are commonly detached from their cognitive roots. This detachment does not imply that the hatred is cognitively empty; it would hardly be recognizable as hatred, much less as the kind of hatred that it is, were it cognitively empty. But its cognitive content is apt to be only very tenuously connected with its target, involving such concepts as evil, for example, without explaining satisfactorily why this target is hated or considered evil.

Since overcoming (allegedly internalized) homophobia is commonly associated with developing lesbian pride, I turn next to consider what it means to have lesbian pride.

What Is Lesbian Pride?

Homophobia among lesbians is commonly regarded as a form of self-hatred. With respect to genuine homophobia, I disagree. I find, rather, that such homophobia raises issues of shame and its presupposed pride. To be subject to shame is not to be without pride; those *without* pride are *shameless*. Genuine homophobia is evidence of having suffered blows to one's pride. But that is not the same as self-hatred.

Lesbian pride, like homophobia, is a troubled concept. Commonly misperceived as exhibitionist, among feminists lesbian pride suggests political chauvinism, which irritates some and embarrasses others. A lesbian said recently that being proud to be lesbian made her feel as foolish as being proud to drink water. Why should lesbians have to be proud?

The answer has been that lesbians have to be proud because of threats to our self-esteem in a hostile environment—because of the alleged danger of internalizing homophobia. For those engaged in lesbian partnering, or eager to maximize the opportunity, coming out of the closet is a more than rational act. Owning with pride a lesbian identity steals thunder from whoever would manipulate one's fears of exposure. Neither chauvinistic nor sexually exhibitionist, the point of coming out is usually to avoid "passing" and duplicity, to prevent extortion, to make political connections, to get others to see oneself in nonintimate contexts as lesbians see each other in such contexts, or to communicate that one is *not* ashamed and refuses to be shamed.

Thus, perceptual and attitudinal shifts in oneself and in others are among the goals of coming out. In this respect, coming out can be likened, somewhat, to what María Lugones has called "world-travel." It was in meditating on Marilyn Frye's essay on arrogance as an obstacle to love that María Lugones introduced the idea of "world"-traveling as a means for U.S. women of color (and, presumably, other members of oppressed groups) to bring about perceptual and attitudinal shifts for the overcoming of arrogance in oneself.[5] By "world"-traveling, she meant a "willful exercise" of a certain flexibility spontaneously acquired by members of a minority in an oppressive society, a flexibility in shifting from one construction of life, in which one is at home although many others are outsiders, to other constructions of life in which some of these former outsiders are at home, or more nearly at home and in which one may figure oneself as an outsider.

To illustrate, she elaborated what it meant for her to "travel" to the "world" of her mother, explaining that she was unable to love her mother well until she did that. She recommended that "world"-travel be animated by an attitude of playfulness, and she apparently presumed a basic attitude of goodwill on the part of travelers toward more permanent inhabitants. Gay Pride parades, often animated by playfulness and frequently a coming-out scene, suggest a different kind of "world"-travel. With some of the same goals, they intrude gay worlds into the mainstream (or at least the Main Street). They reveal to others a bit of how we look in our own worlds—happy, clever, sassy, confident. They confront the arrogance and contempt of many whom we might not wish to invite into lesbian or gay worlds. The attitudes sought in this case are pride and respect, rather than the love and friendship that inspired María Lugones' articulation of the concept of "world"-travel. But some of the obstacles—arrogance and contempt—are the same, and perceptual shifts accompany the emotional shifts in both cases.

Antilesbian hostility can also be resisted as disrespectful to oneself without one's claiming a lesbian identity. I recently came across the following, for example, in a journal article by a feminist philosopher who is not claiming a lesbian identity. "It is likely," she said: "that chosen communities, lesbian communities, for example, attract us in the first place because they appeal to features of ourselves which . . . were inadequately or ambivalently sustained by our unchosen families. . . Thus unchosen communities are sometimes communities which we can, and should, leave."[6]

Such uses of "us" and "ourselves" disarm antilesbian disrespect. Potential resistance thus lies in wider sources of lesbian pride than are suggested by the idea of lesbian community—pride in lesbian possibilities, potentialities, and connections (kinship, friendships, working relationships), even fantasies. One appeal of the idea of a lesbian continuum is that it suggests natural, nonaltruistic extensions of resistance to antilesbian hostility.[7] I also like the idea of such a continuum because without invoking biology it makes sense of my sense that in some sense I have been lesbian as far back as I can recall, although much that I recall is fantasy. Such a continuum allows me pride in my lesbian attachments before I discovered how to do more with them than enjoy them in secret and in terror.

What kind of pride is lesbian pride? Often, it seems to involve a certain reference to freedom from shame, or perhaps, the healing of an injury *to* one's pride. Neither the pride injured, nor the healing of the injury, need involve any sense of elevation over others nor delusions regarding our virtues. Such pride seems an ability to *enjoy ourselves* in a value-laden appreciation of who we are, to enjoy ourselves and our significant relationships in a reasonably full appreciation of what such relationships mean in terms of moral and other values that we take to heart. To be thus proud of being lesbian is to experience the pleasure that being lesbian contributes to our enjoyment of ourselves and our relationships. Such pride seems a fairly modest and good thing to have. Neither arrogant nor exhibitionist, it does not even imply that one is a proud person.[8] Shame, interfering with the enjoyment, injures such pride.

What Is Homophobia?

In those who have known same-sex love or desire, homophobia is a common *source* of shame. But it can also be itself a fear *of* a certain shame. Shame *at* one's own homophobia can thus be complex, "higher order." It can respond to one's "lower order" shame before others whose values one rejects, or to one's fear of such shame.

In recent years, two lesbian feminist books have analyzed "homophobia" in simpler terms, reaching conclusions also opposite to each other. In *Homophobia: A Weapon of Sexism*, Arkansas political organizer Suzanne Pharr sets forth the view that "homophobia" (especially "internalized") is irrational fear and hatred, to be confronted and weeded out before moving on to other political tasks.[9] In *The Social Construction of Lesbianism*, British sociologist Celia Kitzinger rejects that approach, arguing that the concept of "homophobia" is politically naive, because fear of lesbian challenges to patriarchy is not irrational.[10] On her view, so-called "homophobia" is a *rational* fear, for patriarchs and their sympathizers, of antipatriarchal lesbian commitments in sexual politics.

The more conventional view of "homophobia" among lesbians and gays in the United States today is that of Suzanne Pharr. On this view, the failure of the popular women's movement to take "homophobia" seriously *as a weapon of patriarchy* is a major factor in the women's movement's not having achieved more lasting gains. Suzanne Pharr presents "homophobia" as one of "three powerful weapons" used by sexist society to keep the patriarchal nuclear family in place (the other two are "economics" and "violence").[11] Any woman who steps out of line is liable to being labeled "lesbian"; men who break ranks are liable to being taunted as "queers" or "faggots."

Emerging after years in closets to find antilesbian hostility even in the movement against domestic battery, Suzanne Pharr wrote her book to motivate antihomophobia workshops and has toured the United States to encourage them. She is concerned that "internalized homophobia," understood as self-hatred, is a significant factor in lesbian battering and in lesbian communities' reluctance to face up to horizontal abuse and that it keeps lesbians closeted and blocks empathy among feminists.[12] The idea is that lesbian homophobia "internalizes" others' antilesbian hostility (which she thinks of as plain homophobia), much as Freud thought the Superego internalized the Father. Overcoming self-hatred is, on this understanding, analogous to overcoming the Father. It is presented as a common crucial stage in lesbian and gay character development, removing an obstacle to dignity and to integrity in relationships.

Celia Kitzinger, on the other hand, rejects the picture of homophobia as an irrational affliction of the ignorant. She argues that hostilities toward lesbians are *not phobic* because they are grounded in a valid apprehension of lesbians' political challenge to patriarchy. She points out that the "diagnosis" of "homophobia" defuses the lesbian threat by substituting personal for political solutions, thereby discouraging scrutiny of political bases of the fear. The medical model presents phobias as calling for treatment and cure, as though they were like certain allergies, inappropriate reactions to one's environment, evidence of something wrong with the fearer (rather than with the environment).[13] Yet, homophobia is unlike agoraphobia and claustrophobia in that it responds to the real (or potential) dangers that lesbians represent to patriarchal society. Calling antilesbian politics "phobic" seems to let fearers off the hook with respect to judgment and responsibility. What need overcoming, on Celia Kitzinger's view, are the social structures of patriarchy, not fears of lesbians. Lesbian initiative *should* be frightening. At any rate, such fear shows appreciation of how much is at stake. This view rejects the language of "homophobia" altogether.

I feel the force of both views. Yet, each leaves me dissatisfied. The truth in them is a challenge to state, as the meanings of "homophobia" in them are slippery. Neither view, however, is idiosyncratic to either author. Celia Kitzinger does not refer to "internalized homophobia." Suzanne Pharr devotes a chapter to it. Yet neither account really *respects* fears concerning one's own homosexuality. The first regards such fears as irrational. The second would seem to imply that they were naive or confused. I disagree with both. I take seriously fear of being lesbian, which leads me to a certain respect for it.

Taking that fear seriously does not, however, lead me to Suzanne Pharr's faith in individual education as a remedy. I agree with Celia Kitzinger that *what is commonly referred to* as "homophobia" (unmodified) is a kind of hostility that indicates political conflict, confrontation with which requires less psychological change than social change. The truth in Celia Kitzinger's picture gives me serious pause about calling fears of homosexuality "phobic." I share her dislike of the medical model here. I agree that "phobic" as a euphemism for "hostile" can misunderstand hostility and discourage examination of its social and political bases. However, even genuine phobias need not be symptomatic of ill health in the fearer, though they may produce ill health. They need not be irrational. Just as allergies *can* indicate something wrong with the environment, so can phobias. Fear can be oppressive because it is so intense and all-pervasive, because there seems no escape from it. It can *drive* one mad (make one "phobic" in the sense of "fear-ridden") without being itself irrational (in the sense of lacking a rational basis). Such fear can be a response to emotions *in others* that *are* irrational in that *they* lack sound cognitive roots. In short, irrational emotions of others can be rightly terrifying and can make one "phobic" in the sense of "fear-ridden."

Our liability to shame or other emotional pain in being defenselessly exposed to others as despicable, contemptible, or ridiculous does not presuppose that we find those attitudes (contempt, etc.) deserved. One can be shamed simply in being *exposed*, even though one values highly *what* is exposed. One need not be ashamed of one's body, for example, to experience shame in its unexpected or unwanted exposure. Part of homosexual shame is, no doubt, due simply to exposure of facts that one would rather keep private, having unwanted attention called to certain aspects of one's life. Coming out eliminates the surprise element of such exposure (that is, it eliminates the surprise for those who come out—others may well be embarrassed). Coming out as a political gesture also aims to alter others' attention to *what* is exposed by emphasizing the politics rather than the erotics of one's orientation.

Characteristic sources of homosexual shame are public ridicule, blatant contempt, and manifest hatred. However paradoxical it sounds, we can be made to *feel* ridiculous (contemptible, despicable)—thus having cause for shame—without *finding* ourselves ridiculous (contemptible, despicable), just as one can be made to *feel guilty* without believing oneself to *be* guilty. We may be most liable to shame before others whose respect we (at least think we) need or want, whatever we think of some of their values. Yet we can be made to feel uncomfortably conspicuous, self-conscious, aware of ourselves in ways that interfere with the ability to get on with our lives, even before others whose "good opinion" we think, with good reason, that we do not value. Such liabilities are more a function of unavoidable encounters than of our beliefs. Yet, they are often themselves a source of further (higher order) shame.

More than three decades ago, the psychologist Helen Merrell Lynd offered an interesting and helpful account of shame in the first two chapters of her book, *On Shame and the Search for Identity*.[14] Unlike some of her colleagues, she acknowledged the puzzling phenomenon of "double shame" (to which I have already alluded as "higher order" shame), that is, shame at being ashamed, either because one rejects the values on which the original shame is based or because the occasion of the original shame seems trivial (or would seem so to others—which, by the way, she says is characteristic of shame and helps to explain our impulse to hide it). As an example of "double shame," she mentions Virginia Woolf, who was intensely ashamed of caring what critics said about her work. I suspect that double shame is fairly common among lesbians, perhaps as common among feminists and political insurgents, generally, as among artists.

On Helen Merrell Lynd's account, shame is an emotion that permeates one's being. Coming to terms with it reveals things to oneself about one's identity. At any rate, shame *in* one's identity threatens to be uncontainable. Fear of speaking in public, rat phobias, even fear of heights, are relatively containable. That is, they are avoidable by avoiding public speaking, rats, heights. By contrast, fear of being lesbian or gay can *contain the fearer* as much as paranoia or agoraphobia can do. This is a good reason to call it "phobic." And so, I do, despite reservations stemming from unintended suggestions of irrationality. Homophobia can be as debilitating as agoraphobia or claustrophobia. Unlike them, however, genuine homophobia is not irrational.[15] The double shame that can result from a fear of being so debilitated may then make one liable to endless manipulations.

Fear of defenseless exposure to socially tolerated and institutionally sanctioned hostility or disrespect is often called "internalized homophobia." "Internalized homophobia" also sometimes refers, however, to fear of, or inability to enjoy, one's own erotic responses to others of the same sex. These two fears need not be linked. One may enjoy such eroticism enormously when one is not overcome by fear of being hated for doing so.

Without sharing, endorsing, or reproducing in oneself others' contempt or disrespect, we can still be invaded by their attitudes. Having the "right" beliefs in oneself, the power of one's private convictions, can be a shaky defense against invasive, socially backed, hostile emotional power. To see our fear in such contexts as self-inflicted hostility, rather than as a self-protective shield or warning, seems to mistake as masochistic a sound fear of emotional assault from without.

Perhaps genuine homophobia is sometimes a significant factor in the causes of lesbian battering, in explanations of why battered lesbians do not succeed in getting away sooner, and in explanations of poor lesbian community response to lesbian battering. However, if I am right, it would not follow that lesbian *self-hatred* was a causal factor in such matters. When hostility *toward* lesbians is collapsed into a concept, homophobia, that already refers to terror, attention is focussed on the terror rather than on the hostility, the object of terror is assimilated to the target of hostility, and the hostility-terror *dynamic* is erased. Terror then appears a *cause* of lesbian oppression, rather than its debilitating effect.

If such a combination of hatred/fear is said to be internalized by lesbians, it looks as though the result must be self-hatred. Self-hatred then seems a plausible *cause* of lesbian battering, of battered partners' failure to get away, and of lesbian communities' reluctance to face such realities, instead of the *result* of such behavior that genuine self-hatred often is.

When fear of public shame closets lesbians with batterers, the intent is plausibly self-protective, however misguided. And yet, ultimately, more jeopardizing to self-esteem than daily put-downs from abusive partners may be one's willingness to put up with the abuse, whether from loyalty or from fear of worse from without. Horizontal abuse may be the result of misdirected resentment of abuse from above. However, lesbians, like others, can learn abuse and responses to it from parents whose problems had nothing to do with homosexuality. And a certain misplaced lesbian *pride* (rather than self-hatred), together with a well-grounded fear of exposure to antilesbian hatred (genuine homophobia), could also account for poor lesbian community response to horizontal abuse.

For all that, the concept of homophobia is also genuinely imprecise. As mentioned earlier, in society at large, several fears travel under the umbrella of "homophobia": uninformed ones, such as fear of locker-room assault (a *National Enquirer* at the supermarket checkout in late July 1990 screamed, "New Gay Sex Scandal Rocks Tennis: Lesbian Stars Stalk Young Players in Showers"); sophisticated ones, such as fear of one's own erotic responses (for loss of emotional control they may bring); puzzling ones, such as fear that some ordinary person whom one has esteemed (oneself, perhaps) is "homosexual."

Locker-room fears (behavioral fears) are of what homosexuals might *do*—in principle, relatively easily handled by education. There is more reason for more women to fear what heterosexuals do, even without sharing locker rooms. Fear of erotic response, on the other hand, is probably beneficial on the whole, better heeded than overcome in a society where the pornography of everyday life teaches many to respond erotically to what is genuinely harmful. Yet no more than with fear of assault is that danger specific to lesbian interaction. For the third fear, education may offer little help. That one seems to be fear of just *being* (or *becoming*) lesbian, reducible to neither fear of behavior nor fear of erotic response, leaving one at a loss over *why*, apart from consequences, being lesbian should be so frightening. Adrienne Rich observed of "matrophobia" that it "is the fear not of one's mother nor of motherhood but of *becoming one's mother*."[16] Homophobes, likewise, may fear primarily not what homosexuals do or even homosexual attraction but, rather, *being or becoming* homosexual.

The idea that the basic fear is of being contemptible, ridiculous, or despicable in the eyes of others fits with Suzanne Pharr's observation that a weapon patriarchy uses to keep the nuclear family in place is the threat of *labeling* anyone who steps out of line a dyke or queer or faggot. This does not presuppose that "homosexuality" as such is feared. It presupposes fear of the shame or stigma, of the label, fear of being a pariah.

Because of empathy, fear of one's potentialities for pariahdom may also show itself as fear of anyone whose similar potentialities are evident. This can be independent of fear of their behavior toward oneself or of their possible erotic responses to oneself. Ironically, another's fear of me as a lesbian can be due to my mirroring her potentialities. She can even fear *my* capacity to despise *her* for her lesbian potentialities. Thus I do not take the fact that homophobia often shows itself as a fear of others to refute the hypothesis that homophobia is basically a fear of being or becoming lesbian (oneself).

Fear of simply *being* such a target of hatred is no more irrational than fear of the *consequences* of socially sanctioned or tolerated hatred. For, the harm of socially sanctioned hatred is not confined to consequences. The answer to the question why just *being* lesbian can be so scary is that *being the object of a socially sanctioned or tolerated hatred can actually be a deformity in partially constructing who we are by embedding us in ugly social relations.* This is *disfigurement*. Fear of being disfigured is not irrational, however irrational it is to fear others who are disfigured. If we could sue for it, we should collect a mint. What is at stake is not just stoicism in the face of emotional pain. What is at stake is one's identity, which is not simply a function of one's internal picture of oneself or even the picture cherished by one's friends but can include significant unchosen relationships with others, including institutionally defined relationships.

Hating others for their identity does not *necessarily* disfigure the possessors of that identity. Some identities have already disfigured their possessors—identities such as the Nazi SS, for example, or being a member of the KKK—and hatred of them may be well-earned. Lesbian and gay hate stereotypes, however, are powerfully deforming. We have not done nearly enough to earn the hatred described in the *New York Times* article. When our sense of being disfigured lacks social vindication, we may be left with shame both at being hated and at caring about it as much as we sometimes do.

Overcoming Homophobia

Suzanne Pharr has stressed the commonalities in different oppressions. Yet the homophobia that consists in a fear of being homosexual may be something relatively *distinctive* about lesbian and gay oppression. Such fears may be as possible and as widespread as they are partly because of the problematic identity of "the homosexual." It is actually possible to wonder for years "whether one is" in a way that generally lacks an analogue for identities connected with other forms of oppression. Uncertainty has consequences. It exacerbates fear. Fear of death, for example, is exacerbated by uncertainty regarding what if anything follows it, about the process or its timing, as fear of the guillotine was compounded for condemned French prisoners who were not told which night the executioners would come.[17] Fear regarding one's social position can be exacerbated by uncertainty about social identities that are not clearly defined by publicly ascertainable facts but depend, rather, on often private behavior, especially ambiguous private behavior. Fear of being alcoholic may be something like homophobia in this respect.

Resolution of such ambiguity can be an important step toward resisting sources of fear. Knowing who you are helps you know what to expect and get prepared. Resolving the ambiguity can open the way to social connections with others who resolve it similarly. These connections can become important sources of self-esteem. Coming Out as lesbian is one way to resolve such ambiguity. Denial is, of course, another.

A common strategy for saving face is to expose something bad about one's enemies—usually, a cheap solution. The popular fantasy (or insight) that others' hostility toward lesbians is phobic may catalyze lesbian pride but is at best a temporary solution. Arousing fear offers a sense of power, even delight if the terrorized are enemies, as the ever-popular "Leaping [Lesbians]" song demonstrates.[18] Yet, in reality, who has had the power to frighten? If arousing fear can be fun, arousing contempt (often the grim reality) is not. Better bases for pride are needed than exposing weaknesses in others.

A better basis is a strength in oneself. Finding such strength is a challenge in the face of hostile social interpretations of one's behavior. To give something an effective social meaning, we need others to acknowledge that meaning.[19] The undeniable fact of one's survival of oppression presents itself as a possible positive source of pride and one that seems to evade the difficulties of erasure or being devalued by competing interpretations. Yet, survival as a source of pride has its own difficulties. What does it say, for example, about those who have *not* survived, such as Rebecca Wight, the lesbian hiker shot dead by Stephen Roy Carr on the Appalachian Trail?[20] The paradigm of women surviving by outwitting batterers and stalkers suggests pride in ingenuity. Yet not all can take pride in what they must do to survive or in surviving those who died. Consider Annette Green, reduced to killing a lover in self-defense.[21] Without belittling the courage that killing in self-defense can require, you can hardly find having to kill someone you have loved a support of pride in your own survival.

A classic individualist way to create a public basis for pride is compensation—being extra-funny or extra-intelligent, becoming a hero or saint. These strategies have the disadvantage of encouraging others to exploit us, threatening ultimately to lessen rather than build pride. An alternative is to embrace eccentricity, becoming idiosyncratically artsy, for example, in hopes that one's homosexuality may be received as yet another aspect of one's charm or individuality. A strategy with a longer-range future is to create new social relations, communities, that can become sources of pride. It is here that we may confront, in loyalty tests, temptations to exploit each other's liabilities to second-order shame—such as liability to the shame of fearing the shame of having a hated identity.

Fear reminds us of our lack of power. Fear of being a pariah can undermine us in at least two ways. It can remind us of our vulnerability to the hostility of others whose values we reject. And our desire to defuse that hostility threatens to become itself a source of shame, at least to raise the question whether we care too much for the goodwill of those who lack goodwill toward ourselves. Thus we can come to doubt our self-respect and suspect that the contempt of others for us is justified in the end. It can be tempting for lesbians and friends to exploit each other's liability to such self-doubt, threatening the shame of lacking integrity if we do not give of ourselves boundlessly to one another. Liability to fear of shame (before friends) at one's fear of being a pariah can thus encourage a manipulative dynamic of "you care more about them than about us."

Of course, it is possible to care too much for the goodwill of others. It is important not to let one's judgment be corrupted by the desire to make one's ideas palatable to everyone. But there can also be good reason to care about others' goodwill *independently* of what we think of their beliefs or of what they may *do* to us, as long as we must—or we choose to—live among them and confront them regularly. And there can be good reasons to *choose* to live in a way that does not reduce such confrontations to a minimum.

Exposure to ridicule does not necessarily evoke shame. And shame does not necessarily evoke fear. There are worse responses: depression, the apathy of resignation, self-murder. Fear, if not paralyzing, seems a relatively wholesome response. It suggests the vitality of at least an inner fight, of resistance to distortion and disfigurement. Things can get better, of course. Lesbian communities can powerfully fortify our ability to sustain appreciations of the goodness of what others despise. Realizing that we can be and have been made to feel shame in relation to some of our best values, our most important relationships, and our most wonderful experiences can convert fear of homosexual shame into the rage of lesbian pride. The occasional dramatic suddenness of such conversions and the emotional power released in them remind me of religious conversions (and other political conversions—to feminism, for example) in that more than cognition seems to be at work. I turn next to consider this "more."

Emotional Echoing and Empowerment

Even if Celia Kitzinger is right (as I believe she is) that antilesbian hostility indicates political conflict and thus has a rationale, it doesn't follow that *individuals* have their own political reasons for whatever antilesbian (or antigay) hostility they feel (although they may have). Nor does it follow that those who suffer what Suzanne Pharr calls "*internal* homophobia" are politically ambivalent (although they may be). There is a possibility that much antilesbian hostility is only superficially related to the despisers' own perceptions or beliefs. If so, it may be unreachable by the kind of education that is aimed at remedying ignorance and correcting misapprehensions regarding the targets of such hostility. Something more, or different, may be required.

Freudian theory takes the "more" to be a bringing to consciousness for reassessment of material buried in one's psyche decades before. There is, however, a simpler, more social, less "rationalist" way to understand the acquisition and communication of antilesbian hostility. In *The Nature of Sympathy*, twentieth-century phenomenologist Max Scheler described the phenomenon of emotional "infection," picking up and feeling in oneself (reproducing) the joy, for example—or the sadness—of others surrounding us, without any perception of the *basis* of such joy or sadness, or even awareness that what we are doing is *reproducing the feelings of others.*[22] Discarding the medical model, I call such phenomena *echoes* rather than "infections." If joy and sadness can be echoed, why not pride and hatred? Antilesbian hatreds may be to a great extent echoes of others' hatreds, where the *underlying reasons, if any, are not communicated with the feeling.* The echo metaphor captures the idea that with removal of the generating source, the reproduction fades (eventually), that the initial reproduction often magnifies the original in amplitude, and that in any case it tends to have a hollow sound.

Irrational hatreds, like some phobias, are transmittable by echoing. I remember vividly resonating to my mother's bat phobia when I was eight years old. We trembled together behind a door for what seemed hours one hot summer night while one of those creatures circled the ceiling, continually missing the exit. Mother's wild and persistent efforts to tell me how irrational such fear was undermined my terror no more than her own. That terror, electrifying the atmosphere as she wound towels around our hair and dug her nails into my shoulders, spoke to me louder than any of her explanations. Popular culture also plays upon, validates, and reinforces such terror, as the film *Arachnophobia* did recently with spider phobias.[23]

"Internalized homophobia" could refer to lesbians' and gay men's echoing of others' irrational fear of homosexuality. However, one need not be lesbian or gay to experience "internalized homophobia" in that sense, and that is not how the term has been used. Although it is certainly possible for us to resonate to others' irrational fear of us, that fear is also relatively easy for us to evaluate, since we know that we are not dangerous. It is harder to come to terms with a bat phobia, since one can manage easily to avoid contact with bats and thereby avoid being confronted with facts that could undermine the fear. Fears in lesbians and gay men that are more persistent, more difficult to come to terms with, are the fears of others' hatreds. These fears, I have argued, are not irrational and need not have been internalized. There is a connection, however, between echoed irrational fear and the hatreds that we fear rationally. Echoed irrational fear may continue to feed others' hatreds as long as they have no more acquaintance with us than I have with bats.

Emotional echoing is not necessarily dysfunctional. From an evolutionary standpoint, it may be as necessary for the survival of societies as trust in verbal communication. Babies and other animals seem to rely on it regularly. Even adult social relations might deteriorate if regular checking became necessary, as they would were we all to act like Descartes in his stove. Echoing can be as beneficial in individual cases as the transmission of irrational fears and hatreds can be harmful. I remember equally vividly one late morning on a Summer Solstice resonating to a trusted counselor's distress for my health prospects as she learned of the extent to which I was reenacting my mother's fatal cigarette-smoking habit, one and a half to two packs daily, in my case, for nineteen years. My literally *incorporating* that counselor's distress enabled me as nothing else had done to stop smoking, right then and for good. No doubt it also helped that my follow-up self-care included getting rid of carpets, draperies, books, and clothing, repainting my living space, eventually moving, and almost complete withdrawal from environments friendly to smokers. Max Scheler suggests that even environments can be instrumental in producing or reinforcing emotional states—a gloomy day, for example.

A possibility that echoing raises is that even though some individuals are antilesbian for their own political reasons, most antilesbian hostility is as hollow as the joy one absorbs at an office party or the sorrow imbibed at a stranger's funeral. Like instant coffee, "hollow" hostility preserves much of the flavor without the substance (in this case, of cognitive grounds). It is in that respect straightforwardly irrational—it does not rest (in those whose hollow hostility it is) upon reasons at all. Like mountain echoes, it can also initially wildly exaggerate what it reproduces. Many might (many do) disown the reasons for the original response when they are confronted with those reasons.

It is a fine question whether echoed hostility and fear are less well-entrenched than emotions grounded in conviction. Dislodging them may be *more* difficult if what does ground them is unclear. I still carry my mother's bat phobia. On the other hand, being lastingly liberated from a nineteen-year addiction is equally impressive, perhaps more so. It shows that new echoes can help to break the patterns of old ones, despite powerful conflicting social reinforcement of the old ones.

Fear of echoed hostility is not irrational. The irrationality of hatred makes it no less harmful. Being targeted by institutionally sanctioned hatred is still disfiguring, however hollow the hatred. And resonance to echoed hostility is as spontaneous, as disconnected from conviction and choice, as the echoes that evoke it.

Insofar as they are disconnected from conviction and choice, echoes and resonance to them may not be stopped simply by education. Two other kinds of supplementary strategies of resistance, leading in opposite directions, suggest themselves. One is to focus on trying to change institutions in hopes of creating a more favorable emotional climate *for* education, if only by ending the sanctioning of hostility and disrespect that presently have institutional endorsement. The other strategy is to create and cultivate counterechoes, to drown out antilesbian/antigay hostility with our own happy noises, encouraging others to echo positive feelings and attitudes. To be effective as protection in an overwhelmingly antilesbian society, the counterecho approach may require separation from the mainstream, rather than mainstream political involvement. If will-power and reasoning are undependable protection against resonating to the emotions of companions, one should be careful with whom and for how long one keeps company. It may be essential to remove oneself from atmospheres of free-floating contempt, to have regular retreats.

Perhaps there are ways to reconcile the separatist and mainstream activist strategies for resisting antilesbian hostility, for example, by divisions of labor or by compromises. There seems a certain justice in those who have benefited from antilesbian and antigay practices assuming the social burden of changing relevant institutions, although there are obvious motivational problems for that proposal. From a lesbian point of view, the separatist response seems fundamental insofar as it is necessary to secure motivation among lesbians for continuing political resistance. A certain distance from the mainstream enables us better to see genuine homophobia as a self-protective response to echoes, perhaps some in ourselves, of the hostilities of those whose antilesbian and antigay beliefs we may never have shared. It should then come as no surprise if when surrounded by positively affirming echoes, some of us overcome this homophobia with relatively dramatic suddenness, resonating to friendlier emotions consonant with our experience of ourselves and our loves, like waking from a nightmare that leaves a hangover. Nor should it surprise if that "hangover" then gives birth to the rage of lesbian pride.

Just as genuine homophobia is grounded in rational beliefs about the dangers of being hated, lesbian pride and genuinely beneficial rage need to be grounded in rational beliefs about what we do and do not deserve in the way of attitudinal responses from others. Emotional echoing may be an indispensable catalyst in the move from fear and shame to rage and pride. But a catalyst is what it is; it is no substitute for groundings of those emotions in perception and belief.

Chapter 9

the military ban and the rotc:
a study in closeting

In May 1992 U.S. Representative Patricia Schroeder of Colorado introduced a bill that would lift the military ban on lesbians and gay men, enabling them to serve with as much dignity as heterosexual women and men.[1] I had hoped that by the time this chapter saw print, the objectives of that bill would be realized.[2] Lesbian and gay news has never been so public as during recent events: President Clinton, elected with the help of many gay and lesbian votes, addressed the ban at once, terminating the practice of questioning entrants about their sexual orientation and suspending enforcement of the ban elsewhere; members of the armed services (and their children) have continued coming out; gay Seaman Allen Schindler was beaten to death in Japan by a shipmate; Los Angeles Federal District Court Judge Terry Hatter ruled in the case of Keith Meinhold of the Navy that the ban violated equal protection rights guaranteed by the Constitution.

At the present writing, President Clinton has announced his new policy, an anticlimactic compromise, popularly dubbed "don't ask, don't tell, don't pursue." It retains most of the faults of the old policy, even if it stops some of the worst abuses. Intended to halt "witch hunts," it allows gay men and lesbians to serve as long as they stay in the closet. The President seemed disappointed to be unable to do more but also seems justly proud of putting the issue on the agenda and making the point that behavior, not status, is the only tolerable basis for discrimination regarding sexuality. That point may be the critical wedge that the courts need to make further progress. It remains to be seen how courts will judge the differences in treatment that the new policy still sanctions regarding heterosexual and homosexual conduct. Only the Joint Chiefs of Staff seem happy with the new policy, perceiving rightly that it officially alters little, it saves money and grief, and it allows the military to continue to exploit lesbian and gay talent.

Most of the issues remain. The basic ethical ones are not peculiar to the military. A reason for widespread interest in military policy on this issue is that it sets a tone, a standard, an example. It is influential. Policies set here might be emulated. In this case, that is cause for concern. The evils of closeting endanger lesbians and gay men in contexts ranging from athletic programs and nursing schools to religious orders, in many institutions offering careers with hierarchies of authority and same-sex work situations. Even if it is progress for the military, as a model for educational and public service institutions, "don't ask, don't tell, don't pursue" would be a major set-back. Across the U.S.A., lesbians and gay men have been coming out to employers, coworkers, clients, and neighbors to be able to live normally integrated lives, to communicate that "we are everywhere," to fight for lesbian and gay civil rights, and with the hope of ultimately being free of threats of exposure, harassment, and hate crimes. These objectives cannot be achieved where the closet is the norm because *fighting injustice entails visibility.*[3] Emulating the President's new policy could undo two decades of progress. Hence, the need for public attention to the evils of closeting.

My way into issues of military closeting was through campus activism regarding the Reserve Officers Training Corps (ROTC) program at the University of Wisconsin, to which I turn next.

The University of Wisconsin and the ROTC Program

In December 1989 Chancellor Donna Shalala called an all-faculty meeting—the first at Wisconsin in nearly two decades—to discuss the

ROTC program's violation of campus nondiscrimination policies in its exclusions of lesbians and gay men. Optimistic about attendance, she held the meeting in the University Stock Pavilion, responding to a faculty petition circulated by a self-constituted activist committee, which I cochaired.[4] The ban we protested was a policy (not a piece of legislation passed by elected representatives) that originated in the Department of Defense (DOD) during World War II.[5] It extended throughout the uniformed military services, aiming to exclude both "persons who engage in homosexual conduct" and those "who, by their statements, demonstrate a propensity to engage in homosexual conduct."[6] By this policy university students were excludable from benefits (including scholarships) of a program offering courses for university credit. (Under the new policy, students who are not closeted would still be excludable.) Such exclusions, we argued, violate our campus's policy against discrimination on the basis of sexual orientation. That was what made the ROTC program our specific target of protest. We called ourselves Faculty Against Discrimination in University Programs (FADIUP).

The all-faculty meeting revolved around a FADIUP motion asking the University Board of Regents to terminate contracts with the ROTC if its discriminatory policy were not eliminated within four years. It is one thing to object to a policy and another to sever connections with the entire program. Favoring the latter presupposes that the policy is serious indeed and that severing connection would not be worse. The situation of the University of Wisconsin is complicated by its being a land grant institution.[7] Land grant funds are appropriated to colleges "where the leading object shall be, without excluding other scientific and classical studies and including military tactics, to teach such branches of learning as are related to agriculture and mechanical arts" (7 U.S.C. 304). Thus, the university is presently obligated to offer instruction in military tactics.

Were the ROTC program withdrawn, the university would have to do one of three things: (1) find another way to offer instruction in military tactics (as it did prior to the ROTC program), (2) persuade the U.S. government to renegotiate its land grant agreement with respect to the nature of the public service a university could offer to fulfill its obligations, or (3) cease to be a land grant institution. Setting aside the third possibility, FADIUP thought it worth looking into how "instruction in military tactics" might be uncoupled from induction into military service. More ambitiously, the university might negotiate with the government to get it to accept nonmilitary public service training—for example, in education, health care, or other social services—in nondiscriminatory programs with national service upon graduation as a condition of scholarship support, much as current ROTC scholarship students are expected to return service to the government.[8]

FADIUP's motion, with its ultimatum, passed 386–248 at the faculty meeting, but then was overturned on a written ballot distributed by campus mail, with many voting who had not attended the meeting. The ROTC program is therefore still with us, and the university administration has since then pursued ways to encourage change of the DOD's policy in Washington.

There seem obvious advantages, from a humanist perspective, to having military officers trained on college campuses (a policy, incidentally, not altogether popular with many military personnel). Some of these advantages have been offset, however, by the severe homophobia and heterosexism encouraged by the ban, which counteract attitudes of free inquiry. My concern has not been basically with the pros and cons of an ROTC presence on campus. My concern has been with the defamation of lesbians and gay men implicit in the ban and with the moral corruption, especially at the level of career officers, fostered by it. These concerns give members and friends of a land grant university reason to protest such policies vigorously, regardless how they otherwise feel about the ROTC or military service, and regardless even of some problems they may have about lesbian and gay choices.

The faculty meeting was not just an attempt to determine the fate of a particular motion. It was also an attempt to arouse faculty from apathy. Many seemed to feel that although the ROTC exclusion was embarrassing to a liberal campus, it was not worth a fuss because many people found ways to get around it. For some who had not thought about it, the question was real whether the ROTC exclusions *were* unjustified. Finally, some faculty assumed that protesting a program's policies presupposes basically approving of the program itself, and they did not want to give the impression that they approved of the ROTC program. And so, when my turn came to speak, I directed my statement not to the specifics of the motion with its ultimatum but to some basic ethical issues. Speakers were chosen alternately for and against the motion and allotted two minutes each. This was my two minutes' worth:

A South Hall plaque, from the Class of 1955, says, "You shall know the truth, and the truth will make you free."

It has been said that no lesbians or gay men are known to have been discriminated against by the ROTC on this campus.[9] This means that the ROTC has no records of those against whom it has discriminated. Because of the *closet* phenomenon, this is not surprising. Knowing the policy, most lesbian and gay students don't waste time applying; some lie in response to the question, Are you homosexual? Others discover who they are after they are in and do not disclose it. There is a widespread view that if lesbians and gay men would just keep quiet—stay in the closet—what others didn't know wouldn't hurt them, and everyone would be happy. This view grants that there is no sound basis for discrimination, that the problem is the reactions of others. But promoting closeting respects prejudice rather than minority rights. It is not an honorable response.

The ROTC policy rewards lesbian or gay students who lie and threatens to penalize those who would tell the truth. There is a parallel with seventeenth-century England when non-Christians were not permitted to testify in courts of law. Non-Christians willing to lie about their religion were permitted to testify, while those who were *honest* were excluded, on the ground that *their* testimony could not be trusted.

The ROTC's discrimination policy prevents us from knowing who and how many lesbian and gay students on this campus are excluded (or even *in*cluded). It says, in effect, if you are honest enough to tell us who you are, we will exclude you because we will then know you are unreliable.

A policy that encourages and rewards dishonesty about the things that are most important in our lives, whether our religious beliefs or our most intimate relationships, is disgraceful. I, personally, find the University's willingness to maintain contracts with a group who persists in such policies an insult. It would be a joke were it not an insult. It is not funny because it is so dishonorable. Tolerating such policies undermines the search at this university for the truths that are supposed to make us free.

Much in that statement still applies under the new policy. However, my statement did not make distinctions made in the President's new policy. I did not distinguish the specific policy of asking entrants about sexual orientation from the general policy of supporting the closet. The latter was and remains my basic concern. I also now think it misleading to suggest that few lesbians and gay men waste time applying. It may be primarily those who already live openly lesbian or gay lives who would find it a "waste of time" (or worse). Others may routinely apply, drawn to opportunities to work closely with others of the same sex in an environment that offers power and possible adventure, especially women bored by stereotypically feminine work and men bored by stereotypically gay professions.

The Experience of Lesbians and Gay Men in U.S. Military Service

According to the *New York Times* in June 1992, countries permitting lesbian and gay men to serve "with some restrictions" (unspecified) include Austria, Belgium, Denmark, France, Finland, Germany, Italy, Japan, the Netherlands, and Spain.[10] Canada and Australia have since joined their ranks.[11]

The *New York Times* reported in 1990 that "according to Pentagon data, about 1,400 gay men and women are forcibly discharged [from the all the U.S. Armed Services] each year, with lesbians let go at three times the rate of gay men" and that Navy statistics from 1985 to 1989 "show lesbians were discharged at twice the rate of gay men."[12] According to a report released in June 1992 by the General Accounting Office, between 1980 and 1990, "the Pentagon discharged 16,919 enlisted personnel and officers for homosexuality or permitted them to resign."[13] No one knows how many have escaped being discharged or asked to resign. However, recent books by Allan Berube, Mary Ann Humphrey, and Randy Shilts confirm in detail the common knowledge that a great many lesbians and gay men presently serve and always have.[14] Many of their interviewees freely confessed to having lied on their applications; many others, to keeping quiet upon discovering their homosexuality later.

In addressing the university faculty I focused on the moral implications of *closeting*, in part because of the following event. After a Faculty Senate meeting a few weeks before at which FADIUP's protest of the ROTC's discrimination was mentioned, I overheard a colleague say, "When I was in service during World War II, there were lots of gays. Everyone knew. Nobody cared as long as they kept quiet. Why can't they just keep quiet? Why do they have to make a fuss?" This professor seemed unaware of discharges and denials of reenlistment facing lesbians and gay men (whom "everyone knows") after the war, refusals to recommend them for promotions that might trigger expulsion, or the constant terror of exposure, should one fall from grace with one's protectors. More basically, he seemed oblivious to the indignity of having to hide what is easily most important and most central in structuring one's life: whom one loves; in many cases, whom one trusts and depends on more than anyone and with whom one hopes to spend one's life. He did not consider what it would be like to have to hide his spouse or children from employers, students, and coworkers.

For a time, a romantic view of military lesbians and gay men protecting one another and being protected by sympathetic officers was fostered by tales such as the following from Johnny Phelps, who was awarded a purple heart "and several other combat medals from the Pacific" during World War II. While she was working for General Eisenhower in Germany just after the war, she reports, he gave her a direct order to find the lesbians in her WAC battalion in order to get rid of them, to which she responded, "Sir, if the General pleases, I'll be happy to check into this and make you a list. But you've got to know, when you get the list back, my name's going to be first."[15] His secretary, standing next to her, she says, added, "Sir, if the General pleases, Sergeant Phelps will have to be second on the list because mine will be first. You see, I'm going to type it." Sergeant Phelps says she went on to point out to General Eisenhower that theirs was the highest-ranking WAC battalion, that most of its members were decorated, and that in its entire history, it had had no illegal pregnancies, no venereal disease, no negative reports, and that it had received Meritorious Commendations every six months. Hearing this, she says, he "just looked at me and said, 'Forget that order. Forget about it.' " And that was the last they heard of it. Out of almost nine hundred women in that battalion, she estimates, "95 per cent of them were lesbians" (p. 40).

The ban was still new. The war was popular. Camaraderie led many to look past the policy. Such tales give only a partial picture of practices that the ban fostered during the past fifty years. Other officers, perhaps feeling outnumbered, have responded less honorably than Sergeant Phelps.

Because of officers' discretionary powers, not all lesbians and gay men who serve are equally closeted. Secrecy may be unnecessary for many in wartime. According to the *Wall Street Journal* in January 1991, lesbians and gay men who served in the Persian Gulf with their superiors' knowledge of their homosexuality and without actions brought against them were about to be discharged; in July of that year, the *Wall Street Journal* reported that discharge proceedings had begun on gay veterans of Operation Desert Storm.[16] Such hypocrisy calls to mind the well-known case of African American Perry Watkins, drafted and inducted into the Army during the Vietnam War despite his affirma-

tion of his gayness from the beginning. The Army even had him entertain troops in drag. They then refused his reenlistment because of the
homosexuality he had always affirmed. He told Mary Ann Humphrey
that he had applied three times for discharge during the war on the
grounds that he was a homosexual and was denied each time, although
the white men he knew who made the same kind of application had
theirs granted.[17] When they found him useful, the Army found ways to
keep him in; when they found him no longer anything but an embar-
rassment, they tried to keep him out. He appealed the Army's refusal of
reenlistment, and in 1987 the Ninth Circuit Court of Appeals ruled
7–4 in his favor, although not on Constitutional grounds that would
help others' cases.

When the content of a policy is so highly questionable that many of
those charged with enforcing it (such as members of the widespread
lesbian and gay officer networks referred to by Mary Ann Humphrey's
interviewees) cannot be presumed to agree with its rationale, they may
exercise considerable "discretion" in enforcing it. In practice, this means
that when the policy *is* enforced, the real reasons are often irrelevant to
the content of the policy, which becomes a vehicle for the exercise of
many kinds of prejudice, not just prejudice against lesbians and gays.
This compounds abuse. When a policy is unjust to begin with, those
against whom it is arbitrarily enforced suffer at least a double injustice.
Such double injustice is notorious also in the history of capital punishment. With respect to both capital punishment and the exclusionary
policy regarding lesbians and gays, those most liable to suffer have been
those with the least power to mobilize protest. In the United States, it
is often people of color, especially poor people of color. In this respect,
it is not surprising that lesbians are forcibly discharged at many times
the rate of gay men.

Miriam ben-Shalom, president of the Gay, Lesbian, and Bisexual Veterans of America, is another casualty of officer discretion who refused
to leave quietly. She enlisted in the U.S. Army Reserve in 1974. During her second year, when there was a large number of discharges, she
asked why she was not kicked out with the others and says her commanding officer told her, "Oh, there's this regulation, but it's up to the
discretion of the commander. Besides, you're really good at what you
do. We have no arguments with you, so don't worry about it"—imply-
ing that if they did have "arguments" that were insufficient for a discharge, they could trot out the policy against lesbians.[18]

In 1976, Miriam ben-Shalom was discharged when her commander

recommended her for a commendation. Recommendation for a promotion or commendation is a way to initiate a discharge when a "flag"
has been placed on the candidate's file. "A flag is placed on anyone's
personnel file when some action is pending," she explained, "In my case
it had to do with my verbal statements about being a lesbian." Perry
Watkins reports that because of his sexual orientation he was not given
awards and decorations during his last enlistment, explaining, "they
had to consider their 'image.' "[19]

It is often noted that most of those discharged have been enlistees
rather than officers.[20] Those responsible for discharges are sometimes
lesbian or gay officers with an investment to protect against being
outed by indiscretions (or principles) of others. Some have practiced for
decades their own versions of "don't ask, don't tell, don't pursue." Army
recruiter "Elizabeth Strong" (pseud.), for example, told Mary Ann
Humphrey that she never asked applicants "if they were gay" but
would feel no compunction about denying admission to any who
answered the application form's homosexuality questions affirmatively:
"If he is stupid, stupid enough to admit it when everybody knows you
can't do it and be in the military, then he's not smart enough to come
into my Air Force, and that's how I feel."[21] Reports from lesbian and
gay enlistees of their terror of lesbian and gay officers and of a history
of lack of support from those quarters suggest a real fear that lesbian and
gay officers may use their discretionary powers to track down "insufficiently closeted" enlistees. Closeted officers can be in a prime position
to manipulate lesbians or gay men under their authority. Some are
said by Mary Ann Humphrey's interviewees to have bargained with
lesbians or gay men who agreed to spy on others and turn in lists in
exchange for more lenient treatment of themselves (p. 218). Ironically,
lesbian and gay officers who have the most power can come to have the
strongest motives to maintain the closet, deferring to (if not internalizing) socially sanctioned fear and hatred. Thus it is especially important
to address such fears and hatreds in officer training, such as in ROTC
programs. The evils of closeting can take root in especially pernicious
ways at this level, a matter to which I will return.

Thus, the implication of the rhetorical question, "Why can't they
just keep quiet?" that things are basically all right for those who quietly do their jobs well is a long way from the truth. Some of Mary Ann
Humphrey's interviewees indicated that *after they became officers*, they
were put in touch with a network of lesbian or gay officers in many
cities. Such informal networks, often embodying social prejudices of

the time, have not been there for everyone. An African American lesbian in the Navy told Mary Ann Humphrey that she knew of groups in which one could be "totally out and practicing" but that because of racism she did not belong (p. 157). But even officers with major commendations face discharge if they come forward as lesbian or gay or answer direct questions honestly, as in the widely publicized cases of Leonard Matlovich (over ten years' Air Force service, Purple Heart, Bronze Star) and, more recently, Colonel Margarethe Cammermeyer of the National Guard (over twenty-seven years' service, Bronze Star, Veterans Administration Nurse of the Year award) and Tracy Thorne, the naval officer who came out in May 1992 on TV's "Nightline."[22]

An interesting implication of Johnny Phelps' Eisenhower story is that it would not have been in the DOD's interest to enforce its antilesbian and antigay policies uniformly because of the sheer numbers of outstanding and responsible personnel who would have had to be to let go if it did. The military sounds like an outer's paradise: how could the DOD continue to maintain its discriminatory policies if all the lesbians and gay men in positions of responsibility were outed? And yet it has maintained them despite astounding costs. The cost was estimated at $27 million in 1990 for the 1,000 lesbians and gays dismissed, based on an estimated $28,226 to replace an enlisted person and $120,772 to replace an officer.[23] The General Accounting Office estimates that from 1980 to 1990 it cost $498 million to recruit and train replacements for those discharged.[24]

Yet, ethically, these were not the most important costs. More important is the corruption of lesbian and gay officers who are *not* booted out, who perpetuate the defamation of lesbians and gay men. And more important are the lives ruined in consequence of hostile policies selectively enforced.

What's Wrong with Closeting?

"Why can't they just keep quiet?" came from a university colleague knowledgeable in political philosophy, whose analytical skills and political sensitivities I had respected for more than two decades. Overhearing him, I realized that to be taken seriously by faculty on the ROTC issue, I had to address his question. Events since then show his position to be far commoner even than I had guessed. Dishearteningly, it strikes many who have not lived intimately with the issues as a "reasonable compromise."

Setting aside the erroneous assumption that keeping quiet has been sufficient not to get one expelled (and the equally erroneous assumption that failure to keep quiet was sufficient for discharge), I focused on the assumption that living in a closet is not so bad, nor, consequently, tolerating others' being made to do so. This remains the central issue. My colleague's response is not so different from some responses of university students in my classes. Occasionally they have written me notes protesting my "exhibitionism"—as though I had exposed acts rather than facts—when I said or wore something during lecture that identified myself as lesbian, which I am apt to do as naturally as some of my colleagues wear wedding rings and refer to their spouses and children. Informal evidence suggests that the pro-closeting attitude is as common in college athletics as in the ROTC program, and likewise in nursing schools, college dormitories, and generally in same-sex settings that bring members of the university into close physical proximity with one another. The very tone of the question, "Why can't they just keep quiet?" (like the notes from students) reveals how closeting is urged upon lesbians and gay men, *not something we choose for reasons of our own*. We tend to be as private as others about sexual behavior. What is oppressive is being forced to hide our bonds to each other.

There are at least three pernicious aspects of a policy that fosters closeting. First, it rewards lying and penalizes honesty. Even if officers cannot ask the question of entrants, what is to prevent others from asking or situations from arising in which one has either to lie or tell a truth that can lead to expulsion? Lesbians and gay men committed long-term to a military environment will be unable to avoid deception, and deceptions begun will need to be maintained. Such situations tend to be morally corrupting. If intimate relationships are among the most important parts of one's life and one is willing to lie systematically about them to protect one's military standing, the question is raised what else one may be willing to lie about to protect that standing. More importantly, having to enforce against others a policy that one knows applies equally to oneself may lead to psychological "solutions" that involve serious abdications of responsibility, a matter to which I will return.

Second, the policy demeans all lesbians and gay men by upholding a stance that would be justified only if lesbians and gay men were in truth responsible for the fear, disgust, or revulsion of others. In doing so, it encourages the false assumption that lesbians and gay men *are* responsible for those reactions. This is particularly unjust in a context in which lesbians and gay men are hindered from disabusing others of the ignorance on which those fears and hostilities are commonly based. One of the best ways to combat such ignorance is for lesbians and gay men with proven records of honor, service, and achievement to come out. But those who do are subject to expulsion, regardless of their records of honor, service, and achievement. In the past, many of those discovered have been offered honorable discharges or the opportunity to resign in return for leaving quietly. The ban has thus institutionalized homophobia, insulating against criticism a derogatory image that reaches beyond the ROTC to the campus at large, beyond the military to the wider society, and beyond present to future generations.

Third, the policy deters quests for self-knowledge and rewards closed-mindedness. It penalizes an open attitude among youth regarding some of the most important choices of our lives. Insofar as a ban on lesbians and gay men applies in a university campus ROTC program, it confines and insults *all* students, not just those who presently identify as lesbian or gay. Such discrimination turns honest lesbian and gay students into second-class campus citizens (although they pay first-class tuition). It makes dishonest ones vulnerable to manipulation and extortion. And, as I will argue in the next section, it makes potential monsters of career officers.

Living a Lie and "Doubling"

Regarding the sexually inexperienced and those who had not been visibly present in lesbian or gay communities, the military had no effective check on answers to the application form homosexuality question; the applicant's word was all they had at that point. Many entrants lied successfully. Some dared not disclose the truth even to themselves. "Janice" (pseud.) told Mary Ann Humphrey she got involved with an officer "who was so closeted—I can remember her saying to me, 'We're not like those other lesbians. We're not real lesbians. We just love each other.' "[25] For those who lied to get in, or stayed in after discovering forbidden truths about themselves, systematic deception became a way of life (an irony of referring to homosexuality as "an alternative lifestyle").

Under investigatory pressure after others were pushed to identify them, two of Mary Ann Humphrey's lesbian interviewees used marriage as a cover, one with a gay man who also needed a cover, the other with a heterosexual man who seemed unaware of being used. Some got pregnant. Others, less drastically, restyled their hair, put on make-up, flirted with male officers. Nearly all said they dated men as a cover. The new policy will also encourage such charades. Even with a policy of "don't ask," in a heterosexist society any individual entrant will be presumed heterosexual, and the burden to act in accord with that presumption is clear (even if not in detail).

Why do lesbians and gay men put up with living this way? Some do not. Some have quit voluntarily, come forward, or answered direct questions honestly, forcing the hands of others, as in the cases of Leonard Matlovich, Margarethe Cammermeyer, and Tracy Thorne. Yet others have remained, retiring with full benefits.

If their pretenses were literally survival tactics, they might take pride in resourcefulness. But many enlisted *voluntarily*, some because it appeared their best route to an education and career training. They experienced the necessity for pretense as demeaning, not as a source of pride. In some cases, enlistment was their most promising route out of an abusive home, poverty, an intolerant small town environment, or all three. Extortion and manipulation by superior officers may be an upgrading from physical and sexual assault at home. If such a military life compromises the moral character that education ideally develops, many of those so compromised might otherwise receive no education beyond high school (if that). Thus, early misfortunes can make the evils of closeting seem to some a small price to pay for a way out. This makes them exploitable in the maintenance of institutionalized homophobia. Unlike Perry Watkins, who affirmed his gay identity and was thereby unmanipulable, those who succumb to closeting are used, in being abused, to perpetuate oppression and injustice against others.

Not all who live the heterosexual lie have the excuse of escaping a worse situation. Some have professional educations and economically privileged backgrounds (which does not rule out domestic abuse).[26] If some live out parents' ambitions, others pursue their own ideals. Unfortunately, such things offer no assurance of moral sensitivity. Many professionals became war criminals in Nazi Germany. Psychologist Robert Lifton, in studying the Nazi doctors, hypothesized a certain psychological "solution" that educated, intelligent agents living a lie may use to cope with intolerable stress. Although he does not generalize it to other situations, his hypothesis may apply here. My point is not that the behavior of closeted lesbian and gay officers is comparable to the war crimes of the Nazi doctors. It is not comparable, although one can ask disturbing questions about potentialities. What may *be* clearly comparable, however, is the fact of living a severely bifurcated life of hypocrisy, deception, and betrayal and the "solutions" that make such a life both possible and successful, and in the process, destroy moral accountability.

Inquiring into how physicians came to design and participate in Nazi medical experiments, using their skills to kill rather than to heal, Dr. Lifton proposes: "The key to understanding how Nazi doctors came to do the work of Auschwitz is the psychological principle I call 'doubling': the division of the self into two functioning wholes, so that a part-self acts as an entire self."[27]

The idea is that the self who lived inside the death camps divided, psychologically and yet as a functioning whole, from the self who was loving with spouse, children, and the dog at home. The division was not simply between skills called upon in different contexts but between incompatible values and emotional responses. Doubling, he argues, enabled the Nazi doctors to avoid intolerable stress, by avoiding the need to confront contradictions in their own values and practices.

This hypothesis is offered as *explanation* only, not as excuse. Dr. Lifton's ethical view is that the doubler's responsibility "is in no way abrogated by the fact that much doubling takes place outside of awareness"; that, "to live out the doubling and call forth the evil is a moral choice for which one is responsible, whatever the level of consciousness involved" (pp. 418, 423–24). His investigation is intended as a "psychological probing on behalf of illuminating evil" (p. 418). He does not explain, philosophically, how it is possible to be responsible for what takes place outside of awareness. However, there is both legal and moral precedent for his position. What enters awareness is often something over which we have, or can develop, considerable control. Reckless and negligent behavior are examples of conduct for which people are held responsible, both legally and morally, although the dangers and harms the agents failed to avoid were outside their awareness. What one attends to and what one ignores reveal as much about one's character as what one does with what falls within one's awareness. Arrogance is a trait of which its possessors are typically unaware, although self-reflection can make one aware. Thus, even if doubling has elements outside of awareness, they may still be within the agent's responsibility in the wider sense of that which occurs through one's choices or failures to choose, and they may be potentially brought within the agent's awareness. It is possible to choose not to accept responsibility for what is already within one's responsibility in this wider sense. We sometimes hold people responsible for such abdications of responsibility. As I read Dr. Lifton's analysis of doubling, doubling can involve such abdications of responsibility. When it does, it is not innocent.

Dr. Lifton lists five characteristics of doubling: (1) "a dialectic between two selves in terms of autonomy and connection," (2) "a holistic principle," (3) "a life-death dimension," (4) "the avoidance of guilt," and (5) "both an unconscious dimension . . . and a significant change in moral consciousness" (p. 419). He argues that doubling is "holistic," thus distinguishing it from what psychologist Pierre Janet called "dissociation" and what many contemporary psychoanalysts call "splitting." Although he refers to "the mechanism" of doubling, the "mechanism" seems simply to *be* systematic refusal to face contradictions. Doubling appears not to be accompanied by amnestic barriers. Nor does it appear as suddenly and spontaneously as multiple personalities (which, unlike doubling, appear early in childhood).

Most of Dr. Lifton's five characteristics of doubling fit, or are adaptable to, the double lives of lesbian and gay career officers. The guilt or shame they avoid is that of hypocrisy in enforcing against others a policy that demeans themselves as well. The only characteristic not obviously applicable is the "life-death dimension." Yet the recent beating death of gay Seaman Allen Schindler raises unanswered questions about the prevalence of this dimension. Signorile reports that 30 percent of teen suicides are by lesbian and gay youth.[28] Many lesbians and gay men in service are very young. Institutionalized homophobia and hostility can be extremely stressful—for both its targets and its agents. In the summer of 1991 it was reported that "Sgt. Timothy Miller, a 25-year-old officer, allegedly shot his lover, 20-year-old Spc. Terry Wayne Stephenson, days before Miller was to be court-martialed on three counts of sodomy and four counts of indecent conduct . . . Miller apparently shot himself shortly after Stephenson's body was found."[29] How many cases are not reported in such detail? And for those who fear harassment from lesbians or gay men comparable to what is commonly tolerated against women by men, for those who regard such behavior as a normal accompaniment of sexual attraction, fears that lesbians or gay men may be in close physical proximity or positions of power are predictably stressful. Who knows how often military lesbian or gay deaths are presently attributable to the stress of such fears, which could be eliminated by openness, education, and impartial policies regarding sexual abuse?

Dr. Lifton's five characteristics may fit well the double lives of closeted military lesbians and gay men. For those who enter military service because of their ideals, a career of lesbian or gay passing may be made to seem acceptable by the creation of *a special military self*, a shield from stresses that lead others to quit voluntarily, a shield from contradictions in the passer's values and practices. Such a shield can become at the same time *a barrier to integrity and accountability*. Dr. Lifton's hypothesis about how far such doubling can enable one to go in subverting the values of humanity makes it a terrifying prospect to contemplate. Posthumous reports about the late J. Edgar Hoover—not to mention the infamous Roy Cohn—suggest the question whether he may have exemplified such doubling.[30]

Some forms of doubling, Dr. Lifton acknowledges, can be life-saving, "for a soldier in combat, for instance; or for a victim of brutality such as an Auschwitz inmate, who must also undergo a form of doubling in order to survive."[31] This suggests that what is of concern is not doubling in itself but the nature of the "selves" that doubling can create and protect. Those raised under oppressive institutions may view what Dr. Lifton calls "doubling" as on a continuum with fairly ordinary experiences of multiplicity, such as W. E. B. Du Bois' experience of "two-ness": "an American, a Negro; two souls . . . two unreconciled strivings; two warring ideals in one dark body."[32] Philosopher Victoria Davion has argued recently that a multiplicitous self (to use María Lugones' term) *need not* lack integrity, that there are ways to guard against that.[33] However, the case of the Nazi doctors suggests the possibility of using doubling to facilitate an awesome abdication of moral responsibility. By enforcing closeting, an officer training program that attracts lesbians or gay men who are willing systematically to lie, if "need" be, to superiors, coworkers, neighbors, family, and others about central aspects of their lives and who are willing to prove themselves by rooting out others to enforce a policy as defamatory of their own lives as of the lives of those they persecute, may encourage such uses of doubling.[34] It may thus be training potential moral monsters.[35]

Institutionalized Hatred and "The Morale Problem"

The DOD's discrimination policies have not been defended recently by claims of inferior job performance by lesbians or gay men. The official reason in recent years has been, rather, that the *presence* of lesbians and gay men "adversely affects the ability of the Military Services to maintain discipline, good order and morale; to foster mutual trust and confidence among service members, to ensure the integrity of rank and command; to facilitate assignment and worldwide deployment of service members who frequently must live and work under close conditions affording minimal privacy; to recruit and retain members of the Military services; to maintain the public acceptability of military service; and to prevent breaches of security."[36] However, a long history of closeted lesbians and gay men in the military without detrimental consequences to discipline, order, and morale suggests that it is not the *presence* but, if anything, the *perception* of lesbians and gay men that has created a problem. This is borne out in the new policy, which objects not to the presence of lesbians and gay men but to their revelations of who they are to others.

The shift from "presence" to "perception" is an astute move by those who would like to see lesbians and gay men excluded. Lesbians and gay men must be closeted for the old fear of extortion to have any plausibility. If *perception* by others of lesbians and gay men is said to provide a morale problem, closeting appears to be the "solution." Thus, the military seems to have all bases covered: lesbians and gay men who are "out" present a morale problem; those who are "in" present a security problem. Neither argument, however, withstands scrutiny.

There is no serious attempt by the DOD to defend the *bases* of the alleged morale problems, not surprisingly, for such problems have sources in mythology, ignorance, inexperience, and irrationality. Deference to prejudice, however, is not harmless. It fosters horizontal abuse among lesbians and among gay men, and it produces a self-reinforcing cycle of social hatred: discrimination, which is itself stigmatizing, reinforces the existing stigma of being socially hated, which is then cited in defense of discrimination, and so on, without end. Deference to the hatred commonly called "homophobia" *solidifies* it, socially sanctions it, passes it along from generation to generation.

In practical terms, the concern about "morale" comes down to fears of *noncooperation*, at best, and of *sexual harassment and rape*, at worst. Analogously to its earlier resistance to racial integration, the military seems to fear that soldiers will refuse to respect and take orders from lesbian or gay officers. The concerns about fear of sexual harassment or rape, however, are specific to discrimination against gay men and lesbians. As suggested above, it is an interesting question to what extent the latter fears are rooted in the common toleration of sexually abusive behavior *of heterosexual men toward women*, such behavior as was exhibited, for example, by male pilots of the Tailhook Association at their September 1991 convention in Las Vegas, when at least twenty-six women, half of them naval officers, report that they were assaulted while they were "forced through a hotel corridor gantlet of drunken, groping pilots."[37]

Legitimizing antihomosexual fears places responsibility on lesbians and gay men for the ignorance and (anticipated) insubordination of others. Although the "morale" argument need not pretend that the fears and lack of respect are the *fault* of lesbians and gay men, it does hold them responsible instead of holding responsible those who are being irrational or those who are charged with relevant education.

For an ROTC program on a university campus, appeals to problems created by ignorance should have no credibility whatever. The mythologies that perpetuate social hostility toward lesbians and gay men are exposed and examined critically in university courses.[38] If more such courses are needed, a free university is in an excellent position to address that need. Faculty from coast to coast are agitating for lesbian and gay studies programs. On campus, differences in politics and orientation should be productive rather than divisive, addressed through discussion and exchange of points of view, adding to the common fund of knowledge about human experience. The Netherlands offers an example of confronting prejudice with education. Its defense department has published a colorful eight-page brochure, *Homosexualiteit en defense* (Homosexuality in the Defense), which begins:

> Homosexuals in the military—is that possible? Of course it is. Furthermore, it is obvious. The military is a mirror of society. . . . We produced this brochure for homosexuals—to make it clear that they are welcome in the military—and for heterosexuals—to make them realize what kinds of problems their colleagues are facing.[39]

When educational efforts are unsuccessful, the military can require cooperation on pain of discipline for insubordination. Were it necessary to exclude anyone, those refusing cooperation with lesbians and gay men could be excluded, along with perpetrators of assault, regardless of sexual orientation. The point about the locus of responsibility is analogous to that of the feminist response to those who would keep women off the streets to prevent rape: the way to make streets safe is not to keep women off the streets but to keep rapists off the streets. Likewise, the way to a healthier ROTC and military is not to exclude lesbians and gay men but to exclude disrespect for lesbians and gay men and to refuse to tolerate sexual abuse by anyone.

The Ninth Circuit Court of Appeals in its judgment regarding lesbian Army Reserve Captain Dusty Pruitt has recognized the weight of the point about others' prejudices, as others did earlier with respect to analogous "morale" arguments used in defense of racial segregation in the armed forces (removed by President Truman's order in 1948) and barring women from military service. On August 19, 1991 the Ninth Circuit Court ruled that the Army's policy requiring discharge of homosexuals should be subjected to "active" rationality review and in May 1992 upheld that ruling, rejecting the Defense Department's request for a rehearing. On December 7, 1992, the Supreme Court denied the government's appeal, which meant the Army must come up with a new justification for the exclusionary policy or offer Dusty Pruitt a settlement.[40] What the requirement of "active" rational review means, basically, is that the Army cannot continue to rely on traditional arguments that antigay biases of other members of the Army would create problems. Judge Canby, of the Ninth Circuit Court, quoted from *Palmore*: "The Constitution cannot control such prejudices, but neither can it tolerate them. Private biases may be outside the reach of the law, but the law cannot, directly or indirectly, give them effect."[41] The implication is that the Army can no longer appeal to prejudice to justify excluding lesbians and gay men but must find some reasonable ground, such as interference with job performance.

The military is not likely to find anything generally amiss in the job performance records of lesbians and gay men. A substantial body of evidence shows that lesbians' and gay men's performance records are, by the military's own standards, not only not inferior but often outstanding. As I write this, *The Advocate* has a cover story on Joe Zuniga, Sixth U.S. Army Soldier of the Year, who came out in the recent march on Washington.[42] The *New York Times* carried an article in 1990 on the Navy's surface Atlantic fleet being urged to root out lesbians despite their being acknowledged to be "among the command's top performers."[43] It appears that lesbian performance records have not fallen since Johnny Phelps's Eisenhower days. In October 1989 openly gay Congressman Gerry Studds of Massachusetts received a DOD study, "Nonconforming Sexual Orientations and Military Suitability," by Dr. Ted Sarbin, a professor of psychology and criminology, and Dr. Ken Karols, a Navy flight surgeon, of the Defense Personnel Security Research and Education Center (PERESEC). A few months later, he received a second report, "Preservice Adjustment of Homosexual and Heterosexual Military Accessions: Implications for Security Clearance Suitability," by Michael McDaniel, also a DOD researcher, although this report had not been submitted to the Pentagon. Both reports (known as the PERESEC reports) were publicized by representatives Studds and

Patricia Schroeder.[44] The first report concludes that sexuality "is unrelated to job performance in the same way as is being left- or right-handed."[45] The second report suggests that lesbians and gay men display military suitability "that is as good or better than the average heterosexual" (p. x). Decades ago, the Crittenden Report, commissioned by the Navy in 1957—which, according to Rep. Studds, it took twenty years and a court order to pry from Pentagon vaults—had already concluded that "The number of cases of [extortion] as a result of past investigations of homosexuals is negligible. No factual data exist to support the contention that homosexuals are a greater risk than heterosexuals."[46] And in 1991, a Defense Department memo was anonymously leaked to the National Gay and Lesbian Task Force, stating that "the same criteria should be used for gays as for straights in deciding whether to grant security clearances."[47]

And yet, in a way, these reports should offer cold comfort to lesbians and gay men. For, besides exhibiting lesbian and gay talent and achievement, they also show how well lesbians and gay men can be made to turn on other lesbians and gay men. Our reason to oppose a ban on lesbians and gay men is not that *by military standards* we do our jobs as well as if not better than others. More important is that some of the jobs produced by such a ban are morally corrupting for lesbian and gay officers to have to perform. Ability to pass muster in these conditions may testify more to ingenuity than to character.

In view of the rampant deception, self-deception, hypocrisy, lying, spying, manipulation, and extortion fostered by the military's exclusionary policies, the DOD's morale arguments are especially ironic. What could be more demoralizing than the practices resulting from the exclusionary policies themselves? How conducive to morale is an environment in which people known by their colleagues to deserve commendations or promotions are passed over because recommending them might lead to their discharge? How conducive to morale is an environment in which exclusionary policies are known to be arbitrarily enforced? An environment in which "nobody really trusted anybody" because officers plant spies to draw up lists?[48] In which anyone could accuse anyone without evidence and expose them to intense investigation? An environment where informal networks have protected, and will continue to protect, officers who violate regulations they enforce against those they judge not skillful enough at hiding (even if blatant "witch hunts" are discontinued)? One might suspect that were the bans totally lifted and remedial education instituted, military morale would improve several hundred percent.

A State Sexuality?

Finally, it is incompatible with the goals of a state university to penalize students for inquiry regarding sexuality. The University of Wisconsin would not tolerate penalizing students for inquiry into religious beliefs and practices. Were the military to require a certain religious orientation, or even the appearance of one, that would raise serious questions about a state religion. But there should no more be a state sexuality than a state religion.

The morale arguments still holding sway in the new military policy could easily have religious analogues. Many Christians, for example, distrust anyone who professes a lack of faith in Jesus Christ. In a society with a majority of Christians, such distrust might easily be regarded as disturbing the cohesion, order, and so forth of military units, just as a few centuries ago it determined who could testify in courts of law. Imagine a policy permitting private religious beliefs or observances that deviate from the dominant religion but only as long as one keeps *the fact of* such beliefs or observances to oneself. Would anyone seriously maintain today that such a policy differed significantly from religious intolerance?

One's dispositions to form, or not form, intimate partnerships are at least as central to the quality of one's life and one's moral integrity as the freedom to worship, or not worship, as one chooses. Before President Clinton's policy of "don't ask," students who engaged in open inquiry regarding sexuality would have faced exclusion from the ROTC, because many, if honest, would have given hesitant, qualified, or agnostic answers to questions about their own sexuality. Now it is unclear when inquiry about subject of same-sex bonding will have negative repercussions.

The point is not to exempt sexuality—any more than religion—from moral evaluation. On the contrary, freedom to inquire without prejudice is required for informed moral evaluation.

Why Radical Feminists Should Care

I have been asked why I, a long-time feminist with neither military record nor military ambitions, would bother with the ROTC. Why would I *want* lesbians *in*cluded? Is it not contrary to feminist values? Or, at best hopelessly reformist, where a more revolutionary approach is needed?

My response is complex. First, some questioners may confuse femi*nism* with femin*inity*. Fighting against men is incompatible with popular ideals of *femininity* and widely (although not universally) held to be the prerogative of the *masculine*. (Fighting among women, on the other hand, is often encouraged by those adhering to the same ideals). Such ideals are widely enforced among white women of the middle classes and used by them to judge others. Feminists have long objected that "femininity," so understood, is a political construction of femaleness used to keep women subordinate and subservient to men.[49] During the past two decades, the women's self-defense movement has instituted in most major cities of the United States physical and attitudinal training programs, often cooperating with rape crisis centers, with the objective of enlarging women's options to include effectively fighting back against assailants.[50] Many women have aptitudes for physical activities from which we have been traditionally discouraged to keep us in our place— aptitudes for sports, for example, and for battle, as well. Lesbians have always been outstanding among athletes and warriors, although often not visible as lesbians. The Amazon tradition, although less popular than the Sapphic, is a major strand of lesbian culture, extending from the ancient Amazons through many "cross-dressers" of modern times to contemporary lesbians in U.S. and other military forces.[51] History documents amazons—formidable bands of women warriors—in every age, in every part of the globe.[52] Even if fighting against men were "unfeminine," it would not follow that it is either unfemale or unfeminist.

The second part of my response begins by pointing out that it is one thing to choose not to exercise an option and another not to have the option. I want lesbians not to be excluded from the options of ordinary citizens in good standing. In a society defended by armed forces, that includes military options. My concern is not that of a reformer who sees opportunities for lesbian advancement in reformed military institutions. My concern is what exclusion means for who we are. To be excluded in advance from a public program for no good reason is demeaning to those excluded and to all who share the identity on the basis of which they are excluded. Such exclusions help to construct a disfiguring image of all who share the excluded identity. Thus, even were a student not interested in ROTC, it is still in the interest of that student for the option not to be foreclosed on grounds of sexual orientation. What is at stake is one's dignity in communities in which one lives daily, one's very identity in those respects in which it is a social construction.[53]

Nevertheless, those who have never considered seriously the opportunity for military training may not know how they would evaluate the option. Where military service is the *only* public service to which citizens may be obligated, those denied access to military service may become beholden to others for public defense and security. Although during wartime Rosie and other women previously slated for domestic service were welcomed as riveters and so forth, their services were not recognized as military. No veterans' benefits attached to it. After the war, they were sent home so that returning soldiers could reclaim such jobs as they had held previously. The debt traditionally exacted from women who do not serve militarily has been feminine service. A feminist who acknowledges a debt to be honored might prefer to "pay her way" in military service, as many women did during World War II. The concept of "military service" might be radically transformed if service obligations were democratic and distributed in an egalitarian manner. In a war genuinely supported by the people, who would be home to defend but children, the old, and the ill? Caring for them might have to be recognized as wartime military service, with full benefits, awards, purple hearts, and the rest.[54]

If it is not obvious that a feminist would in principle oppose serving militarily, neither does it follow from rejecting "femininity" that she would embrace modern weapons or the values war has most often implemented. The uses of violence, military and otherwise, raise issues over which feminists, like others, are deeply divided. Many would agree with Professor Gerda Lerner, who argued passionately in a public campus address a few years ago that in modern warfare, it is too often the case that *there is no defense of women, children, and old people who are not soldiers themselves, that these are the people most likely to be killed in the event of war fought with modern technology.*[55]

I do not rest my case on the value of actually exercising the option to become a member of the ROTC or any branch of military service. Rather, I emphasize the importance of not being excluded from honorable candidacy for such service, whether on the basis of one's identity or on the basis of self-respecting verbal acknowledgments of that identity. Feminist values do not obviously exclude eligibility for military service. Exclusion by the government is a denial of the normal options of citizenship. On a campus with an ROTC program, such exclusion becomes a denial of the normal options of students in good standing. Wrongful exclusions contribute to an unjust social construction of the excluded as dishonorable, abnormal, or somehow shameful, which affects all areas of their lives, not just their choices of courses.

It is sometimes objected that were it demeaning to exclude lesbians and gay men, it would also be demeaning to exclude from service those with such physical disabilities as blindness, deafness, or loss of the use of limbs. For, these disabilities are no more the fault of those who suffer them than being lesbian or gay is the fault of those excluded on that account, and others might use such exclusions also to support wrongful stigmatizing.

At least two things are wrong with this argument. First, citing the absence of fault is misleading. For, it suggests both that choice is not involved in becoming lesbian or gay or in incurring a disability, and that were there such a choice, one would be at fault to make it. Yet a foreseeable disability may be incurred as a consequence of justifiable choices (as when one is injured in performing a meritorious act), the roles of choice in becoming lesbian or gay are disputed among lesbians and gay men, and were it not for hardships imposed and inconveniences experienced by others, there might be no more to regret about living with any of many forms of disability than about living one's life as lesbian or gay. (On choice in becoming lesbian, see chapters 2 and 3.) Second, appealing to the predicament of those with disabilities is intended as a *reductio ad absurdam*, assuming without argument that it *is* justifiable to exclude from service those lacking ordinary physical abilities. However, the argument that wrongful exclusion from the normal options of citizenship contributes to an unjust social construction of those excluded can also be heard to support the inclusion, as much as possible, of those with physical disabilities. Many today prefer to be recognized as differently abled; they are able to perform a wide range of services when others are open to the possibilities and cooperate.[56] There may also be services that can be well-performed by some who have been dismissed in the past as mentally disabled.[57]

Finally, it is true that lesbians and gay men who serve militarily would acquire access to veterans' educational programs, health services, and jobs presently available on a preferential basis to veterans. Preferential hiring is controversial among white men when its recipients are nonveteran women or people of color. But veterans have had preferen-

tial treatment for decades. The Veterans' Preference Act of 1944 specified that for certain jobs, nonveterans were not to be considered unless
no veterans were available.[58] This may be a good reformist argument.
However, although I do not dispute its justice, it is not the kind of consideration that motivates my concern.

What benefits could be expected from abolishing all exclusionary policies regarding lesbian and gay men in all student programs, including
the ROTC? I have no special reason to expect that lesbian and gay students would sign up in great numbers to contribute their talents to the
ROTC, although perhaps they would. I would not be surprised, however, if many already in came out (I do not mean dropped out)—at
least, if the military also took seriously its duty to protect lesbians and
gay men against assault. Eliminating the stress of a double life with its
terror of exposure, its associated manipulative powers, and its barriers
to deserved promotions and commendations can be expected to affect
performance positively. Speaking from experience, coming out for me
in my work—now more than a decade and a half ago—has had a very
positive effect on my ability to be productive. Even more importantly,
removing the need for "doubling," to use Dr. Lifton's term, would
improve the integrity and accountability of lesbian and gay officers in
military service. Ethically, the latter is one of the two most important
benefits.

The other is that removal of the need to hide would strike a blow
against institutionalized fear and hatred and the public disfigurement of
lesbians and gay men not only on campus but in the larger world. Lesbians and gay men would be recognized to have the normal rights of
citizens in good standing, whether or not they serve militarily. The next
generation would inherit less public defamation than ours did. Dimin-
ishing the disfigurement of lesbians and gay men and penalizing instead
those who refuse to respect us would potentially extend far beyond
campus and military, as generations graduated and moved out into the
world or returned to civilian life, taking with them attitudes developed
on campuses and in military environments into communities everywhere. This is why, as a feminist lesbian who is also an educator, I care
about this issue.

Chapter 10

other people's secrets: the ethics of outing

Among gay men, support for outing appears to be growing. Among lesbians, one scarcely hears it discussed at all, perhaps because lesbians have had less to gain by hiding. I think there are also other reasons. Despite the moral concerns about closeting explored in the previous chapter, I am not enthusiastic about outing. Neither am I dead set against it. This chapter examines why and advocates some scruples for those who cannot resist this tempting, heretical, as yet uncodified practice.

Background

Outing is the practice of publicizing without their consent the gayness of named individuals, booting them "out of the closet."[1] A few years ago, Chicago's *Outline*, a now defunct gay periodical, "regularly listed approximately 20 famous people they believe to be gay in a weekly feature titled 'Peek-a-Boo.' "[2] When journalist Michelangelo Signorile outed deceased Malcolm Forbes in New York's *OutWeek* in March 1990, the practice captured media attention from the *Washington Post* to the *San Francisco Chronicle*.[3]

The concept of outing is now established in popular culture. Within gay communities (on the whole, still apparently more opposed to the practice than supportive of it) many would restrict outing to public figures who, as Barney Frank (one of two openly gay congressmen) put it, "shamefully use the fact or accusation of homosexuality as a weapon against others."[4] For Signorile, however, candidates for outing have included celebrities and other public figures, not in reprisal for offensive deeds but on the basis of principled objections to media enforcement of the closet and on pragmatic political grounds. Celebrities may be strategically positioned to be role models, to show that indeed "we are everywhere." Gay men or lesbians may be implicated in a newsworthy story where their heterosexuality would have been alluded to or implied as a matter of course had they been heterosexual. In other instances, outing may be a means to or a consequence of exposing hypocrisy in governmental or other organizations, as in Signorile's outing of Assistant Secretary of Defense Pete Williams.[5]

Like Signorile, Larry Gross, who has also written extensively on the topic, maintains that the intention has never been to out ordinary folk, such as one's schoolteacher neighbor who might lose her job or lose custody of her children as a result.[6] However, philosopher Richard Mohr argues that "a gay person living in the truth will out nearly everyone he or she knows to be gay," as a plain matter of dignity and living morally—at least, as long as the government is not shooting gays.[7]

And yet, the dignity of outing is also problematic—or so I will argue. Like terrorism, outing lends itself to anonymity, giving it potentialities that should be at least embarrassing to conscientious practitioners. The only trick may be to capture media attention. And mainstream media now seem bored with it. Perhaps, like "streaking" in the early 1970s, widely publicized outings will soon have been a short-lived fad. Yet, unlike streaking, outing raises issues that are morally complex, interesting, and, unfortunately, enduring. As Gross put it, "Outing has a long past, if only a short history."[8]

The idea is as old as "passing," and passing, as old as stigmatized identities. For those who share a socially stigmatized identity but do not pass, the question arises whether to protect the passing of others, particularly if the stigmatized identity is in truth honorable enough even though public opinion treats it as dishonorable, abnormal, or shameful. Recent outings of public figures have seized the initiative, volunteering unsolicited information. Previously, individuals worried not so much whether to take such initiatives as how far to go in protecting others' secrets and how to respond to direct queries about others whom they believed to be passing. Now the question presents itself whether honor requires making a point of *not* protecting passing.

Not protecting a secret does not always result in outing. Even remarks to friends and acquaintances may produce little publicity. Yet who can predict the consequences of what we say? Often, we are ignorant of what has been said already, of the funds of information to which we contribute. By disregarding others' secrets, we become willing participants in outing even if we don't carry it all the way. Thus, some of the same issues arise for everyday violations of gay and lesbian "gag rules," to use Mohr's term, as for Signorile's journalistic outing.

Two basic questions for the ethics of outing are (1) whether it wrongs those who are outed and (2) whether those who are already out would wrong themselves in protecting others who pass. Concentrating on gay men, Mohr defends a negative answer to the first question, interpreted as whether outing gays violates their defensible privacy rights, and a positive answer to the second, interpreted as the question whether protecting passers violates one's own gay dignity.[9] He does not support "outing" others medical records to reveal HIV statuses, arguing that to do so would violate doctor-patient privacy (pp. 17–18). This apparently leaves it open, however, that when the source of information is not one's access to medical records, or a similarly privileged position, a dignity defense of "outing" could apply here, also. Nor does Mohr support "hypocrisy outings" of gay politicians, arguing, rather, that a right to privacy regarding one's sexual orientation would not be defeated by hypocrisy (pp. 23–24). This appears to leave it open that if no right to privacy protects sexual orientation, outing to expose hypocrisy could be justified, particularly if it reveals a major lack of integrity in elected officials.[10] Forgoing appeals to political strategy, Mohr builds his case for outing squarely on dignity, offering at once the most sweeping and, philosophically, the most sophisticated defense I have encountered.

Yet, I remain unconvinced on both counts. I find that outing can easily wrong those who are outed, even apart from privacy rights, and that protecting passers can be as dignified as the alternatives. More is at issue than privacy rights and individual integrity. Other sources of indignity can enter in besides those of lesbian and gay closets, including misogyny, class oppression, and cultural or racial oppression. I favor a defeasible presumption of reticence about lesbian and gay secrets in nonlesbian and nongay contexts that are riddled with multiple sources of injustice. I agree with Mohr, however, on the moral centrality of dignity, and I owe much to his work on that topic.[11]

Why Dignity?

Neither the language of privacy rights nor that of dignity is found much in contemporary lesbian feminist ethics. Dignity has been associated in modern moral philosophy with justice, rights, and autonomy. A significant body of feminist philosophy, including the work of Sarah Hoagland, favors moving beyond justice, rights, and autonomy.[12] Yet, dignity need not be tied only to justice and its associated concepts. In the context of outing, "dignity" refers to a solid sense of one's worth that is independent of utility, pleasure, or even happiness, and to accordingly worthy demeanor. Dignity applies to relationships as well as to individuals. It transcends ideologies. The dignity defense of outing rests, first, on the judgment that lesbian and gays closets are a major *indignity* and, second, on the argument that it demeans oneself and one's relationships to abide by a "gag rule" protecting passers in the same way that it would do to pass oneself.

Why *dignity*? Not all oppressed groups fasten on this concept. Dignity is important for those who have been ridiculed and demeaned, presented as alternately insubstantial, a joke, and disgusting. Dignity conveys weight (or substance), elevation (here, elevation out of the mud, not elevation over others), seriousness, reciprocity.[13] A gay Catholic organization bears the name Dignity, and other gay groups have included the term "dignity" in their titles. It is not only that lesbians and gay men have been wrongly perceived and portrayed as ridiculous, although that is true. More importantly, when we hide what is most valuable and central in our lives, we may find our own comportment ridiculous and unworthy of our relationships.

Dignity as a basic value refers to the absence of various indignities, rather than to the presence of anything special, such as pomp and circumstance. It is associated with self-respect, which is commonly understood in the same way (that is, by contrast with ways of lacking it). John Stuart Mill appealed to dignity to rebut the objection that utilitarian ethics was a "pig philosophy."[14] For Mill, "dignity" referred to that sense leading human beings to prefer pleasures involving intellect, even at the cost of a greater *quantity* of pleasure on the whole.[15] Immanuel Kant's *wurde*, commonly translated as "dignity," refers to a worth that he contrasted with "price." For Kant, *wurde* is that value of rational subjects in virtue of which no equivalent can be put in their place, unlike "price," the value of objects, which is a merely market value.[16]

Dignity, however, is not just a function of individual will or nature. It is also a function of social standing, how one is received by others, how one is able to interact socially. Socially, dignity suggests the ability to hold up one's head, to look others in the eye, with a certain immunity or resistance to shame. Dignity is also a matter of degree, and it can attach to many aspects of one's identity. The dignity of a social identity also transcends the dignity of individuals. Harm to gay or lesbian dignity is not simply a sum of the harms that individuals suffer. Nor is protecting such dignity reducible to protecting individuals.

Thus, dignity can be threatened on many fronts. Mohr acknowledges that dignity-protecting behavior is in principle limitable by other considerations of dignity, although he finds it unlikely that such considerations will often argue persuasively against outing. Perhaps such considerations are more evident in lesbian experience and in the experience of others who face injustice and oppression on multiple fronts, whose political identities are complex and who are consequently vulnerable to multiple indignities, than they are in the experience of gay white men. When silence is demeaning to those reduced to it to avoid worse indignities, they are not responsible for the indignity. The choice to remain silent may be, unfortunately, as dignified as any open to them. I will return to this after looking more closely at passing and outing.

Passing and What Is Problematic About It

A common first reaction to outing is to find it a morally disgusting betrayal. Yet, few shut their ears to it in particular instances. For, the passing that outing disrupts is often itself highly problematic.

Secrecy about socially stigmatized identities or histories protects the livelihood, social connections, and family connections of the passer. When an identity is stigmatized, as with many minority ethnic identities and health histories or statuses (such as being diabetic, alcoholic, epileptic, or HIV positive), passing becomes problematic not only for the passer, who is drawn into systematic deception, but for others who share the identity as well. For, their cooperation is usually required. Thus, many who for one reason or another cannot pass and, ironically, some who resist oppression by *refusing* to pass, may be called on to protect the passing of others.

Successful passing hides one's status as a target of oppression. As

Mohr points out, for an oppressor, the next best thing to eliminating a group may be to render it imperceptible. A group imperceptible to its own members is politically impotent. A cultural group may be killed by being cut off from its roots, losing the meanings of inherited practices, as contemporary Indian Catholics of New Mexico who are descended from sixteenth-century Mexican "Conversos" have been cut off from their Jewish roots. In addition to being practicing Catholics, many have for centuries also practiced Jewish customs privately at home, isolated from Jewish community, *no longer knowing what the customs mean or even that they are Jewish*.[17] The same may be true of their Indian customs inherited from cultures that are no longer as clearly identifiable as Jewish cultures are today. Although lesbians and gay men are not in danger of dying out, lesbian and gay cultures share that danger. For centuries, we have had to rediscover lesbian and gay cultures, or reinvent them.

As Mohr insists, however, more is at issue than political strategy. Dignity, as he has argued elsewhere, may remain even when justice fails.[18] And if the stigmatizing of one's identity is *demeaning*, the question arises whether *failure to protest* is *also* demeaning, even if protest is ineffective as an instrument of social change.

In a different context, political philosopher Bernard Boxill argues that failure to protest oppression directed against oneself may rob one of evidence of one's self-respect.[19] Passers often do not begin by sharing their oppressors' values. Hiding can reflect deserved distrust or contempt of others rather than shame regarding what one hides. And yet, letting major wrongful images and judgments of oneself stand uncontested eventually endangers one's sense of self-worth in the way that a continuous pretense of servility does. Discussing the controversial "Sambo" personality, Boxill argues that even if Sambo is a fraud, his clowning a mask "to salvage his dignity," even if he is engaged in a "deadly serious game" in which "the perfect stroke of rebellion must ideally appear to the master as the ultimate act of submission," Sambo himself must have occasion to wonder what evidence he has that this pretense is *only* a pretense and not a true picture of who he has become, for "unless it is already known to be pretense, apparent servility is evidence of servility."[20] Reflecting on the contrasting views of W. E. B. DuBois and Booker T. Washington about protesting racism, Boxill argues that those who have to appease oppressors by not offending them come to need evidence of their own self-respect: "When an individual desires to know whether he has self-respect, what he needs is not evidence of his worth in general but evidence of his faith in his worth" and protest "may be an excellent way of confirming that one has faith in one's worth" (p. 195).

Passing is analogous to (perhaps an instance of) at least a pretense of servility. Like servility (real or pretended), it impedes one's ability to protest. Lacking evidence of our faith in our own worth, we become superficial or fall prey to self-doubt. Either way, we are demeaned. Complicity in others' passing can likewise threaten our sense of self-worth, as it easily engages us in hypocrisy regarding values applying as much to ourselves as to those we help to hide.

Passing and complicity can also demean others who share the identity. Failure to resist an oppressive requirement has the consequence of supporting it. When a requirement of secrecy would be justified only were the secret shameful, compliance conveys that the secret *is* shameful, however unintended the message. As an act of defiance, outing may set right some of this wrong. Yet, the question remains whether in doing so it wrongs those who are outed. Some even object to outing the dead, who cannot defend themselves against our mistakes or interpretations and reinterpretations of who they were.

Outing the Dead

If Aristotle could ask whether the fortunes of descendants affect the happiness of the dead, we can ask whether outing the dead does them wrong.[21]

The case that brought outing to public notice was the outing of someone who had died (Malcolm Forbes). Yet, it is paradoxical, perhaps equivocal, to call this "outing." For the person is no longer around to bring out. All that can come out is the secret. The person is gone, neither "in" nor "out." Nevertheless, revealing a dead person's secrets can change the way that life, now ended, is perceived by others, and insofar as the meaning of a life is a social construction, it might be argued that outing can have implications even for lives that have ended. The meaning goes on, so to speak, even after the life has stopped.

Here, it seems to me, the dignity defense of "outing" is least problematic. Objections to tarnishing the deceased's memory seem to assume that having been gay or lesbian is a stain. The concern of some survivors, however, may be to avoid the indignity of exposing that the deceased led a double life. This indignity (which the deceased cannot experience) does need to be weighed against other indignities, such as those involved in the continuing support of the closet (which is experienced by many). A memory can also be undeservedly trashed. Yet, there may be no way to vindicate the deceased's truth without risking that. Objections to social inconveniences suffered by survivors who are not themselves lesbian or gay suggest that they care too much for the favor of those whose opinions demean the memory of the deceased, and such concern seems itself demeaning to that memory.

The main consideration regarding outing the dead, however, is not what it does to or for them, as such, but what it does to or for others. Resolution of the question whether to out the dead has implications for education and research and consequently, for the general fund of knowledge available to a society. A serious scholar of lesbian or gay culture will inevitably out and raise questions about many deceased. Gag rules here stifle scholarship and perpetuate major distortions of fact, past and present. Outing the dead is an excellent way to demonstrate, especially to the very young, that honorable people and honorable relationships have been lesbian or gay. It has the great merit of not risking the exposure of those outed to loss of livelihood or other opportunities, to bodily gay-bashing, to interference with child custody, or even to disinheritance.

In teaching lesbian culture, I routinely encourage library detective work: figuring out where to find the lesbians, where to find lesbian history, literature, philosophy, and so on. Most of it is still not identified in catalogues except where the word "lesbian" appears in relevant titles. I encourage students to evaluate material by and about women for possible lesbian content, to recognize clues in code words, for example, and to work with a family resemblance conception of "lesbian" that embraces many kinds of relationships (see chapter 1). One could claim with merit that I incite students to engage in outing the dead, as I present sharing the results of such searches and evaluations in class presentations as an honorable activity (even though we have not shared them with the newspapers).

Occasionally a student reports that another teacher objects to my treating as lesbian a writer, such as Emily Dickinson, who did not apply that "label" to herself. The objection may not be intended as a moral one so much as the logical one that it is ahistorical to identify people as lesbian or gay when they lived in a social context that did not recognize such identities. However, I do not hear similar objections to less stigmatizing "labels," such as "modernist" and "postmodernist." In any case, identifying past lives as lesbian or gay need not be ahistorical in the sense of ignoring social contexts, the options they defined, past vocabularies, and so on. We can seek to understand what it was or was not possible to hide and reveal about same-sex erotic and sexual attachments in other periods.[22] Not wronging the dead is basically a matter of getting it right regarding what it was like for them, appreciating their standpoints and struggles, and that is worth striving for.

An important difference between recent gay outing and the way I "out" the dead in teaching lesbian culture is that the evidence with which I work in teaching is already published—letters, diaries, poetry, fiction, biographies, essays—rather than previously unpublished personal papers, memories, or implied confidences. This is not paradigm outing, although, like paradigm outing, it involves revelation and sometimes exposes secrets. Researchers in archives of *un*published materials have opportunities genuinely to out a lesbian life or relationship.

Such an opportunity confronted Doris Faber when the Lorena Hickok archives were opened in 1978. Researching new material for a biography of Eleanor Roosevelt (ER), Doris Faber discovered in the newly opened archives a passionate set of love letters between "Hick" and ER. When her efforts to have the correspondence resealed until the year 2000 were unsuccessful, she dropped her plans to write the biography of ER and wrote instead a biography of Lorena Hickok—as ER's *friend*, intending to minimize as much as possible "Hick's" role in ER's life.[23] In a "Personal Note," she cites her concern about what others might have done with such letters "taken out of context" had she not assumed this responsibility (pp. 331–32). Evidently, she hoped to prevent a posthumous outing of the relationship. However, revealing that "ER's friend" lived in the White House for four years during the Roosevelt presidency and gave ER a ring studded with diamonds (which ER wore on her little finger), and offering choice quotes from the letters, which she annotated to explain away lesbian implications, her book became one of the funniest unintentional outings in contemporary biography.

Directors of art museums no doubt confront decisions comparable to those of library archivists. Ponder, for a moment, the following, from the British Chief Magistrate at the trial of the publisher Jonathan Cape in 1928 regarding Radclyffe Hall's banned lesbian novel, *The Well of Loneliness*: "There is a room at Naples to which visitors are not admitted as a rule, which contains fine bronzes and statues, all admirable works of art, but all grossly obscene."[24] How many works of art are hidden in back rooms because someone did not want the artist, or the artist's subjects, to become known as homosexual? Given the vast body of heterosexual art, including art depicting rape, shamelessly on display throughout the world, it would be astonishing if famous sculptors left no gorgeous bronzes and statuary depicting men in same-sex sexual behavior.

Here, the ethical issues seem relatively straightforward ones of honesty in correcting or amplifying the historical record and confronting public fears and hostilities. Outing the dead can no longer make *them* suffer, rob *them* of choices and opportunities, or interfere with the course of *their* lives and *their* relationships with others, and these are the main differences, ethically, from outing the living. Of course, not only may it embarrass survivors but also, depending on the timing, it may not be possible to out the dead without also outing some of the living. For this and other reasons, the practice can be expected to affect record-keeping and estate-planning, and it does. Lorena Hickok, who died at the age of seventy-five, specified that the cartons of letters that she donated to the Franklin D. Roosevelt Library in Hyde Park, New York, remain sealed until ten years after her death. However, she also wanted them perfectly open to interested researchers thereafter.

Uptake and Source

It may not matter ethically who outs the dead, and where the information is primarily of interest to scholars, uptake may be difficult to gauge. However, in outing the living, the source of the revelation is logically important to the concept, and it contributes to the moral interest of the practice. And uptake is necessary to achieving its point.

Consider, first, the logical significance of uptake. As with streaking, the context of the act matters. If you run naked across a dark residential street at three in the morning when everyone else is asleep, it is not *really* streaking. You need witnesses. And they need to be surprised. Paradigm streakers might run naked at high noon through a busy restaurant or around the capitol square. If you offer information that no one acknowledges, it is not yet outing. Thus, Mohr defines "outing" as "making publicly acknowledged the sexual orientations of a homosexual without regard to whether the person is willing to have this information publicly acknowledged."[25] "Making acknowledged" implies uptake, as when a newspaper prints the information as news. Uptake does not imply persuasion, but it does imply being taken seriously, treated as credible.

Consider next the logical significance of the source. Mohr's definition does not include the gay or lesbian identity of the outer, and yet that is generally assumed in his and in most discussions using the term "outing." The gay or lesbian identity of the source clearly contributes certain kinds of moral interest to the practice. It underlies initial reactions of moral disgust and the sense of a betrayal, for example. It is at work in the idea that an apparently mitigating factor is that outers seem not to be asking others to risk what they do not risk themselves.[26] It is central to the dignity defense. It is also tied to the meaning of the concept. Anyone can reveal others' gay or lesbian secrets. But calling it "outing" implies violating a presumption of secret-keeping, and not just anyone is in a position to violate such a presumption. Those who regard homosexual behavior as dangerous or disgusting do not generally belong to communities that have presumptions favoring lesbian and gay secret-keeping. When such individuals tell what they know, it is not outing, even if the content of the revelation is the same. It has been said that the military is guilty of more outing over the years than lesbian and gay activists. However, the military viewed itself, during the history of its inquisitions, as exposing violations of its own policies, not as violating a presumption of secrecy that it officially shared.[27] Bargaining with gay men and lesbians for names of others does rely on outing, however, and participation of closeted lesbian and gay military personnel in identifying and prosecuting others generally is rightly enough considered outing.

The question whether attorneys should have a right to question prospective jurors about their sexuality would raise paradigm issues of outing only if the parties on whose behalf they were to be questioned were lesbian or gay (or were so connected as to be in a position to violate presumptions of lesbian or gay secrecy). As long as lesbians and gay men lack protection against discrimination and are poorly protected against hate crimes, a right to question prospective jurors about their sexual orientation could be expected to deter many lesbians and gay men from willing jury service.

Coming Out vs. Outing

As elaborated in the previous chapter, coming out, publicly embracing one's lesbian or gay experience, identity, or connections as honorable, challenges the stigma against these things.[28] Coming out is done in print, public lectures, interviews, conversation, even parades with banners proclaiming "Gay is Good."[29] Usually, it is less exhibitionist (although it raises more eyebrows) than common heterosexual displays of marriage and parenthood. It may be misperceived as sexually exhibitionist. However, what it displays is an identity, history, or heritage, not sexual acts. Outings are often similarly misperceived. Dispelling the confusion between revealing an identity and revealing agents engaged in sexual acts is important to Mohr's argument that outing does not violate defensible privacy rights.[30] Outing offers no peep shows. It does not give bedroom access. It exposes facts, not acts. And the facts exposed are not only sexual but as often social or affiliational and frequently political.

Coming out and outing are often done for political goals, with or without concern for dignity. For those who regard coming out as instrumental to political resistance or revolution, the choice whether to come out appears to exemplify a "prisoner's dilemma" confronting the oppressed.[31] Drawing on work by philosopher Allen Buchanan, Boxill, in a discussion of race and class, presents the dilemma as follows: if only a few join, the revolution will fail and their efforts will be wasted; if enough join, the revolution will succeed, and their efforts will be superfluous.[32] Thus everyone appears to have sufficient self-interested reason not to join, regardless of what others do, with the result that there will be no revolution, which is, by hypothesis, contrary to the interests of all the oppressed. However, Boxill goes on to point out, this formulation ignores that for many oppressed, joining is *hardly a cost*, as they have little that valuable to lose. The first part of the formulation—that if only a few join, their efforts will be wasted—may describe a consideration that does not move them. They can afford such "waste." In the present case, those with least to lose are not passing. Those least likely to be able to pass may come out voluntarily in order to be politically effective. Outing others might then seem to them an ingenious way to enlist support for the revolution: why wait for volunteers when you can blow their cover so they will no longer have so much to lose?

Or, so it may seem *a priori*. In fact, as others have observed, outed celebrities often respond with unremitting denials and sometimes resort to such cover-ups as marriage.[33] Organizing with others is good reason to *come* out but not, as Mohr points out, good reason to out others, who may not be moved to exploit their new status politically. Longtime passers may not feel oppressed by the closet (though they may feel oppressed by outers). Still, having to protect passers can impede the political effectiveness of those who already live openly as gay or lesbian. Signorile found that it hindered him as an activist journalist.[34] For such reasons, activists may be tempted to out public figures, regardless of the politics of those they out.

A moral difference between coming out and outing, however, is that the price of disclosure is paid by oneself in the first case but by others in the second, and although one has the consent of the first party (oneself), one lacks it (by hypothesis) for others. It may seem to mitigate this difference that outers who are themselves out appear to be exposing others only to costs they have shown a willingness to risk themselves. I will have occasion to revisit that assumption, however.

Suppose one agrees that the closet is demeaning and that this is a good reason to come out (or refuse to go in). Does it follow that it also is a good reason for outing? Is outing, as Mohr put it, an expectable consequence of lesbians and gay men living morally, so long as the government is not shooting lesbians and gay men? What if hate-groups and stalkers, such as Stephen Roy Carr (who shot Rebecca Wight and Claudia Brenner), are doing the killing that the government is not doing?[35] What if the government is ready to deport lesbians or gay men who are not citizens to lands considerably less tolerant? Or forcibly discharge citizens from military service, refusing their pensions even at the point of retirement after decades of honorable or even exemplary service? These are not rare circumstances. Rather than arguing that such risks do not count when dignity is at stake, one might note, in the spirit of Boxill's argument, that such risks to lesbians and gay men are *already* substantial, even without outing—Stephen Roy Carr, for example, appears to have drawn his own conclusions—so that if something important might be gained from outing, perhaps such risks ought not to defeat it.

Yet, there are difficult questions of distributing responsibility for resisting the indignities that lesbian and gay people have suffered. It is one thing to *take* responsibility for resisting the indignities in one's own life. It is another to lay such responsibility on others with respect to the indignities in theirs.

Hiding, no matter how justified, is not a dignified way to live. In hiding, one lives furtively, treads carefully, looks constantly over one's shoulder. This is not dignified behavior. Dignity suggests the metaphor of holding up one's head—being open, unguarded, at ease, not nervous or anxious. Aristotle's famous description of the proud man captures a paradigm of dignity: "it would be most unbecoming for a proud man to fly from danger, swinging his arms by his sides. . . . He must also be open in his hate and in his love. . . . Further, a slow step is thought proper to the proud man, a deep voice, and a level utterance."[36]

However, although hiding is undignified, it need not stem from shame or deficient self-respect. One who enters a witness protection program, for example, may have done the honorable thing in testifying, even though the consequence is a life spent in hiding.[37] Still, though the need to hide is attributable to others' wrongdoing, hiding may *produce* shame and undermine self-respect in one who hides precisely *because* it requires undignified behavior. One can be ashamed of not being able to hold up one's head, regardless of the cause. Constant fear raises self-doubts about courage, undermining self-respect. Such consequences raise the question whether even hiding produced by honorable choices is ultimately worth it. Self-respect and honor may lead one to reject such a life.

But where coming out would be honorable or self-respecting, it does not follow that it is honorable to out those who fail to do the honorable thing themselves. As Mill argued in *On Liberty*, separate justifications are in order for the judgment that an action is wrong and the further judgment that others' preventing that action would be right.[38] The latter does not follow straight off from the former. Applied to the case at hand, separate justifications are in order for the judgments that passing is wrong and that outing is right. Mill's condition, that to be justifiably preventable, conduct must be harmful to others, is satisfied where passing demeans not only the passer but others as well. Still, this condition is at most necessary, not sufficient. There remains the question whether interference may not do a greater harm, even to dignity, than it prevents. There is also the question whether we might find less harmful ways than outing individuals to undo the damage to lesbian and gay dignity that passing supports.

In many contexts, it is important to contrast considerations of *welfare* with considerations of *dignity*. One may be poor and unfortunate in many respects without losing one's dignity. In the case of the harm done by socially sanctioned hatred, however, that contrast is not sharp. Even Mill did not adhere strictly to a utilitarian understanding of welfare but counted the cultivation of a sense of dignity a great benefit and its loss or injury a serious harm. Harms to basic well-being, such as bodily integrity, *are* indignities. Recall Deuteronomy's prohibition against punishing an offender with more than forty lashes, lest "your neighbor . . . be degraded in your sight."[39] Outing facilitates gay-bashing, which, like more than forty lashes, assaults both life and dignity. An irony of arguing that outing need not violate defensible privacy rights is the implied suggestion that the outed are still protected in their privacy.

This ignores the outlaw status of lesbians and gay men. Outlaws are unprotected in their persons, let alone their privacy, by legal rights. Even though facilitating hostile access is not the point of principled outing, can outers morally wash their hands of it?

"Dirty hands" from exposing the outed to hate crimes may not imply that the act is unjustified, all things considered. Analogous stances have been defended by some who would resist terrorism. Even though individuals are irreparably wronged—as they may be when hostage-takers' demands are not met—the same may be true of the alternatives, and the alternatives may also be worse.[40] However, insofar as what is problematic about complicity in passing is that it supports oppressive concealment, there may be better ways than outing living individuals to undermine forced closeting. Three other ways to do this are to *come out oneself* and try to persuade others to do so, to out the *dead* judiciously, and to seek publicity for lesbian and gay *groups* (and for lesbians and gays as members of other groups) rather than for lesbian and gay individuals. To be most effective, to convey an appropriate sense of how widely we are distributed and how honorable our lives can be, we should come out in many contexts, seek to expose many kinds of past lives, and publicize many groups of us, conveying our presence in many walks of life, rather than emphasizing one abstract figure, such as ten percent. The point that "we are everywhere"—which disrupts stereotypes, myths, and public denials—may be communicable by information using percentages in many areas without names and by using representative names of those deceased and those who choose to live openly. To take an example, the Society for Lesbian and Gay Philosophy exists publicly as a satellite of the American Philosophical Association (APA), although its membership list is confidential. The Central Division of the APA, in which the Society was founded, waived its usual membership list requirement for the organization's application (although membership in the Society is open to all in the profession), accepting instead a report of how many we were, with a token list of members whose identities were already public.

There is also something to be said for others having to become more conscious that they *do not* know which of their neighbors we are. Fed up with finding herself continually an involuntary auditor of racist remarks, light-skinned artist and philosopher Adrian Piper distributed "calling cards" that said, in part, "I am black. I am sure you did not realize this when you made/laughed at/agreed with that racist remark. I regret any discomfort my presence is causing you just as I am sure you regret the discomfort your racism is causing me."[41] Gay and lesbian adaptations are readily imaginable. Without exposing others against their will, such innovative strategies may be sufficient to embarrass the average bigot and put a damper on the kind of humor that supports passing.

Outing individuals may be necessary to prevent or stop cruelty, to address or redress major injustices. Outing was necessary for Karen Thompson to address the needs of her partner Sharon Kowalski after the car accident that left Sharon Kowalski brain-damaged, unable to move her limbs or communicate in usual ways.[42] Outing may be necessary to address partner battery or stalking. And where tax-supported institutions use closeted lesbians and gay men to persecute others of us, outing may be necessary to expose and sabotage that corruption.

Who Is Revealed?

In outing the dead, what is outed is a history. In outing the living, however, one outs a *person* with potentialities still unfolding. For some, outing may be just the push they need for growth, as for Representative Gerry Studds, who was outed and embraced the consequences with honor.[43] In other cases, however, outing is more a liability than an asset to gay dignity.

"Outing," like "coming out," comes from the expression "living in the closet." Yet, the closet metaphor is no longer very apt for many of the lives it is still commonly invoked to describe. The metaphor suggests a life that is hidden away. But "living in the closet" has become a euphemism for lying and deception on the part of people whose lives are in many ways very public.

"Living in the closet" is not an apt metaphor for passers who are already out in gay or lesbians communities, those who live in what Signorile refers to as "the Revolving Closet," who are closeted on the job from nine to five but out in town at night.[44] Historically, it was not the desires of lesbians or gay men for security that led to the closet. It was the desire of kin to keep things "all in the family" to preserve their own reputation. We used to come out into gay or lesbian communities instead of keeping our secrets at home or locked in our hearts. When I first discovered "closets" in the 1950s, being closeted meant not yet having had an overtly homosexual relationship, not having disclosed one's desires to anyone; it meant living in a fantasy world much of the time. "Coming out" meant both "seeing the light" and getting *involved*—which makes better sense of the metaphor than simply "going public," which is all that "coming out" often seems to mean today.

Closets restrict mobility. In closets, we watch life through a keyhole instead of participating actively. Closets call to mind the proverbial skeleton hidden *by others*. Those who hide on the job often protect their own interests more than those of their families. With access to gay or lesbian communities, we are not so impoverished as in closets. Communities offer mobility and colleagues, relationships of trust and affection, checks on our perceptions. They can be sites of revolutionary politics. Passers who visit only pass through; they do not live there much, or they could not pass. But *neither are they closeted*. Those who "pass" are *mobile*. This is what it *means* to "pass." They do not just observe. They participate in many worlds. They lead at least double lives. A *mask* is a better metaphor than a closet. For some, after years, it may be masks all the way down, or better, to the core. An onion (or artichoke) may be an even better metaphor.

Probably few of us are such thorough onions or artichokes. Outing, like coming out, has degrees. In urban centers many whose lives are not on the whole very public are out to friends and acquaintances but remain closeted (masked) with respect to parents or bosses, where there is less choice in the relationship and much hinges on it.

Thus, "outing" is usually unmasking, blowing someone's cover, usually someone with a sufficiently public life that the cover is substantial. And what *do* we find underneath? A problem with blowing someone's cover when you value what was covered and care about the person is that you risk "outing" the person not only as gay or lesbian but also as a moral coward, a liar, a chameleon, a sleaze—depending on how the cover was maintained, how much of a lifetime was invested in it, who was deceived and why. At least, you risk making the person *appear* sleazy. It is difficult to imagine such revelations doing valuable things for gay dignity. Few have displayed the character of a Gerry Studds in turning the event into an occasion for public rebirth. When a pretense has become basic to one's lifestyle, one can expect others rightly to wonder what else one has concealed, especially if the concealment was for personal or political advancement. Passers who are truly cowards or opportunists are skeletons on the loose in lesbian and gay communities, better shoved *into* closets, if we could.

Of course, some hide not for themselves but to protect partners whose situations are more precarious than their own with respect to career loss, disinheritance, loss of child custody or of child visitation rights, and so on—all knowledge that outers may easily lack.

It is not only gay or lesbian dignity that injudicious outings jeopardize. Outing risks disrespecting others' self-concepts or choices where no deception is involved. Some with lesbian or gay experience lead basically heterosexual lives and make a point of not wanting to mislead lesbians or gay men about that. Others embrace bisexuality. Some refuse labels. Although not everyone's sexual identity is ambiguous, such identities lack a sharpness that would enable one to answer clearly to "is she, or isn't she?" wherever she has not declared herself.[45] A difficulty with outing—as with coming out—is that it oversimplifies and easily misleads. This is not usually a good reason not to *come* out. But it may be a good reason to be careful about outing others. Outing often reveals enough to set a public on fire, but seldom enough for the public to understand what the information means in the lives of those outed, who may have no interest in publicly clarifying matters.

A further problem is that the *kind* of uptake required for the intended outing may not be the kind that is forthcoming, with the consequence, again, that attempted outings easily misfire. Outing is what many contemporary philosophers, following Oxford analytic philosopher John Austin, would call an "illocutionary act," that is, "the performance of an act *in* saying something as opposed to performance of an act *of* saying something."[46] Saying "I do" in the context of a marriage ceremony is an illocutionary act, not simply a self-description. It is an act that, in this case, changes one's status. The problem with the illocutionary act of outing is that one may easily end up doing something unintended and failing to do what one did intend, thanks to conflicting understandings and widespread misunderstandings of the concepts, "gay," "lesbian," and "homosexual." The meaning of "lesbian," for example, is presently both in flux and in dispute. Lesbian feminist communities are working to reshape its meaning independently of medical, psychiatric, and legal histories. For many, lesbian life is not focused on sex. When shared understandings cannot be presumed, uptake may be wrong, with the result that individuals become saddled with false and even strange reputations, such as being "a man in a woman's body," being totally preoccupied with sex, or being sexually aggressive, promiscuous, or even a child molester.[47] Where such ideas are still prevalent, "living in the truth" requires more than outing can achieve.

Because stigmas usually rest on false beliefs, openness is often the best way, if not the only way, to correct them. This is often a major reason to come out, to be in a better position to dispel misunderstandings of who we are. However, as suggested above, it may be a poor reason to out others, who may not be motivated to fight stereotypes. Many who are closeted *subscribe* to myths and stereotypes but consider themselves exceptions. Like outing cowards, outing self-deceivers may be more a liability than an asset to gay dignity and public education, even if it is just the dash of cold water that some need.

What Is Revealed?

Can we be confident that outing will not disrespect others' privacy? The claim that lesbian or gay secrets can be revealed without invading privacy rests on the idea that all outing gives others access to is an *identity or orientation*, not the bedroom, of the outed. Abstract facts and identities are all we generally mean to reveal even in *coming* out.[48] However, it may be difficult to avoid subjecting the outed to gossip regarding specific relationships. Privacy at this level is not legally protected but is commonly valued and widely respected.

To gain credibility, it may be difficult to stick to abstractions or even to particulars that are already publicly known. One easily slides into telling stories. Nothing convinces of the veracity of the teller like knowledge of specific detail, especially details previously inaccessible. Names in a gay newspaper may be enough for gay community. But outsiders want more. Scandal sheets expose particular affairs shamelessly, characteristically revealing *only* details, letting readers infer identities and histories.

Going public with something removes a lot of control over it. The following case is illustrative. In 1985 the Naiad Press published *Lesbian Nuns: Breaking Silence*, an anthology of autobiographical narratives edited by ex-nuns Rosemary Curb and Nancy Manahan. Aiming for publicity and wide sales, the Press sold serial rights to *Forum* magazine, which happened to be owned by Penthouse International, and *Forum* printed excerpts under a dayglo orange heading, "Sex Lives of Lesbian Nuns," focusing on sexual experience in the convent and cutting "almost all references to platonic friendships, spirituality, convent ethics, and feminist views."[49] Barbara Grier of Naiad is quoted as saying, "there is no way that you can take non-prurient material and make it prurient" (p. 91). Others who read both *Lesbian Nuns* and the *Forum* magazine article disagreed. According to one reader, "In the pages of *Forum*, the stories of three lesbian ex-nuns become the literary equivalent of the female body parts that appear regularly in mainstream advertising and men's magazines" (p. 91). Subsequently, at least one contributor to *Lesbian Nuns* was reported to have lost her teaching job. It was not just publication that was at issue (Naiad had already published the book) but *excerpting* in a context that distorted the meaning of the work and the lives portrayed. Because outing generally carries the risk of excerpting our lives in ways disrespectful of ordinary privacy, it may be as likely to subject us to indignities as to vindicate a sense of our worth.

What About Trust?

If outing jeopardizes trust in lesbian or gay community, it jeopardizes conditions that have made lesbian and gay dignity as possible as it is today.

Many rules protect trust in society at large. Ordinarily, secret-keeping that requires lying is considered problematic. Telling a secret to avoid lying requires balancing considerations all of which respect trust. Volunteering information promiscuously is of a different order from responding to direct requests from legitimately interested parties. Some deserve truthful responses where one would not be wise to offer truths unasked. Silence that is not a source of others' distorted values is of a different order from declarations that presuppose those values. And those who remain silent need not be selling out for security or advantage, even though others may use their silence for oppressive ends. Where such nuanced distinctions are frequently important, trust is not spontaneous. It must be earned over time.

Special conventions protect trust among members of a stigmatized group. Mohr points out that the "gag rule" protecting passers is a convention of gay communities, and that this rule, rather than promises to individuals, is usually the source of gay complicity in others' passing. He urges violating this convention. When conventions are violated, new issues of trust arise. Violating a convention as a matter of conscience is a little like civil disobedience. In civil disobedience, it can be important to put others on notice of one's intentions, so they do not mistakenly rely upon one in ways that they otherwise might. Until relatively recently, lesbian and gay secret-keeping was generally reciprocal. Now that many live openly, such reciprocity cannot be presumed. Despite continued widespread observance of the "gag rule," among those who live openly there is no longer consensus about keeping others' secrets. Perhaps passers should know better than to so entangle their lives with those openly lesbian or gay as to risk being outed inadvertently. Equally, perhaps those who are open should know better than to become beholden to those who live in closets. If being open about oneself is not sufficient notice to others, or if one goes public in the midst of relationships and transactions, one could put others on notice explicitly, saying: (continue to) associate with me at your risk; I will go out of my way neither to out you nor to help you maintain your cover.

It may be, as Mohr acknowledges, that as a result of widespread outing, some would be reluctant to come out into lesbian or gay communities. This, he argues, would result in improved quality of the community: the price of admission would be higher.[50] This argument sounds high-minded. However, the quality of the community is a function also of what it can do for its members. Many who refused to join such a community would no doubt form their own—many, mutually isolated communities, returning to pre-1950s gay life.[51] Only recently have we have able to refer casually to "the" lesbian or gay community. Advantages of larger communities include—besides greater funds, more workers, improved communications, and easier outreach—enabling younger generations to know where to turn. High rates of lesbian and gay teen suicides, for example, indicate that what is at stake in preserving such a haven is not just material advantage.[52] My town has a grant-giving organization supporting lesbian and gay educational and health projects and supported in turn by subscriptions from working lesbians and gay men, including many who support such causes anonymously. These projects improve possibilities for many to live with dignity. As long as public taxes do not support lesbian and gay interests, distrust discouraging lesbians and gay men with access to resources from forming such organizations would be a major loss, not to politics in a sense that is opposed to dignity, but to a politics that has at its heart enhancing lesbian and gay dignity.

Cruising may have produced more well-defined conventions of trust for men than lesbian life has produced among women. I know nothing corresponding to the rule Mohr cites about no talking in bathhouse orgy rooms.[53] Aside from such variations, the considerations discussed so far seem more or less the same for lesbians as for gay men. However, when I think of trust specifically in relation to women in a sexist society, I think not so much of rules or conventions as of feminist bonding that would be jeopardized by women offering information to a male-dominated public about stigmatized histories of other women. There is something ancient about such betrayals. Both men and women have been betraying women to men for ages. Although patriarchy has a long and strong history of same-sex bonding among men, women have had hard work to develop mutual trust against the background of stereotypes as devious, untrustworthy manipulators. Outing threatens to confirm the indignity of those stereotypes and to do so doubly, first by revealing the lesbian who outs others as betraying other lesbians' trust and second, by revealing outed lesbians as having led duplicitous lives. Analogous considerations apply to members of other oppressed groups. Like women, relatively powerless men—the poor, for example, and members of stigmatized minorities—have also been stereotyped as liars. Recall Nietzsche's memorable stereotype of the "lying, common man."[54]

It may be objected that stereotypes of untrustworthiness cut both ways where protecting passing requires lies. In such a case, untrustworthiness seems an issue whether one lies or not. However, lesbians who protect the cover of lesbians (or gay men) in a misogynist, heterosexist society do not jeopardize the trust of that society; as lesbians, we have no such trust to lose. Outing, on the other hand, betrays lesbians (or gay men) to a society that has a history of using us against each other, encouraging divisiveness, making us easier to dominate. Resisting misogyny, many lesbians share information widely with women—lesbian or not—but hardly at all with men. If misogyny removes temptations among lesbians to out each other to men or to a male-dominated public, racism similarly removes temptations for lesbian and gay people of color to out each other to a society dominated by white privilege.

Appreciation of misogyny also gives gay men reason not to out lesbians, as appreciation of white racism gives white lesbians and gay men reason not to out those of color. Gay men who are white tend to be "everywhere," as the slogan goes, in all kinds of jobs and positions. "We are everywhere" is less true of lesbians, not so much because we are lesbian—that is often not evident—but because we are female. And it is less true of lesbians and gay men of color, of working-class lesbians and gay men, disabled lesbians and gay men, older lesbians and gay men, fat lesbians and gay men. Many occupations and qualifying programs have only recently been open to any but healthy young able-bodied middle-class white men. Equal opportunity for desirable positions is often little more than rhetoric. The desirability of positions is measurable not just in income but also in freedom, responsibility, and the self-fulfilling potentialities—one could say, the dignity—of the work. Women and gay men who are not white, middle class, young, slim, or able-bodied, and who lose such positions have far fewer and less desirable options remaining. Of course, full-time occupations ought not to be divided into those that offer meaningful work and those that do not. But it does nothing toward correcting this pattern to out those in positions that do offer meaningful work. More likely, it allows the positions to be passed on to others for whom they will mean less, because of the richer range of options that would remain to them in any case.

Recall that one thing making the dignity argument sound dignified was that lesbians or gay men who are already out appear to be in a good position to out others, in that they seem not to be asking others to take risks or suffer losses that they have not taken or suffered themselves. It should be evident by now that such an appearance is superficial. It results from seeing lesbians and gay men as only lesbian or gay and not also as having or lacking the social privileges or liabilities attaching to gender, class, color, ethnicity, and so on. A deeper look suggests that few are well-positioned to out very many others. It is probably no accident that the outing game seems to have been played mostly by relatively privileged white men.

To take the position that it is all right to out others as a matter of course can have as a consequence that anyone who is lesbian or gay may be forced, in self-defense, to prioritize that aspect of their lives. For some, being lesbian or gay may rightly not seem to them the most significant aspect of their lives, especially after it has not been news to them for many years. Even if oppressions are interconnected, as individuals we usually need to set priorities to be effective. The "gag rules" that protect the callous, the complacent, and the greedy also respect and can protect our choices about which honorable battles to enter.

Lesbian and gay communities are not communities of origin for their vast majorities. Lesbian and gay histories are not histories of "peoples." Like Deaf Culture, lesbian and gay culture develops in communities consciously chosen, politically formed by individuals who have other communities of origin.[55] Lesbian and gay communities also tend to be culturally biased in favor of their majorities. Even when they are concerned to combat oppression in a general way, as many are, they may not offer the best environments for members of many cultural groups to develop pride in their origins and work together to resist oppression or racism.

The best existing environments for such work are sometimes, unfortunately, homophobic and heterosexist. Silence about one's sexuality in such a context need not be for the sake of security or advantage; both are likely to be at risk in resisting racism. Controlling the timing of one's own coming out may be crucial to being able to assert one's dignity under other aspects of one's identity with their own associated histories of oppression.[56] Outers who do not share the same communities of origin are apt to be in a poor position to gauge such timing.

To deny that those who pass or are complicit in passing are selling out is not to deny that the silence is demeaning. However, it is the *need* for silence that is responsible for the indignity. It is demeaning that such hiding or silence should ever be one's best option. Our possibilities for living with dignity are not simply a function of our individual attitudes and choices. They are also, to some extent, a matter of moral luck, a function of many heritages. Some groups have more opportunity than others to live with dignity.

When it is possible, living in the truth is generally easier. Hiding is stressful. "Commit a crime," observed Emerson, "and the earth is made of glass."[57] But living in the truth is also a privilege, not always securable simply by speaking out.

I have argued that outing individuals may be an unnecessarily harmful way to assert lesbian or gay dignity, that it can be as undignified as complicity with passing, that the circumstances of the multiply oppressed may offer the choice of effectively asserting dignity under some facets of one's identity only at the cost of maintaining silence about others, and that indignity may not be entirely avoidable by the individual efforts of some. I conclude that valuing lesbian or gay dignity will seldom support publicizing the identities of friends and acquaintances to a public that will spit on them, or even telling the truth when asked outright by most members of such a public. In a world of multiple oppressions and misfortunes, many not readily apparent, I favor a *presumption* of reticence *about others* who choose not to live openly in nonlesbian and nongay publics. Lesbian and gay communities make possible the openness needed for faith in ourselves, and they do so not as a result of outing but thanks to many who voluntarily live openly.

I also favor a *general* public reticence regarding living others, rich or poor, who may be targets of, or have heritages of, *any* kind of oppression, whose circumstances one seldom knows as fully as one may think. Such reticence is overridable in cases like Sharon Kowalski's or where other serious and preventable or remediable injustice is at stake. Yet I would not override it for the sake of "living in the truth" in a mendacious public.

Chapter 11

consensual sadomasochism: charting the issues

I have saved this subject for last because the topic has been so contested among lesbians (and among feminists, generally; it has not been much contested—at least in print—among gay men), and I wanted to be able to draw freely, in discussing it, on material from earlier chapters. In a decade of teaching lesbian culture, I have found no topic more divisive in the classroom than consensual sexual sadomasochism. Yet on no topic has it been more difficult to generate discussion. There are many reasons.

First, lesbian sexuality suffers from a vocabulary problem, making it difficult to discuss any lesbian sexuality and tempting to borrow others' vocabularies, which are often inadequate or inappropriate.[1] Second, Women's Studies students tend to be acutely aware of potentialities for causing offense through insensitivity. They realize that the class may include survivors of incest and other child abuse, rape, or partner battery, survivors who are not sadomasochists. Some students simply find the idea of sadomasochism repulsive. The class may also include survivors of child abuse who are participants in consensual sadomasochism. Some participants in sadomasochism also identify as feminists and are deeply offended at the suggestion that they support or engage in rape or battery. Many sexual sadists and masochists see themselves as members of a sexual minority victimized by prejudice. Survivors of abuse, on the other hand, may be vulnerable to flashbacks and may find sadomasochist play outrageously disrespectful. Yet discussion of issues raised by lesbian sadomasochism cannot proceed with clarity without mention of examples of sadomasochistic drama and of playful attitudes. Finally, students who oppose sadomasochism may suspect its defenders of trying to *engage* them in sadomasochism through argument and by being outrageous, and defenders may suspect critics of wanting to be so engaged. These issues put both students and teacher between a rock and a hard place. The stress of negotiating such tensions in the classroom led me finally to remove the topic from the syllabus. The ethical and political issues surrounding the topic, however, deserve to be addressed.

The difficulties for nonsadomasochists have been primarily with sadism and with psychodrama that appears to make light not only of rape and incest but also of histories of oppression, such as American slavery and the Nazi Holocaust, drawing upon those histories to construct sex-games.[2] Many feminists tend to regard masochism as an example of the damage inflicted by oppression.[3] Many also think of it as passive, whereas sadism appears active, more easily identified with oppressors. The term "sadomasochism" diverts attention from sadism to masochism, subtly suggesting that masochism is basic, which may not be true. One of the most sophisticated definitions of "sadism" (evidently that of a connoisseur) includes masochism as a form of sadism, the definition offered by Iwan Bloch ("Eugen Duhren") and quoted by Havelock Ellis in his *Love and Pain*:

> A connection, whether intentionally sought or offered by chance, of sexual excitement and sexual enjoyment with the real or only symbolic (ideal, illusionary) appearance of frightful and shocking events, destructive occurrences and practices which threaten or destroy the life, health, and property of man and other living creatures, and threaten and interrupt the continuity of inanimate objects, whereby the person who from such occurrences obtains sexual enjoyment may either himself be the direct cause, or cause them to take place by means of other persons, or merely be the spectator, or, finally, be, voluntarily or involuntarily, the object against which these processes are directed.[4]

The final clause encompasses masochism, suggesting vicarious hostility to self, and the inclusion of witnessing leaves open with which party, if either, the spectator identifies. Havelock Ellis proposed the term "algolagnia," literally "pain-lust," as a substitute for "sadism" and "masochism." However, "algolagnia," like Bloch's definition, seems to ignore humiliation and servitude, widely recognized forms of sadism and masochism. And like "sadomasochism," "algolagnia" blurs distinctions between sadists and masochists. Sadism and masochism raise issues worth considering separately. If masochism is more confusing, sadism is ethically more troubling.

The term "sadomasochism" became popular with Freud's speculation that sadistic and masochistic desires can exist in the same person, that one can move under certain conditions from masochism to sadism or in the reverse direction.[5] Thus, as a Freudian, one might speak of an individual's sadomasochist potentialities. The term "sadomasochism" as adopted by contemporary "sadomasochist liberationists," however, refers to *a contractual relationship* between two (or more) parties. Sadomasochism so understood has been the subject of political activist defense by members of both sexes in the United States for at least two decades. The earliest support group of which I am aware is New York City's Till Eulenspiegel Society formed in the early 1970s, open to both sexes, whether gay, bisexual, or heterosexual. The Samois support group of San Francisco has been probably the most politically vocal lesbian group, publishing a pamphlet *What Color Is Your Handkerchief?* in 1979 and shortly thereafter, the anthology, *Coming to Power.*[6]

Although there is no general presupposition in sadomasochist contracts that the parties will exchange roles, individual contracts can allow for role changes, and some "tops" (sadists, a.k.a. "S's") report that they began as "bottoms" (masochists, a.k.a. "M's").[7] One reason for the move from "bottom" to "top," apparently, is the relative dearth of "tops," especially among women. In sadomasochist culture, however, such roles, like those of butch and femme (with which they need not coincide), can be fairly settled, signaled to others through dress codes or by various ornaments. *What Color Is Your Handkerchief?* described such a code whereby lesbians sadomasochists signal their preference for being a "top" or "bottom" by displaying a colored handkerchief in the right or left pocket and the kind of activity preferred by the color of the handkerchief.[8]

"Sadomasochism" in this chapter refers to certain pleasures of erotic or sexual desire and erotic or sexual behavior, not to general hostility or self-destructiveness. I have elected to treat lesbian sadomasochism not as an example of horizontal hostility but as a puzzling set of practices whose participants generally wish each other well and respect each other's choices. It is a matter of concern, however, that the only things distinguishing the behavior of an **S** from battery and other abuse may be the motivations of the parties and the consent of the **M**. Disagreement is widespread among lesbians, as among feminists generally, over whether (or within what limits) this motivation and consent can make sadomasochistic play all right, ethically, and over the question what attitudes and policies are appropriate for outsiders to take, especially feminists who are not part of the culture. Pat Califia added to the second edition of *Coming to Power* a long essay summarizing a history of collision with San Francisco feminists over attempts of Samois to rent feminist space and to participate in lesbian-feminist events, such as marches.[9] A better candidate for horizontal hostility than consensual sadomasochism may be the sparring that has gone on for more than a decade between lesbian sadomasochist liberationists and lesbian feminists who oppose sadomasochism. Addressing such differences is now among the issues.

My own approach to sadomasochism initially, to the extent that I thought about it, was the liberal, "sexual preference" approach. I have not participated in sadomasochist culture. My knowledge of it comes from participants' writings. Yet, I am no stranger to sadomasochistic sexual desires and fantasies, nor to their sexual enactment, although my direct experience has been neither extensive nor intensive. For the better part of two decades I have distanced myself from such experiments as a result of forming a different view, more social, less individualistic, in the context of two political struggles: the struggle of feminists against women's complicity in patriarchy and that of gay men and lesbians against homophobic presentations of homosexuality as violent and dangerous.

My present approach perceives sexual sadomasochism as enacting, in an eroticized and often playful make-believe fashion, roles of dominance and subordinance that characterize not only authoritarian adult-child relationships within the family or authoritarian religious relationships but, more generally, the norms of a patriarchal, misogynist society that is also riddled with homophobia, racism, anti-Semitism, and other forms of oppression. On this understanding, sadomasochistic desires have roots not simply in individual psychologies but in society at large; they are not mysterious givens but social constructions. The direction of my ethical concern has shifted, accordingly, more to the process of their construction than to that of their enactment. However, beliefs about the meanings and consequences of their enactment remain critical to this social concern. In what follows, I try to clarify, conceptually, what "consensual sadomasochism" is, to distinguish issues pertaining to masochism from those pertaining to sadism, and to sort out some of the critical empirical questions regarding both. While I do not answer the empirical questions, I explore what might follow, ethically, if certain answers were true.

The Paradox of Masochism

Richard von Krafft-Ebing coined the term "masochism" late in the nineteenth century after the German novelist Leopold von Sacher-Masoch (1836–1896 or 1905), who portrayed the phenomenon in some of his novels, the best-known of which is *Venus in Furs* (1870).[10] In Sacher-Masoch's novels, the masochist is a man who seeks, receives, and enjoys punishment and humiliation from a woman who willingly dishes them out; the man becomes ever more attached to her as a result. This is paradoxical. Masochism, unlike sadism, sounds like a self-contradictory concept: how can one enjoy one's own pain or suffering if one's pain or suffering is, by definition, a sensation or other experience that one does not enjoy? How can one want to suffer, if suffering is, by definition, not getting what one wants? That some apparently do want and enjoy it is the paradox of masochism. No such perplexity attaches to sadism, which requires only that one person enjoy causing pain to *others*.

One response to the paradox of masochism is to accept the contradiction as real and deny that masochism is genuinely possible. There remains, then, to explain phenomena that *appear* masochistic. Two ways readily suggest themselves. One cites a pleasurable physiological response to pain, claiming that this pleasure is the ultimate object of so-called masochistic desires and that pain is tolerated only as a means to this pleasurable response. The other is to argue that what a so-called masochist really wants is to *please the sadist*, perhaps that only the sadist wants to cause pain.

On the physiological response theory, one writer reports that the release of "opiate-like" endorphins throughout the central nervous system in response to stress can produce a "profound sense of well-being," and that this experience may produce an attraction, even an addiction, that looks like, behaves like, an attraction to pain but is really a desire for the euphoria produced by the endorphins.[11] On this hypothesis, what is sought *for its own sake* is the euphoria; pain is merely instrumental. Presumably, if the euphoria could be obtained without the pain, say by injecting a drug, that would be just as satisfying.

The euphoria caused by release of endorphins may explain the apparent attraction of some "masochists" to physically painful experiences. However, this hypothesis has limitations. Not all masochistic activity involves physical pain. As Bloch's lengthy definition indicates, the source of excitement may be an *illusion* of pain, a threat, something shocking. Just as common are scenes of humiliation, servitude, and nonphysical punishments. The endorphin hypothesis seems incapable of explaining the attraction where there is no physical pain—unless emotional stress also releases endorphins. Even then, it may be only *part* of the attraction. Alternatively, the endorphin high may explain only what enables some masochists to *tolerate* pain without explaining why they want to tolerate it in the first place.

The hypothesis of pleasing the sadist may appear more plausible for sadomasochistic play that does not involve the infliction of significant physical pain or stress but involves other sorts of suffering, such as humiliation. If what the apparent masochist wants is the *approval* of the sadist, and she would be as happy to obtain this approval without having to suffer for it, the appearance of masochism is false. One might say that she only incidentally plays the *role* of a masochist, that she does it without being masochistic. However, if her desire is to please the sadist *as such* (as a sadist), this desire is as paradoxical as a simpler desire for pain or suffering. This masochist does not want to please just anyone, but only a sadist; presumably, she would not be as happy to please the sadist without suffering. If the sadist's sadism is essential to the masochist's desire to please her, submitting to pain is not just *instrumental* but is *what it means* to please the sadist.

For masochistic desire to be an intelligible, coherent notion, one needs a sophisticated theory of desire. Such a theory acknowledges a distinction between "higher order" and "lower order" desires.[12] A "higher order" desire is not a better one but simply one that is relatively *abstract* and has as its object—or as part of its object—another, usually more concrete, desire. Thus, if the desire for a cigarette is a lower order desire (very concrete), the desire to quit smoking, in a way that involves no longer wanting to smoke or even positively wanting not to smoke, is higher order (as is the desire to be able to enjoy or to continue to enjoy smoking). The *objects* of the latter desires, to want or to want not to, are themselves other desires. The object of a higher order desire need not be the *existence or cessation*, however, of another desire. The object can be instead the *frustration or gratification* of another (continuing) desire. The point is that a higher order desire is one the object of which makes essential reference to yet another desire. Thus, the desire to continue to gratify one's desire to smoke is higher order, as is the desire to have one's continuing desire for something frustrated. The latter can be an example of a masochistic desire. It need not be, of course, if one has an ulterior aim, such as improving one's health. However, if I want my desire for something to be frustrated *in order to experience the frustration*, this higher order desire is masochistic. In *frustrating* the relevant *lower* order desire, I am *gratifying* a *higher* order one. Thus, I *both* get what I seek (on a higher level) and deny myself (on a lower one).

Just as desires can be higher or lower order, so can *will* or *choice*, and so can *valuing*. A higher order choice (or expression of will) is one that has as part of its object yet another choice. Legislation is an example of higher order choice. It consists of choices that specify what people are or are not permitted to choose. Higher order valuing has as (at least part of) what is valued (or disvalued) yet another value. An example of higher order valuing is being ashamed of one's vanity. Nietzsche's project of the revaluation of values was a project in higher order valuing.

Wanting to be humiliated or violated in ways that do not involve physical pain can be understood analogously to desiring pain. To value being humiliated is to value (higher order) a thwarting of one's (relatively lower order) self-esteem. To choose to be violated is a higher order choice to allow certain of one's lower order choices to be violated or to allow certain of one's boundaries to be crossed without one's lower order consent.

A sadomasochistic sexual contract expresses higher order choices. Mutually agreed upon "safe words" (to be discussed more below) used by an **M** to signal an **S** to stop or cease escalating activity, make possible further higher order choices. So understood, masochism is *conceptually* no more paradoxical than legislation or the idea of a social contract. For social contracts and legislation express higher order choices that certain lower order choices be thwarted in certain ways. The obvious difference, of course, is that one does not enter into a social contract, or consent to legislation, *in order to experience* this thwarting of certain lower order choices or *in order to thwart* them. One hopes, rather, that such occasions will not arise or can be minimized. But *why* one engages in sadism or masochism is a *motivational* puzzle, not a conceptual one.

The Contract: Sanitizing Sadism

Female masochism has received more discussion than female sadism, at least from feminists. An exception is Lorena Saxe's recent inquiry into whether female sadists should be admitted to feminist events, such as music festivals.[13] It is frequently observed that many more participants in sadomasochistic culture prefer the masochist role, especially among women.[14] Men who want a female dominatrix frequently have to hire a prostitute, who would not otherwise be interested.

If voluntary masochism presents a metaphysical paradox, the sadism of consensual sadomasochism presents an ethical one. Consensual sadomasochism adds to the conceptual complexities of masochism the ethical complexities of a claim to make sadism acceptable by way of a contract. How can it be right to cause unnecessary suffering deliberately? The fact that someone is unnecessarily being made to suffer creates a presumption that the person is being wronged. This presumption is said to be rebuttable by a *contract*, to which the **M** consents, explicitly, or implicitly. The questions arise, then, whether, to what extent, with what limitations, under what conditions, if any, such a contract can rebut presumptions of wrongdoing. Recall that, in law, even surgery would be a technical battery were it not for the patient's consent.[15]

Again, one response is to deny that apparently sadistic activities are really sadistic. The idea here is that the sadist basically aims to *please* the masochist and that making her suffer is simply a means to doing so. However, because sadistic desires to please masochists are the mirror image of the latter's desires to please sadists, the sadist is not off the hook simply by claiming that she aims only to please. Her aim to cause suffering is no more incidental to her aim to please than the masochist's aim to submit to suffering is incidental to hers.

Some uses of the abbreviation "S&M" appear less than candid about what counts as sadomasochism. One participant in a forum on sadomasochism, for example, claimed that "S&M" has become a generic term for "any inventive sexuality involving spoken or acted-out fantasy, psychodrama, domination and submission, sex toys, or conscious role-playing."[16] This could lead one to think that masturbating with a vibrator or playing hide-and-seek with a sex partner might be examples of sadomasochism. The distinguishing characteristics uniting items on this list, it seems, are *imagination, make-believe,* and *playfulness.* In Western culture, perhaps anything that departs from the "missionary position" could count. Thus practitioners contrast sadomasochism with "vanilla sex."

This make-believe and play understanding of sadomasochism is comparable to an understanding of pornography popular among consumers as simply an explicit portrayal of sexuality that is playful (hence, *Playboy*) rather than utilitarian, or is intended to arouse sexual desire rather than, say, simply to educate. Feminist philosophers concerned about pornography as a purveyor of misogyny have worked to expose that what such definitions omit is ethically more important than what they acknowledge, namely, that the material that pornography eroticizes, treats playfully, and presents in a positive light is, in reality, derogatory, demeaning, or degrading to women, and that this is *no mere coincidence* but is *an important aspect of the turn-on*.[17] The target of feminist protest has not been playfulness, inventiveness, or explicitness as such. It has been material or activity that treats as a source of enjoyment the pain, humiliation, or violence, real or fantasized, that is inflicted on someone who is playing a woman or playing a slave (even if, as if often the case in overt sadomasochistic psychodrama and literature, the someone is in fact male and socially powerful).

Another way to avoid talking about pain, humiliation, and violence is to define "sadomasochism" in terms of *power*. Lesbian sadomasochists of Samois tend to hold the view that basic to all forms of sadomasochism is an eroticizing of power and powerlessness. The sadomasochist contract is presented as an "exchange of power."[18] Like the playfulness definition, this can be misleading also. Giving up and exercising power need not involve pain, humiliation, or violence. Still, seeing the sadomasochistic contract as an exchange of power can be clarifying, as long as we understand that the power is exchanged for sadistic and masochistic ends.

"Power" is ambiguous between a more general sense and a narrower sense. For evaluating the sadism of sadomasochism, it matters what happens with power in each of these senses. In the most abstract sense, power is *potency*, the ability to act. "Energy" and "vitality" are near synonyms of "power" in this sense. In a narrower sense, power refers to "control," the more specific abilities to determine or check the flow of energy or to determine its direction toward various goals. The implications of having power in each of these senses are different. Those in control, for example, often control the energies of others and may do it with relatively little energy of their own.

Candlepower, horsepower, and womanpower are measures of power as energy, not of power as control. When Audre Lorde wrote of the erotic (in general) as empowering, she meant that it is energizing, not that it is controlling.[19] Political power, on the other hand, is power in the "control" sense, the ability to determine the uses of energy by means of political norms. The power "negotiated" in "consensual sado-masochism" is also, presumably, power in the "control" sense, which is also exercised to a great extent by way of norms. Questions, then, for evaluating a sadomasochist contract include not only how it distributes control but also what its consequences are for the empowerment or disempowerment of the parties in the "energy" or "vitality" sense, per-haps especially whether it disempowers the masochist.

Defining "sadomasochism" in terms of power sounds promising for evaluating the sadism of sadomasochism. For "oppression" is also defin-able in terms of power. To be oppressed is to be rendered impotent, to have one's power in the "energy" sense severely curtailed and depressed in a lasting way. To be oppressed is—as Marilyn Frye has argued—to be diminished, reduced, molded, immobilized.[20] Consent may often rebut charges of exploitation, but it does not nullify oppression. And consent *of* the oppressed is, presumably, not freely given.

Let us consider, then, what occurs in a sadomasochist exchange of power. On one interpretation, an "exchange of power" between sexu-al partners seems harmless enough. It may be characteristic of sexual interaction in general: taking turns being in control of the other's feel-ings or sensations. One does not necessarily give up the ability to con-trol in giving up the "right" to exercise control, i.e., in allowing anoth-er to be *in* control, any more than one need give up one's driver's license in order to allow a partner to do the driving (one need aban-don only the wheel). Such exchanges need involve no pain, humilia-tion, or violence or even a fantasy thereof. The activity may be highly aggressive, vigorous, playful, teasing, and so forth without being at all hostile, violent, humiliating, or painful (unless one counts as "pain" any stimulation of the pain receptors in the skin, in which case, stroking is "painful," too). I see no basis yet for attributions of either of sadism or masochism.

The sadomasochist contract, however, need not involve any ex-change of *roles*, any taking of turns. The sadomasochistic exchange, as such, is different; it characterizes the relationship between a "top" and "bottom" as such, without presupposing that they are going to trade places. Each party gives up one kind of power in exchange for anoth-er. The **S** gets power over (control over) the **M** at the level of the **M**'s *lower order choice*, in exchange for submitting to the **M**'s *higher order choic-es* (her form of control over the **S**), which are expressible through the use of "safe words." Both agree, at a higher level yet, to abide by this exchange. Often, the script of sadomasochist drama is provided by the **M**, although who provides the script can vary, as long as the **M** retains a veto.

This understanding of the contract seems to impose limits on what an **S** is permitted to do. To *retain* the ability to check the **S**, an **M** must be aware of what is being done. Likewise, to honor an **M**'s higher order choices, an **S** also must be aware of what she is doing and of what the **M** wants at the higher level. The judgment of both must remain unimpaired. These conditions should rule out significant consumption of alcohol or other drugs. Some **S**'s, as a matter of principle, abstain from alcohol or other drug consumption prior to and during sadomasochistic sex, and insist that their partners do likewise. These conditions may also seem to rule out treatment that would prevent the **M** from using her safe words or the **S** from understanding them in time.

Abdication of lower level choice by an **M** *need* not be disempowering. Carrying out another's orders may require considerable energy. However, some classic activities of sadomasochism, such as bondage, do curb agency, not simply control, at least temporarily. Being tied and gagged with a hood over one's head severely impedes communication. A clear safe word should be more specific than a groan or a wiggle. To prevent fatal accidents and keep open the possibility of communication, a sadomasochist agreement should also include advance safety understandings, such as that no one will be left tied up unattended or left face down in soft material that might hamper breathing. Scrupulous **M**'s are expected to inform **S**'s in advance of disabilities, disorders, or vulnerabilities, such as allergies, diabetes, or heart trouble. These precautions are taken from an essay on safety in *Coming to Power*, whose author insists that such advice is only common sense.[21] For those seeking the thrill of danger, however, that may not be obvious. Concern for basic safety and keeping open the lines of communication may compete with the pleasures sought. Constant higher order communication may disrupt the spirit of play, intruding too much reality. All that is clear is that *if* higher order consent is to be *continuously* consulted, such precautions set limits. What is not clear is that consensual sadomasochists will be interested in continuous consultation.

Because the **S** is supposed to submit to the **M**'s safe words, and because the **M** often writes the script, some maintain that the **M** has more power. However, that is not obvious, either. Who can best protect herself when things go wrong? When the other party, through anger, frustration, or ineptitude, violates the contract? Aside from with-holding information, who is in the best position to violate it? Retaining the *ability* to resist the **S** would seem prudent in case the **S** does not respond or respond rapidly enough to the **M**'s safe words, although an **M** may not be much interested in prudence. The usual response of lesbian sadomasochists has been that an **S** who does not respect an **M**'s limits soon finds herself partnerless (which may be cold comfort to an individual **M**). That suggests, however, a more general consideration. One's power is in part a function of alliances with others. Fear of retaliation might restrain an **S** who is tempted to go beyond the contract or disregard safe words.

The situation of men who enjoy playing the **M** in relation to female prostitutes is instructive here. In a society that systematically gives men power over women, men usually have enough ability to retaliate that a female **S** is, ultimately, very much in their power. On this basis, John Stoltenberg has argued that sadomasochism may be liberating for men in a way that it cannot be for women in a patriarchy.[22]

The position of prostitutes in relation to clients is exacerbated by the fact that they are outlaws. Lesbians are also outlaws. As long as a lesbian **M** can rely on the safe word convention, she has its power at her disposal. But what makes that convention reliable? What power backs it? Bat-Ami Bar On, in considering this difficulty, finds first, that the ability to set limits by safe words is only a negative power (veto) and second, that the *power* of the safe word is not even possessed by the individual masochist as such but at most by the class of masochists and only insofar as sadists depend for their own gratification on the existence and cooperation of masochists. In a class situation, she argues, this is like the power that stems from the dependence of the oppressors on the oppressed. Such dependence "secures the oppressed class against total destruction, although it does not secure *all* of its members against total destruction. And it secures none of its members treatment that is fair, enhancing of freedom and respectful of persons . . . This is the same kind of protection that slaves have in a slave-based economy and which Jews in Nazi Germany *lacked* because they were considered utterly disposable."[23]

Where a particular kind of sadomasochistic activity diminishes a lesbian **M**'s agency, placing her at the mercy of the **S**'s scruples and competence, the exchange is critically unequal, even though a lesbian **S** has no better social alliances than a lesbian **M**. Setting aside the case of a suicidal **M**, the **S** is often better able to act. Whereas the **M** may be in jeopardy of unintended injury, or even death, should the **S** become angry, careless, or misunderstand, the **S** in such contingencies risks at most being charged with assault, battery, or murder, offenses seldom prosecuted successfully when they are committed in privacy during sexual activity.

Perhaps the fact that sadomasochist contracts are *outlaw* contracts should give would-be **S**'s and **M**'s reason to be cautious about relying on them. It might be argued that a condition of rational consent to a contract is adequate assurance that parties to such contracts will in general abide by them, that the contract conventions will be upheld, some reliable sanction imposed if a contract is violated. However, this argument ignores the rationality of risk-taking. Further, the outlaw aspect may contribute to the thrill of it all. If enjoyment of risk is a major motivation for engaging in sadomasochism in the first place, the lack of backing for the safe word convention might add to the risks enjoyed. An **M** may enjoy being at the mercy of her **S**'s goodwill and competence. She may even enjoy being at the mercy of luck, perhaps seeing her life in general that way, anyhow.

To summarize, although conditions required by the sadomasochist contract and its conventions in principle impose some limits on harmful behavior, they do so only on the interpretation of the contract as requiring the possibility of continuous communication. Reliance upon the consent principle, however, would seem to rule out subjecting unconsenting parties to witnessing the enactment of sadomasochist contracts and or even, in some cases, to witnessing the resulting damage. Such witnessing, as Iwan Bloch's definition acknowledges, is itself one of the forms that sadomasochistic sexual behavior can take. Observing this scruple may require considerable restraint in coming out behavior and in political demonstrations by sadomasochists.

Were an **M** to consent in full knowledge of the risks, it would seem difficult to maintain, if things turn out badly for her, that she was wronged by the **S**, or that the **S** acted unethically (whatever one may think of her sources of pleasure). This leaves open the possibility, however, that both are wronged by a larger society that is responsible for the construction of their desires in the first place. Whether outsiders to consensual sadomasochism who are members of such a society can have good reason to intervene to stop, prevent, or limit consensual sadomasochism would seem to depend, in part, on the wider social consequences of sadomasochistic indulgence. I turn next to hypotheses about such consequences.

Social Consequences: Catharsis, Addiction, or Harmless Compulsion?

From a contract to undergo surgery, the expected consequence is the patient's improved health (and a sizable fee for the surgeon). The expectable consequences of sadomasochism, however, other than sexual pleasure, are a subject of much dispute.

The most vigorously opposing views most frequently expressed in my classes and in the literature fall roughly into two camps, the *catharsis* (or "safety valve") camp and the *addiction* camp. Both catharsis and addiction suggest a medical model, which has not been generally characteristic of lesbian feminist approaches to sexuality. Actually, the idea of illness is not basic to the disagreement. These terms capture deep disagreement about the relationships of sadomasochistic "pretend hostility" to *real* hostility and about the social consequences of sexual sadomasochism.

On the addiction view, sadomasochism is itself a problem; on the catharsis view, it remedies other problems. On the catharsis view, sadomasochistic desires are thought to have sources external to the sadomasochistic drama itself—for example, in mistreatment suffered or witnessed involuntarily by the agent early in life—and sadomasochistic play is said to be a way to get rid of hostilities safely.[24] The addiction hypothesis, on the contrary, holds that sadomasochistic play itself gives rise to sadomasochistic desires, intensifying those enacted, with a frightening potential to reinforce real hostility.[25] The conflict between these views was expressed poignantly in a study of extreme and extensive sadomasochistic activity of male politicians with prostitutes in Washington D.C.: "Is it a principle of catharsis which is operating here, or does this behavior lead to an accumulation of pressure which eventually may cause them to lose control in situations where a disciplined rationality is essential to our very survival?"[26]

Also, there is more than one addiction model. Perhaps some forms of sadomasochism, such as those involving acute physical stress or pain, are more likely to be addictive than others in a physiological way, as the endorphin hypothesis suggests. This might account for the tendency of some masochists to become involved in heavier scenes over time. It would not, however, explain similar escalations of sadism, except indirectly (that is, insofar as the sadist was responding to, or identifying with, the escalating desires of a masochist). The American Psychiatric Association's *Diagnostic and Statistical Manual* notes under its entry for

"Sexual Masochism" that some "may engage in masochistic acts for many years without increasing the potential injuriousness of their acts," while others "increase the severity of the masochistic acts over time or during periods of stress."[27] But under the entry for "Sexual Sadism," the *DSM-III-R* claims that "usually, however, the severity of the sadistic acts increases over time" (p. 287). If the difference between these claims is warranted, there may be different addictive mechanisms for sadism and for masochism.

The addiction model of sadomasochism need not rest on a physiological hypothesis, such as the endorphin hypothesis. More simply, it may rest on the observation that erotic or sexual behavior that is satisfying tends to be self-reinforcing. This view would apply to both sadistic and masochistic satisfactions. Erotic fixations seem capable of behaving like addictions in that those who become fixated report being at a loss for how to alter such desires, when they want to.[28] Perhaps not all participants, however, are fixated. According to one study based on interviews with men in the middle 1970s, only 16% indicated that they would like sex exclusively with sadomasochism, while 32% indicated that they would like predominantly such sex and another 32% indicated that they would like sex equally often with and without sadomasochism.[29]

Those who take sadomasochism simply as a mysterious given of human variation, a *sexual preference*, a matter of taste, tend to regard lesbianism, bisexuality, and heterosexuality in the same way.[30] Thus many are puzzled at the apparent hypocrisy or arbitrariness of feminists who support lesbianism but oppose sadomasochism. Thinking of sadomasochism as a sexual preference suggests the liberal view that participants have only the responsibility not to visit unwanted harm on others, that the exercise of their preferences is otherwise a matter of individual liberty, nothing for others to be concerned about as long as participants are consenting adults acting in private. Thus the liberal view encourages a nonjudgmental attitude, or toleration, within limits. It also assumes that participants *can* keep from visiting unwanted harm on others, an assumption that seems unwarranted as long as the sources of such desires are not understood.

In the context of a sexually oppressive or repressive society, the liberal view may give way to a movement to provide social support for the self-esteem of sadomasochists and to offer socially supported spaces for the exercise of sadomasochism. Thus liberalism may give way to sexual liberationism, which supplants nonjudgmentalism with a positive endorsement. To gain social support, it usually helps to be able to claim to offer a social benefit. This is what the *catharsis* view does in maintaining that consensual sadomasochism provides a safe outlet for potentially harmful and destructive impulses. For an **S**, the catharsis view provides a justification additional to the consent of the **M**. It enables an **S** to hold that the acceptability of the sadism of sadomasochism is also a function of its cathartic value with respect to hostile impulses of the sadist and self-destructive ones of the **M**. The catharsis view need not deny the sadism of the **S**; catharsis, like happiness, may require a certain motivational detachment of the parties from that end. That is, catharsis may be more likely if one does not deliberately aim at it, just as happiness is more likely if one does not pursue it too self-consciously.[31] Yet, the parties might regard the cathartic effects of sadomasochism as tending to *justify* to others what they do, staving off their interference, if not positively enlisting their support.

Many lesbian feminist sexual liberationists today, like their feminist critics, hold a social, rather than individualistic, view of the roots of sadomasochism. Appealing to catharsis, however, they conclude that consensual sadomasochism in an oppressive society deserves the support of feminists and others who would resist that oppression. Some maintain that the make-believe of sadomasochism can be sources of insight into oppression, that they can indicate a healthy independence of the players from the abuse mimicked, and that they can actually heal damage of oppression.[32] One contributor to *Coming to Power* claimed that sadomasochistic sex had enabled her and her partner to save their relationship from destruction by jealous hostilities that were generated by their nonmonogamous behavior.[33]

Thus, whether outsiders are endangered or protected by consensual sadomasochism seems to depend on whether the catharsis or the addiction view is closer to the truth. On the catharsis view, acting out sadomasochistic desires with a consenting and knowledgeable partner *decreases* the likelihood that the parties will support or engage in violence against *un*consenting others. On the addiction view, sadomasochistic desires are fostered to a great extent *by* sadomasochistic activity itself, consensual or not, as the desire for a drug is fostered by using it, and they can become stronger with participation, much as one can come to need more and more of a drug in order to get the same satisfaction that a lower dose produced initially.

On the addiction view, then, the question arises whether "sadomasochist addicts" will seek their pleasures outside the bounds of the contract, as drug addicts who would otherwise be law-abiding may be led into crime to support their addiction. Will they find themselves enjoying real domination or subordination in oppressive societies, domination and subordination without consent? Will sadomasochistic play foster make-believe with respect to real power imbalances and oppression, encouraging indulgence of the fantasy that the power of others is held by consent of the dominated? A contributor to *Lesbian Ethics* appears to acknowledge this danger as a problem calling for watchfulness.[34] This is not only a concern for would-be **S**'s and **M**'s, however. It is a concern for outsiders.

Not only does the addiction model suggest that outsiders may be harmed, but also it suggests that the ethical validity of the contract is undermined. A contract between free and equal adults who know what they are doing ordinarily is taken to nullify complaints of either party against the other, a rule understood in law as the rule that "consent nullifies harm." More specifically, it nullifies injustice. Certain considerations are commonly understood to limit the ability of a contract to rebut the presumption that anyone is harmed unjustly: the parties must be adequately *informed* and their consent must be *free* (uncoerced).

For addictive behavior, neither of these conditions may be met adequately. For the information requirement, the parties would have to be aware not only of immediate likely consequences but also of the likelihoods of addiction, information not readily available in a society that does not support dissemination of information about sexual sadomasochism. Addictions also diminish freedom to withdraw, raising the question whether the freedom condition is met adequately—for *either* party. If the **M**'s addiction undermines her consent, the presumption of wrongdoing may also be undermined by the **S**'s addiction. For, the **S**'s addiction would call into question her responsible agency. The observation that addictions diminish freedom to withdraw suggests that over time, what began as a consensual activity may cease to be clearly consensual, not because of communication problems but because of diminished responsible agency on the part of either or both parties.

Catharsis and addiction are not the only possible hypotheses, however. Neither may be right as a generalization about everything that participants have wanted to include under the umbrella of sadomasochism. Another suggestion is that sexual sadism and masochism are *compulsions*, rather than addictions, and that like handwashing compulsions, they may not get worse over time, even if they stubbornly resist eradication.[35] Sadistic and masochistic compulsions, however, still raise some of the same disturbing questions as addictions: will indulging such compulsions encourage one also to enjoy vicariously the involuntary suffering of others in society at large and thus compete with one's motivation to prevent such suffering? Do such compulsions underlie the current popularity of violence in films and novels? Do they thereby encourage a spread of such compulsions to new generations?

As a generalization, the catharsis hypothesis seems to oppose the addiction and compulsion hypotheses, in that catharsis is supposed to be good for society, whereas compulsion is not supposed to offer any particular social benefit, and addiction seems likely to be socially bad. Yet some combination of these views may be closer to the truth. Some sexually sadistic or masochistic desires may have sources in childhood abuse, as the catharsis hypothesis tends to hold, and some kinds of playful sadomasochistic enactment may also reinforce such desires and even intensify them instead of providing a "safety valve" or catharsis.

Similar questions may be asked about the effects of expressing (real) anger. Does failure to express anger bottle it up until it explodes destructively, whereas letting oneself get angry gets rid of the anger safely? Or, on the contrary, does expressing anger reinforce it, making one even angrier, instead of getting rid of it, increasing instead of decreasing the likelihood of destructive behavior? Is repeatedly expressing anger simply a compulsion that some people have? Perhaps none of these hypotheses is true of all kinds of anger or of all ways of suppressing or expressing it. Perhaps there are ways in which each can be true. And the same may be true of the variety of activities that have been called "sadomasochistic."

A Possible Reconciliation

My conclusions are in the form of more questions and hypotheticals. I find far more ethical questions surrounding this topic than are usually discussed. It may be apparent by now that there are as many questions of right and wrong as there are agents involved and kinds of sadomasochistic activity. There are questions for masochists, for sadists, for outsiders who believe they may be harmed, for supporters and beneficiaries of the norms that sadomasochism reenacts, and for victims of those norms. And there may be as many ethical questions for each of these parties as there are others with whom they interact. For sadists and masochists, there are questions regarding their treatment of each other but also regarding their responses to outsiders and regarding their responses to genuine oppression. For outsiders, there are not only questions regarding their interaction with sadomasochists but also regarding their interaction with those who support the oppressive norms that sadomasochistic drama mimics.

What has received most attention are the implications of the addiction and catharsis hypotheses for the ethics of sadists' and masochists' treatment of each other and for the ethics of their interactions with outsiders and of outsiders' with them. If sadomasochistic sexuality undermines resistance to oppression by eroticizing domination and subordinance, that is cause for social as well as individual concern. However, it does not follow that social concern should be focused on, or directed primarily to, consensual sadomasochism itself. Both the addiction and catharsis models suggest that sadomasochism signals underlying social distress. Even if consensual sadomasochism creates and intensifies potentially harmful and destructive desires, and even if participants in consensual sadomasochism are in that way complicit in maintaining the forces of oppression, sexual sadomasochism does not appear to be a *fundamental source* in an oppressive society of the hostilities to which it gives vent.

The addiction model suggests that social concern be directed primarily to the relevant social norms of domination and subordinance and to those who profit most from their continuance. Those who profit most from drug addiction are neither addicts nor those who sell directly to addicts but those who control both and who need fear no serious opposition to anything they do from those who are hooked and dependent on them for a regular fix. Likewise, those who profit most from sadomasochism may not be its participants, either, but those whose oppressive social practices are a source of fantasy for participants and who need fear little serious opposition from those whose fantasies they feed.[36]

The catharsis model is also suggestive in other ways than those emphasized by sadomasochists with respect to wider social concerns. For, like the addiction model, it suggests the question, once asked by Audre Lorde in an interview on sadomasochism, "Who benefits from lesbians beating on each other?"[37] Who profits from this "catharsis"? *Who* might otherwise have been the *target* of sadomasochists' hostilities?

An interesting answer is suggested in a criticism that Sarah Hoagland once brought against sadomasochism as an irresponsible illusion whereby we get to play at having power over each other instead of seeking the real political power needed to end oppression.[38] If she is right, sadomasochism can sublimate desires for real political power. Consequently, those with real political power in an oppressive society would benefit most from the sadomasochism of others, as antifeminists may profit most from feminists battling one another over sadomasochism. Without the catharsis of sadomasochism, participants' hostilities might have been directed against social oppression. But, if we become addicted or compulsively fixated in sadomasochism, eroticizing roles of dominance and subordinance, whatever hostility spills over the bounds of contracts seems more likely to be directed against those who would resist oppression. Thus, sadomasochism may purge us of revolutionary impulses, not only by getting rid of our hostilities but also by redirecting them, channeling them ultimately against ourselves and those who should be our allies. If so, what sadomasochism eliminates are hostile impulses that might otherwise be used in politically productive ways to bring about real social change. This would make the sadomasochism of others safe for oppressors.

On the other hand, if empirical investigation were to reveal that participants in sexual sadomasochism are in general as politically resistant to oppression as their feminist critics, that might suggest that neither the catharsis model nor the addiction model captures well the consequences of sadomasochistic activity for real hostility or real destructiveness.

Even if the addiction and catharsis models do capture cooperatively such consequences—if sadomasochistic practice does reinforce socially oppressive norms, refocus potential revolutionaries, keep them too preoccupied and too attached to existing structures to seek real social change—the most important social intervention for critics is not into consensual sexual sadomasochistic activity but into the oppressive norms that sadomasochism eroticizes: norms of servitude, cruelty, misogyny, racism, and so on. What is required to make sadomasochist contracts unattractive to lesbians and unprofitable to oppressors may be nothing less than a restructuring of society, or the creation of a new one.

Notes

introduction

1. The murder of Christine Rothschild, to my knowledge, remains unsolved.

2. The student was David Fine. For a page-turning account of those times, see Tom Bates, *Rads: The 1970 Bombing of the Army Math Research Center at the University of Wisconsin and Its Aftermath* (New York: HarperCollins, 1992). According to Bates (p. 446), David Fine earned a law degree at the University of Oregon, was then denied admission to the Oregon Bar, and went to work as a paralegal with a Portland firm specializing in patent law.

3. I did, however, supplement the philosophy with autobiographical writings and letters, such as Claude Brown's *Manchild in the Promised Land* (New York: Macmillan, 1965) and *Soledad Brother: The Prison Letters of George Jackson* (New York: Coward-McCann, 1970).

4. For more on experimental pedagogy with roots in feminist activism, see Claudia Card, "The Feistiness of Feminism," *Feminist Ethics*, ed. Claudia Card (Lawrence: University Press of Kansas, 1991), pp. 3–31.

5. See Claudia Card, "Removing Veils of Ignorance," *Journal of Social Philosophy* 22, no. 1 (Spring 1991), 155–61.

1 ■ what is lesbian culture?

1. Sahli Cavallaro, Deborah Edel, Joan Nestle, Pamela Oline, and Julia Stanley [Julia Penelope], *Lesbian Herstory Archives Newsletter*, letter to "Sisters," June 1975 (New York: Lesbian Herstory Educational Foundation, 1975).

2. *Lesbian Herstory Archives Newsletter* no. 13 (June 1992), pp. 1–3.

3. Elizabeth Lapovsky Kennedy and Madeline D. Davis, *Boots of Leather, Slippers of Gold: The History of a Lesbian Community* (New York: Routledge, 1993).

4. *Lesbian-Feminist Clearinghouse*, Brochure, Women's Studies Program, Pittsburgh, no date (probably 1981).

5. I have its brochure for 1978.

6. There were also others in other states; these are the ones mentioned in *NLFO News* no. 4 (June/July 1979), p. 2.

7. "Culture," *Random House Webster's College Dictionary* (New York, 1991), p. 330.

8. Ann Ferguson, *Sexual Democracy: Women, Oppression, and Revolution* (Boulder, Colo.: Westview, 1991), pp. 133–54.

9. See, for example, Vern Bullough and Bonnie Bullough, "Lesbianism in the 1920's and 1930's: A Newfound Study," *Signs* 2, no. 4 (Summer 1977), 895–904, reporting on a 1938 manuscript based on interviews with twenty-five lesbians from a community in Salt Lake City.

10. H. L. A. Hart, *The Concept of Law* (Oxford: Clarendon Press, 1961), pp. 55–56. Thanks to Laurence Thomas for reminding me of this valuable distinction that he also uses in his analysis of American slavery in his *Vessels of Evil: A Psychology of Slavery and the Holocaust* (Philadelphia: Temple University Press, 1993).

11. *Mädchen in Uniform*, dir. Leontine Sagan, German with English subtitles, 1931. For the sections cut, see Vito Russo in *The Celluloid Closet: Homosexuality in the Movies* (New York: Harper & Row, 1981), pp. 56–58. The film is based on Christa Winsloe's play of the same title, also expanded as the novel, *The Child Manuela*, trans. Agnes Neill Scott (New York: Farrar & Rinehart, 1933).

12. "Letter to a Friend from a Newly Married Nineteenth-Century American Woman," in *The Genteel Female*, ed. Clifton Furness (New York: Knopf, 1931), endpaper. Thanks to Sue Lanser for calling this to my attention long ago.

13. Gertrude Stein, *Selected Writings*, ed. Carl Van Vechten (New York: Random House, 1962), pp. 563–68.

14. Richard Bridgman, *Gertrude Stein in Pieces* (New York: Oxford University Press, 1970), p. 96, note 1.

15. See Audre Lorde, *Zami: A New Spelling of My Name* (Trumansburg, N.Y.: Crossing Press, 1982).

16. See Paula Gunn Allen, *The Sacred Hoop* (Boston: Beacon Press, 1986); Judy Grahn, *Another Mother Tongue: Gay Words, Gay Worlds* (Boston: Beacon Press, 1984), especially pp. 49–72; and Walter L. Williams, *The Spirit and the Flesh: Sexual Diversity in American Indian Culture* (Boston: Beacon Press, 1986), especially pp. 233–51.

17. Grahn, *Another Mother Tongue*, p. 56.

18. A recent example is Shane Phelan's *Identity Politics: Lesbian Feminism and the Limits of Community* (Philadelphia: Temple University Press, 1989). See also Ann Ferguson, "Patriarchy, Sexual Identity, and the Sexual Revolution," *Signs* 7, no. 1 (Autumn 1981), 159–72 and Jacqueline Zita's response, "Historical Amnesia and the Lesbian Continuum," same issue, pp. 172–87.

19. Diana Fuss, *Essentially Speaking: Feminism, Nature and Difference* (New York: Routledge, 1989).

20. See *Forms of Desire: Sexual Orientation and the Social Constructionist Controversy*, ed. Edward Stein (New York: Routledge, 1992).

21. Michel Foucault, *The History of Sexuality*, tr. Robert Hurley (New York: Random House, 1978). See also Jeffrey Weeks, *Coming Out: Homosexual Politics in Britain from the Nineteenth Century to the Present* (London: Quartet Books, 1977); John D'Emilio, *Sexual Politics, Sexual Communities: The Making of a Homosexual Minority in the United States, 1940–1970* (Chicago: University of Chicago, 1981); and *The Making of the Modern Homosexual*, ed. Kenneth Plummer (London: Hutchinson, 1981).

22. Thomas S. Szasz, *The Manufacture of Madness* (New York: Delta, 1970).

23. Interestingly, his word for what he did was different from mine for what I did.

24. Richard Mohr, *Gay Ideas: Outing and Other Controversies* (Boston: Beacon Press, 1992), pp. 221–42.

25. Plato, *Symposium* 189c–193d, in *The Collected Dialogues of Plato*, ed. Edith Hamilton and Huntington Cairnes (New York: Bollingen, 1961), pp. 542–46.

26. Compare Marilyn Frye, *The Politics of Reality: Essays in Feminist Theory* (Trumansburg, N.Y.: Crossing Press, 1983), especially, pp. 155–61, on distinctions men have and have not found worth marking,

27. *Forms of Desire*, ed. Stein, pp. 341–43.

28. John Boswell, "Concepts, Experience, and Sexuality," in *Forms of Desire*, ed. Stein, pp. 133–73.

29. Cf. John Rawls' definition of "institution" in *A Theory of Justice* (Cambridge, Mass.: Harvard University Press, 1971), p. 55: "a public system of rules which defines offices and positions with their rights and duties, powers and immunities, and the like."

30. Adrienne Rich, *Of Woman Born: Motherhood as Experience and Institution* (New York: Norton, 1976).

31. Marilyn Frye, *Willful Virgin: Essays in Feminism* (Freedom, Calif.: Crossing Press, 1992), pp. 59–75.

32. See John Boswell, *Christianity, Social Tolerance, and Homosexuality: Gay People in Western Europe from the Beginning of the Christian Era to the Fourteenth Century* (Chicago: University of Chicago, 1980), p. 43, n. 6; and Bruce Rogers, *The Queen's Vernacular: A Gay Lexicon* (San Francisco: Straight Arrow Books, 1972), pp. 93–95.

33. "Homosexual" became the preferred term in (often hostile) legal and psychological contexts. Many of us find it too clinical-sounding (unlike "gay" and "lesbian"). It can also be used to homogenize lesbians and gay men.

34. On this and other terms referring to human females, see Julia Penelope, *Speaking Freely: Unlearning the Lies of the Fathers' Tongues* (New York: Pergamon, 1990).

35. Monique Wittig, *The Straight Mind and Other Essays* (Boston: Beacon Press, 1992).

36. Monique Wittig and Sande Zeig, *Lesbian Peoples: Material for a Dictionary* (New York: Avon, 1979).

37. Alice Walker, *In Search of Our Mothers' Gardens* (San Diego: Harcourt, Brace, Jovanovich, 1983), p. xii.

38. Mary Barnard, "A Footnote to These Translations," in *Sappho: A New Translation*, trans. Barnard (Berkeley: University of California Press, 1958), pp. 95–106.

39. The suggestion is by way of taking the "I" in the poem to refer to Sappho herself, which, of course, it need not.

40. *Random House Webster's College Dictionary* gives "homosexual" as one meaning of "gay" ("Gay," p. 552) and reports that "gay" so used has ceased to be slang. It still considers "dyke" slang as well as "disparaging and offensive," not recognizing that that depends on who uses it and how ("dyke," p. 417). Among dykes, "dyke" is affectionate and honorific.

41. See *Sappho: A New Translation* for a helpful short bibliography and index of proper names. See also *Greek Lyric*, with an English translation by David A. Campbell (4 vols.; Cambridge, Mass.: Harvard University Press, 1982), 1:ix–xix and 1:2–205.

42. See, for example, Judith P. Hallett, "Sappho and Her Social Context: Sense and Sensuality," *Signs* 4, no. 3 (Spring 1979), 447–64, and the reply by Eva Stehle Stigers, same issue, pp. 465–71.

43. On ancient Amazons, see *Herodotus*, trans. A. D. Godley, 4 vols. (Cambridge, Mass.: Harvard University Press, 1921), 2:311–17 and *Diodorus of Sicily*, trans. C. H. Oldfather, 12 vols. (Cambridge, Mass.: Harvard University Press, 1935), 2:29–37, 2:393–97, and 2:431–33, all on Black Sea Amazons, and *Diodorus*, 2:245–61 on North African Amazons.

44. Helen Diner, *Mothers and Amazons: The First Feminine History of Culture*, trans. John Philip Lundin (Garden City, N.Y.: Anchor, 1973), pp. 95–111. *Diodorus*, 2:245–61. *The Geography of Strabo*, trans. Horace Leonard Jones (8 vols.; Cambridge, Mass.: Harvard University Press, 1988), 5:233–39. Justin, *A History of the World*, trans. G. Turnbull (London: S. Birt and B. Dod, 1746); Justin's history is believed to be an epitome of a work by an earlier Greek historian, Pompeius Trogus. The Theseus legend is in *Plutarch's Lives*, trans. Bernadotte Perrin (11 vols.; Cambridge, Mass.: Harvard University Press, 1982), 1:59–67.

45. Diodorus Siculus and Strabo say the Amazons seared off one breast to facilitate shooting a bow. Diodorus says this is how the Amazons got their name. They interpret "amazon" as Greek, meaning "breastless." In "Linguistic Problems with Patriarchal Reconstructions of Indo-European Culture," *Women's Studies International Quarterly* 3 (1980), 227–37, Susan Wolfe and Julia Stanley [Penelope] say that "hamazon" in Old Persian means "woman warrior."

46. Pausanias, *Guide to Greece*, tr. Peter Levi (2 vols.; New York: Penguin, 1971), *passim*.

47. Abby Wettan Kleinbaum, for example, begins *The War Against the Amazons* (New York: McGraw-Hill, 1983), "The Amazons is a dream that men created, an image of a superlative female that men constructed to flatter themselves." A survey of arguments commonly used to deny the existence of the ancient Amazons is offered by Pierre Samuel, *Amazones, Guerrieres et Gaillardes* (Bruxelles: Presses Universitaires de Grenoble, 1975), pp. 57–76.

48. *The Geography of Strabo*, 5:237.

49. Emmanuel Kanter, *The Amazons* (Chicago: Kerr, 1926), p. 58. See John L. Myres, *Herodotus: The Father of History* (Chicago: Regnery, 1953), pp. 44–45, for an allusion to such an explanation.

50. Guy Rothery, *The Amazons in Antiquity and in Modern Times* (London: Francis Griffiths, 1910).

51. See Lysias, "Funeral Oration for the Men Who Supported the Corinthians," 4–6 in *Lysias*, trans. W. R. M. Lamb (Cambridge, Mass.: Harvard University Press, 1960), pp. 33–34; and Isocrates, "Panegyricus" and "Panenthenaicus" in *Isocrates*, 3 vols.; vols. 1–2, trans. George Norlin; vol. 3 trans. Larue Van Hook (Cambridge, Mass.: Harvard University Press, 1982–1991), 1:159–61 and 2:493.

52. For a lesbian perspective on Joan of Arc, see Vita Sackville-West, *Saint Joan of Arc* (Garden City, N.Y.: Country Life Press, 1936). Louise Labé, *Love Sonnets* (New York: New Directions, 1947). Catalina de Erauso, *The Nun Ensign*, ed. and trans. James Fitzmaurice-Kelly (London: Fisher-Unwin, 1908). Margaret Goldsmith, *Christina of Sweden* (Garden City, N.Y.: Doubleday, 1933). Thomas Dekker and Thomas Middleton, *The Roaring Girl*, ed. Andor Gomme (New York: Norton, 1976; first published 1611),

53. Daniel Defoe, *General History of the Robberies and Murders of the Most Notorious Pyrates* [sic] (first published 1724; reprinted New York: Garland, 1972), pp. 117–34. See also Susan Baker, "Anne Bonny & Mary Read: They Killed Pricks," in *Women Remembered: A Collection of Biographies from The Furies*, ed. Nancy Myron and Charlotte Bunch (Baltimore, Md.: Diana Press, 1974), pp. 77–89.

54. Théophile Gautier, *Mademoiselle de Maupin*, trans. Joanna Richardson (Middlesex, Eng.: Penguin, 1981). A brief summary of the life of La Maupin is included in Bram Stoker's *Famous Imposters* (London: Sidgwick & Jackson, 1910), pp. 235–41.

55. *Six Plays by Lillian Hellman* (New York: Modern Library, 1960), pp. 5–86. For history and evaluation of the Edinburgh case, see Lillian Faderman, *Scotch Verdict* (New York: Quill, 1983). Lillian Hellman's play concludes with one teacher committing suicide, which departs from history. The teachers won their case, although it ruined their lives. The film, *The Children's Hour* (dir. William Wyler; 1962; with Audrey Hepburn and Shirley MacLaine) follows Lillian Hellman's play, rather than history. An earlier version, *These Three* (dir. William Wyler; 1936), avoided lesbianism altogether and made premarital sex the issue.

56. See *The Hamwood Papers of the Ladies of Llangollen and Caroline Hamilton*, ed. Eva Mary Bell (London: Macmillan, 1930). Colette, *The Pure and the Impure*, trans. Herma Briffault (New York: Farrar, Straus & Giroux, 1966), pp. 109–29, discusses their relationship. Doris Grumbach's novel, *The Ladies* (New York: Dutton, 1984), is based on their lives.

57. *Correspondence of Fraulein Gunderode and Bettina von Arnim*, trans. Margaret Fuller (Ossoli) (1842; reprinted Boston: Burnham, 1861). On Gunderode's suicide, see Bettina Brentano's letter to Goethe's mother, in Bettina (Brentano) von Arnim, "Letter to Frau Rath," in *Goethe's Correspondence with a Child* (2 vols.; Boston: Ticknor and Fields, 1961), 1:49–67. Gunderode's suicide is alluded to in Anna Elizabet Weirauch's novel, *The Scorpion*, trans. Whittaker Chambers (rev. ed.; New York: Willey, 1948), a work that takes its title from an insect that is said to commit suicide rather than permit itself to be captured and tortured.

58. For an interesting hypothesis about who inspired Emily Dickinson's erotic poetry, see Rebecca Patterson, *The Riddle of Emily Dickinson* (Boston: Houghton Mifflin, 1951). For examples of pronoun alteration, see *The Poems of Emily Dickinson*, including variant readings critically compared with all known manuscripts, ed. Thomas H. Johnson (Cambridge, Mass.: Belknap, 1958), pp. 376–77.

59. A short biographical sketch appears in *Lesbian Lives: Biographies of Women from The Ladder*, ed. Barbara Grier and Colette Reid (Baltimore, Md.: Diana Press, 1976), pp. 26–31.

60. Ethel Smyth, *Mass in D, The March of the Women, The Boatswain's Mate; Mrs. Waters' Aria*, (London: Virgin Classics LTD VC 7 91188–2, 1991).

61. Shari Benstock, *Women of the Left Bank: Paris, 1900–1940* (Austin: University of Texas Press, 1986).

62. See Amy Lowell, *The Complete Poetical Works* (Boston: Houghton Mifflin, 1925), esp. pp. 209–18.

63. See Faderman, *Odd Girls and Twilight Lovers: A History of Lesbian Life in Twentieth-Century America* (New York: Columbia University Press, 1991), pp. 62–92: Eric Garber, "A Spectacle in Color: The Lesbian and Gay Subculture of Jazz Age Harlem," *Hidden from History: Reclaiming the Gay and Lesbian Past*, ed. Martin Bauml Duberman, Martha Vicinus, and George Chauncey Jr.

(New York: New American Library, 1989), pp. 318–31; and *The AC/DC Blues: Gay Jazz Reissues* (Brooklyn, N.Y.: Stash ST-106, 1977), Side A, bands 1, 3, 6 and Side B, band 3.

64. See *Lesbians in Germany: 1890's-1920's*, ed. Faderman and Brigitte Eriksson (Tallahassee, Fla.: Naiad Press, 1990); and James Steakley, *The Homosexual Emancipation Movement in Germany* (Salem, N.H.: Ayer, 1982).

65. Faderman discusses critically some of the work of early sexologists in *Surpassing the Love of Men: Romantic Friendship and Love Between Women from the Renaissance to the Present* (New York: Morrow, 1981), pp. 239–53 and pp. 314–31. See Richard von Krafft-Ebing, *Psychopathia Sexualis* (New York: Putnam, 1965) and Havelock Ellis, "Sexual Inversion," in *Studies in the Psychology of Sex* (2 vols.; New York: Random House, 1936), 1:4:iii–xi and 1–384.

66. Consider, for example, Jeanette Foster, *Sex Variant Women in Literature* (2d ed.; Baltimore: Diana Press, 1975); Faderman, *Surpassing the Love of Men*; Barbara Grier's bibliography, *The Lesbian in Literature* (3d ed.; Tallahassee, Fla.: Naiad Press, 1981); and Dell Richards' *Lesbian Lists: A Look at Lesbian Culture, History, and Personalities* (Boston: Alyson, 1990).

67. Janice Raymond, *A Passion for Friends: Toward a Philosophy of Female Affection* (Boston: Beacon Press, 1986), p. 244, n. 26. Jan Raymond now prefers the idea of "gyn/affection" to that of a "lesbian continuum." Adrienne Rich, "Compulsory Heterosexuality and Lesbian Existence," *Signs* 5, no. 4 (Summer 1980), 631–60. See also Ann Ferguson, Jacqueline Zita, and Kathryn Pyne Addelson, "On 'Compulsory Heterosexuality and Lesbian Existence': Defining the Issues," *Signs* 7, no. 1 (Autumn 1981), 158–99.

68. For the last view, see Phelan, *Identity Politics*.

69. Faderman, *Surpassing the Love of Men*.

70. On the Sappho model, see Elaine Marks, "Lesbian Intertextuality," in *Homosexualities and French Literature: Cultural Contexts/Critical Texts*, ed. George Stambolian and Elaine Marks (Ithaca, N.Y.: Cornell University Press, 1979), pp. 353–77.

71. Ludwig Wittgenstein, *Philosophical Investigations*, trans. G. E. M. Anscombe (Oxford: Blackwell, 1958), pp. 31–33.

72. In adopting the family resemblance metaphor to explain the meanings of "lesbian," I intend no endorsement of the politics of the family, especially of the patriarchal family.

73. Friedrich Nietzsche, *On the Genealogy of Morals*, trans. Walter Kaufmann and R. J. Hollingdale (New York: Viking, 1969), p. 80.

74. On "reversals," see Mary Daly, *Beyond God the Father: Toward a Philosophy of Women's Liberation* (Boston: Beacon Press, 1973), pp. 95–97; and *Gyn/Ecology: The Metaethics of Radical Feminism* (Boston: Beacon Press, 1978), p. 8.

75. See *Lesbian Lives*, ed. Grier and Reid, for sketches of M. Carey Thomas

and Alice James. On Miss Marks and Miss Woolley, see Anna Mary Wells, *Miss Marks and Miss Woolley* (Boston: Houghton Mifflin, 1978).

76. Eve Kosofsky Sedgwick, *Epistemology of the Closet* (Berkeley: University of California Press, 1990), p. 1.

77. I do not count Schopenhauer's bizarre half dozen pages on "pederasty" (a term he appears to use as synonymous with male homosexuality) appended to his essay "The Metaphysics of Sexual Love," in *The Will as World and Representation*, trans. E. F. J. Payne (2 vols.; New York: Dover, 1966), 2: 560–67.

2 ▪ *lesbian attitudes and* the second sex

1. Simone de Beauvoir, *The Second Sex*, trans. and ed. H. M. Parshley (New York: Modern Library, 1969), p. 424.

2. Beauvoir, p. 406. Parshley translated *"l'assumer"* as "accepting it," which is not the same. For the original chapter from which Parshley's translation is condensed, see Beauvoir, *Le deuxieme sex* 2 vols. (Paris: Gallimard, 1949), 1:481–510.

3. Parshley translated *"la femme qui se fait lesbienne"* as "the woman who turns lesbian" (Beauvoir, *ibid.*, p. 419).

4. "Women have always loved women," opens Elaine Marks' "Lesbian Intertextuality," George Stambolian and Elaine Marks, ed., *Homosexualities and French Literature: Cultural Contexts/Critical Texts* (Ithaca, N.Y.: Cornell University Press, 1979), pp. 353–77.

5. Marilyn Frye, *The Politics of Reality: Essays in Feminist Theory* (Trumansburg, N.Y.: Crossing Press, 1983), pp. 152–74. Monique Wittig, *The Straight Mind and Other Essays* (Boston: Beacon Press, 1992), pp. 9–20.

6. In *Being and Nothingness*, trans. Hazel Barnes (New York: Philosophical Library, 1956), Sartre concluded that human beings in relationships are doomed to alternate between sadism and masochism. Beauvoir challenged that view in *The Second Sex*.

7. *The Nicomachean Ethics of Aristotle*, trans. Sir David Ross (Oxford: Clarendon Press, 1925), p. 50.

8. *Oxford English Dictionary* (New York: Oxford University Press, 1971), p. 553.

9. Elizabeth Telfer, "Friendship," *Proceedings of the Aristotelian Society*, New Ser. 71 (1970–71), 223–41. See p. 230, "This acknowledgement involves, not so much the *formation* of a policy, as endorsement of or consent to a policy which is by then enshrined in practice."

10. See Joyce Trebilcot, "Taking Responsibility for Sexuality," in *Philosophy and Sex*, ed. Robert Baker and Frederick Elliston, 2d ed., rev. (Buffalo, N.Y.: Prometheus, 1984), pp. 421–30.

11. For discussion of this combination of exploitation and failure to take responsibility, see Loretta Ulmshneider, "Bisexuality," in *Lesbianism and the*

Women's Movement, ed. Nancy Myron and Charlotte Bunch (Baltimore, Md.: Diana Press, 1975), pp. 85–88.

12. *The Nicomachean Ethics of Aristotle*, p. 194.

13. Ludwig Wittgenstein, *Philosophical Investigations*, trans. G. E. M. Anscombe (Oxford: Blackwell, 1958), pp. 31–32.

14. Adrienne Rich, "Compulsory Heterosexuality and Lesbian Existence," *Signs* 5, no. 4 (1980), 631–60.

3 ▪ *choosing lesbianism*

1. On *Lavender Jane Loves Women* (New York City, Project 1, 1975), Alix Dobkin sings Liza Cowan's song, "Hug-EE-Boo," Side II, Band 9. Cf Anne Koedt, Ellen Levine, and Anita Rapone, eds., *Radical Feminism* (New York: Quadrangle, 1973), p. 240.

2. Sandra Bartky, *Femininity and Domination: Studies in the Phenomenology of Oppression* (New York: Routledge, 1990), p. 55.

3. Kathleen Barry, *Female Sexual Slavery* (Englewood Cliffs, N.J.: Prentice-Hall, 1979).

4. Bartky, *Femininity and Domination*, pp. 45–47.

5. "Renée" was also the pseudonym of Pauline Tarn (Renée Vivien), 1877–1909, poet and lover of Natalie Barney, 1876–1972.

6. Bishop Joseph Butler, *Fifteen Sermons Preached at Rolls Chapel* (first published in 1726), with introduction, analyses, and notes by W. R. Matthews (London: G. Bell, 1967), pp. 149–63.

7. For elaboration of this conception of ignorance, see Marilyn Frye, *The Politics of Reality: Essays in Feminist Theory* (Trumansburg, N.Y.: Crossing Press, 1983), pp. 52–83 and 152–73.

8. Bartky, *Femininity and Domination*, p. 58.

9. William James, *The Will to Believe and Other Essays in Popular Philosophy* (New York: Longmans, 1905), pp. 1–31.

10. George Herbert Mead, *Mind, Self, and Society* (Chicago: University of Chicago Press, 1934). Edwin M. Schur, *Labeling Deviant Behavior* (New York: Harper and Row, 1971).

11. John Rawls, *A Theory of Justice* (Cambridge, Mass: Harvard University Press, 1971), p. 55; "Two Concepts of Rules," *Philosophical Review* 64, no. 1 (January 1955), 3, n. 1.

12. Richard Mohr, *Gay Ideas: Outing and Other Controversies* (Boston: Beacon Press, 1992), pp. 222–23.

13. Betty Mahmoody, *Not Without My Daughter* (New York: St. Martin's Press, 1987).

14. Adrienne Rich, "Compulsory Heterosexuality and Lesbian Existence," *Signs* 5, no. 4 (Summer 1980), 631–60.

15. Cf. Rawls, "Two Concepts of Rules," on the perspectives of the legislator and the judge, and on distinguishing between justifying an act falling

under a practice and justifying the practice itself. See chapter 11, below, for further development of the idea of levels of choice—higher and lower order choices, valuations, and desires.

4 ▪ *lesbian ethics*

1. Renée Vivien (pseudonym of Pauline Tarn), *A Woman Appeared to Me*, trans. Jeanette H. Foster (Tallahassee, Fla.: Naiad Press, 1982). Colette, *The Pure and the Impure*, trans. Herma Briffault (New York: Farrar, Straus, Giroux, 1967), pp. 79–98 (on Renée Vivien) and pp. 109–29 (on the Ladies of Llangollen). On Germany, see, for example, *Lesbians in Germany: 1980's-1920's*, trans. and ed. Lillian Faderman and Brigitte Eriksson (Tallahassee, Fla.: Naiad Press, 1980). Simone de Beauvoir, *The Second Sex*, trans. and ed. H. M. Parshley (New York: Modern Library, 1968), pp. 404-24.

2. Mary Wollstonecraft, *A Vindication of the Rights of Woman: An Authoritative Text, Backgrounds, Criticism*, ed. Carol H. Poston (New York: Norton, 1975).

3. See Virginia Woolf, "Mary Wollstoncraft," in *Virginia Woolf: Women and Writing*, ed. Michele Barrett (New York: Harcourt, Brace, Jovanovich, 1979), pp. 96–103, and Eleanor Flexner, *Mary Wollstonecraft* (New York: Coward, McCann and Geoghegan, 1972). Mary Wollstonecraft died ten days after the birth of her second daughter.

4. The Ladies of Llangollen, who eloped from Ireland to Wales in the 1770s, are a well-known exception.

5. Margaret Fuller, "The Great Lawsuit: Man versus Men. Woman versus Women," *Dial* 4 (July 1843), 1–47; *Woman in the Nineteenth Century* (New York: Norton, 1971), esp. pp. 115–16 and 169–70.

6. *Correspondance of Fraulein Gunderode and Bettina Von Arnim*, trans. Fuller (1842; reprinted, Boston: T. Burnham, 1961). In her Preface, Fuller says Caroline was a Canoness "mixing freely in the world at her pleasure," p. viii. Jeanette Foster clarifies that Caroline was "one of several daughters of a moderately affluent widow, who spent the latter part of her short life in a 'Kloster' (not a religious house but a dignified retreat for well-born spinsters such as has been charmingly pictured by Isak Dinesen in *Seven Gothic Tales*)," *Sex Variant Women in Literature* (2d ed.; Baltimore, Md.: Diana Press, 1975), p. 125.

7. Fuller, journal exerpt, in *Gay American History: Gay Men and Lesbians in the U.S.A.*, ed. Jonathan Katz (New York: Crowell, 1976), p. 466.

8. Fuller, *Woman in the Nineteenth Century*, pp. 72–81.

9. Fuller, *Woman in the Nineteenth Century*, pp. 172, 128, 41, and 43.

10. John Stuart Mill, *The Subjection of Women* (first published in 1969), in John Stuart Mill and Harriet Taylor Mill, *Essays on Sex Equality*, ed. Alice Rossi (Chicago: University of Chicago Press, 1970), p. 215.

11. Fuller, *Woman in the Nineteenth Century*, p. 95.

12. Fuller, *Woman in the Nineteenth Century*, p. 97. In 1849 or 1850 in Italy,

Margaret Fuller is said to have secretly married the Marchese d'Ossoli, with whom she had a son, Nino. All three died in a shipwreck in 1850 off the shore of Fire Island, a sand bar off the coast of Long Island.

13. Charlotte Perkins Gilman, *The Living of Charlotte Perkins Gilman* (New York: Arno Press, 1972), especially, pp. 44–60 and 78–89.

14. Gilman, *The Living of Charlotte Perkins Gilman*, p. 81.

15. See Ann J. Lane, "The Fictional World of Charlotte Perkins Gilman," in *The Charlotte Perkins Gilman Reader* (New York: Pantheon, 1980), pp. ix–xlii, and Carl N. Degler, "Introduction to the Torchbook Edition,"in Gilman, *Women and Economics: A Study of the Economic Relation Between Men and Women as a Factor in Social Evolution* (New York: Harper, 1966), pp. vi–xxxv.

16. Gilman, *The Yellow Wallpaper* (Old Westbury, N.Y.: Feminist Press, 1973), with Afterword by Elaine Hedges, pp. 37–63. "The Yellow Wallpaper" was first published in *The New England Magazine* (May 1892).

On Mitchell's "rest cure" and its social context, see G. J. Barker-Benfield, *The Horrors of the Half-Known Life: Male Attitudes Toward Women and Sexuality in Nineteenth-Century America* (New York: Harper and Row, 1976), especially, pp. 129–30.

17. Gilman, *Women and Economics*, pp. 169–294.

18. *Herland*, serialized in *The Forerunner* (a monthly magazine edited and mostly written by Charlotte Gilman), was first published as a book in 1979 (New York: Pantheon) with an introduction by Ann Lane.

19. Magnus Hirschfeld, introducing a letter from Emma Goldman to the *Yearbook for Sexual Intermediate Types*, in *Gay American History*, ed. Katz, p. 378. Emma Goldman was married in the 1880s for about a year to a fellow immigrant, Jacob Kershner. Her autobiography reports that an "inverted womb" prevented her from conceiving children but that because she saw no room for a child in a life that "would never know harmony in love for very long" and because she expected that "strife and not peace would be my lot," she refused an operation, *Living My Life* (2 vols.; New York: Dover, 1970), 1:187.

20. Goldman, letter to Magnus Hirschfeld, in *Gay American History*, ed. Katz, p. 379.

21. Goldman, *Living My Life*, 2:555–56.

22. Almeda Sperry, letters to Emma Goldman, in *Gay American History*, ed. Katz, pp. 523–30.

23. "Uranian" ("*Urning*" in German), a term for "homosexual" introduced by late nineteenth-century German sexologists, is apparently taken from Plato's *Symposium*, in which Aristodemus refers to the "heavenly Aphrodite" (who desires the soul) as "Uranian" by contrast with the "earthly Aphrodite" (who desires the body). *Collected Dialogues of Plato*, ed. Edith Hamilton and Huntington Cairns (New York: Pantheon, 1961), pp. 534–39.

24. She relates in her autobiography that when the government was searching for her after Alexander Berkman's failed attempt to assassinate Henry Clay Frick, she hid in a house of prostitutes and supported herself by sewing for them, *Living My Life*, 1:104.

25. For Emma Goldman's feminist views, see "The Traffic in Women," "Woman Suffrage," "The Tragedy of Women's Emancipation," and "Marriage and Love," first published in *Mother Earth* (the anarchist journal she founded and edited from 1906–15), reprinted in Goldman, *Anarchism and Other Essays* (New York: Dover, 1969). These should be read in conjunction with her anarchist essays, "Anarchism: What It Really Stands For" and "The Psychology of Political Violence" (same volume).

26. Woolf, *Three Guineas* (New York: Harcourt, Brace, and World, 1938).

27. Woolf, *Orlando: A Biography* (first published in 1928) (New York: Harcourt, Brace, Jovanovich, 1956). *A Room of One's Own* (New York: Harcourt, Brace, and World, 1929).

28. Quentin Bell, *Virginia Woolf: A Biography* (New York: Harcourt, Brace, Jovanovich, 1972), p. 119.

29. See Louise DeSalvo, *Virginia Woolf: The Impact of Childhood Sexual Abuse on Her Life and Work* (Boston: Beacon Press, 1989).

30. See Margaret Simons, "Lesbian Connections: Simone de Beauvoir and Feminism," *Signs* 18, no. 1 (Autumn 1992), 136–61.

31. Sara Ruddick's *Maternal Thinking: Toward a Politics of Peace* (Boston: Beacon Press, 1989) discusses virtues that the tasks of mothering ideally develop. These are as ethical as political.

32. Marilyn Frye, *Willful Virgin: Essays in Feminism* (Freedom, Calif.: Crossing Press, 1992), p. 144. Sarah Lucia Hoagland, *Lesbian Ethics: Toward New Value* (Palo Alto, Calif.: Institute for Lesbian Studies, 1988).

33. Frye, *Willful Virgin*, pp. 144–45.

34. Frye, *Willful Virgin*, pp. 14, 16. On p. 14, politics is presented as a medium of forces that "determine what can be done and by whom"; on p. 16, "The politics of anything is about will and value: aligning, allying, and engaging individual and collective will with that which is of value, which includes engaging will in the making of value."

35. "Getting It Right" (Frye, *Willful Virgin*, pp. 13–27) first appeared in *Signs* 17, no. 4 (Summer 1992), 781–93; an ancestor of "A Response to *Lesbian Ethics*: Why Ethics?" (Frye, *Willful Virgin.*, pp. 138–46), appeared in *Hypatia* 5, no. 3 (Fall 1990), 132–37.

36. Frye, *Willful Virgin*, p. 14; p. 26, n. 4.

37. Frye, *Willful Virgin*, p. 14. Cf. Michel Foucault, *The History of Sexuality*, trans. Robert Hurley (New York: Vintage, 1980).

38. Friedrich Nietzsche, *On the Genealogy of Morals*, trans. Walter Kaufmann and R. J. Hollingdale (New York: Vintage, 1969), pp. 24–56.

39. Mary Daly, *Beyond God the Father: Toward a Philosophy of Women's Lib-

eration (Boston: Beacon Press, 1973), pp. 44–60.

40. See Laurence Thomas, *Vessels of Evil* (Philadelphia: Temple University Press, 1993) on the Holocaust and American slavery as paradigmatic evils of different kinds.

41. Linda Brent (pseudonym of Harriet Brent Jacobs), *Incidents in the Life of a Slave Girl*, ed. L. Maria Child (New York: Harcourt Brace Jovanovich, 1973), pp. 88, 179.

42. Brent (Jacobs), p. 205. The woman, identified in the narrative as "Mrs. Bruce," did it anyhow (for $300), with the result that Harriet Jacobs was legally freed from those who would have re-enslaved her had they caught her. Upon hearing of this transaction, Harriet Jacobs writes, "I had objected to having my freedom bought, yet I must confess that when it was done I felt as if a heavy load had been lifted from my weary shoulders." That such relief should be a "confession" indicates the principles with which it competed.

43. Minnie Bruce Pratt, "Identity: Skin Blood Heart," in Elly Bulkin, Pratt, and Barbara Smith, *Yours in Struggle: Three Feminist Perspectives on Anti-Semitism and Racism* (Brooklyn, N.Y.: Long Haul Press, 1984), pp. 14–15.

44. Claudia Card, "Gender and Moral Luck," *Identity, Character, and Morality: Essays in Moral Psychology*, ed. Owen Flanagan and Amelie Oksenberg Rorty (Cambridge, Mass.: MIT Press, 1991), pp. 199–218, esp. p. 209.

45. The term should be "mutual combat," although "mutual battering" is the term often heard. See chapter 6.

46. *Lesbian Ethics*, ed. Fox (a.k.a. Jeanette Silveira), 3x annually, since Fall 1984, LE Publications, Box 4723, Albuquerque, N.M. 87196. *Gossip: A Journal of Lesbian Feminist Ethics* was issued twice annually by Onlywoman Press, London, beginning in 1986, for approximately six issues. Other journals that have been receptive to essays in lesbian ethics include *Sinister Wisdom: Journal for the Lesbian Imagination in the Arts and Politics*, ed. Elana Dykewomon, Berkeley, Calif., 1976 to present (49 issues as of Spring/Summer 1993); *Trivia: A Journal of Ideas*, ed. Lise Weil and Linda Nelson, Amherst, Mass., 1982 to present (20 issues as of 1992); *The Canadian Journal of Feminist Ethics* (title changed to *Feminist Ethics* in 1987), ed. Kathleen Martindale and Martha Saunders, 1986–89; *Hypatia: A Journal of Feminist Philosophy*, ed. Linda Lopez Macalister, University of South Florida, 3x annually 1986–91 and quarterly since 1991; *Signs: Journal of Women in Culture and Society*, ed. Ruth-Ellen Boetcher Joeres and Barbara Laslett, Minneapolis, quarterly, since 1975. and the *Journal of Homosexuality*, ed. John de Cecco, San Francisco, quarterly, since 1975.

47. Adrienne Rich, "Women and Honor: Some Notes on Lying," *Heresies*, 1:1 (January 1977), 23–26, reprinted in Rich, *On Lies, Secrets, and Silence: Selected Prose 1966–1978* (New York: Norton, 1979), pp. 185–94. Frye, "Some Thoughts on Separatism and Power," *Sinister Wisdom* no. 6 (Summer 1978), 30–39, reprinted as "Some Reflections on Separatism and Power," Marilyn Frye, *Politics of Reality: Essays in Feminist Theory* (Trumansburg, N.Y.:

Crossing Press, 1983), pp. 95–109.

48. *For Lesbians Only: A Separatist Anthology*, ed. Sarah Lucia Hoagland and Julia Penelope (London: Onlywomen Press, 1988).

49. *Lesbian Philosophies and Cultures*, ed. Jeffner Allen (Albany, N.Y.: State University of New York Press, 1990) offers diverse perspectives in lesbian ethics, including essays by many of these authors as well as many more. See also Gloria Anzaldúa, *Borderlands/La Frontera: The New Mestiza* (San Francisco: Spinsters/Aunt Lute, 1987); Mary Daly, *Gyn/Ecology: The Metaethics of Radical Feminism* (Boston: Beacon Press, 1978); Daly, *Pure Lust: Elemental Feminist Philosophy* (Boston: Beacon Press, 1984), and her autobiography, *Outercourse: The Be-Dazzling Voyage* (San Francisco: Harper, 1992); two books of essays by Audre Lorde, *Sister Outsider: Essays and Speeches* (Trumansburg, N.Y.: Crossing Press, 1984) and *A Burst of Light* (Ithaca, N.Y.: Firebrand, 1988), as well as her autobiographical *The Cancer Journals* (Argyle, N.Y.: Spinsters Ink, 1980) and *Zami: A New Spelling of My Name* (Watertown, Mass.: Persephone Press, 1982); Joan Nestle, *A Restricted Country* (Ithaca, N.Y.: Firebrand, 1987); Julia Penelope, *Call Me Lesbian: Lesbian Lives, Lesbian Theory* (Freedom, Calif.: Crossing Press, 1992); Janice G. Raymond, *The Transsexual Empire: The Making of the She-Male* (Boston: Beacon Press, 1979) and *A Passion for Friends: Toward a Philosophy of Female Affection* (Boston: Beacon Press, 1986); and Joanna Russ, *Magic Mommas, Trembling Sisters, Puritans & Perverts: Feminist Essays* (Trumansburg, N.Y.: Crossing Press, 1985). For essays by María Lugones, Joyce Trebilcot, and Jacquelina Zita, see the Selected Bibliography.

In *A Chorus of Stones: The Private Life of War* (New York: Doubleday, 1992), Susan Griffin does not identify herself as lesbian but writes of having a lesbian sister. Griffin's writings, especially *Woman and Nature: The Roaring Inside Her* (New York: Harper and Row, 1978) and the poems of *Like the Iris of an Eye* (New York: Harper and Row, 1976), have had a significant impact on lesbian ethics.

50. Susan Cavin, *Lesbian Origins* (San Francisco: Ism Press, 1985). Lillian Faderman, *Odd Girls and Twilight Lovers: A History of Lesbian Life in Twentieth-Century America* (New York: Columbia University Press, 1991); *Scotch Verdict* (New York: Quill, 1983); and *Surpassing the Love of Men: Romantic Friendship and Love Between Women from the Renaissance to the Present* (New York: Morrow, 1981); Judy Grahn, *Another Mother Tongue: Gay Words, Gay Worlds* (Boston: Beacon Press, 1984) and *The Highest Apple: Sappho and the Lesbian Poetic Tradition* (San Francisco: Spinsters Ink, 1985).

51. See, for example, Susan Griffin, *Woman and Nature*; and H. Pat Hynes, *The Recurring Silent Spring* (New York: Pergamon, 1989).

52. Kathleen Martindale and Martha Saunders, for example, in "Realizing Love and Justice: Lesbian Ethics in Upper and Lower Case," *Hypatia* 7, no. 4 (Fall 1992), 148–71, protest the lack of attention to justice in "Upper Case" lesbian ethics.

53. For example, in *Maternal Thinking*, Sara Ruddick notes that lesbians can be mothers, too, and yet lesbians are not among her paradigms.

54. Joyce Trebilcot, "Dyke Methods," *Hypatia* 3, no. 2 (Summer 1988), 1–13.

55. For gay ethics, see Richard Mohr, *Gays/Justice: A Study of Ethics, Society, and Law* (New York: Columbia University Press, 1988) and *Gay Ideas: Outing and Other Controversies* (Boston: Beacon Press, 1992).

56. See Elizabeth Däumer, "Queer Ethics, or The Challenge of Bisexuality to Lesbian Ethics," *Hypatia* 7, no. 4 (Fall 1992), 91–105.

57. See Frye, *Politics of Reality*, pp. 128–51.

58. Carol Gilligan, *In a Different Voice: Psychological Theory and Women's Development* (Cambridge, Mass.: Harvard University Press, 1982). See also Gilligan, Janie Victoria Ward, and Jill McLean Taylor with Betty Bardige, *Mapping the Moral Domain: A Contribution of Women's Thinking to Psychological Theory and Education* (Cambridge, Mass.: Harvard Graduate School of Education, 1988); and *Making Connections: The Relational Worlds of Adolescent Girls at Emma Willard School*, ed. Gilligan, Nona P. Lyons, and Trudy J. Hanmer (Troy, New York: Emma Willard School, 1989).

59. Nel Noddings, *Caring: A Feminine Approach to Ethics and Moral Education* (Berkeley: University of California Press, 1984).

60. Noddings, *Women and Evil* (Berkeley: University of California Press, 1989).

61. The complementarity view is suggested at the end of *In a Different Voice*. The view that the two ethics offer alternative gestalts is suggested in Gilligan, "Moral Orientation and Moral Development," in *Women and Moral Theory*, ed. Eva Feder Kittay and Diana T. Meyers (Totowa, N.J.: Rowman and Littlefield, 1987), pp. 19–33.

62. Nel Noddings describes her care ethics as feminine and appears not to see a conflict between "feminine" and "feminist."

63. Hoagland, "Some Thoughts About 'Caring,' " in *Feminist Ethics*, ed. Claudia Card (Lawrence: University Press of Kansas, 1991), pp. 246–63. For lesbian perspectives on heterosexual motherhood, see *Mothering: Essays in Feminist Theory*, ed. Trebilcot (Totowa, N.J.: Rowman & Allanheld, 1984) and Rich, *Of Woman Born: Motherhood as Experience and Institution* (New York: Norton, 1976). For a lesbian perspective on lesbian motherhood, see Phyllis Burke (the nonbiological mother), *Family Values: Two Moms and Their Son* (New York: Random House, 1993).

64. Allen, *Lesbian Philosophy: Explorations* (Palo Alto, Calif.: Institute for Lesbian Studies, 1986), pp. 27–59.

65. As, for example, Woolf, *Three Guineas*, and Ruddick, *Maternal Thinking*. See also Olive Schreiner, *Woman and Labour* (London: Virago, 1978; originally, T. Fisher Unwin, 1911), pp. 151–78 (on women and war).

Although war and street crime kill and maim women and children, writers who take war and street crime as their paradigms of violence tend to focus on men as victims, as though the harm to women and children were primarily the loss of husbands and fathers.

66. The journal *Lesbian Ethics* has had Readers' Forums and special issues on these topics. Much of Pat Califia's *Sapphistry: The Book of Lesbian Sexuality* (Tallahassee, Fla.: Naiad Press, 1980) is on practical sapphic ethics.

67. "Economics" has roots in the ancient Greek "*oikos*" (house) and "*nomos*" (law). Similarly, "ecology" is, etymologically, the "study of the house."

5 ▪ *lesbian friendships: separations and continua*

1. Sarah Lucia Hoagland, *Lesbian Ethics: Toward New Value* (Palo Alto, Calif.: Institute of Lesbian Studies, 1988).

2. María C. Lugones and Elizabeth V. Spelman, "Have We Got a Theory for You! Feminist Theory, Cultural Imperialism and the Demand for 'the Woman's Voice'," in *Hypatia Reborn: Essays in Feminist Philosophy*, ed. Azizah Y. al-Hibri and Margaret A. Simons (Bloomington: Indiana University Press, 1990), pp. 18–33.

3. Margy, "Can Lesbians Be Friends?" *Lesbian Connection* 2, no. 4 (August 1976), 13–14, and "Can Lesbians Be Friends: Part II," *Lesbian Connection* 2, no. 6 (November 1976), 10–11.

4. Jan Raymond noted, in personal correspondence, that women in heterosexual relationships often do not sever a relationship for things over which women in lesbian relationships would immediately do so. The natural instability of lover relationships that are heterosexual may be often counteracted by pressures on women to maintain intimate connections with men.

5. Esther Heffernan, *Making It in Prison: The Square, the Cool, and the Life* (New York: Wiley, 1972), pp. 87–106.

6. Rose Giallombardo, *Society of Women: A Study of a Women's Prison* (New York: Wiley, 1966), pp. 133–89. See also David A. Ward and Gene G. Kassebaum, *Women's Prison: Sex and Social Structure* (Chicago: Aldine, 1965).

7. Ju-K'ang T'ien, "Female Labor in a Cotton Mill," supplementary chapter in Kuo-Hang Shih, *China Enters the Machine Age: A Study of Labor in Chinese War Industry*, trans. and ed. Hsiao-Tung Fei and Francis L. K. Hsu (Cambridge, Mass.: Harvard University Press, 1944), pp. 178–95.

8. Giallombardo, *Society of Women*, pp. 174–75.

9. Strictly, monogamy is a form of marriage. Legally disabled from marrying each other, lesbians nevertheless commonly use the term loosely, and I follow that usage without scare-quotes hereafter.

10. John Rawls, *A Theory of Justice* (Cambridge, Mass.: Harvard University Press, 1971), p. 20.

11. Janice G. Raymond, *A Passion for Friends: Toward a Philosophy of Female Friendship* (Boston: Beacon Press, 1986), pp. 149–201.

12. For some of her ideas on lesbian ethics, see Janice Raymond and Patri-

cia Hynes, "Convent Values and Lesbian Ethics," in *Lesbian Nuns: Breaking Silence*, ed. Rosemary Curb and Nancy Manahan (Tallahassee, Fla.: Naiad Press, 1985), pp. 349–62.

13. Raymond, *A Passion for Friends*, p. 8.

14. For more on the prohibition against "particular friendships," see Raymond and Hynes, "Convent Values and Lesbian Ethics" and other contributions to *Lesbian Nuns*, ed. Curb and Manahan.

15. For lesbians' accounts of why they joined the military, see Mary Ann Humphrey, *My Country, My Right to Serve: Experiences of Gay Men and Women in the Military, World War II to the Present* (New York: HarperCollins, 1988); and Randy Shilts, *Conduct Unbecoming: Lesbians and Gays in the U.S. Military, Vietnam to the Persian Gulf* (New York: St. Martin's Press, 1993).

16. According to Jan Raymond, during the twelfth century, the idea of containing female religious activity within convent walls gained ground and "in 1289 Pope Boniface VIII made the rule of enclosure mandatory for all women who wished to live a canonically approved religious life," a rule that was "not enforced within religious communities of men" (*A Passion for Friends*, pp. 99–100).

On marriage resisters, Jan Raymond cites as ground-breaking the research of Marjorie Topley, "The Organisation and Social Function of Chinese Women's *Chai T'ang* in Singapore" (Ph.D. dissertation, University of London, 1958) and "Marriage Resistance in Rural Kwangtun," in *Women in Chinese Society*, ed. Margery Wolf and Roxane Witke (Stanford: Stanford University Press, 1975).

17. Raymond, *A Passion for Friends*, p. 153.

18. Hannah Arendt, *The Human Condition* (Chicago: University of Chicago Press, 1958), pp. 50–67.

19. Arendt, *The Jew as Pariah: Jewish Identity and Politics in the Modern Age*, ed. Ron Feldman (New York: Grove Press, 1978); Virginia Woolf, *Three Guineas* (New York: Harcourt, Brace & World, 1938), pp. 106 ff.

20 Hoagland, *Lesbian Ethics*, pp. 24–68.

21. Hoagland, *Lesbian Ethics*, p. 3. See also *For Lesbians Only: A Separatist Anthology*, ed. Hoagland and Julia Penelope (London: Onlywomen Press, 1988).

22. Marilyn Frye, *The Politics of Reality: Essays in Feminist Theory* (Trumansberg, N.Y.: Crossing Press, 1983), pp. 95–109.

23. Raymond, *A Passion for Friends*, pp. 153–4; on "the freedom and untouchability of outcasts," she quotes Arendt, *Jew as Pariah*, p. 90.

24. Raymond, *A Passion for Friends*, p. 154. She adds, "—or should I say that this past is one that most women know little about?"

25. Raymond, *A Passion for Friends*, p. 154, again quoting Arendt (*Jew as Pariah*, p. 27).

26. Elizabeth Mavor, *The Ladies of Llangollen* (Middlesex, England: Pen-

guin, 1973).

27. Eleanor Butler, Sarah Ponsonby, and Caroline Hamilton, *The Hamwood Papers of the Ladies of Llangollen and Caroline Hamilton*, ed. Eva Mary Bell (London: Macmillan, 1930).

28. Shari Benstock, *Women of the Left Bank: Paris, 1900–1940* (Austin: University of Texas Press, 1986), pp. 268–307.

29. See Frye, *Politics of Reality*, pp. 152–74, and Hoagland, *Lesbian Ethics*, pp. 114–56.

30. *The Autobiography of Malcolm X* with the assistance of Alex Haley (New York: Grove Press, 1964), p. 246: "To *segregate* means to control. Segregation is that which is forced upon inferiors by superiors. But *separation* is that which is done voluntarily." Cf. *Malcolm X: The Last Speeches*, ed. Bruce Perry (New York: Pathfinder, 1989), pp. 38–39: "We don't go for segregation. We go for separation. Separation is when you have your own. You control your own economy; you control your own politics; you control your own society; you control your own everything." Also Frye, *The Politics of Reality*, p. 96: "Feminist separation is . . . initiated or maintained, at will, *by women*. (Masculist separatism is the partial segregation of women from men and male domains *at the will of men*. This difference is crucial.)"

31. On material resources, see, for example, Frye, *Willful Virgin: Essays in Feminism* (Freedom, Calif.: The Crossing Press, 1992), pp. 28–38.

32. María Lugones, "Playfulness, 'World'-Travelling, and Loving Perception," *Hypatia* 2, no. 2 (Summer 1987), 3–19.

33. Jan Raymond seems to agree that separatism need not be isolationist or unworldly, noting that she had only identified unworldly dissociation with *some* separatists, although she seems reluctant to use the language of separatism in presenting contexts supportive of female friendships, perhaps finding it misleading. Raymond, "Response," *Hypatia* 3, no. 2 (Summer 1988), 139–43.

34. See Claudia Card, "Gratitude and Obligation," *American Philosophical Quarterly* 25, no. 2 (April 1988), 115–27, for further development of the contrast between intimate and formal relationships and between the formal and informal obligations to which they give rise.

35. Arendt, *The Human Condition*, pp. 51–52 and 241–43.

36. For example, Cicero, "On Friendship," in *On Friendship and Old Age*, trans. Harry G. Edinger (Indianapolis: Bobbs Merrill, 1967), pp. 3–39; and Michel de Montaigne, "Of Friendship," in *The Complete Essays of Montaigne*, trans. Donald M. Frame (Stanford, Calif.: Stanford University Press, 1965), pp. 135–44.

37. Aristotle's misogyny and elitism have been well-explored by others. See, e.g., Elizabeth V. Spelman, *Inessential Woman: Problems of Exclusion in Feminist Thought* (Boston: Beacon Press, 1988). Although I do not go over that ground again here, his misogyny and elitism help explain why Aristotle did not develop some of the potentialities of a theory of friendship of interest to lesbians.

38. *The Nicomachean Ethics of Aristotle*, trans. Sir David Ross (London: Oxford University Press, 1925), pp. 192–247. See also Aristotle's *Eudemian Ethics*, Bk. VII; *Magna Moralia* Bk. II, chs. 11–17; and *Rhetoric* Bk. II, ch. 4; all in *The Complete Works of Aristotle*, 2 vols., ed. Jonathan Barnes (Princeton, N.J.: Princeton University Press, 1984), 2:1956–81, 2:1912–21, and 2:2200–02.

39. Aristotle tends to see lover relationships as subject also to another kind of instability insofar as he assumes that they exemplify "mixed" friendships, where the love is not the same on both sides and the motives of each party are different.

40. Aristotle, *Eudemian Ethics* VII:6, in Barnes, *Complete Works*, 2:1965.

41. Aristotle, *Politics* I:13, in Barnes, *Complete Works* 2:1999–2000.

42. Rawls, *A Theory of Justice*, pp. 472–79.

43. Aristotle, *Eudemian Ethics* VI:10, in Barnes, *Complete Works*, 2:1968.

44. Aristotle, *Rhetoric* II:4, in Barnes, *Complete Works*, 2:2200–02.

45. Adrienne Rich, *The Dream of a Common Language: Poems 1974–1977* (New York: Norton, 1978).

46. Elizabeth Telfer, "Friendship," *Proceedings of the Aristotelian Society*, New Ser. 71 (1970–71), 223–41. She includes under shared activity mutual contact, reciprocal services, and joint pursuits.

47. Telfer, "Friendship," 229–30.

48. Aristotle, *Eudemian Ethics* VII:2, in Barnes, *Complete Works*, 2:1958–59.

49. *The Nicomachean Ethics of Aristotle*, pp. 55–58.

50. Simone Weil, *Gravity and Grace* (London: Ark, 1987), pp. 105–11; Frye, *Politics of Reality*, pp. 72–83, 170–73; Hoagland, *Lesbian Ethics*, 120–43.

51. On the damage such a lover can do, see Phaedrus' speech in Plato, *Phaedrus* (231a–234c), in *The Collected Dialogues of Plato*, ed. Edith Hamilton and Huntington Cairnes (New York: Bollingen, 1961), pp. 479–82.

52. In support of having several friends, Aristotle notes that we share different things with different friends: "one man is like another in body, and another like him in soul, and one like him in one part of the body or soul, and another like him in another," *Eudemian Ethics* VII:10, in Barnes, 2:1974. Yet, these may be only friendships of pleasure or utility.

53. Aristotle thought one had to live with friends to know them well enough for true friendship. With widespread literacy and technologically improved transportation and communication, that may be less true today.

6 ▪ *horizontal violence: partner battering and lesbian stalking*

1. Information on Catherine Rouse and Joan Kebick is from Madison newspapers: *Capital Times*, Jan. 14, 1989, pp. 1, 4; *Wisconsin State Journal*, Jan. 14, 1989, pp. 1–2 and Jan. 17, 1989, pp. 1–2.

2. On Annette Green and Ivonne Julio, see Claire Renzetti, *Violent Betrayal: Partner Abuse in Lesbian Relationships* (Newbury Park, Calif.: Sage, 1992),

pp. 75, 111, 113; Ruthann Robson, *Lesbian (Out)Law: Survival Under the Rule of Law* (Ithaca, N.Y.: Firebrand, 1992), pp. 157–64; and *Geraldo* transcript #569 (for show aired Nov. 21, 1989), Journal Graphics, 267 Broadway, New York, N.Y. 10007.

Claire Renzetti reports that in 1991 Annette Green was granted a new trial, accepted a five-year sentence for manslaughter, and was released in late 1991. Since Annette's first trial, two other lesbians have successfully used the battered woman defense, although no deaths were involved: Priscilla Forbes, who was successfully defended in February 1991 in Boise, Idaho, against a charge of stabbing her partner in the back, and Sherry Sperling in Los Angeles, who was charged with misdemeanor battery (Renzetti, *Violent Betrayal*, p. 113).

3. Robson, *Lesbian (Out)Law*, p. 160. Claire Renzetti, who appeared on Geraldo's show with Annette Green, observed that, "In crimes against women . . . the victim, typically, has to prove that she is a . . . worthy victim because, in our society . . . being female is a devalued status. . . . the more devalued statuses you add to femaleness, the more difficult time you have proving your worthiness. . . . homosexuality or sexual preference is one additional devalued status. In Annette's case, she is also Hispanic. She's a minority woman; another devalued status. She's poor; another devalued status" (*Geraldo*, transcript #569, p. 4).

4. For example, in 1989–90, the Minnesota Coalition for Battered Women (Hamline Park Plaza, 570 Asbury, Suite 201, St. Paul, Minn. 55104) put together a training manual (unpublished), "Confronting Lesbian Battering," ed. Pamela Elliott, Coordinator of the Coalition's Lesbian Battering Intervention Project, containing definitions, brief articles from small periodicals, practical guidelines, and survivor narratives.

5. David Island and Patrick Letellier, *Men Who Beat the Men Who Love Them* (New York: Harrington Park Press, 1991). *Naming the Violence: Speaking Out About Lesbian Battering*, ed. Kerry Lobel (Seattle, Wash.: Seal Press, 1986), grew out of a 1983 meeting of the Lesbian Task Force of the National Coalition for Domestic Violence. Seal Press has also published *Getting Free: A Handbook for Women in Abusive Relationships* (1986) and *The Ones Who Got Away: Women Who Left Abusive Partners* (1987), both by Ginny NiCarthy [*sic*], both including selections on lesbian battering.

6. Robson, *Lesbian (Out)Law*, pp. 171–75, also criticizes mediation in other contexts involving violence as individualizing, privatizing, and depoliticizing.

Adopting a feminist participatory research model, Claire Renzetti and the Working Group agreed on a division of responsibilities whereby the Working Group would return what was learned from the study to members of lesbian communities, and Claire Renzetti would publish the results in book form for colleagues in sociology.

7. Island and Letellier take the controversial position that batterers have a curable psychological disorder. Not optimistic about the *likelihood* of cure,

however, they unambiguously advise survivors to sever contact forever with former partners who battered them.

8. Melanie Kaye/Kantrowitz, *The Issue Is Power: Essays on Women, Jews, Violence and Resistance* (San Francisco: Aunt Lute, 1992), pp. 34–40.

9. Alice Miller, *For Your Own Good: Hidden Cruelty in Child-Rearing and the Roots of Violence*, trans. Hildegarde and Hunter Hannum (New York: Farrar, Straus, Giroux, 1983) and *Thou Shalt Not Be Aware: Society's Betrayal of the Child*, trans. Hildegarde and Hunter Hannum (New York: New American Library, 1984).

10. However, children may also experience abuse at schools or religious institutions and from babysitters, neighbors, neighborhood children, and so on, which may not show up in studies, depending on the questions asked.

11. Kaye/Kantrowitz, *The Issue Is Power*, p. 36.

12. Julia Penelope and Sarah Hoagland call attention to uses of the passive voice that obscure agency, often used to render hostile agents invisible. See Sarah Hoagland, *Lesbian Ethics: Toward New Value* (Palo Alto, Calif.: Institute of Lesbian Studies, 1988), pp. 17–18, and Julia P. Stanley [Julia Penelope], "Prescribed Passivity: The Language of Sexism," in *Views on Language*, ed. Reza Ordoubadian (Murfreesboro, Tenn.: Inter-University Publishing, 1975), pp. 96–108.

13. Elliott, ed., "Confronting Lesbian Battering," p. 35. This abuse is also graphically described by Tobias Wolff in *This Boy's Life: A Memoir* (New York: Atlantic Monthly Press, 1989), pp. 85 ff. and pp. 134–36.

14. Elliott, ed., "Confronting Lesbian Battering," pp. 37–38.

15. Renzetti, *Violent Betrayal*, p. 21.

16. Lydia Walker, "Battered Women's Shelter and Work with Battered Lesbians," in *Naming the Violence*, ed. Lobel, p. 76.

17. For example, Karen Lee Asherah, "The Myth of Mutual Abuse," *Matrix* (February 1988), in Elliott, ed,., "Confronting Lesbian Battering," pp. 56–58. Claire Renzetti and contributors to *Naming the Violence* agree.

18. Kaye/Kantrowitz, *The Issue Is Power*, p. 34.

19. Robson, *Lesbian (Out)Law*, pp. 161–62.

20. Barbara Hart, "Lesbian Battering: An Examination," in *Naming the Violence*, ed. Lobel, pp. 173–89.

21. Nomi Porat, "Support Groups for Battered Lesbians," in *Naming the Violence*, ed. Lobel, p. 83, and Linda and Avreayl, "Organizing Safe Space for Battered Lesbians: A Community Based Program," *Naming the Violence*, p. 107.

22. Hart, "Lesbian Battering," p. 189.

23. Joseph R. Nolan and Jacqueline M. Nolan-Haley, *Black's Law Dictionary: Definitions of the Terms and Phrases of American and English Jurisprudence, Ancient and Modern*, 6th ed. (St. Paul: West, 1990), pp. 152–53.

"Battery" is both a civil and a criminal concept, with accordingly different standards of proof, different penalties (money damages as opposed to imprisonment, for example), and different theoretical bases (private wrongs as opposed to public wrongs). Where police protection is needed, the criminal concept is the salient one.

24. See, for example, "batter" and "battery," in *Random House Webster's College Dictionary* (New York, 1991), p. 117.

25. In law, an *assault*, as a threat or attempt, is distinguished from *battery*, as its physical enactment. More on this below.

26. Juries believing in the rightness of the self-defense plea have been driven to find the defendant not guilty *by reason of insanity*, when her act appeared among the sanest of her life. See, for example, Faith McNulty, *The Burning Bed* (New York: Bantam, 1981), on Francine Hughes of Michigan, acquitted of murder although she killed her batterer as he slept.

27. The point here is not that domestic battering is a form of *enslavement*. It is not; it does not grant batterers a legal right to sell the partner or their children. The point is that battering can create and maintain a dominance pattern in domestic partnerships, just as it helped maintain owner dominance under American slavery, without necessarily relying on continual physical violence.

28. J. D. Mabbott, "On Punishment," *Mind* n.s. 48 (1939), 152–67.

29. Joyce McConnell, "Beyond Metaphor: Battered Women, Involuntary Servitude and the Thirteenth Amendment," *Yale Journal of Law and Feminism* 4, no. 2 (Spring 1992), 207–53,

30. Lenore E. Walker, *The Battered Woman* (New York: Harper, 1979), pp. 55–70. Her views are based on studying women battered by men. See also Lenore E. Walker, *Terrifying Love: Why Battered Women Kill and How Society Responds* (New York: Harper & Row, 1989).

31. Melanie Kaye/Kantrowitz, *The Issue Is Power*, p. 76, n. 2., cites "psychiatrist Carole Warshaw, *New York Times*, March 15, 1992" as claiming that "The greatest risk of getting killed is when the woman attempts to leave. . . . The husband or the partner can't tolerate the idea of her leaving."

32. *Black's Law Dictionary*, p. 153; "assault," pp. 114–15. Like battery, assault is both a civil and a criminal concept. (For the *crime* of assault, for example, it is not necessary that the victim be apprehensive, if the assailant intends to harm. For the *tort* of assault, the victim's apprehension is necessary.)

33. See, for example, Herbert Morris, "Punishment for Thoughts," *The Monist* 49, no. 3 (July 1965), 342–76, or Gerald Dworkin and David Blumenfeld, "Punishment for Intentions," *Mind* 75, no. 299 (July 1966), 396–404.

34. In 1971 Gerald MacCallum's unpublished writings on violence first drew my attention to the suddenness aspect. These essays are now published in Gerald C. MacCallum, Jr., *Legislative Intent and Other Essays on Law, Politics, and Morality*, ed. Marcus G. Singer and Rex Martin (Madison: University of Wisconsin Press, 1993).

35. A cruelty in France under the guillotine was that condemned prison-

ers were not told which night they would be executed. The official position was that this spared prisoners the anxiety of knowing. In reality, it enhanced control over the prisoners by holding them in constant terror. See Albert Camus, "Reflections on the Guillotine," in *Resistance, Rebellion, and Death*, trans. Justin O'Brien (New York: Modern Library, 1960), pp. 131–79.

Some survivors of battering try to take control of the timing by provoking an eruption of the violence that they know is inevitable.

36. Renzetti, *Violent Betrayal*, p. 117.

37. For a good discussion of this, see Susan Forward and Joan Torres, *Men Who Hate Women and the Women Who Love Them* (New York: Bantam, 1986). Naive in its assumptions regarding heterosexuality and male dominance and in its mother-blaming, this book's documentation of patterns of abuse is nevertheless superb.

38. *Windows*, dir. Gordon Willis (United Artists, 1980). Elizabeth Ashley plays the lesbian stalker, who tries to murder her heterosexual victim.

39. Richard Wade Farley, for example, shot and killed seven workers in addition to shooting and critically wounding Laura Black at her workplace after stalking her eight years. See Bob Trebilcock, "I Love You to Death," *Redbook* no. 178 (March 1992), 100–103, 112, 114. In other cases reported between 1990 and 1992, several stalkers killed themselves upon being cornered by police after killing, or attempting to kill, their prey.

40. Melinda Beck with Debra Rosenberg, Farai Chideya, Susan Miller, Donna Foote, Howard Manly, and Peter Katel, "Murderous Obsession," *Newsweek* 120 (July 13, 1992), 61. Christiane N. Brown, "New Laws to Protect You from Stalkers," *Good Housekeeping* 217, no. 2 (August 1993), 155–56.

41. "Stalker," Transcript for Show #187 (New York: CBS News; March 4, 1992), Journal Graphics, 1535 Grant St., Denver, CO 80203–1843.

42. Sharon Gless, then 46, who played Christine Cagney on the TV series, "Cagney and Lacey," was reportedly stalked by Joni Leigh Penn, then 30, who eventually broke into Gless's house, although the house was unoccupied at the time. See Jeannie Park, Lois Armstrong, Doris Bacon, and Eleanor Hoover, "A Fan's Long, Suicidal Obsession with Actress Sharon Gless Leads to a Tense Police Standoff," *People Weekly* 33 (April 16, 1990), 62–63. Film actor Teri Garr had been reportedly stalked for five years in 1990 by a fan whose aliases included Brook Morgan Hull and Susan Hull. See Susan Schindehette and Doris Bacon, "Vanna White and Teri Garr Ask the Courts to Protect Them from Fans Who Have Gone Too Far," *People Weekly* 34 (July 16, 1990), 40–41.

43. See Anastasia Toufexis, "A Fatal Obsession with the Stars," *Time* 134 (July 31, 1989), 43–44.

44. Claire Safran, "A Stranger Was Stalking Our Little Girl," *Good Housekeeping* 215 (November 1992), 266.

45. Those using psychiatric models of analysis call it "erotomania" when the stalker is deluded into believing that the erotic passion is mutual.

46. According to *Black's Law Dictionary*, p. 717, the Federal Fair Debt Collection Practices Act prohibits debt collectors from using certain harassment tactics. Holding intelligence agents accountable is, apparently, more difficult. Curt Gentry, *J. Edgar Hoover: The Man and the Secrets* (New York: Norton, 1991) discusses FBI tactics under Hoover.

47. Randy Shilts, *Conduct Unbecoming: Gays and Lesbians in the U.S. Military, Vietnam to the Persian Gulf* (New York: St. Martin's Press, 1993).

48. Claudia Brenner, "Eight Bullets" in *Hate Crimes: Confronting Violence Against Lesbians and Gay Men*, ed. Gregory M. Herek and Kevin T. Berrill (Newbury Park, Calif.: Sage, 1992), 11–15. Stephen Roy Carr was convicted of first-degree murder and sentenced to life imprisonment with no possibility of parole, even though "the judge excluded as inadmissible any arguments by the defense that the victims' sexual orientation or behavior had provoked the attack," *Lesbian Connection* 11, no. 4 (January/February 1989), 3–4. *Lesbian Connection* 11, no. 2 (September/October 1988), 2–3, reported that Claudia Brenner and Rebecca Wight first saw Stephen Carr after Rebecca had gone to the outhouse naked on the morning of May 13, thinking they were alone in the woods, that they then moved their campsite and again saw him, this time with a rifle, and that he shot them at 8 P.M. that night.

49. On ethical issues raised by horizontal stalking in another context, see Peter Wyden, *Stella* (New York: Simon & Schuster, 1992), about a Jewish woman used by Nazis to find Jews in Berlin.

50. Mike Tharp, "In the Mind of a Stalker," *U.S. News and World Report* 112 (Feb. 17, 1992), 28–30.

51. Psychiatrist Helen Morrison, quoted in Safran, "A Stranger Was Stalking Our Little Girl," p. 266.

52. Tharp, "In the Mind of a Stalker," p. 28. He does not identify the study.

53. Bob Trebilcock, "I Love You to Death," p. 102.

54. I had read and commented on two prepublication manuscripts of this work but was not then thinking about lesbian violence and had not begun writing about it.

55. Hoagland, *Lesbian Ethics*, pp. 39–49.

56. The last chapter begins: "I have been focusing on how the concept of 'control' permeates our lives. In chapter two I discussed control from a position of subordination. . . . In chapter three I discussed paternalism, an attempt to control, from a position of dominance. . . . In chapter four I discussed the fragmentation of reasoning and emotions involved with the idea of 'self-control.' . . . In this chapter I want to discuss the function of patriarchal ethics as social control. . . . to develop my suggestion that the function of Lesbian

Ethics be, not social control, but rather the development of lesbian integrity and agency." Hoagland, *Lesbian Ethics*, p. 247.

57. Hoagland, *Lesbian Ethics*, pp. 1–3.

58. See Hoagland, *Lesbian Ethics*, p. 256, for an example.

59. In recent correspondence, Sarah Hoagland has indicated that her intention was to focus on lesbian interactions *before* they reached the stage of battering, to develop an ethic that would make violence less likely.

60. Stanley M. Elkins, *Slavery: A Problem in American Institutional and Intellectual Life*, 2d ed. (Chicago: University of Chicago Press, 1968), pp. 81–139; Bruno Bettelheim, "Individual and Mass Behavior in Extreme Situations," *Surviving and Other Essays* (New York: Vintage, 1980), 48–83.

61. Plato, *Theatetus* 149–152, in *The Collected Dialogues of Plato*, ed. Edith Hamilton and Huntington Cairnes (New York: Bollingen, 1961), pp. 853–54.

62. In *Lesbian Ethics* Sarah Hoagland acknowledges limits to the value of attending (pp. 130–31): others may need privacy, we may need to shield ourselves, we cannot always be a party to another's choices, and so on. Although she commented on the negative effects on the batterer of being attended by her victim, however, she did not comment on the batterer's own problematic attending.

63. See Mary Daly, *Gyn/Ecology: The Metaethics of Radical Feminism* (Boston: Beacon Press, 1978), pp. 139–41, 163–65, 198–99, and 301–302, on women as "token torturers" in footbinding, genital mutilation, the European witchcraze, and in Nazi Germany. Although I would not analyze these torturers as "tokens," I agree that their choices have roots in their own oppression, and that such choices have been significant for women's attitudes toward women.

64. This may remind one of Melanie Kaye/Kantrowitz's idea of rechanneling hostilities against oppressive institutions.

65. Hoagland, *Lesbian Ethics*, p. 117.

66. On lesbian invisibility, see Marilyn Frye, *The Politics of Reality: Essays in Feminist Theory* (Trumansburg, N.Y.: The Crossing Press, 1983), pp. 152–174.

67. Hoagland, *Lesbian Ethics*, pp. 12–13.

68. Alvin Poussaint, *Why Blacks Kill Blacks* (New York: Emerson Hall, 1972), pp. 69–80.

69. I know of only two cases that are clear exceptions and a possible third. The first is the case of Pauline Parker and Juliet Hulme of New Zealand who were in love and who in 1954, when they were aged fifteen and sixteen, murdered the mother of Pauline Parker, apparently because she was trying to keep them apart. They were convicted and sentenced to prison terms, which they have served. See Julie Glamuzina and Alison J. Laurie, *Parker and Hulme: A Lesbian View* (Auckland, New Zealand: New Women's Press, 1991).

The second is the case of Catherine May Wood and Gwendolyn Graham, nursing home aides at Alpine Manor, Grand Rapids, Michigan, who were convicted in 1989 of the murder in 1987 of several elderly patients, ostensibly as a game. They are serving prison terms. The account presented by journalist Lowell Cauffiel in *Forever and Five Days* (New York: Zebra, 1992) treats the lesbian relationship between the two women as enabling Cathy Wood to manipulate Gwen Graham into doing the killings; however, he also reveals that Cathy Wood confessed to being a "child abuser," that Gwen Graham reported having been sexually abused by her father when she was a child, and that a psychiatrist suggested that the victims were "mother figures" to their killers.

A possible third instance is the infamous, never solved, case of Lizzie Borden, who was legally acquitted of the ax murders of her father and stepmother on August 14, 1982 in Fall River, Massachusetts. An account that develops a hypothesis about how Lizzie might have done it and also documents Lizzie's attachments to Nance O'Neill and other women is Victoria Lincoln, *A Private Disgrace: Lizzie Borden by Daylight* (1967; reprinted New York: International Polygonics, 1986). Victoria Lincoln thought Lizzie might have been subject to epileptic spells, during which she was capable of violence and about which she had amnesia. My own hypothesis is that if Lizzie committed the murders and suffered amnesia about it, she may have been a survivor of incest by her father and, like many other incest survivors, she may have been multiple.

70. Melanie Kaye/Kantrowitz, *My Jewish Face and Other Stories* (San Francisco: Spinsters/Aunt Lute, 1990), pp. 85–96.

71. In *The Issue is Power*, Melanie Kaye/Kantrowitz writes, "In Portland, we formed a group called the Godmothers, who would protect battered women in their own homes" (p. 48).

72. Kaye/Kantrowitz, *My Jewish Face*, p. 87.

73. Kaye/Kantrowitz, *My Jewish Face*, pp. 94–100. In *The Issue Is Power*, pp. 48–49, she mentions aggressive measures women have taken, or appear to have taken, in various cities, and she raises moral and prudential difficulties that taking such steps present. More such discussion is needed.

7 ■ *female incest and adult lesbian crises*

1. Some investigators specify that for abuse, a perpetrator must be at least five years older, which allows that both can be children. See John Briere and Marsha Runtz, "Post Sexual Abuse Trauma" in *Lasting Effects of Childhood Sexual Abuse*, ed. Gail Elizabeth Wyatt and Gloria Johnson Powell (Newbury Park, Calif.: Sage, 1988).

2. Sarah Lucia Hoagland, *Lesbian Ethics: Toward New Value* (Palo Alto, Calif.: Institute of Lesbian Studies, 1988).

3. That is how I read it when I wrote "Defusing the Bomb: Lesbian Ethics

and Horizontal Violence," *Lesbian Ethics* 3, no. 3 (Summer 1989), 91–100.

4. In recent correspondence, Sarah Hoagland has indicated that her intention was to address potential sources of difficulty *before* they reached abusive stages.

5. Maya Angelou, *I Know Why the Caged Bird Sings* (New York: Random House, 1970). On child credibility, see Jean Goodwin, "Credibility Problems in Multiple Personality Disorder Patients and Abused Children," in *Childhood Antecedents of Multiple Personality*, ed. Richard Kluft (Washington, D.C.: American Psychiatric Press, 1985).

6. Susan Forward and Craig Buck, *Betrayal of Innocents: Incest and Its Devastation* (New York: Penguin, 1979), pp. 115–29. This is also true of acts described in the survivor narrative by Kate Moran, "Mary Poppins and My Childhood in Hell," *Lesbian Ethics* 5, no. 1 (Summer 1993), 76–81.

7. Claudia Card, "Intimacy and Responsibility: What Lesbians Do," *At the Boundaries of Law*, ed. Martha Albertson Fineman and Nancy Sweet Thomadsen (New York: Routledge, 1991), pp. 77–94.

8. Nancy Chodorow, *The Reproduction of Mothering: Psychoanalysis and the Sociology of Gender* (Berkeley: University of California Press, 1978).

9. This is an example of "moral luck"—a richly suggestive concept introduced by Bernard Williams in "Moral Luck," *Proceedings of the Aristotelian Society*, Supplementary Volume L (1976), 115–35 and elaborated by Thomas Nagel, "Moral Luck," *Moral Questions* (Cambridge, Eng.: Cambridge University Press, 1979), pp. 24–38, and Martha Nussbaum, *The Fragility of Goodness: Luck and Ethics in Greek Tragedy and Philosophy* (Cambridge, Eng.: Cambridge University Press, 1986).

10. An exception is Forward and Buck, *Betrayal of Innocents*, pp. 115–129. On maternal physical abuse, see, e.g., Adrienne Rich, *Of Woman Born: Motherhood as Experience and Institution* (New York: Norton, 1976), pp. 260–86.

11. Flora Rheta Schreiber, *Sybil* (New York: Warner, 1974).

12. In addition to *Sybil*, book-length narratives of multiple personalities with histories of childhood sexual abuse include *When Rabbit Howls*, by the Troops for Truddi Chase (New York: Dutton, 1987), Kathy Evert & Inie Bijkerk, *When You're Ready: A Woman's Healing from Childhood Physical and Sexual Abuse by Her Mother* (Walnut Creek, Calif.: Launch Press, 1987), and Joan Frances Casey, *The Flock: Autobiography of a Multiple Personality* (New York: Knopf, 1991). See, also, *Multiple Personality Disorder from the Inside Out*, ed. Barry M. Cohen, Esther Giller and Lynn W. [sic] (Baltimore, MD: Sidran Press, 1991). *Sybil* and *When You're Ready* present histories of female incest.

13. *Diagnostic and Statistical Manual of Mental Disorders* (3d ed., rev.; Washington, D.C.: American Psychiatric Association, 1987), p. 271. I do not, however, assume that multiple personality must be a disorder.

Those who believe that adult-child sexual relationships need not be abusive rightly cite the bias imported by a focus on clinical data. However, many nonclinical survivor narratives also recount unambiguous memories of abuse.

14. In addition to narratives mentioned above, general accounts of multiple personality by observers with a clinical orientation include Eugene L. Bliss, *Multiple Personality, Allied Disorders, and Hypnosis* (New York: Oxford, 1986); Kluft, *Childhood Antecedents of Multiple Personality*; Frank W. Putnam, *Diagnosis and Treatment of Multiple Personality Disorder* (New York: Guilford, 1989); and Colin A. Ross, *Multiple Personality Disorder: Diagnosis, Clinical Features, and Treatment* (New York: Wiley, 1989).

15. By 1990 the International Society for the Study of Multiple Personality and Dissociation had a membership approaching 2,000. For addresses of organizations and periodicals, see the pamphlet, *United We Stand: A Book for People with Multiple Personalities*, ed. Eliana Gil (Walnut Creek, Calif.: Launch Press, 1990) (P.O. Box 31493, Walnut Creek, CA 94598).

16. Unpublished work includes materials assembled by M. Reynolds (who identifies herself as a survivor), "The Reality: The Truths about Satanic/Ritualistic Abuse and Multiple Personality Disorder," Portland, Ore.; copyrighted 1991.

17. Stephen Braude, *First Person Plural: Multiple Personality and the Philosophy of Mind* (New York: Routledge. 1991). This is, to my knowledge, the first philosophical book ever devoted to the topic and possibly the only philosophical writing since the days of William James to take multiple personality very seriously. Informative although dry, Braude discusses theories of physicians who mostly ignore the roots in childhood abuse. Braude notes those roots but conducts his subsequent investigations as though they were irrelevant. Although his work is a serious study—unlike William Peter Blatty's novel, *The Exorcist* (New York: Harper & Row, 1971) and the film based on it—such abstraction is morally disturbing. It makes me think of the brass bull of the tyrant Phalaris of Acragas (early 6th century BCE, Sicily), which sounded like it was "singing" to those who heard unknowingly the screams of victims roasting inside.

18. Adam Crabtree, *Multiple Man: Explorations in Possession and Multiple Personality* (London: Holt, Rinehart, & Winston; 1985), pp. 62–138. Under the occult, he includes occult aspects of established religions, such as Catholicism. This book also indicates awareness of histories of childhood abuse but does little with that awareness. See also Blatty, *The Exorcist*, p. 259, for a curious passage on how to distinguish possession from psychological illnesses.

19. Andrea Dworkin, *Woman Hating* (New York: Dutton, 1974), pp. 118–50; Mary Daly, *Gyn/Ecology: The Metaethics of Radical Feminism* (Boston: Beacon Press, 1978), pp. 178–222; *The Malleus Maleficarum of Heinrich Kramer and James Sprenger*, trans. Montague Summers (New York: Dover, 1971).

20. Sigmund Freud, *The Origins of Psychoanalysis—Letters to William Fliess, Drafts and Notes: 1887–1902*, ed. Marie Bonaparte, Anna Freud, and Ernst Kris; trans. Eric Mosbacher and James Strachey (London: Imago, 1954).

21. See Moran, "Mary Poppins and My Childhood in Hell"; Anne [no last name], "Talking about Evil," *Lesbian Ethics* 5, no. 1 (Summer 1993), 82–89; Chris Cuomo, "Ritual Abuse—Making Connections," *Lesbian Ethics* 4, no 3 (Spring 1992), 45–53. See also Elizabeth S. Rose (pseudonym), "Surviving the Unbelievable: A First-Person Account of Cult Ritual Abuse," *Ms* 3, no. 4 (January/February 1993), 40–45.

22. For general accounts, see Larry Kahaner, *Cults that Kill: Probing the Underworld of Occult Crime* (New York: Warner, 1988); Carl A. Rashke, *Painted Black: From Drug Killings to Heavy Metal—The Alarming True Story of How Satanism Is Terrorizing Our Communities* (San Francisco: Harper & Row, 1990); and Daniel Ryder, *Breaking the Circle of Satanic Abuse: Recognizing and Recovering from the Hidden Trauma* (Minneapolis: CompCare Publishers, 1992).

23. Los Angeles County Commission for Women, quoted in Rose, "Surviving the Unbelievable," 41.

24. Rose, "Surviving the Unbelievable," 41.

25. Anne, "Talking about Evil," 83.

26. Kate Millett, *The Basement: Meditations on a Human Sacrifice* (Rev. ed.; New York: Touchstone, 1991). This work contains graphic descriptions of torture.

27. Wyatt and Powell, *Lasting Effects of Child Sexual Abuse*, p. 11.

28. Robert S. Mayer, *Satan's Children: Case Studies in Multiple Personality* (New York: Putnam, 1991), pp. 17–57.

29. Anne, "Talking about Evil," 82.

30. See Michelle Smith (pseudonym) and Lawrence Pazder, *Michelle Remembers* (New York: Pocket Books, 1981); for the story of Jenny Walters Harris, see Judith Spencer, *Suffer the Child* (New York: Pocket Books, 1989). See also Moran, "Mary Poppins and My Childhood in Hell." Kate Moran, who was adopted, reports that when she confronted her mother later in life with the abuse, she met with denial. That was my experience, also, and my mother, referring to abuse, said of her own mother, "Mother believes her own lies."

31. On seasoning and criminalizing prostitutes, see Kathleen Barry, *Female Sexual Slavery* (Englewood Cliffs, N.J.: Prentice-Hall, 1979), pp. 73–136.

32. For essays on the history of the Blood Libel, see Alan Dundes, ed., *The Blood Libel Legend: A Casebook in Anti-Semitic Folklore* (Madison: University of Wisconsin Press, 1991).

33. On reversals of truth as a general method of mystification by oppressors, see Mary Daly, *Gyn/Ecology: The Metaethics of Radical Feminism* (Boston: Beacon Press, 1978), p. 8. The classic example of a "reversal" is the birth of Eve from the body of Adam (or of Athena from Zeus).

34. Denis Diderot, *The Nun*, trans. Leonard Tancock (New York: Penguin, 1974). Clemence Dane (pseudonym of Winifred Ashton), *Regiment of Women* (New York: Macmillan, 1932).

35. Rashke discusses the McMartin preschool case, *Painted Black*, pp. 62–67.

36. Christa Winsloe, *The Child Manuela: The Novel of "Maedchen in Uniform*," tr. Agnes Neill Scott (New York: Farrar & Rinehart, 1933). "Mädchen in Uniform," dir. Leontine Sagan, 1931, German with English subtitles. The film's ending was changed from a suicide ending to a rescue; the novel retains the suicide ending.

37. Peggy Reeves Sanday, *Fraternity Gang Rape: Sex, Brotherhood, and Privilege on Campus* (New York: New York University Press, 1990), pp. 135–73. Peggy Sanday interviewed former fraternity brothers who revealed having been gang-sodomized by older fraternity brothers as part of their initiation. I am not aware of reports of sexual abuse in campus sororities.

38. Andrea Dworkin, *Mercy* (New York: Four Walls, Eight Windows, 1991), p. 158. In an otherwise illuminating and informative essay on mercy and justice, Martha Nussbaum wrote recently of this book that "there is no mercy in it," in "Equity and Mercy," *Philosophy and Public Affairs* 22, no. 2 (Spring 1993), 83–125; the quoted claim is on p. 83. She seems to have missed this passage—which, for me, was a central one—along with the pacifism which the main character of the book gradually comes to reject, after countless instances of overlooking and forgiveness of abuse.

39. Ian Hacking, "The Invention of Split Personalities," in *Human Nature and Natural Knowledge: Essays Presented to Marjorie Grene on the Occasion of Her Seventy-Fifth Birthday*, ed. Alan Donagan, Anthony N. Perovich, Jr., and Michael V. Wedin (Dordrecht, Holland: D. Reidel, 1986), pp. 63–85.

40. Anne, "Talking about Evil," 83–84, 89.

41. See Kahaner, *Cults that Kill*.

42. See *Hitler's Apologists: The Anti-Semitic Propaganda of Holocaust "Revisionism"* (New York: Anti-Defamation League, 1993); Deborah Lipstadt, *Denying the Holocaust: The Growing Assault on Truth and Memory* (New York: Free Press, 1993); and Pierre Vidal-Naquet, *Assassins of Memory: Essays on the Denial of the Holocaust*, trans. Jeffrey Mehlman (New York: Columbia University Press, 1992).

43. Margaret Alice Murray, *The Witch Cult in Western Europe: A Study in Anthropology* (Oxford: Clarendon Press, 1921).

44. Chris Cuomo, "Ritual Abuse: Making Connections," pp. 49–50.

45. Ardel Thomas, "Dangerous Connections: Lesbian Sado-Masochism and Mother-Daughter Incest," *Lesbian Ethics* 4, no. 3 (Spring 1992), 79–86.

46. Evert and Bijkerk, *When You're Ready*. Pat Califia, *Macho Sluts* (Boston: Alyson, 1988).

47. Lorena Saxe, "Sadomasochism and Exclusion," *Hypatia* 7, no. 4 (October 1992), 59–72.

48. Sarah Hoagland, "Sadism, Masochism, and Lesbian Feminism," in *Against Sadomasochism: A Radical Feminist Analysis*, ed. Robin Ruth Linden,

Darlene R. Pagano, Diana E. H. Russell, and Susan Leigh Star (East Palo Alto, Calif.: Frog in the Well Press, 1982), pp. 153–63.

49. See Hoagland, *Lesbian Ethics*, esp., pp. 1–3, 114–56.

50. On the theme of rejecting justice or questioning its value, see, in addition to Sarah Hoagland's *Lesbian Ethics*, Nel Noddings, *Caring: A Feminine Approach to Ethics and Morality* (Berkeley: University of California Press, 1984).

51. Theodor Reik, *Listening with the Third Ear* (New York: Farrar, Straus, 1948).

8 ▪ *homophobia and lesbian/gay pride*

1. *New York Times*, July 10, 1990, pp. B1, 9.

2. See, for example, Ronald de Sousa, *The Rationality of Emotion* (Cambridge, Mass.: MIT Press, 1990).

3. See, for example, Susan Griffin, *Woman and Nature: The Roaring Inside Her* (New York: Harper & Row, 1978).

4. Sigmund Freud, *Group Psychology and the Analysis of the Ego*, trans. James Strachey (New York: Bantam, 1960).

5. María Lugones, "Playfulness, 'World'-Travelling, and Loving Perception," *Hypatia* 2, no. 2 (Summer 1987), 3–19. Marilyn Frye, *The Politics of Reality* (Trumansburg, N.Y.: Crossing Press, 1983), pp. 52–83.

6. Marilyn Friedman, "Feminism and Modern Friendship: Dislocating the Community," *Ethics*, 99, no. 2 (1989), 289.

7. Adrienne Rich, "Compulsory Heterosexuality and Lesbian Existence," *Signs* 5, no. 4 (Summer 1980), 631–60.

8. See Gabriele Taylor, *Pride, Shame, and Guilt: Emotions of Self-Assessment* (Oxford: Clarendon, 1983), ch. 2, for discussion of distinctions between pride as a character trait and feelings of pride.

9. Suzanne Pharr, *Homophobia: A Weapon of Sexism* (Inverness, Calif.: Chardon Press, 1988).

10. Celia Kitzinger, *The Social Construction of Lesbianism* (London: Sage, 1987), pp. 57–65. Cf. Celia Kitzinger, "Heteropatriarchal Language: The Case Against 'Homophobia'," *Gossip: A Journal of Lesbian Feminist Ethics* #5 (n.d.), 15–20; and Richard Mohr, *Gays/Justice: A Study of Ethics, Society, and Law* (New York: Columbia University Press, 1988), p. 12.

11. Pharr, *Homophobia*, p. 9.

12. For a similar view on "internalized homophobia" and lesbian battering, see Mindy Benowitz, "How Homophobia Affects Lesbians' Response to Violence in Lesbian relationships," in *Naming the Violence: Lesbians Speak Out About Battering*, ed. Kerry Lobel (Seattle, Wash.: Seal, 1988), pp. 198–201.

13. Celia Kitzinger cites A. P. MacDonald and R. G. Games, "Some Characteristics of Those Who Hold Positive and Negative Attitudes Toward Homosexuals," *Journal of Homosexuality* 1, no. 1 (1974), 9–27; and G. Weinberg, *Society and the Healthy Homosexual* (New York: Anchor, 1973) on the

introduction of the concept of homophobia by mental health professionals in the early 1970s.

14. Helen Merrell Lynd, *On Shame and the Search for Identity* (New York: Harcourt, Brace & World, 1958).

15. Many feminists have wanted to say the same thing about female paranoia in a rape culture: it is debilitating, but, unfortunately, also well-grounded.

16. Rich, *Of Woman Born: Motherhood as Experience and as Institution* (New York: Bantam, 1977), pp. 2377–38. She cites poet Lynn Sukenik, "Feeling and Reason in Doris Lessing's Fiction," *Contemporary Literature* 14, no. 4 (1973), 519, as her source of the term, "matrophobia."

17. See Albert Camus, "Reflection on the Guillotine," *Resistance, Rebellion, and Death*, trans. Justin O'Brien (New York: Modern Library, 1960), pp. 131–79.

18. Sue Fink and Joelyn Grippo, "Leaping" (1977), with familiar Halloween chords, sung by Meg Christian on *Face the Music* (Olivia Records, 1977), Side II, Band 4.

19. See Claudia Card, "Intimacy and Responsibility: What Lesbians Do" in Martha Fineman and Nancy Thomadsen, eds., *At the Boundaries of Law: Feminism and Legal Theory* (New York: Routledge, 1990), pp. 77–94.

20. Claudia Brenner, "Eight Bullets," *Hate Crimes: Confronting Violence Against Lesbians and Gay Men*, ed. Gregory M. Herek and Kevin T. Berrill (Newbury Park, Calif: Sage, 1992), pp. 11–15.

21. Ruthann Robson, *Lesbian (Out)Law: Survival Under the Rule of Law* (Ithaca, N.Y.: Firebrand, 1992), pp. 158–65.

22. Max Scheler, *The Nature of Sympathy*, trans. Peter Heath (Hamden, Conn.: Archon, 1970), pp. 15 ff.

23. *Arachnophobia* (dir. Frank Marshall; 1990).

9 ■ *the military ban and the rotc: a study in closeting*

1. I have requested a copy of the text of this bill but have not received it.

2. The present revisions are as of July 1993. Most of this chapter was written during the summer of 1992. For the text of the President's new guidelines, see *New York Times*, July 20, 1993, p. A12.

3. For elaboration and defense of this point in regard to civil rights, see Richard Mohr, *Gays/Justice: A Study of Ethics, Society, and Law* (New York: Columbia University Press, 1988), esp., pp. 162–88.

4. Usually, I was the only female present at meetings of this committee. Cochair Joe Elder did most of the work. Rick Villasenor launched the committee, as one of his last projects as an undergraduate, persuading me to lend my name, as others later persuaded me to lend my efforts, to the cause. After the all-faculty meeting, an ad hoc faculty committee was appointed to pursue the issues, chaired by Professor Michael Olneck. I served on this committee, also.

5. However, in 1950 Congress created the Uniform Code of Military Justice, a code that prohibits both homosexual and heterosexual oral and anal sex. See Chris Bull, "And the Ban Played On," *The Advocate*, no. 624 (March 9, 1993), 38, for this and other milestones in the history of the military ban.

6. From Defense Department policy, quoted by Rep. Gerry Studds, "Forward," *Gays in Uniform: The Pentagon's Secret Reports*, ed. Kate Dyer (Boston: Alyson, 1990), p. xiv. The policy does not extend to nonuniformed advisers, such as Assistant Secretary of Defense Pete Williams, outed by Michelangelo Signorile in *The Advocate* no. 584 (Aug. 27, 1991), 34–44, to protest Defense Department hypocrisy.

7. Many universities and colleges that are not land grant institutions have refused an ROTC program or have taken a position similar to that of FADI-UP's motion. Dartmouth College, for example, told the Defense Department that "it will discontinue the campus program if there is no change by April 1993," according to the *Windy City Times*, Oct. 3, 1991, p. 10. In 1993, it extended its phaseout plan until April 1994, according to John Gallagher, "ROTC: R.I.P?" *The Advocate,* no. 637 (Sept. 7, 1993), 51.

8. At the present writing, the Senate is debating a program of national service that would encourage young people to volunteer for public service work in return for, among other things, educational vouchers.

9. Two state senators, in a letter of Dec. 6, 1989 to the president of the Board of Regents, maintained that "After checking, we are not aware of a single instance in which a homosexual who enrolled in ROTC courses was not commissioned by the program because of sexual preference."

10. Eric Schmitt, "Barring Homosexuals Called Costly to Military," *New York Times*, June 20, 1992, p. A6.

11. It was reported during the summer of 1992 that Britain "will no longer prosecute military personnel for engaging in gay sex, but will continue to discharge all personnel discovered to be gay," *Lesbian/Gay Law Notes* (Summer 1992), 54.

12. Jane Gross, "Navy Is Urged to Root Out Lesbians Despite Abilities," *New York Times*, Sept. 2, 1990, p. A9. Estimates since then have placed the figure for the discharge of lesbians as high as ten times the rate of gay men (Signorile, "The Outing of Assistant Secretary of Defense Pete Williams," p. 36).

13. Gallagher, "GAO: Military Spent $500 Million Discharging Gays," *The Advocate* no. 608 (July 30, 1992), 20.

14. Allan Berube spent ten years interviewing lesbian and gay veterans and reviewed hundreds of letters between gay GIs for his *Coming Out Under Fire: The History of Gay Men and Women in World War II* (New York: Free Press, 1990). Mary Ann Humphrey, after she was booted out of the Army Reserve when a former male colleague outed her to satisfy a grudge, began gathering interviews (about a third presented under pseudonyms) for her book, *My Country, My Right to Serve: Experiences of Gay Men and Women in the Military,*

World War II to the Present (New York: Harper Collins, 1990). The currently definitive work covering the period from the 1960s through the Gulf War is Randy Shilts, *Conduct Unbecoming: Gays and Lesbians in the U.S. Military, Viet Nam to the Persian Gulf* (New York: St. Martin's Press, 1993). Shilts is said to have interviewed over 500 closeted gay and lesbian servicepeople in his research (Signorile, "The Outing of Assistant Secretary of Defense Pete Williams," p. 36).

15. Humphrey, *My Country, My Right to Serve*, p. 40.

16. Signorile, "The Outing of Assistant Secretary of Defense Pete Williams," p. 36.

17. Humphrey, *My Country, My Right to Serve*, pp. 248–57.

18. Humphrey, *My Country, My Right to Serve*, p. 188.

19. Humphrey, *My Country, My Right to Serve*, p. 254.

20. "Officers seem to receive more lenient treatment. Only 227 officers were discharged or resigned because they are gay, 1% of the total figure of discharges," reports Gallagher, "GAO: Military Spent $500 Million Discharging Gays," p. 21.

21. Humphrey, *My Country, My Right to Serve*, p. 246.

22. On Leonard Matlovich, see Humphrey, *My Country, My Right to Serve*, pp. 151–55. I take my information on Col. Margarethe Cammermeyer from a clipping from David Olson, "Lesbian Colonel Booted After 27 Years of Service," *Windy City Times*, Sept. 26, 1991, p. 4, and on Tracy Thorne, from Tracie Cone, "He's an Officer . . . and a Homosexual: Naval Aviator Challenges His Dismissal," *Wisconsin State Journal*, Aug. 9, 1992, pp. F1–2.

23. Eric Schmitt, "Barring Homosexuals Called Costly to Military," *New York Times*, June 20, 1992, p. A6.

24. Gallagher, "GAO: Military Spent $500 Million Discharging Gays," p. 20.

25. Humphrey, *My Country, My Right to Serve*, pp. 129–30.

26. Cf. James Woods, *The Corporate Closet: The Professional Lives of Gay Men in America* (New York: Free Press, 1993).

27. Robert Jay Lifton, *The Nazi Doctors: Medical Killing and the Psychology of Genocide* (New York: Basic Books, 1986), p. 418.

28. Signorile, *Queer in America: Sex, the Media, and the Closets of Power* (New York: Random House, 1993), p. 81.

29. Signorile, "Handcuffs, Murder, and Suicide," *The Advocate* no. 584 (Aug. 27, 1991), 38.

30. See, for example, Curt Gentry, *J. Edgar Hoover: The Man and the Secrets* (New York: Plume, 1991) and Anthony Summer, *Official and Confidential: The Secret Life of J. Edgar Hoover* (New York: Putnam's, 1993).

31. Lifton, *The Nazi Doctors*, p. 420.

32. W. E. B. Du Bois, *Writings* (New York: Library of America, 1986), pp. 364–65.

33. Victoria Davion, "Integrity and Radical Change" in *Feminist Ethics*, ed. Claudia Card (Lawrence: University Press of Kansas, 1991), pp. 180–92. See also María Lugones, "Structure/AntiStructure and Agency under Oppression," *Journal of Philosophy* 87, no. 10 (October 1990), 500–507.

34. For an interesting discussion of Dr. Lifton's analysis of "doubling" and its implications for moral responsibility, see Laurence Mordekhai Thomas, *Vessels of Evil: American Slavery and the Holocause* (Philadelphia: Temple University Press, 1993), pp. 92–116.

35. It would seem to follow from this argument that career spies are, at least potentially, also moral monsters. This is probably true, contrary to popular mythology of spy hero worship.

36. Dyer, *Gays in Uniform*, p. xiv, quoting from Defense Department policy.

37. Bill Turque, "Running a Gantlet of Sexual Assault," *Newsweek* 119 (June 1, 1992), 45.

38. The University of Wisconsin Women's Studies Program offers not only the lesbian culture course discussed in chapter 1 but also, occasionally, an interdisciplinary course on male homosexuality taught jointly by male faculty from three departments. Other Women's Studies courses and courses in many departments also draw upon lesbian and gay writings to address lesbian and gay issues.

39. "News in Brief," *The Advocate* no. 608 (July 30, 1992), 32–33.

40. *Lesbian/Gay Law Notes* (January 1993), l.

41. *Palmore* v. *Sidoti*, 466 U.S. 433 (1984). Quoted in *Lesbian/Gay Law Notes* (September 1991), 55.

42. Gallagher, "Dream On: Soldier of the Year Joe Zuniga secs his hope for a military career dashed as Clinton Compromises on the ban," *The Advocate* no. 634 (July 27, 1993), 32–38.

43. Gross, "Navy Is Urged to Root Out Lesbians Despite Abilities."

44. Both reports are in Dyer, *Gays in Uniform*, pp. 3–135; the first report is exerpted in Humphrey, *My Country, My Right to Serve*, pp. 260–66.

45. Dyer, *Gays in Uniform*, p. ix.

46. For Rep. Studds on how long it took to get the Crittenden Report, see Humphrey, *My Country, My Right to Serve*, p. viii. For the quotation from the report, see Dyer, *Gays In Uniform* p. xvi. The term originally used in the report was "blackmail."

47. David Olson, "Memo Undermines Military's Ban on Gays," *Windy City Times* (Sept. 19, 1991). (My clipping lacks the page number).

48. Humphrey, *My Country, My Right to Serve*, p. 182.

49. See, for example, Sarah Lucia Hoagland, *Lesbian Ethics: Toward New Value* (Palo Alto, Calif.: Institute of Lesbian Studies, 1988), pp. 69–113. An earlier classic discussion is Kate Millett's *Sexual Politics* (Garden City, N.Y.: Doubleday, 1970), pp. 23–58.

50. On women's self-defense, see Andra Medea and Kathleen Thompson, *Against Rape* (New York: Farrar, Straus, Giroux, 1974); Linda Tschirhart Sanford and Ann Fetter, *In Defense of Ourselves: A Rape Prevention Handbook for Women* (New York: Doubleday, 1979), and *Her Wits about Her: Self-Defense Success Stories by Women*, ed. Denise Cagnon and Gail Groves (New York: Harper & Row, 1987).

Men Stopping Rape is an organization also committed to many goals of the women's self-defense movement and to taking responsibility for educating men about sex and gender oppression. See also John Stoltenburg, *Refusing to be a Man: Essays on Sex and Justice* (New York: Penguin, 1990).

51. See chapter 1. On twentieth-century lesbians in military service, see Lillian Faderman, *Odd Girls and Twilight Lovers: A History of Lesbian Life in Twentieth-Century America* (New York: Columbia University Press, 1991), pp. 118–38.

Miriam ben-Shalom reports having fought in the Israeli Army almost a year and a half before enlisting in the U.S. Army Reserve (Humphrey, *My Country, My Right to Serve*, p. 187).

52. Guy Rothery, *The Amazons in Antiquity and Modern Times* (London: Griffiths, 1910).

53. For impassioned and well-developed arguments concerning gay dignity, see Richard Mohr, *Gays/Justice*, pp. 315–37 and *Gay Ideas: Outing and Other Controversies* (Boston: Beacon Press, 1992), pp. 11–48.

54. Virginia Woolf proposed in *Three Guineas* (New York: Harcourt, Brace, & World, 1938) that motherhood be recognized and paid as a state service (p. 110) and, in discussing military uniforms and hierarchies, invited readers to imagine responses to mothers wearing on their shoulders a tuft of horsehair for each child (pp. 20–21).

55. Public lecture, State Historical Society Auditorium, University of Wisconsin-Madison, April 4, 1991.

56. Literature on deaf culture protests the stigma of "disabled." See Carol Padden and Tom Humphries, eds., *Deaf in America: Voices from a Culture* (Cambridge, Mass.: Harvard University Press, 1988). For similar and related protests, see *With Wings: An Anthology of Literature by and About Women with Disabilities*, ed. Marsha Saxton and Florence Howe (New York: Feminist Press, 1987) and *With the Power of Each Breath: A Disabled Women's Anthology*, ed. Susan E. Browne, Debra Connors, and Nanci Stern (Pittsburgh: Cleis Press, 1985).

57. See Carol Van Kirk, "Sarah Lucia Hoagland's *Lesbian Ethics: Toward New Value* and Ablemindism," *Hypatia* 5, no. 3 (Fall 1990), 147–52.

58. 5 U.S.C. Sec. 3310 (1972), cited by James Nickel, "Preferential Policies in Hiring and Admissions: A Jurisprudential Approach," *Columbia Law R.* 75 (1975), 534–558, reprinted in *Today's Moral Problems*, 2d ed., ed. Richard A. Wasserstrom (New York: Macmillan, 1979), p. 231, n. 5.

10 ▪ *other people's secrets: the ethics of outing*

1. According to Michelangelo Signorile, *Queer in America: Sex, the Media, and the Closets of Power* (New York: Random House, 1993), p. 73, the term "outing" was first used in *Time* magazine. See William A. Henry III, "Forcing Gays Out of the Closet," *Time* 135 (Jan. 29, 1990), 67.

2. Jon E. Grant, " 'Outing' and Freedom of the Press: Sexual Orientation's Challenge to the Supreme Court's Categorical Jurisprudence," *Cornell Law Review* 77, no. 1 (November 1991), 103–41, note 11.

3. See, for example, "The Ins and Outs of Outing the Ins," *San Francisco Chronicle*, Aug. 12, 1991, p. E12; "Gays, Privacy, and the Free Press," *Washington Post*, April 8, 1990, p. B7.

4. Quoted by Henry in "Forcing Gays Out of the Closet," p. 67.

5. Signorile, "The Outing of Assistant Secretary of Defense Pete Williams," *The Advocate* no. 584 (Aug. 27, 1991), 34–44.

6. According to Signorile, "journalistic outing is not aimed at all gay people who are not following an 'agenda,' but at *public figures* and only when pertinent to a story that may or may not have anything to do with an 'agenda'— liberal or conservative," *Queer in America*, p. 149.

Larry Gross writes, in reference to the hypothetical "high school gym teacher who is a closeted lesbian living quietly with her lover and children by a former marriage" that "neither the mainstream press nor the militant gay activists who promote outing would endorse exposing [such] nonpublic lesbian and gay people" and that "the proponents of outing make no case for exposing people whose closets are truly necessary camouflage," *Contested Closets: The Politics and Ethics of Outing* (Minneapolis: University of Minnesota Press, 1993), pp. 2–3.

7. Richard Mohr, *Gay Ideas: Outing and Other Controversies* (Boston: Beacon Press, 1992), pp. 34, 39.

8. Gross, *Contested Closets*, p. 5.

9. Mohr, *Gay Ideas*, pp. 11–48.

10. Mohr, however, seems not to find hypocrisy in politics a major problem but sees it as "part and parcel of public political life." *Gay Ideas*, p. 24.

11. See also Mohr, *Gays/Justice: A Study of Ethics, Society, and Law* (New York: Columbia University Press, 1988), esp., pp. 315–37.

12. Sarah Lucia Hoagland, *Lesbian Ethics: Toward New Value* (Palo Alto, Calif.: Institute of Lesbian Studies, 1988). Also skeptical of the value of justice and rights are philosophers Nel Noddings, *Caring: A Feminine Approach to Ethics and Moral Education* (Berkeley: University of California Press, 1984) and Sara Ruddick, *Maternal Thinking: Toward a Politics of Peace* (Boston: Beacon Press, 1989). For a promising feminist reconception of justice, see Iris Marion Young, *Justice and the Politics of Difference* (Princeton: Princeton University Press, 1990). For lesbian concern with justice, see Kathleen Martindale and

Martha Saunders, "Realizing Love and Justice: Lesbian Ethics in the Upper and Lower Case," *Hypatia* 7, no. 4 (Fall 1992), 148–71 and Ruthann Robson, *Lesbian (Out)Law: Survival Under the Rule of Law* (Ithaca, N.Y.: Firebrand, 1992).

13. An extended and illuminating philosophical discussion of dignity is Aurel Kolnai, "Dignity," *Philosophy* 51, no. 197 (July 1976), 251–71.

14. The objection presupposes slanderous judgments of pigs (which Mill does not contest) who, according to philosopher Peter Singer, are in fact intelligent and also clean when they have adequate living space. See Singer, *Animal Liberation: A New Ethics for Our Treatment of Animals* (New York: Avon, 1975), pp. 113–21.

15. *The Philosophy of John Stuart Mill: Ethical, Political and Religious*, ed. Marshall Cohen (New York: Modern Library, 1961), pp. 331–34.

16. Immanuel Kant, *The Moral Law: Kant's Groundwork of the Metaphysic of Morals*, trans. H. J. Paton (3d ed.; London: Hutchinson, 1956), pp. 102–3.

17. See Maria Steiglitz, "New Mexico's Secret Jews," *Lilith* 16, no. 1 (Winter 1991), 8–12; and La Escondida, "Journal Toward Wholeness: Reflections of a Lesbian Rabbi," *Twice Blessed: On Being Lesbian, Gary, and Jewish* , ed. Christie Balka and Andy Rose (Boston: Beacon Press, 1989), pp. 218–27.

18. Mohr, *Gays/Justice*, pp. 315–37.

19. Bernard Boxill, "Self-Respect and Protest," in *Philosophy Born of Struggle: Anthology of Afro-American Philosophy from 1917*, ed. Leonard Harris (Dubuque, Iowa: Kendall/Hunt, 1983), pp. 190–98.

20. Boxill, "Self-Respect and Protest," p. 197. It is controversial whether the "Sambo" personality, as described by Stanley M. Elkins in *Slavery: A Problem in American Institutional and Intellectual Life* (3d rev. ed.; Chicago: University of Chicago Press, 1976), was ever widespread among descendants of enslaved Africans in the United States. For further discussion, see Howard McGary and Bill E. Lawson, *Between Slavery and Freedom: Philosophy and American Slavery* (Bloomington: Indiana University Press, 1992).

21. *The Nicomachean Ethics of Aristotle*, trans. W. D. Ross (London: Oxford, 1925), pp. 22–23.

22. Jacqueline Zita, "Historical Amnesia and the Lesbian Continuum," *Signs* 7, no. 1 (Autumn 1981), 172–87, offers an extended response to this objection.

23. Doris Faber, *The Life of Lorena Hickok: ER's Friend* (New York: Morrow, 1980), "A Personal Note and Some Acknowledgments," pp. 329–34. See Blanche Wiesen Cook, *Eleanor Roosevelt*, Vol. 1: 1884–1933 (New York: Viking, 1992), pp. 448–500, for a level and sympathetic account of the Lorena Hickok–Eleanor Roosevelt relationship.

24. Dolores Klaich, *Woman Plus Woman: Attitudes Toward Lesbianism* (New York: Simon & Schuster, 1974), p. 188, quoting H. Montgomery Hyde in

Norman Birkett (London: Hamilton, 1964), p. 254. *The Well of Loneliness,* banned in England for many years, passed the New York courts in 1929 and has been almost continuously in print in the United States. My edition is New York: Pocket Books, 1950.

25. Mohr, *Gay Ideas.* p. 21. This improves upon the definition offered by Grant, " 'Outing' is the intentional exposure by gay people of the sexual orientation of public figures" (" 'Outing' and Freedom of the Press," p. 104).

26. Mohr does not appeal to this idea.

27. On such inquisitions, see Randy Shilts, *Conduct Unbecoming: Gays and Lesbians in the U.S. Military* (New York: St. Martin's Press, 1993); and Mary Ann Humphrey, *My Country, My Right to Serve: Experiences of Gay Men and Women in the Military, World War II to the Present* (New York: Harper Collins, 1990). Unofficially, of course, many in the military apparently have shared such presumptions of secrecy.

28. Derivatively, we can speak of coming out as the parent, child, or sibling of one who is lesbian or gay; there is room here also to defy presumptions of secrecy and for courage and pride, as opposed to fear and shame.

29. On the history of this slogan, see Martin Duberman, *Stonewall* (New York: Dutton, 1993).

30. Mohr, *Gay Ideas,* pp. 12–15.

31. On "prisoner's dilemma," see Luce & Raiffa, *Games and Decisions: Introduction and Critical Survey* (New York: Wiley, 1957), pp. 88–113.

32. Boxill, "The Race-Class Question," in *Philosophy Born of Struggle: An Anthology of African American Philosophy from 1917,* ed. Leonard Harris (Dubuque, Iowa: Kendall/Hunt, 1983), p. 114. Boxill cites Allen Buchanan, "Revolutionary Motivation and Rationality," *Marx, Justice and History,* ed. Marshall Cohen, Thomas Nagel, and Thomas Scanlon (Princeton: Princeton University Press, 1980), pp. 268–69.

33. Mohr claims that no famous celebrity has joined gay political causes as a result of being outed, *Gay Ideas,* p. 43.

34. Signorile, *Queer in America,* pp. 3–93.

35. See chapter 6. See also Gary David Comstock, *Violence Against Lesbians and Gay Men* (New York: Columbia University Press, 1991) and *Hate Crimes: Confronting Violence Against Lesbians and Gay Men,* ed. Gregory M. Herek and Kevin T. Berrill (Newbury Park, Calif.: Sage, 1992).

36. *The Nicomachean Ethics of Aristotle,* pp. 91–94.

37. John Grisham's novel, *The Client* (New York: Doubleday, 1993), dramatizes such a choice.

38. *The Philosophy of John Stuart Mill,* pp. 196–200 and 271–93.

39. *Holy Bible*: New Revised Standard Version (Nashville, Tenn.: Thomas Nelson, 1989), p. 180 (Deuteronomy 25:2–3).

40. On "dirty hands," see Michael Stocker, *Plural and Conflicting Values* (Oxford: Clarendon Press, 1990), pp. 9–36 and 51–84.

41. Carla Maria Verdino-Sullwold, "Dislocations: Dialogue of Disparate Visions," *Crisis* 99, no. 1 (January 1992), p. 8.

42. See Karen Thompson and Julie Andrzewjewski, *Why Can't Sharon Kowalski Come Home?* (San Francisco: Spinsters/Aunt Lute, 1988) for history of the case to April 1988. Since then, a judge who wished to deny Karen custody (which she finally received), complained that in prosecuting the case, Karen had outed Sharon—although there was, obviously, no other way to bring the case.

43. Mohr, *Gay Ideas*, pp. 41–42.

44. Signorile, *Queer in America*, p. 204.

45. Grant, " 'Outing' and Freedom of the Press," p. 122, discusses problems about determining whether someone is really gay that turn on lack of consensus or clarity about what it means to be gay, as distinct from having performed a particular action.

46. John Austin, *How to Do Things with Words* (Oxford: Clarendon Press, 1962), p. 99. Thanks to Dennis Stampe for reminding me of this.

47. Even so distinguished a philosopher as Schopenhauer used the term "pederasty" (*die Paderastie*) as though it were synonymous with homosexuality. See the Appendix to his essay, "The Metaphysics of Sexual Love," in *The World as Will and Representation*, trans. E. F. J. Payne (2 vols.; New York: Dover, 1966), 2:560–67.

48. The newly announced (July 1993) military policy regarding gay men and lesbians notwithstanding, identifying oneself verbally as lesbian or gay is not ordinarily considered "homosexual conduct." Ordinarily, homosexual conduct is understood as sexual acts or acts leading toward sexual acts.

49. Susanna J. Sturgis, "Breaking Silence, Breaking Faith: The Promotion of Lesbian Nuns" and "Lesbian Nuns: Some Documents in the Case," *Lesbian Ethics* 1, no. 3 (Fall 1985), 89–107.

50. Mohr, *Gay Ideas*, p. 45.

51. See, for example, Vern Bullough and Bonnie Bullough, "Lesbianism in the 1920s and 1930s: A Newfound Study," *Signs* 2, no. 4 (1977), 895–904.

52. According to Signorile, "Thirty percent of the teen suicides in America are among lesbian and gay kids, even though homosexuals make up only 10 percent of the population (this is according to a U.S. government-sponsored study)," *Queer in America*, p. 81. He does not name the study.

53. Mohr, *Gay Ideas*, p. 29.

54. Friedrich Nietzsche, *On the Genealogy of Morals*, trans. Walter Kaufmann and Robert Hollingdale (New York: Vintage, 1969), p. 29.

55. Thanks to John Jakovina for calling my attention to the literature of Deaf Culture. See, for example, Carol Padden and Tom Humphries, *Deaf in America: Voices from a Culture* (Cambridge, Mass.: Harvard University Press, 1988).

56. María Lugones offers a creative solution to this kind of problem in

"Hispaneando y lesbiando: Sarah Hoagland's *Lesbian Ethics*," *Hypatia* 5, no. 3 (Fall 1990), 138–46.

57. *Complete Works of Ralph Waldo Emerson* (2 vols.; New York: Wise, 1929), 1:160.

11 ▪ *consensual sadomasochism: charting the issues*

1. See Marilyn Frye, *Willful Virgin: Essays in Feminism* (Freedom, Calif.: Crossing Press, 1992), pp. 109–19, on impoverished vocabulary for what lesbians do.

2. For an example of such protest, see Alice Walker, "A Letter of the Times, or Should This Sado-Masochism Be Saved?" *You Can't Keep a Good Woman Down: Stories by Alice Walker* (New York: Harcourt Brace Jovanovitch, 1981), pp. 118–23.

3. Sandra Lee Bartky, *Femininity and Domination: Studies in the Phenomenology of Oppression* (New York: Routledge, 1990), pp. 45–62, presents such a view of feminine masochism.

4. Havelock Ellis, "Love and Pain," in *Studies in the Psychology of Sex* (2 vols.; New York: Random House, 1942), 1:2:105–6, quoting E. Duhren (pseudonym of Iwan Bloch), *Der Marquis de Sade und Seine Zeit* (3d ed.; 1901), p. 449.

5. Sigmund Freud, *New Introductory Lectures on Psychoanalysis*, trans. W. J. H. Sprott (New York: Norton, 1933), pp. 142 ff; and *Basic Writings of Sigmund Freud*, trans. and ed. A. A. Brill (New York: Modern Library, 1938), pp. 569–71.

6. *What Color Is Your Handkerchief: A Lesbian S/M Sexuality Reader*, ed. Samois (Berkeley, Calif.: Samois, 1979); *Coming to Power: Writings and Graphics on Lesbian S/M* (2d ed. rev. and expanded; Boston: Alyson Publications, 1982). "Samois," from Pauline Reage, *The Story of O*, trans. Sabine d'Estree (New York, 1965), is the place where O is tortured.

7. I use "**M**" (hereafter, without quotation marks) to refer to one playing the masochist in a contract and, likewise, "**S**" to refer to one playing the sadist.

8. The code is reproduced in *Coming to Power*, p. 66.

9. Pat Califia, "A Personal View of the History of the Lesbian S/M Community and Movement in San Francisco," in *Coming to Power*, pp. 243–81.

10. According to James Cleugh, *The Marquis and the Chevalier: A Study in the Psychology of Sex as Illustrated by the Lives and Personalities of the Marquis de Sade (1740–1814) and the Chevalier von Sacher-Masoch (1836–1905)* (New York: Duel, Sloan and Pearce, 1952), Sacher-Masoch was incarcerated in an asylum for the insane at Mannheim in 1895 and his death publicly reported soon thereafter, although he did not in fact die until 1905. On the term "masochism," see Richard von Krafft-Ebing, *Psychopathia Sexualis: A Medico-Forensic Study*, trans. Harry E. Wedeck (New York: Putnam, 1965), p. 159.

11. Lawrence Mass, "Coming to Grips with Sadomasochism," in *S and M:*

Studies in Sadomasochism, ed. Thomas Weinberg and G. W. Levi Kamel (Buffalo, N.Y.: Prometheus, 1983), pp. 53–54.

12. The notion of higher order desires is from Harry G. Frankfurt, *The Importance of What We Care About: Philosophical Essays* (New York: Cambridge University Press, 1988), pp. 11–25.

13. Lorena Saxe, "Sadomasochism and Exclusion," *Hypatia* 7, no. 4 (Fall 1992), 59–72.

14. Paul Gebhard, for example, claims, "Sadists are far rarer than masochists, and female sadists are so highly prized that masochists will travel hundreds of miles to meet them." Gebhard, "Sadomasochism," in *S and M*, ed. Weinberg and Kamel, p. 36.

15. Joseph R. Nolan and Jacqueline M. Nolan-Haley, *Black's Law Dictionary: Definitions of the Terms and Phrases of American and English Jurisprudence, Ancient and Modern* (6th ed.; St. Paul, Minn.: West, 1990), p. 153. See also chapter 6, above, on battery.

16. Ian Young, "Forum on Sadomasochism," *Lavender Culture*, ed. Karla Jay and Allen Young (New York: Jove/HBJ, 1978), p. 85. He contrasts this with a narrower sense according to which "S&M" is sex involving pain, either physical (such as slapping or spanking) or symbolic (such as enacted domination or restraint of one partner by another).

17. See, for example, Helen E. Longino, "Pornography, Oppression, and Freedom: A Closer Look," in *Take Back the Night: Women on Pornography*, ed. Laura Lederer (New York: Morrow, 1980), pp. 40–54.

18. The glossary in *What Color Is Your Handkerchief* defined "S/M" as "a form of eroticism based on an eroticized exchange of power negotiated between two or more sexual partners," p. 7. Contributors to *Coming to Power*, also, tend to work with an understanding of "S/M" as an exchange of power.

19. Audre Lorde, *Sister Outsider: Essays and Speeches* (Trumansburg, N.Y.: Crossing Press, 1984), pp. 53–59.

20. Frye, *The Politics of Reality: Essays in Feminist Theory* (Trumansburg, N.Y.: Crossing Press, 1983), pp. 1–16.

21. Janet Bellwether, "Love Means Never Having to Say Oops: A Lesbian's Guide to S/M Safety," in *Coming to Power*, pp. 69–79.

22. John Stoltenberg, "Sadomasochism: Eroticized Violence, Eroticized Powerlessness," in *Against Sadomasochism: A Radical Feminist Analysis*, ed. Robin Ruth Linden, Darlene R. Pagano, Diana E. H. Russell, and Susan Leigh Star (East Palo Alto, Calif.: Frog in the Well Press, 1982), pp. 124–30.

23. Bat-Ami Bar On, "Feminism and Sadomasochism: Self-Critical Notes," in *Against Sadomasochism*, ed. Linden et al., p. 79.

24. Gerald and Caroline Greene, *S-M: The Last Taboo* (New York: Grover, 1974), esp. pp. 45–61.

25. Marissa Jonel (pseudonym) reports that for her the practice was addictive, habituating, "I was frightened when I felt myself feeling less and need-

ing more real pain to get excited. It's like drugs—you develop a quick tolerance to the pain." Jonel, "Letter from a Former Masochist," in *Against Sadomasochism*, ed. Linden et al., p. 18.

26. James, Bess, and Saltus, *A Sexual Profile of Men in Power* (1978), quoted by Lawrence Mass in "Coming to Grips with Sadomasochism," *S and M*, ed. Weinberg and Kamel, p. 49.

27. *Diagnostic and Statistical Manual* (3d ed. rev.; Washington, D.C.: American Psychiatric Association, 1987), p. 286.

28. For an interesting discussion of the concept of addiction, see Robert E. Goodin, *No Smoking: The Ethical Issues* (Chicago: University of Chicago Press, 1989), pp. 95–100.

29. Andreas Spengler, "Manifest Sadomasochism of Males: Results of an Empirical Study," in *S and M*, ed. Weinberg and Kamel, pp. 57–72. See table IX, p. 68.

30. This view is expressed by Pat Califia, "A Secret Side of Lesbian Sexuality," in *S and M*, ed. Weinberg and Kamel, p. 129.

31. For a classic discussion of this point, see Bishop Joseph Butler, Sermon #11, in *Fifteen Sermons Preached at Rolls Chapel* (first published in 1726) (London: G. Bell & Sons, 1976), pp. 164–83.

32. Pat Califia, for example, writes "Why would anyone want to be dominated, given the risks? Because it is a healing process. As a top, I find the old wounds and unappeased hunger I nourish, I cleanse and close the wounds. I devise and mete out appropriate punishment for old, irrational sins. . . . A good scene doesn't end with orgasm—it ends with catharsis." "A Secret Side of Lesbian Sexuality," p. 134.

33. Susan Farr, "The Art of Discipline: Creating Erotic Dramas of Play and Power," in *Against Sadomasochism*, ed. Linden et al., p. 186.

34. Jeanne F. Neath, "Let's Discuss Dyke S/M and Quit the Name Calling: A Response to Sheila Jeffreys," *Lesbian Ethics* 2, no. 3 (Summer 1987), p. 97.

35. Sandra Bartky, in personal correspondence, called my attention to this possibility.

36. It is possible, of course, for addicts to resist addiction, and yet, the generalization holds.

37. Audre Lorde and Susan Leigh Star, "Interview with Audre Lorde," in *Against Sadomasochism*, ed. Linden et al., p. 67.

38. Sarah Hoagland, "Sadism, Masochism, and Lesbian Feminism," in *Against Sadomasochism*, ed. Linden et al., p. 160.

Selected Bibliography

of lesbian ethics, politics, and the arts

1. reference works

Card, Claudia. "Selected Bibliography of Lesbian Philosophy and Related Works," *Hypatia* 7, no. 4 (Fall 1992), 212–22.

Daly, Mary in cahoots with Jane Caputi. *Webster's First New Intergalactic Wickedary of the English Language*. Boston: Beacon Press, 1987.

Fletcher, Lynne Yamaguchi and Adrien Saks. *Lavender Lists: New Lists About Lesbian and Gay Culture, History, and Personalities*. Boston: Alyson, 1990.

A Gay Bibliography: Eight Bibliographies on Lesbianism and Male Homosexuality. New York: Arno Press, 1975.

Grier, Barbara, ed. *The Lesbian in Literature*, 3d ed. Tallahassee, Fla.: Naiad Press, 1981.

Richards, Dell. *Lesbian Lists: A Look at Lesbian Culture, History, and Personalities*. Boston: Alyson, 1990.

Roberts, JR, comp. *Black Lesbians: An Annotated Bibliography*. Tallahassee, Fla.: Naiad Press, 1981.

Rogers, Bruce. *The Queen's Vernacular: A Gay Lexicon* (San Francisco: Straight Arrow Books, 1972).

Sillman, Amy. "Bibliography on Lesbian Art and Artists." *Heresies* No. 3 (Fall 1977): 115–17.

Wittig, Monique and Sande Zeig. *Lesbian Peoples: Material for a Dictionary.* New York: Avon, 1979. First published in France as *Brouillon pour un dictionnaire des amants,* 1976.

II. *periodicals*

The Advocate: The National Gay and Lesbian News Magazine. Ed. Gerry Kroll. Los Angeles: since c.1967. Biweekly.

The Amazon Quarterly: A Lesbian Feminist Arts Journal. Ed. Gina Covina and Laurel Galana. Oakland, Calif.: 1972–74.

Azalea: Magazine by Third World Lesbians. New York: 1977–? Quarterly.

Canadian Journal of Feminist Ethics. Ed. Kathleen Martindale and Martha Saunders. Montreal, Quebec: 1986–88; Calgary, Alberta: 1988–89. Title changed to *Feminist Ethics* in 1987.

Chrysalis: A Magazine of Women's Culture. Los Angeles: 1977–80. (10 issues). Includes many relevant articles.

Common Lives, Lesbian Lives: A Lesbian Feminist Quarterly. Ed. Lesbian Collective. Iowa City: 1981 to present.

Conditions: feminist magazine of writing by women with emphasis on writing by lesbians. Founding eds. Elly Bulkin, Jan Clausen, Irena Klepfisz, Rima Shore. New York: 1977–90 (17 issues).

GLQ: A Journal of Lesbian and Gay Studies. Ed. Carolyn Dinshaw and David Halperin. New York: Gordon and Breach Science Publishers. Quarterly, since Summer 1993.

Gossip: Journal of Lesbian Feminist Ethics. Onlywoman Press, 38 Mount Pleasant, London WC1X OAP, U.K.: 1986 to ca. 1988 (at least 5 issues).

The Journal of Homosexuality. Ed. John P. de Cecco, Center for Research and Education in Sexuality, San Francisco State University: 1975 to present. Quarterly.

The Ladder. 1956–72. First published by Daughters of Bilitis, a lesbian organization founded in 1955 in San Francisco by Phyllis Lyon and Del Martin. Monthly. Reissued 1975 in 9 vols. New York: Arno Press.

Lambda Book Report: A Review of Contemporary Gay and Lesbian Literature. Ed. Jim Marks. Washington D.C.: since 1991. Bimonthly.

Lesbian Connection. Ambitious Amazons, Helen Diner Memorial Women's Center, East Lansing, Mich.: 1976 to present. Bimonthly newsletter.

Lesbian and Gay Studies Newsletter. Ed. Margaret Morrison, Dept. English, North Carolina Wesleyan College, Rocky Mount, NC 27804. 1973 to present. Research newsletter of MLA Gay/Lesbian Caucus. 3x annually.

Lesbian Ethics. Ed. Fox (a.k.a. Jeanetter Silveira). LE Publications, Albuquerque, N.M.: 1984 to present. 3x vol.

Lesbian Herstory Archives Newsletter. Lesbian Herstory Educational Foundation, Inc., New York: 1975-present. Irreg.

The Lesbian Tide. Los Angeles: 1971–81. Bimonthly newsletter.

Matrices: Lesbian Feminist Resource and Research Newsletter. Ed. Jacqueline Zita, University of Minnesota, Minneapolis. 1977 to present.

Quest: A Feminist Quarterly. Washington D.C.: 1974–1980s. Many relevant articles.

Signs: Journal of Women in Culture and Society. 9, no. 4 (Summer 1984). Special Issue: The Lesbian Issue. 18, no. 4 (Summer 1993), Special Issue: Theorizing Lesbian Experience. Other issues occasionally have relevant articles.

Sinister Wisdom: Journal for the Lesbian Imagination in the Arts and Politics. Ed. Elana Dykewomon, Berkeley, Callif. 1976 to present (49 issues as of Spring/Summer 1993).

Society for Lesbian and Gay Philosophy Newsletter. Ed. John Pugh, John Carroll University, University Heights, OH 44881. 1988 to present. Semiannual.

Trivia: A Journal of Ideas. Ed. Lise Weil and Linda Nelson. Amherst, Mass.: 1982 to present. (20 issues, as of 1992).

III. amazons

1. Ancient Amazons

Arctinus. *Aethiopis.* Summarized in *Hesiod: The Homeric Hymns and Homerica.* Trans. Hugh G. Evelyn-White. Cambridge, Mass.: Harvard University Press, 1974, pp. 507–509.

Bennet, Florence Mary. *Religious Cults Associated with the Amazons.* New York: Columbia University Press, 1912.

Cavin, Susan. *Lesbian Origins.* San Francisco: Ism Press, 1985, pp. 63–80.

Diodorus of Sicily. 12 vols. Trans. C. H. Oldfather. Cambridge, Mass.: Harvard University Press, 1967, 2:29–37; 2:245–61; 2:393–97; 2:431–33.

The Geography of Strabo. 8 vols. Trans. Horace Leonard Jones. Cambridge, Mass.: Harvard University Press, 1988, 5:233–39.

Herodotus. Trans. A. D. Godley. 4 vols. Cambridge, Mass.: Harvard University Press, 1982, pp. 309–317.

Isocrates. 2 vols. Vols. 1–2, trans. George Norlin; vol. 3, trans. Larue Van Hook. Cambridge, Mass.: Harvard University Press, 1982–1991, 1:159–61; 2:493.

Justin. *A History of the World.* Trans. G. Turnbull. London: S. Birt and B. Dod, 1746, pp. 21–25.

Kanter, Emmanuel. *The Amazons: A Marxian Study.* Chicago: Kerr, 1926.

Lysias. Trans. W. R. M. Lamb. Cambridge, Mass.: Harvard University Press, 1960, pp. 33–34.

Markale, Jean. *Women of the Celts.* Trans. A. Mygind, C. Hauch, and P. Henry. Rochester, Vt.: Inner Traditions International, 1986.

Pausanias. *Guide to Greece.* 2 vols. New York: Penguin, 1971.

Plutarch's Lives. 11 vols. Trans. Bernadotte Perrin. Cambridge, Mass.: Harvard University Press, 1982. 1:59–67.

Rothery, Guy. *The Amazons in Antiquity and Modern Times.* London: Griffiths, 1910.

Samuel, Pierre. *Amazones, guerrieres et gaillardes.* Bruxelles: Presses Universitaires de Grenoble, 1975.

Sobol, Donald. *Amazons of Greek Mythology.* London: Thomas Yoseloff, 1972.

Zografu, Mina. *Amazons in Homer and Hesiod: A Historical Reconstruction.* Athens, 1972.

2. Modern Amazons

Bennett, Betty T. *Mary Diana Dods: A Gentleman and a Scholar.* New York: Morrow, 1991.

Cameron, Anne. *Daughters of Copper Woman.* Vancouver: Press Gang, 1981.

Daly, Mary. *Outercourse: The Be-Dazzling Voyage.* San Francisco: Harper, 1992.

David, Elizabeth Gould. *The First Sex.* Baltimore, Md.: Penguin, 1971.

Dekker, Thomas and Thomas Middleton. *The Roaring Girl.* Ed. Andor Gomme. New York: Norton, 1976; first published 1611.

Erauso, Catalina de. *The Nun Ensign.* Trans. James Fitzmaurice-Kelly. London: Fisher Unwin, 1908.

Forde, Daryll and P. M. Kaberry, eds. *West African Kingdoms in the Nineteenth Century.* Oxford: Oxford University Press, 1967, pp. 86–89

Gautier, Théophile. *Mademoiselle de Maupin.* Trans. Joanna Richardson. Middlesex, Eng.: Penguin, 1981.

Gilbert, Oscar Paul. *Women in Men's Guise.* London: Bodley Head, 1932.

Goldsmith, Margaret. *Christina of Sweden.* Garden City, N.Y.: Doubleday, 1935.

Hall, Radclyffe. *The Well of Loneliness.* New York: Pocket Books, 1950; first published 1928.

Katz, Jonathan, ed. *Gay American History: Lesbians and Gay Men in the U.S.A.* New York: Crowell, 1976. "Passing Women," pp. 209–79.

Kleinbaum, Abby Wettan. *The War Against the Amazons.* New York: McGraw-Hill, 1983.

Mann, Herbert. *The Female Review: Life of Deborah Sampson.* (1797; reprinted New York: Arno, 1972).

Rae, Isobel. *The Strange Story of Dr. James Barry: Army Surgeon, Inspector-General of Hospitals, Discovered on Death to Be a Woman.* London: Longmans, 1958.

Sackville-West, Victoria. *Saint Joan of Arc.* Garden City, N.Y.: Country Life Press, 1936.

Stoker, Bram. *Famous Imposters.* London: Sidgwick and Jackson, 1910.

Thompson, Charles J. S. *Mysteries of Sex.* London: Hutchinson, 1938.

Wheelwright, Julie. *Amazons and Military Maids: Women Who Dressed as Men in Pursuit of Life, Liberty, and Happiness*. London: Pandora, 1989.

Williams, Walter L. *The Spirit and the Flesh: Sexual Diversity in American Indian Culture*. Boston: Beacon Press, 1986. "Amazons of America: Female Gender Variance," pp. 233–51.

IV. sappho and sapphic tradition

1. Sappho and Her Commentators

Hallett, Judith P. "Sappho and Her Social Context: Sense and Sensuality." *Signs* 4, no. 3 (Spring 1979):447–64.

Page, Denys. *Sappho and Alcaeus: An Introduction to the Study of Ancient Lesbian Poetry*. Oxford: Clarendon Press, 1955, pp. 3–146.

The Poems of Sappho. Trans. Susy Q. Groden. Indianapolis: Bobbs-Merrill, 1966.

Robinson, David M. *Sappho and Her Influence*. New York: Cooper Square, 1963.

Sappho. *Greek Lyric*. Trans. David A. Campbell. 4 vols. Cambridge, Mass.: Harvard University Press, 1982, 1:ix–xix and 1:2–205.

Sappho: A New Translation. Trans. Mary Barnard. Berkeley, Calif.: University of California Press, 1958.

Sappho: Poems and Fragments. Trans. Josephine Balmer. London: Brilliance Books, 1984.

Steigers, Eva Stehle. "Romantic Sensuality, Poetic Sense: A Response to Hallett on Sappho." *Signs* 4, no. 3 (Spring 1979):465–71.

Weigall, Arthur. *Sappho of Lesbos: Her Life and Times*. New York: Stokes, 1932.

Wharton, Henry Thornton. *Sappho: Memoir, Text, Selected Renderings, and a Literal Translation*, 4th ed. Chicago: A. C. McClurg, 1898.

2. Modern Sapphic Tradition

Barney, Natalie Clifford. *Adventures of the Mind*. Trans. John Spalding Gatton. New York: New York University Press, 1992.

Barney, Natalie Clifford. *A Perilous Advantage: The Best of Natalie Clifford Barney*. Trans. and ed. Anna Livia. Norwich, Vt.: New Victoria Publishers, 1992.

Colette. *The Pure and the Impure*. Trans. Herma Briffault. New York: Farrar, Straus, & Giroux, 1967, pp. 79–98. (On Renée Vivien.)

Dickinson, Emily. *The Complete Poems*. Ed. Thomas H. Johnson. Boston: Little, Brown, 1960.

Gidlow, Elsa. *Sapphic Songs: Eighteen to Eighty*. Mill Valley, Calif.: Druid Heights Books, 1982.

Grahn, Judy. *The Highest Apple: Sappho and the Lesbian Poetic Tradition*. San Francisco: Spinsters Ink, 1985.

Grahn, Judy; Gertrude Stein. *Really Reading Gertrude Stein: A Selected Anthology with Essays by Judy Grahn*. Freedom, Calif.: Crossing Press, 1989.

Labé, Louise. *Love Sonnets*. New York: New Directions, 1947.

Lorde, Audre. *Chosen Poems—Old and New*. New York: Norton, 1982.

Lowell, Amy. *The Complete Poetical Works*. Boston: Houghton Mifflin, 1955.

Marks, Elaine. "Lesbian Intertextuality." In *Homosexualities and French Literature: Cultural Contexts/Critical Texts*, ed. George Stambolian and Elaine Marks. Ithaca, N.Y.: Cornell University Press, pp. 353–77.

Olivia (pseudonym of Dorothy Bussy Strachey). *Olivia*. New York: Sloane, 1949.

Parker, Pat. *Movement in Black*. Trumansburg, N.Y.: Crossing Press, 1983.

Patterson, Rebecca. *The Riddle of Emily Dickinson*. New York: Houghton Mifflin, 1951.

Rich, Adrienne. *The Dream of a Common Language, Poems 1974–1977*. New York: Norton, 1978.

Stein, Gertrude. "As a Wife Has a Cow, a Love Story." In *Selected Writings of Gertrude Stein*, ed. Carl Van Vechten. New York: Vintage, 1972, pp. 541–45.

Stein, Gertrude. *Lifting Belly*, ed. Rebecca Mark. Tallahassee, Fla.: Naiad Press, 1989.

Stein, Gertrude. "Tender Buttons." In *Selected Writings*, pp. 459–509.

Vivien, Renée (b. Pauline Tarn). *At the Sweet Hour of Hand in Hand*. Trans. Sandia Belgrade. Naiad Press, 1979.

Vivien, Renée. *The Muse of the Violets*. Trans. Margaret Porter and Catharine Kroger. Tallahassee, Fla.: Naiad Press, 1977.

Vivien, Renée. *A Woman Appeared to Me*. Trans. Jeannette H. Foster. Tallahassee, Fla.: Naiad Press, 1982.

Vivien, Renée. *The Woman of the Wolf and Other Stories*. Trans. Karla Jay and Yvonne M. Klein. New York: Gay Presses of New York, 1983.

Winsloe, Christa. *The Child Manuela: The Novel of "Maedchen in Uniform."* Trans. Agnes Neill Scott. New York: Farrar and Rinehart, 1933.

V. passionate friendship

Bell, Eva Mary, ed. *The Hamwood Papers of the Ladies of Langollen and Caroline Hamilton*. London: Macmillan, 1930.

Colette. *The Pure and the Impure*. Trans. Herma Briffault. New York: Farrar, Straus, & Giroux, 1967, pp. 109–29. (On the Ladies of Langollen.)

Curb, Rosemary and Nancy Manahan, eds. *Lesbian Nuns: Breaking Silence*. Tallahassee, Fla.: Naiad Press, 1985.

Faber, Doris. *The Life of Lorena Hickok: E.R.'s Friend.* New York: Morrow, 1980.

Faderman, Lillian. *Scotch Verdict: Miss Pirie and Miss Woods v. Dame Cumming Gordon.* New York: Quill, 1983.

Faderman, Lillian. *Surpassing the Love of Men: Romantic Friendship and Love Between Women from the Renaissance to the Present.* New York: Morrow, 1981.

Giallombardo, Rose. *Society of Women: A Study of a Women's Prison.* New York: Wiley, 1966, pp. 133–89.

Gunderode, Caroline and Bettina (Brentano) von Arnim. *Correspondance of Fraulein Gunderode and Bettina von Arnim.* Trans. Margaret Fuller. 1842; reprinted, Boston: Burnham, 1961.

Heffernan, Esther. *Making It in Prison: The Square, the Cool, and the Life.* New York: Wiley, 1972, pp. 87–106.

Hellman, Lillian. "The Children's Hour." In *Six Plays by Lillian Hellman.* New York: Modern Library, 1960, pp. 5–86.

Lugones, María C. and Elizabeth V. Spelman. "Have We Got a Theory for You! Feminist Theory, Cultural Imperialism, and the Demand for 'the Women's Voice.' " In *Hypatia Reborn: Essays in Feminist Philosophy*, ed. Azizah al-Hibri and Margaret Simons. Bloomington: Indiana University Press, 1990, pp. 18–33.

Margy. "Can Lesbians Be Friends?" *Lesbian Connection* 2, no. 4 (August 1976): 13–14.

Margy. "Can Lesbians Be Friends? Part II." *Lesbian Connection* 2, no. 6 (November 1976):10–11.

Mavor, Elizabeth. *The Ladies of Llangollen.* Middlesex, Eng.: Penguin, 1973.

McNaron, Toni A. H. *The Sister Bond: A Feminist View of a Timeless Connection.* New York: Pergamon, 1985.

Raymond, Janice G. *A Passion for Friends: Toward a Philosophy of Female Affection.* Boston: Beacon Press, 1986.

Ruth. In *The Holy Scriptures According to the Masoretic Text.* Philadelphia: Jewish Publication Society of America, 1955, pp. 1087–91.

Sarton, May. "A Divorce of Lovers." In *Collected Poems (1930–1973).* New York: Norton, 1974, pp. 201–9.

Stein, Gertrude. "Fernhurst" and "Q.E.D." In *Fernhurst, Q.E.D., and Other Early Writings.* New York: Liveright, 1971, pp. 1–49 and 53–133.

Stein, Gertrude. "Miss Furr and Miss Skeene." In *Selected Writings*, pp. 561–68.

Stein, Gertrude. *Three Lives.* New York: Vintage, copyright 1909 and 1936 by Gertrude Stein.

T'ien, Ju-K'ang. "Female Labor in a Cotton Mill." Supplementary chapter in Kuo-Hang Shih, *China Enters the Machine Age: A Study of Labor in Chinese War Industry.* Trans. and ed. Hsiao-Tun Fei and Francis L. K. Hsu. Cambridge, Mass.: Harvard University Press, 1944, pp. 178–95.

Wells, Anna Mary. *Miss Marks and Miss Woolley*. Boston: Houghton Mifflin, 1978.

Wollstonecraft, Mary. *Mary, A Fiction*. New York: Schocken, 1977; first published in 1788.

Zita, Jacqueline. "Female Bonding and Sexual Politics." *Sinister Wisdom* 14 (Summer 1980):8–16.

VI. theater, visual arts, music

Abbott, Berenice. *Photographs*. New York: Horizon, 1970.

Biren, Joan E. (JEB). *Eye to Eye: Portraits of Lesbians*. Washington, D.C.: Glad Hag Books, 1979.

Biren, Joan E. *Making a Way: Lesbians Out Front*. Washington D.C.: Glad Hag Books, 1987.

Blackbridge, Persimmon and Sheila Gilhooly. *Still Sane*. Vancouver: Press Gang Publishers, 1985.

Boffin, Tessa and Jean Fraser. *Stolen Glances: Lesbians Take Photographs*. London: Pandora, 1991.

Brooks, Romaine. *Portraits-Tableaux-Dessins*. New York: Arno, 1975. (Reprinted from a copy in the Library of the Philadelphia Museum of Art.)

Charke, Charlotte. *A Narrative of the Life of Mrs. Charlotte Charke (Youngest Daughter of Colley Cibber, Esq.)*. Gainesville, Fla.: Scholar's Facsimiles and Reprints, 1969; first published 1755.

Cooper, Emmanuel. *The Sexual Perspective: Homosexuality and Art in the Last 100 Years in the West*. London: Routledge & Kegan Paul, 1986.

Corinne, Tee. *Women Who Loved Women*. Copyright 1984 by Tee Corinne.

Curtin, Kaier. *"We Can Always Call Them Bulgarians": The Emergence of Lesbians and Gay Men on the American Stage*. Boston: Alyson, 1987.

Fine, Elsa Honig. "Edmonia Lewis (1843–c.1900)." In Fine, *The Afro-American Artist: A Search for Identity*. New York: Holt, Rinehart, and Winston, pp. 63–67.

Dyer, Richard, ed. *Gays and Film*. London: British Film Institute, 1980.

Dyer, Richard. *Now You See It: Studies on Lesbian and Gay Film*. New York: Routledge, 1990.

Grier, Barbara and Colette Reid, eds. *The Lavender Herring: Lesbian Essays from The Ladder*. Baltimore, Md.: Diana Press, 1976, pp. 284–357.

Hadleigh, Boze. *The Lavender Screen: The Gay and Lesbian Films: Their Stars, Makers, Characters, and Critics*. New York: Citadel Press, 1993.

Hadleigh, Boze. *The Vinyl Closet: Gays in the Music World*. San Diego, Calif.: Los Hombres Press, 1991.

Heresies: A Feminist Publication on Arts and Politics. No. 3 (Fall 1977). Special Issue on Lesbian Art and Artists.

Leach, Joseph. *Bright Particular Star: The Life and Times of Charlotte Cushman.* New Haven: Yale University Press, 1970.

Lewis, Samella. "(Mary) Edmonia Lewis (1843–1900?)." In Lewis, *Art: African American.* New York: Harcourt Brace Jovanovich, 1978, pp.39–43.

Ovenden, Graham, ed. *Clementina: Lady Hawarden.* New York: St. Martin's Press, 1974.

Russo, Vito. *The Celluloid Closet: Homosexuality in the Movies.* New York: Harper & Row, 1981; rev. ed. New York: Perennial Library, 1987.

Secrest, Meryle. *Between Me and Life: A Biography of Romaine Brooks.* Garden City, N.Y.: Doubleday, 1974.

Smyth, Ethel. *The Memoirs of Ethel Smyth.* Abridged and introduced by Ronald Crichton. New York: Viking, 1987.

Souhami, Diana. *Gluck 1895–1978: Her Biography.* London: Pandora, 1988.

Tilt: An Anthology of New England Women's Writing and Art. Lebanon, N.H.: New Victoria Publishers, Inc., 1978.

VII. violence and abuse

Primarily items directly relevant to lesbian violence and abuse of lesbians are listed here. Many further references to materials on battering, stalking, incest, and cult ritual abuse are to be found in the notes for chapters 6 and 7.

Anne [no surname]. "Talking About Evil." *Lesbian Ethics* 5, no. 1 (Summer 1993):82–89.

Cauffiel, Lowell. *Forever and Five Days.* New York: Zebra, 1992.

Comstock, Gary David. *Violence Against Lesbians and Gay Men.* New York: Columbia University Press, 1991.

Cuomo, Chris. "Ritual Abuse: Making Connections." *Lesbian Ethics* 4, no. 3 (Spring 1992):45–53.

Daly, Mary. *Gyn/Ecology: The Metaethics of Radical Feminism.* Boston: Beacon Press, 1978, pp. 107–312.

Elliott, Pamela, ed. "Confronting Lesbian Battering: A Manual for the Battered Women's Movement." St. Paul: Minnesota Coalition for Battered Women. (Not published.)

Evans, Lee and Shelley Bannister. "Lesbian Violence, Lesbian Victims: How to Identify Battering in Relationships." *Lesbian Ethics* 4, no. 1 (Spring 1990):52–65.

Evert, Kathy and Inie Bijkerk. *When You're Ready: A Woman's Healing from Childhood Physical and Sexual Abuse by Her Mother.* Walnut Creek, Calif.: Launch Press, 1987.

Forward, Susan and Craig Buck. *Betrayal of Innocence: Incest and Its Devastation.* Rev. New York: Penguin, 1988, pp. 115–29.

Glamuzina, Julie and Alison J. Laurie. *Parker and Hulme: A Lesbian View.* Auckland, New Zealand: New Women's Press, 1991.

Herek, Gregory M. and Kevin T. Berrill, eds. *Hate Crimes: Confronting Violence Against Lesbians and Gay Men.* Newbury Park, Calif.: Sage, 1992.

Island, David and Patrick Letellier. *Men Who Beat the Men Who Love Them: Battered Gay Men and Domestic Violence.* New York: Harrington Park Press, 1991.

Kaye/Kantrowitz, Melanie. *The Issue Is Power: Essays on Women, Jews, Violence and Resistance.* San Francisco: Aunt Lute Books, 1992.

Klepfisz, Irena. "Anti-Semitism in the Lesbian/Feminist Movement." In *Nice Jewish Girls: A Lesbian Anthology*, ed. Evelyn Torton Beck. Rev. and updated. Boston: Beacon Press, 1989, pp. 51–57.

Kushner, Leah Pesa. *Dragonchild: One Lesbian's Journal of Survival Through a Childhood of Battering and Sexual Abuse.* Iowa City: Iowa City Women's Press, 1984.

Lincoln, Victoria. *A Private Disgrace: Lizzie Borden by Daylight.* New York: International Polygonics, 1986.

Lobel, Kerry, ed. *Naming the Violence: Speaking Out About Lesbian Battering.* Seattle: Seal Press, 1986.

McNaron, Toni. "Mother Rite" and "For My Mother." In *Voices in the Night: Women Speaking About Incest*, ed. Toni A. H. McNaron and Yarrow Morgan. Minneapolis: Cleis Press, 1982, pp. 47, 172–76.

Moran, Kate. "Mary Poppins and My Childhood in Hell." *Lesbian Ethics* 5, no. 1 (Summer 1993):76–81.

Park, Jeannie, Lois Armstrong, Doris Bacon, and Eleanor Hoover. "A Fan's Long Suicidal Obsession with Actress Sharon Gless Leads to a Tense Police Standoff." *People Weekly* 33 (April 16, 1990):62–3.

Renzetti, Claire. *Violent Betrayal: Partner Abuse in Lesbian Relationships.* Newbury Park, Calif.: Sage, 1992.

Reynolds, M. "The Reality: The Truths About Satanic/Ritualistic Abuse and Multiple Personality Disorder." Revised. Copyright M. Reynolds 1991. (Not published.)

Robson, Ruthann. *Lesbian (Out)Law: Survival Under the Rule of Law.* Ithaca, N.Y.: Firebrand Books, 1992.

Rich, Adrienne. *Of Woman Born: Motherhood as Experience and as Institution.* New York: Norton, 1976, pp. 260–86.

Schindehette, Susan and Doris Bacon. "Vanna White and Teri Garr Ask the Courts to Protect Them from Fans Who Have Gone Too Far." *People Weekly* 34 (July 16, 1990):40–41.

Schreiber, Flora Rheta. *Sybil.* New York: Warner, 1974.

Smith, Michelle (pseudonym) and Lawrence Pazder. *Michelle Remembers.* New York: Pocket Books, 1980.

Spencer, Judith. *Suffer the Child.* New York: Pocket Books, 1989.

Thomas, Ardel. "Dangerous Connections: Lesbian S/M and Mother-Daughter Incest." *Lesbian Ethics* 4, no. 3 (Spring 1992), 79–86.

VIII. cultural history

Anzaldúa, Gloria. *Borderlands/La Frontera: The New Mestiza*. San Francisco: Spinsters/Aunt Lute, 1987.

Benstock, Shari. *Women of the Left Bank: Paris, 1900–1940*. Austin: University of Texas Press, 1986.

Berube, Allan. *Coming Out Under Fire: The History of Gay Men and Women in World War Two*. New York: Free Press, 1990.

Boswell, John. *Christianity, Social Tolerance, and Homosexuality: Gay People in Western Europe from the Beginning of the Christian Era to the Fourteenth Century*. Chicago: University of Chicago Press, 1980.

Brown, Judith C. *Immodest Acts: The Life of a Lesbian Nun in Renaissance Italy*. New York: Oxford, 1986.

Chung, C., A. Kim, and A. K. Lemeshewsky, eds. *Between the Lines: An Anthology by Pacific/Asian Lesbians of Santa Cruz*. Santa Cruz, Calif.: Dancing Bird Press, 1987.

Cook, Blanche Wiesen. *Eleanor Roosevelt*, Vol. 1: 1884–1933. New York: Viking, 1992, pp. 102–24, 448–500.

D'Emilio, John. *Making Trouble: Essays on Gay History, Politics, and the University*. New York: Routledge, 1992.

D'Emilio, John. *Sexual Politics, Sexual Communities: The Making of a Homosexual Minority in the United States, 1940–1970*. Chicago: University of Chicago Press, 1983.

Duberman, Martin Bauml, Martha Vicinus, and George Chauncey, Jr., eds. *Hidden from History: Reclaiming the Gay and Lesbian Past*. New York: New American Library, 1989.

Duberman, Martin. *Stonewall*. New York: Dutton, 1993.

Faderman, Lillian. *Odd Girls and Twilight Lovers: A History of Lesbian Life in Twentieth-Century America*. New York: Columbia University Press, 1991.

Faderman, Lillian and Brigitte Eriksson, eds. *Lesbians in Germany: 1890s–1920s*. Tallahassee, Fla.: Naiad Press, 1990.

Foster, Jeannette. *Sex-Variant Women in Literature*. New York: Vantage, 1956.

Frontiers: A Journal of Women's Studies. 4, no. 3 (Fall 1979). Lesbian History Issue.

Grahn, Judy. *Another Mother Tongue: Gay Words, Gay Worlds*. Boston: Beacon Press, 1984.

Grier, Barbara and Coletta Reid, eds. *Lesbian Lives: Biographies of Women from The Ladder*. Baltimore, Md.: Diana Press, 1976.

Gross, Larry. *Contested Closets: The Politics and Ethics of Outing*. Minneapolis: University of Minnesota, 1993.

Humphrey, Mary Ann. *My Country, My Right to Serve: Experiences of Gay Men and Women in the Military, World War II to the Present.* New York: Harper & Row, 1990.

Katz, Jonathan Ned, ed. *Gay/Lesbian Almanac: A New Documentary.* New York: Harper & Row, 1983.

Kennedy, Elizabeth Lapovsky and Madeline D. Davis. *Boots of Leather, Slippers of Gold: The History of a Lesbian Community.* New York: Routledge, 1993.

Klaich, Dolores. *Woman + Woman: Attitudes Toward Lesbianism.* New York: Simon & Schuster, 1974.

Lorde, Audre. *The Cancer Journals.* Argyle, N.Y.: Spinsters Ink, 1980.

Lorde, Audre. *Zami: A New Spelling of My Name.* Trumansburg, N.Y.: Crossing Press, 1982.

Marcus, Eric. *Making History: The Struggle for Gay and Lesbian Equal Rights 1945–1990: An Oral History.* New York: Harper & Row, 1992.

Martin, Del and Phyllis Lyon. *Lesbian/Woman.* New York: Bantam, 1972.

McNaron, Toni. *I Dwell in Possibility: A Memoir.* New York: Feminist Press, 1992.

Mellow, James R. *Charmed Circle: Gertrude Stein and Company.* New York: Avon, 1975.

Penelope, Julia and Susan J. Wolfe, eds. *The Original Coming Out Stories.* Expanded ed. Freedom, Calif.: Crossing Press, 1989.

Penelope, Julia and Sarah Valentine, eds. *Finding the Lesbians: Personal Accounts from Around the World.* Freedom, Calif.: Crossing Press, 1990.

Richards, Dell. *Superstars: Twelve Lesbians Who Changed the World.* New York: Carol & Graf, 1993.

Schwarz, Judith. *Radical Feminists of Heterodoxy: Greenwich Village 1912–1940.* Rev. ed. Ed. Claudia Lamperti and Beth Dingman. Norwich, Vt.: New Victoria, 1986.

Shilts, Randy. *Conduct Unbecoming: Gays and Lesbians in the U.S. Military.* New York: St. Martin's Press, 1993.

Signorile, Michelangelo. *Queer in America: Sex, the Media, and the Closets of Power.* New York: Random House, 1993.

Steakley, James. *The Homosexual Emancipation Movement in Germany.* New York: Arno, 1975.

Tobin, Kay and Randy Wicker. *The Gay Crusaders.* New York: Paperback Library, 1972

IX. philosophy and theory

Abelove, Henry, Michele Aina Barale, and David M. Halperin, eds. *The Lesbian and Gay Studies Reader.* New York: Routledge, 1993.

Allen, Jeffner, ed. *Lesbian Philosophies and Cultures.* Albany, N.Y.: State University of New York Press, 1990.

Allen, Jeffner. *Lesbian Philosophy: Explorations.* Palo Alto, Calif.: Institute of Lesbian Studies, 1986.

Allen, Paula Gunn. *"Hwame, Koshkalaka,* and the Rest: Lesbians in American Indian Cultures." In *The Sacred Hoop: Recovering the Feminine in American Indian Traditions.* Boston: Beacon Press, 1986, pp. 54–75.

Atkinson, Ti-Grace. *Amazon Odyssey.* New York: Links Books, 1974.

Balka, Christie and Andy Rose, eds. *Twice Blessed: On Being Lesbian, Gay, and Jewish.* Boston: Beacon Press, 1989.

Beauvoir, Simone de. "The Lesbian." Ch. 15 in *The Second Sex.* Trans. H. M. Parshley. New York: Knopf, 1952.

Beck, Evelyn Torton. *Nice Jewish Girls: A Lesbian Anthology.* Rev. and updated, Boston: Beacon Press, 1989.

Birkby, Phyllis, Bertha Harris, Jill Johnston, Esther Newton, and Jan O'Wyatt, eds. *Amazon Expedition: A Lesbian Feminist Anthology.* New York: Times Change Press, 1973.

Black, Evelyn. "Sexuality and Gender in Certain Native American Tribes: The Case of Cross-Gender Females." *Signs* 10, no. 1 (Autumn 1984):27–42.

Bunch, Charlotte and Nancy Myron, eds., *Class and Feminism: A Collection of Essays from The Furies.* Baltimore, Md.: Diana Press, 1974.

Butler, Judith. *Gender Trouble: Feminism and the Subversion of Identity.* New York: Routledge, 1990.

Card, Claudia, ed. *Adventures in Lesbian Philosophy.* Bloomington: Indiana University Press, 1994.

Card, Claudia. "The Feistiness of Feminism." In *Feminist Ethics,* ed. Claudia Card. Lawrence: University Press of Kansas, 1991.

Card, Claudia. "Fidelity." In *Encyclopedia of Ethics,* ed. Lawrence C. Becker with Charlotte B. Becker. 2 vols. New York: Garland, 1992, 1:373–75.

Card, Claudia. "Intimacy and Responsibility: What Lesbians Do." In *At the Boundaries of Law: Feminism and Legal Theory,* ed. Martha Albertson Fineman and Nancy Sweet Thomadsen. New York: Routledge, 1991.

Card, Claudia. "Oppression and Resistance: Frye's Politics of Reality." *Hypatia* 1, no. 1 (Spring 1986):149–66.

Card, Claudia. "Pluralist Lesbian Separatism." In *Lesbian Philosophies and Cultures,* ed. Jeffner Allen. Albany: State University of New York Press, 1990.

Copper, Baba. *Over the Hill: Reflections on Ageism Between Women.* Freedom, Calif.: Crossing Press, 1988.

Cornwell, Anita. *Black Lesbian in White America.* Tallahassee, Fla.: Naiad Press, 1983.

Covina, Gina and Laurel Galana, eds. *The Lesbian Reader: An Amazon Quarterly Anthology.* Oakland, Calif.: Amazon Press, 1975.

Cruikshank, Margaret, ed. *Lesbian Studies: Present and Future.* Old Westbury, N.Y.: Feminist Press, 1982.

Daly, Mary. *Gyn/Ecology: The Metaethics of Radical Feminism*. Boston: Beacon Press, 1978.

Daly, Mary. *Pure Lust: Elemental Feminist Philosophy*. Boston: Beacon Press, 1984.

Dart, Trudy and Sandee Potter, eds. *Woman-Identified Women*. Palo Alto, Calif.: Mayfield, 1984.

Douglas, Carol Anne. *Love and Politics: Radical Feminist and Lesbian Theories*. San Francisco: Ism Press, 1990.

Ferguson, Ann. "Is There a Lesbian Culture?" Ch. 7 in Ferguson, *Sexual Democracy: Women, Oppression, and Revolution*. Boulder: Westview Press, 1991, pp. 133–58.

Frye, Marilyn. *The Politics of Reality: Essays in Feminist Theory*. Trumansburg, N.Y.: Crossing Press, 1983.

Frye, Marilyn. *Willful Virgin: Essays in Feminism*. Freedom, Calif.: Crossing Press, 1992.

Fuss, Diana, ed. *Inside/Out: Lesbian Theories, Gay Theories*. New York: Routledge, 1991.

Grier, Barbara and Colette Reid, eds. *The Lavender Herring: Lesbian Essays from The Ladder*. Baltimore, Md.: Diana Press, 1976.

Harding, Sandra. "Thinking from the Perspective of Lesbian Lives." Ch. 10 in *Whose Science? Whose Knowledge?* Ithaca, N.Y.: Cornell University Press, 1991, pp. 249–67.

Hoagland, Sarah Lucia. *Lesbian Ethics: Toward New Value*. Palo Alto, Calif.: Institute of Lesbian Studies, 1988.

Hoagland, Sarah Lucia and Julia Penelope, eds. *For Lesbians Only: A Separatist Anthology*. London: Onlywomen Press, 1988.

Hypatia: A Journal of Feminist Philosophy 7, no. 4 (Fall 1992). Special Issue: Lesbian Philosophy, ed. Claudia Card.

Jay, Karla and Allen Young, eds. *Lavender Culture*. New York: Jove/HBJ, 1979.

Johnston, Jill. *Lesbian Nation: The Feminist Solution*. New York: Simon and Schuster, 1973.

Kehoe, Monika, ed. *Historical, Literary, and Erotic Aspects of Lesbianism*. New York: Harrington Park Press, 1986.

Kitzinger, Celia. *The Social Construction of Lesbianism*. London: Sage, 1987.

Koertge, Noretta. "Constructing Concepts of Sexuality: A Philosophical Commentary." In *Homosexuality/Heterosexuality: Concepts of Sexual Orientation*, ed. David P. McWhirter, Stephanie A. Sanders, and June Machover Reinisch. New York: Oxford University Press, 1990.

Linden, Robin Ruth, Darlene R. Pagano, Diana E. H. Russell, and Susan Leigh Star, eds. *Against Sadomasochism: A Radical Feminist Analysis*. East Palo Alto, Calif.: Frog in the Well Press, 1982.

Lindenbaum, Joyce P. "The Shattering of an Illusion: The Problem of Competition in Lesbian Relationships." In *Competition: A Feminist Taboo?* Ed. Valerie Miner and Helen E. Longino. New York: Feminist Press, 1987.

Lorde, Audre. *Sister Outsider: Essays and Speeches*. Trumansburg, N.Y.: Crossing Press, 1984.

Lorde, Audre. *A Burst of Light: Essays*. Ithaca, N.Y.: Firebrand Books, 1992.

Lugones, María. "Playfulness, 'World'-Travelling, and Loving Perception." *Hypatia* 2, no. 2 (Summer 1987):3–19.

Lugones, María. "Hablando Cara a Cara/Speaking Face to Face: An Exploration of Ethnocentric Racism." In *Making Face, Making Soul/Haciendo Caras: Creative and Critical Perspectives by Women of Color*, ed. Gloria Anzaldua. San Francisco: Aunt Lute Foundation, 1990.

Lugones, María. "Hispaneando y Lesbiando: On Sarah Hoagland's *Lesbian Ethics*." *Hypatia* 5, no. 3 (Fall 1990):138–46.

Lugones, María C. "Structure/Anti-Structure and Agency Under Oppression." *Journal of Philosophy* 87, no. 10 (October 1990):500–507.

Lugones, María Cristina and Elizabeth V. Spelman. "Competition, Compassion, and Community: Models for a Feminist Ethos." In *Competition: A Feminist Taboo?*, ed. Valerie Miner and Helen E. Longino. New York: Feminist Press, 1987.

Mohr, Richard. *Gays/Justice: A Study of Ethics, Society, and Law*. New York: Columbia University Press, 1988.

Mohr, Richard. *Gay Ideas: Outing and Other Controversies*. Boston: Beacon Press, 1992.

Mohr, Richard. *A More Perfect Union: Why Straight Americans Must Stand Up for Gay Rights*. Boston: Beacon Press, 1994.

Myron, Nancy and Charlotte Bunch, eds. *Lesbianism and the Women's Movement*. Baltimore, Md.: Diana Press, 1975.

Nestle, Joan. *A Restricted Country*. Ithaca, N.Y.: Firebrand Books, 1987.

Penelope, Julia. *Call Me Lesbian: Lesbian Lives, Lesbian Theory*. Freedom, Calif.: Crossing Press, 1992.

Penelope, Julia and Susan J. Wolfe, eds. *Lesbian Culture: An Anthology*. Freedom, Calif.: Crossing Press, 1993.

Pierce, Christine and Sara Ann Ketchum. "Separatism and Sexual Relationships." In *Philosophy and Women*, ed. Sharon Hill and Marjorie Weinsweig. Belmont, Calif.: Wadsworth, 1978.

Pharr, Suzanne. *Homophobia: A Weapon of Sexism*. Inverness, Calif.: Chardon Press, 1988.

Phelan, Shane. *Identity Politics: Lesbian Feminism and the Limits of Community*. Philadelphia: Temple University Press, 1989.

Pratt, Minnie Bruce. *Rebellion: Essays 1980–1991*. Ithaca, N.Y.: Firebrand Books, 1991.

Ramos, Juanita, ed. *Compañeras: Latina Lesbians: An Anthology*. New York: Latina Lesbian History Project, 1987.

Raymond, Janice G. *The Transsexual Empire: The Making of the She/Male.* Boston: Beacon Press, 1979.

Rich, Adrienne. *Blood, Bread, and Poetry: Selected Prose 1979–1985.* New York: Norton, 1986.

Rich, Adrienne. *On Lies, Secrets, and Silence: Selected Prose 1966–1978.* New York: Norton, 1979.

Roof, Judith. *A Lure of Knowledge: Lesbian Sexuality and Theory.* New York: Columbia University Press, 1991.

Roscoe, Will, ed. *Living the Spirit: A Gay American Indian Anthology.* New York: St. Martin's Press, 1988.

Sedgwick, Eve Kosofsky. *Epistemology of the Closet.* Berkeley: University of California Press, 1990.

Trebilcot, Joyce. "Conceiving Women: Notes on the Logic of Feminism." *Sinister Wisdom* 11 (Fall 1979):43–50.

Trebilcot, Joyce. "Notes on the Meaning of Life." *Lesbian Ethics* 1, no. 1 (Fall 1984):90–91.

Trebilcot, Joyce. "Taking Responsibility for Sexuality." In *Philosophy and Sex*, 2d ed., ed. Robert Baker and Frederick Elliston. Buffalo, N.Y.: Prometheus, 1984.

Trebilcot, Joyce. "Hortense and Gladys on Dreams." *Lesbian Ethics* 1, no. 2 (Spring 1985):85–87.

Trebilcot, Joyce. "Partial Response to Those Who Worry That Separatism May Be a Political Cop-Out: Expanded Definition of Activism." *off our backs* (May 1986). Reprinted in *Gossip* 3 (n.d.):82–84.

Trebilcot, Joyce. "Dyke Economics: Hortense and Gladys on Money." *Lesbian Ethics* 3, no. 1 (Spring 1988):1–13.

Trebilcot, Joyce. "Dyke Methods." *Hypatia* 5, no. 1 (Spring 1990):1–13.

Trebilcot, Joyce. "More Dyke Methods." *Hypatia* 5, no. 3 (Fall 1990):147–52.

Trebilcot, Joyce. "Stalking Guilt." *Lesbian Ethics* 5, no. 1 (Summer 1993):72–75.

Trujillo, Carla, ed. *Chicana Lesbians: The Girls Our Mothers Warned Us About.* Berkeley, Calif.: Third Woman Press, 1991.

Wittig, Monique. *The Straight Mind and Other Essays.* Boston: Beacon Press, 1992.

Wolfe, Susan J. and Julia Penelope Stanley. "Linguistic Problems with Patriarchal Reconstructions of Indo-European Culture." *Women's Studies International Quarterly* 3, nos. 2/3 (1980):227–37.

Zita, Jacqueline. "Historical Amnesia and the Lesbian Continuum." *Signs* 7, no. 1 (Winter 1981):172–78.

Zita, Jacqueline. " 'Real Girls' and Lesbian Resistance." *Lesbian Ethics* 3, no. 1 (Spring 1988):85–96.

Zita, Jacqueline. "Lesbian Angels and Other Matters." *Hypatia* 5, no. 1 (Spring 1990):133–39. (Response to Joyce Trebilcot, "Dyke Methods.")

Index

Abuse: emotional, 109, 112; psychological, 109, 112–13; verbal, 113,
116; *see also* Battering; Childhood
abuse; Female incest; Stalking
Addelson, Kathy, 5
Addiction, sadomasochism as,
231–37
African Americans, 208; domination, 124; killing of black women
and men, 129; in military service,
175–76, 178; Sambo personality,
124, 199; separatism and nationalism, 94; "two-ness," Du Bois'
concept of, 184; "womanist"
used by, 21

Agency: ethic of, 125; Frye's theory
of, 66; institutions and, 89
Algolagnia, 220
Allen, Jeffner, 72, 78
Allen, Paula Gunn, 16
Amazonian ethics, 75–76, 78–79
Amazonian lesbians, 31–33, 46, 190
Amazons, 24–25, 29, 144; labrys, 5
Ambitious Amazons, 11
American Philosophical Association
(APA), 76, 208
American Psychiatric Association,
37, 137, 231; *Diagnostic and Sta-
tistical Manual of Mental Disorders*,
137, 231–32

Amnesia, 131, 137, 143

Angelou, Maya, 134

Anti-stalking laws, 118

Anzaldua, Gloria, 72

APA, *see* American Philosophical Association

Arendt, Hannah, 91, 94–96; *The Human Condition*, 96

Aristotle, 42; on friendship, 45, 85, 96–105; *Nicomachean Ethics*, 99–101, 103; on the proud man, 206; *Rhetoric*, 100

Arnim, Bettina von, *see* Brentano, Bettina

Ashton, Winifred, *Regiment of Women*, 142

Attending, 103, 125–29; loss of attention, 128; redirection of attention, 94

Attitude, 42–43; bisexuals, 45; choice and, 43; evaluation, 44; heterosexuality as, 38, 42; homosexuality as, 44; lesbianism as, 36–39, 41–42, 44–46

Austin, John, 211

Baniszewski, Gertrude, 140

Baniszewski, Paula, 140, 142

Barnes, Djuna, 27

Barney, Natalie Clifford, 27, 30, 33, 93, 153

Barry, Kathleen, 49

Bartky, Sandra, 52

Battering, 112–13, 115; *see also* Childhood abuse; Domestic battering; Partner battering; Stalking

Beardless men, 25

Beauvoir, Simone de, 21, 34, 36–46, 65; *The Second Sex*, 36–40, 46

Bell, Quentin, 64

ben-Shalom, Miriam, 176–77

Berdache, 16

Berube, Allan, 174

Bettelheim, Bruno, 124

Birtha, Becky, 12

Bisexuality, 45, 51, 211; Emma Goldman, 63

Black and White Men Together, 76

Blacks, *see* African Americans

Bloch, Iwan, 219–20, 223, 230

Blood, Fanny, 60

Blood Libel, 141

Bonheur, Rosa, 33

Bonny, Ann, 26

Boswell, John, 18–19, 54

Bourges, Clemence de, 26, 33

Boxill, Bernard, 199, 205–6

Bradley, Katherine, 27, 33

Braude, Stephen, 138

Brenner, Claudia, 119, 206

Brentano, Bettina, 27, 61

Brooks, Romaine, 27, 93

Buchanan, Allen, 205

Buck, Craig (and Forward), *Betrayal of Innocents*, 134

Buffalo Oral History project, 12

Butch and femme roles, 84–85, 220

Butler, Eleanor, 27

Butler, Joseph, 52

Cable, Wittgenstein's metaphor of, 31, 75

Califia, Pat, 145, 221; *Macho Sluts*, 145

Cammermeyer, Margarethe, 178, 181

Card, Claudia, "Feminist Ethical Theory: A Lesbian Perspective," 5

Career women, Goldman's idea of, 64

Care ethics, 76–77

Carr, Stephen Roy, 119, 164, 206

Catharsis, sadomasochism as, 231–37

Cavin, Susan, 72

Childhood abuse, 108; battering, 134; cult ritual abuse, 137–44;

female incest, 131–37, 142, 144–47; heterosexual abuse, 136; incidence, 140; rape, 134

China, female friendships, 86, 90, 98, 104

Choice, 192; as act, 41, 48; Aristotle's notion of, 42; of attitude, 43; de Beauvoir's understanding of, 36–42 exercising, 48; levels of exercise of, 56–57; as option, 41, 48–49

Christina, Queen of Sweden, 26, 30

Clinton, Bill, 169–70

Closeting, 93, 157, 161, 197, 209–10; in military service, 170, 175, 177, 180–81, 183–86; pernicious aspects of, 178–80 in ROTC, 174; *see also* Passing

Code, *see* Encoding

Colette: *The Pure and the Impure*, 59; *Vagabonde*, 44

Coming out, 155, 159, 163, 193, 211–12 degrees of, 210; meaning of, 209; vs. outing, 204–9

Coming to Power (anthology), 220–21, 228, 233

Communities, lesbian and gay, *see* Gay communities; Lesbian communities

Compulsions, sadomasochistic, 234–35, 237

Compulsory heterosexuality, 40–41, 56

Consciousness raising (CR), 4–5, 49

Construction, social, *see* Social construction

Continuum, lesbian, *see* Lesbian continuum

Control, 126–28, 133; adult-child abuse, 134, 136; internal battles among feminists, 146; sadomasochism, 227

Convents, 212; friendships, 89–90, 98, 104

Cooper, Edith Emma, 27, 33

CR (consciousness raising), 4–5, 49

Crabtree, Adam, *Multiple Man*, 138

Crittenden Report, 188

Cruikshank, Peg, 12

Cult ritual abuse, 137–44

Culture, meanings of, 12; *see also* Lesbian culture

Cuomo, Chris, 72, 144

Curb, Rosemary (and Manahan), *Lesbian Nuns: Breaking Silence*, 212–13

Daly, Mary, 68, 72, 138, 141

Davion, Victoria, 184

Davis, Madeline D. (and Kennedy), *Boots of Leather, Slippers of Gold: The History of a Lesbian Community*, 12

Defense, Department of (DOD), 171, 178, 184–85, 187–88

Dekker, Thomas (and Middleton), *The Roaring Girl*, 26

Detective work, 14, 201

Dickinson, Emily, 27, 30, 201

Diderot, Denis, *The Nun*, 141

Dignity, 214; and outing, 195–200, 206–7, 210, 216–17

Dignity (organization), 197

Diner, Helen, 24

Diodorus Siculus, 24–25

Disfigurement, 193; fear of, 162

Dissociation, psychological, 138, 143, 183

Dissociation from the world, 91, 95

Dobkin, Alix, 47

DOD (Dept. of Defense), 171, 178, 184–85, 187–88

Domestic battering, 71; Walker's cycle theory, 114, 116; *see also* Partner battering

Domination, 124, 127, 145; in partner battering, 111–12, 116–17; in sadomasochism, 221

Double shame, Lynd's notion of, 159–60

Doubling, psychological principle of, 182–84, 193

Du Bois, W. E. B., 184, 199

Dworkin, Andrea, 138; *Mercy*, 143

Dyke, 21–23, 33; ethics, 71; separatists, 44, 46

Echoing, emotional, *see* Emotional echoing

Eckstein-Diener, Berthe, *see* Diner, Helen

Eisenhower, Dwight D., 175

Elkins, Stanley M., 124

Ellis, Havelock, 28, 219–20; *Love and Pain*, 219

Elsie Publishing Institute, 11

Emerson, Ralph Waldo, 217

Emotional echoing, 165–68

Empathy: and fear, 162; in friendship, 99

Encoding, 15

Endorphins, 222–23, 231–32

Environmental ethics, 73, 79

Erauso, Catalina de, 26, 30

Essence, 30

Essentialism, 17

Ethics, 66–68, 71; of outing, 196; *see also* Feminist ethics; Lesbian ethics

Evert, Kathy, 145

Evil, 68–69, 77

Exhibitionism, 154, 179; coming out, 205

External aspects of rules, Hart's notion of, 14, 28

Faber, Doris, 202

Faculty Against Discrimination in University Programs (FADIUP), 171–72, 174

Faderman, Lillian, 29, 72

FADIUP, *see* Faculty Against Discrimination in University Programs

Familying, Heffernan's notion of, 86

Family resemblance, 30–31; friendships, 45, 97; lesbian attitudes, 46

Farstein, Linda, 120

Fear, 158–59, 161–63; echoing, 166; and lack of power, 164; as response to ridicule, 165; *see also* Homophobia

Female friendship, Raymond's study of, 88–96; *see also* Lesbian friendship

Female incest, 131–37, 142, 144–47; cult ritual abuse, 137–44; documentation, 137

Feminism, 21–22, 37, 49, 51; changing passions, difficulty in, 52; internal disagreements, 145–46; internalized homophobia, 157; military exclusionary policies, 189–93; pornography, 226; sadomasochism, 218–19, 221, 233

Feminist ethics, 65, 73–78; *see also* Lesbian ethics

Feminist organizations, 133; *see also* Lesbian organizations

Ferguson, Ann, 13, 15

"Field, Michael," 27, 33

Fontaine, Coralyn, 12

Forbes, Malcolm, 194, 200

Forward, Susan (and Buck), *Betrayal of Innocents*, 134

Foucault, Michel, 17–19, 66; *History of Sexuality*, 17

Frank, Barney, 195

Freud, Sigmund, 157, 165; Fliess correspondence, 138–39, 144; sadomasochism, 220

Friendship: in animals, 102; Aristotle's analysis of, 45, 96–105; with coupled lesbians, 84–85; history, 101; with noncoupled lesbians,

84; public requirement, 96; Raymond's study of, 88–96; sharing, 102; virtues of, 99, 103–4; *see also* Lesbian friendship

Frith, Mary, 26

Frye, Marilyn, 20, 23, 31, 39, 92, 227; on arrogance, 155; attending, 103; ethics and politics, 58, 65–67, 70–72; "Getting It Right," 66; separatism, 94–95; "Some Thoughts on Separatism and Power," 72

Fuller, Margaret, 27, 59–61; "The Great Lawsuit," 60; *Woman in the Nineteenth Century*, 60–61

Fuss, Diana, 17

Gautier, Théophile, *Mademoiselle de Maupin*, 27

Gay, as sexual term, 15, 21, 23

Gay-bashing, 207; shooting of Brenner and Wight, 119, 164, 206

Gay communities, 209–10, 214, 216–17

Gay ethics, 76

Gay men, battering, 105; *see also* Military services; Outing

Genealogy, Nietzsche's concept of, 31–32

Giallombardo, Rose, 86

Gilligan, Carol, 76–78

Gilman, Charlotte Perkins, 59, 105; *Herland*, 63; *Women and Economics*, 62; "The Yellow Wallpaper," 62

Goldman, Emma, 59, 63–64; "The Tragedy of Women's Emancipation," 64

Goodness, 68; utilitarian and nonutilitarian conceptions of, 69–70

Gordon, Dame Helen Cumming, 27

Grahn, Judy, 16, 23, 72

Greene, Annette, 106–7, 164

Grier, Barbara, 212

Griffin, Susan, 72

Gross, Larry, 195

Gunderode, Karoline von, 27, 61

Gwinn, Mary, 33

Gyn/affection, Raymond's notion of, 88–96

Habits, Hart's notion of, 14

Hacking, Ian, 143

Hall, Radclyffe, *The Well of Loneliness*, 28, 202

Harlem Renaissance, 28

Harris, Jenny Walters, 141

Hart, Barbara, 111–12, 114, 118

Hart, H. L. A., 14, 28; *The Concept of Law*, 14

Hatred, 151, 154, 157, 161–62; *see also* Homophobia; Self-hatred

Hatter, Terry, 169

Hedges, Elaine, 62

Heffernan, Esther, 85

Hegel, Georg Wilhelm Friedrich, 38–39

Hellman, Lillian, *The Children's Hour*, 27

Heteroreality, Raymond's concept of, 94

Heterosexuality: abuse of women by men, 185; attitudinal aspects, 37; battery, 110; choice, 38, 41; compulsoriness, 40–41, 56; de Beauvoir's understanding of, 38–41; subordination of women, 49

Hickok, Lorena, 202–3

Higher order desires, 223–24

Hirshfeld, Magnus, 63

Hoagland, Sarah, 21–23, 65–66, 133; attending, 103, 125–26; control, 126–27; domination, 124; ethics, 197; lesbian ethics, 71–73, 77, 92, 123–25; *Lesbian Ethics: Toward New Value*, 65–66,

Hoagland, Sarah (*continued*)
71–72, 123–24, 126, 128, 133;
lesbian friendship, 83; and Penelope, *For Lesbians Only: A Separatist Anthology*, 72; oppression,
128; revolutionary ethics, 67;
sadomasochism, 146, 236; separatism, 94; "world"-travel, 95
Holism, 73, 153, 183
Holocaust, the, 69, 144
Homophobia, 75, 151–54, 156–63;
emotional echoing, 165–68;
institutionalized, 180–81, 183,
185; overcoming, 153–65
Homosexuality: as attitude, 44; de
Beauvoir's understanding of,
36–46; as identity, 18; inherited
vs. acquired, 37; options, absence
of, 49; origins and causes, 17
Homosexual rights, 59; Goldman's
defense of, 63–64
Hoover, J. Edgar, 184
Horizontal abuse, hostility, violence,
106–30; deference to, 185;
defined, 107–8; and lesbian ethics,
122–23; reluctance to acknowledge, 157, 161; sadomasochism as
example of, 220–21; *see also* Partner battering; Stalking
Hostility, 126–28; antilesbian,
155–56; in classroom, 142; and
partner battering, 112, 117; *see
also* Hatred; Homophobia
Humphrey, Mary Ann, 174,
176–78, 180
Hwame (Mohave Indian), 16
Hynes, H. Patricia, 72

Identity: dignity and, 198; hatred
and, 162; *see also* Sexual identity
Illocutionary acts, Austin's notion
of, 211
Incest, 132, 134; *see also* Female
incest

Indian Catholics, New Mexico, 199
Institutions: and friendship, 87–91,
95, 97, 101–2; interactions with,
55–56; options and, 54–55; sexual identities, 19, 31
Internal aspects of rules, Hart's
notion of, 14
Internalized homophobia, 153,
157–58, 160, 165; emotional
echoing, 166
Island, David (and Letellier), *Men
Who Beat the Men Who Love
Them*, 107

Jackson, Bessie, 28
Jacobs, Harriet, 70
James, Alice, 33
James, William, 53
Janet, Pierre, 183
Jay, Karla, 12
Justice, 100, 146; and dignity, 197;
ethics, 76–77
Justin, 24

Kant, Immanuel, 197
Kanter, Emmanuel, 25
Karols, Ken (and Sarbin), "Noncon-
forming Sexual Orientations and
Military Suitability," 187–88
Katz, Jonathan, 63
Kaye/Kantrowitz, Melanie, 108,
110; *My Jewish Face and Other
Stories*, 129; "War Stories, 197_,"
129–30
Kennedy, Elizabeth Lapovsky (and
Davis), *Boots of Leather, Slippers of
Gold: The History of a Lesbian
Community*, 12
Kinship structure, friendship and,
85–87
Kitzinger, Celia, 157–58, 165; *The
Social Construction of Lesbianism*,
157
Kleinbaum, Abby, 25

Kowalski, Sharon, 209, 217
Krafft-Ebing, Richard von, 28, 222

Labé, Louise, 26, 33
Labeling: the dead, 201; Schur's theory of, 54
Labrys, 5
Ladies of Llangollen, 27, 30, 33, 93
Land grant institutions, 171
LC newsletter, *see Lesbian Connection* newsletter
Lerner, Gerda, 191
Lesbian, meaning and use of term, 16, 21–23, 48, 211
Lesbian and Gay Philosophy, Society for, 76, 208
Lesbian communities, 87, 92–93; attraction of, 156; coming out in, 209–10, 214; formal relationships within, 96; friendship, 105; internalized homophobia, 157; and lesbian pride, 165; and outing, 216–17; "world"-travel within, 95
Lesbian Connection (LC) newsletter, 11, 83–84
Lesbian continuum, 29–30, 46, 156
Lesbian culture, 11–35; cultures of resistance, 15–16; detection, 14–15, 201–2; developments, 12–13; ethical problem, 16–17; ethnicity and diversity, 16–23; family resemblance metaphor, 31–32; genealogy, 28–34; logical problem, 16–17; teaching, 14, 23–28
Lesbian ethics, 71–79; horizontal violence, 122–29; institutions and, 89; outing, 196–98, 203–17; skepticism regarding, 65–71; sadomasochism, 225, 235; separatism, 92; *see also* Feminist ethics
Lesbian Ethics (journal), 145

Lesbian-Feminist Study Clearinghouse (LFSC), 12
Lesbian friendship, 83–88; Aristotelian analysis, 96–105; lover relationships and, 98, 103–5; with nonlesbians, 84; nonsexual, 85; sexuality and, 89
Lesbian Herstory Archives (LHA), 11
Lesbian identity, 28, 32, 34
Lesbianism: choice of, 41, 47–57, 192; de Beauvoir's understanding of, 36–46; freedom, 40–41; option, 41, 49–51; as rebellion, 56
Lesbian organizations, 11–12
Lesbian peoples, Wittig's proto-dictionary on, 21, 23
Lesbian pride, 154–56, 161, 168; survival as source of, 164
Lesbian studies programs, 13–15, 23–28, 201–2
Letellier, Patrick (and Island), *Men Who Beat the Men Who Love Them*, 107
LHA (Lesbian Herstory Archives), 11
Lifton, Robert, 181–84
Likens, Sylvia, 140
Lobel, Kerry, 107; *Naming the Violence: Speaking Out About Lesbian Battering*, 107–9, 117
Logical positivists, emotive theory of, 153
Lorde, Audre, 16, 72, 226, 236
Loring, Katherine, 33
Love, privacy of, 96
Lowell, Amy, 27
Lower order desires, 223
LSFC (Lesbian-Feminist Study Clearinghouse), 12
Lugones, María, 72, 83, 95, 155, 184
Luther, Martha, 62
Lynd, Helen Merrell, 159–60; *On Shame and the Search for Identity*, 159

Mabbott, J. D., 113
McConnell, Joyce, 114
McNaron, Toni, 72
Mädchen in Uniform (film), 15, 142
Mahmoody, Betty, 55
Maiden Rock Collective, 12;
    Women's Learning Institute, 72
Malcolm X, 94
Malleus Maleficarum, 138
Manahan, Nancy (and Curb), *Lesbian Nuns: Breaking Silence*, 212
Marks, Miss, 33
Marriage, 54–56, 59–60; as coverup, 180, 205; Fuller's idea of, 61; Goldman's opposition to, 64; and worldlessness, 91
Marriage resisters, Chinese, 90, 98
Masochism, 47, 49, 219–20, 222–24; *see also* Sadomasochism
Matlovich, Leonard, 178, 181
Maupin, Mlle de, 27
Mayer, Robert, 141
Mead, George Herbert, 53
Medusa, 32
Meinhold, Keith, 169
Memories, recovered, *see* Recovered memories
Michigan Music Festival, 11
Middleton, Thomas (and Dekker), *The Roaring Girl*, 26
Midwest Society of Women in Philosophy (SWIP), 5, 72
Midwife, 125
Military service, 90, 169–70, 174–78; closeting, 180–81, 183–84; countries permitting lesbians and gay men to serve, 174; deception, 180–81; discharge of lesbians and gay men, 174, 178; educational effort, in Netherlands, 186; feminists' concern with exclusionary policy, 189–93; lesbian and gay officers, 177–78, 181, 183–84, 193;

morale, and lesbians and gay men, 184–88; noncooperation with lesbians and gay men, 185–86; outing, 204; performance records of lesbians and gay men, 187–88; ROTC program, 170–74; security risk of homosexuals, 187–88; sexual harassment and rape, fear of, 185; stalking, 119
Mill, John Stuart, 61, 197; *On Liberty*, 207
Miller, Alice, 108
Miller, Timothy, 183
Millett, Kate, 140; *The Basement*, 140
Misogyny, 47, 49, 53, 75, 215
Mohr, Richard, 18, 54, 195–96, 198–99, 203, 205–6, 213–14
Moll Cutpurse, 26
Monogamy, 60; and friendships, 87; Goldman's opposition to, 64; nonmonogamy, 78
Morality, 67–69; *see also* Ethics; Feminist ethics; Lesbian ethics
Mother-daughter incest, 134–37, 142, 144–46
Multiple personalities, 137–39, 143–44, 183
Murray, Margaret, 144

National Gay and Lesbian Task Force, 188
National Institutes of Justice, 118
National Lesbian Feminist Organization, 12
Native Americans 15, 16
Nazism, 49, 69, 124, 162; Lifton's study of Nazi doctors, 181–84
Nestle, Joan, 72
Netherlands, homosexuals in the military, 186
Nietzsche, Friedrich, 31–32, 215, 224; *On the Genealogy of Morals*, 32; morality, 58, 68–70

Noddings, Nel, 76–78
Nuns, 212; *see also* Convents

On, Bat-Ami Bar, 72, 229
Operation Desert Storm, 175
Oppression, 69–70, 128, 163–64;
    homophobia as response to, 153;
    passing and, 198–99, 208; power
    and, 227
Outing, 194–98, 209–13; alternatives
    to, 208; coming out vs., 204–9;
    the dead, 200–203; degrees of,
    210; necessary cases of, 209; risks
    of, 206, 211; trust and, 213–17;
    uptake and source, 203–4
Outline, 194
Outweek, 194

Parker, Pat, 72
Partner battering, 106–17; homo-
    phobia, 160–61; internalized
    homophobia, 157; lesbian ethics,
    122–29
Passing, 14–15, 155, 195–200, 205,
    208–10; indignity of, 217; protec-
    tion of, 213–15; *see also* Closeting
Passionate friendship, 29, 31, 33,
    46, 88; lesbian ethics, 75–76,
    78–79
Patriarchy, 49, 52–53; bonding
    among men, 215; homophobia,
    157–58; lesbian options in, 56
Pausanias, 24
Penelope, Julia, 12, 23; and
    Hoagland, *For Lesbians Only: A
    Separatist Anthology*, 72–73
PERESEC reports, 187
Persian Gulf War, 175
Pharr, Suzanne, 157–58, 162–63,
    165; *Homophobia: A Weapon of
    Sexism*, 157
Phelps, Johnny, 175
Philadelphia Working Group on
    Lesbian Battering, 107

Philia, Aristotle's discussion of, 97
Phobias, 158–60; echoing, 166; *see
    also* Homophobia
Photography, nude, of children,
    135
Physical disabilities, and exclusion
    from military service, 192
Piper, Adrian, 208
Pirie, Jane, 27
Plato, 125; *Symposium*, 18
Political correctness, 66, 70, 72–73
Politics: conflict and antilesbian hos-
    tility, 165; dissociation from the
    world, 92; ethics and, 65–71;
    Frye's view of, 66–67; outing
    and coming out, goals of, 205
Ponsonby, Lady Sarah, 27
Pornography, 79, 145, 161, 226
Poussaint, Alvin, "Why Blacks Kill
    Blacks," 129
Powell, Gloria, 140
Power: as energy vs. control,
    226–27; experience of, in partner
    battering, 116–17; lack of, as
    source of fear, 164; sado-
    masochism and, 226–29, 236–37
Pratt, Minnie Bruce, 70–71
Predator model of partner battering,
    117
Pride: Aristotle's description of
    proud man, 206; control as
    source of, 127; *see also* Lesbian
    pride
Prisons, 3, 6; women prisoners, 85,
    86; *see also* Familying
Privacy: and friendships, 87, 104; of
    love, 96; and outing, 196–97,
    205, 207–8, 212; separatist com-
    munities, 94
Pruitt, Dusty, 186–87
Public aspect of friendship, 87, 96;
    separatist communities, 94
Punishment: of children, 135; theo-
    ries of, 2–4, 6; threat of, 113

Queer ethics, 76

Racism, 178, 199, 208, 215, 217
Rainey, Ma, 28, 30
Rawls, John, 54, 87, 100
Raymond, Janice, 29, 72, 94; female friendship, analysis of, 88–96, 98, 104; *A Passion for Friends: Toward a Philosophy of Female Friendship*, 88, 90
Reade, Mary, 26
Recovered memories, 137, 139, 141, 143
Reik, Theodor, 146
Renzetti, Claire, 107, 116; *Violent Betrayal: Partner Abuse in Lesbian Relationships*, 107–9
Reserve Officers Training Corps (ROTC), 170–74, 177, 186, 189; closeting, 178–80, 184; feminist concern with exclusionary policy, 189–93
Respect, 96; *see also* Self-respect
Revolving closet, 209
Rich, Adrienne, 20, 29, 40, 46, 56, 72, 102; matrophobia, 161; *Of Woman Born: Motherhood as Experience and Institution*, 20; "Women and Honor: Some Notes on Lying," 72
Ritual cult abuse, *see* Cult ritual abuse
Robson, Ruthann, 107, 111
Romantic friendship, 29; *see also* Passionate friendship
Roosevelt, Eleanor, 202
ROTC, *see* Reserve Officers Training Corps
Rothery, Guy, 25
Ruddick, Sara, *Maternal Thinking: Toward a Politics of Peace*, 65, 78
Rules, Hart's notion of, 14
Russ, Joanna, 72
Russell, Ada, 27

Ruth and Naomi, biblical story of, 26, 29–30, 33, 78
Sacher-Masoch, Leopold von, *Venus in Furs*, 222
Sackville-West, Vita, 64–65
Sadism, 219–20, 222, 225–30; *see also* Sadomasochism
Sadomasochism, 79, 109–10, 135, 145–46, 218–22; social consequences, 231–35; *see also* Masochism; Sadism
Safety: in lesbian community, 123–24; in sadomasochism, 228–30
Sambo personality, 124, 199
Samois, 220–21, 226
Sanday, Peggy, 143
Sapphic ethics, 75, 78–79
Sapphic lesbians, 21–22, 31, 33, 46
Sappho of Lesbos, 15–16, 22, 24, 29–30
Sarbin, Ted (and Karols), "Nonconforming Sexual Orientations and Military Suitability," 187–88
Sartre, Jean-Paul, 39
Satanic cults, 137, 139–40
Saxe, Lorena, 145, 225
Schaeffer, Rebecca, 119
Scheler, Max, 165, 167; *The Nature of Sympathy*, 165
Schindler, Allen, 169, 183
Schroeder, Patricia, 169, 188
Schur, Edwin M., 53–54
Sedgwick, Eve, 34
Segregation, *see* Separatism
Self-deceit, 52
Self-defense, 110–12, 190
Self-hatred, 157, 160–61; homophobia as, 154
Self-love, 53
Self-respect, 199; hiding and, 207
Separatism, 44, 46, 71, 92–94; distinguished from segregation, 94;

formal relationships, 95–96; friendships, 92; response to homophobia, 168; Virginia Woolf, 64; "world"-travel, 95

Sexual abuse, 109; *see also* Abuse; Battering; Childhood abuse; Female incest; Stalking

Sexual identity, 17–20; *see also* Lesbian identity

Sexual orientation: as attitude, 42–43; choice in, 41–42, 48–57; responsibility for, 36–37, 43; voluntarism, 47

Shalala, Donna, 170

Shame, 154, 156, 159–65; hiding and, 207

Shilts, Randy, 119, 174

Signorile, Michelangelo, 194–96, 205, 209

Sisterhood, feminist ideal of, 86

Slang, 23

Slavery, 69–70, 124

Smith, Michelle, 141–43

Smyth, Dame Ethel, 27, 65

Social construction, 17–20, 22; and choice, 53–54; interconnected families of lesbians, 31; multiple personality, 143; sadomasochistic desires, 221; world, the, 91

Socrates, 32, 125–26

Spelman, Vicky, 83

Sperry, Almeda, 63

Stalking, 117–22, 128–30, 144

Stein, Edward, 19

Stein, Gertrude, 15, 27, 44; "Miss Furr and Miss Skeene," 15

Stephenson, Terry Wayne, 183

Stoltenberg, John, 229

Strabo, 24–25

Streaking, 195, 203

Studds, Gerry, 187–88, 209–10

Student-teacher relations, 142, 145; stalking, 120–22

Subordination, 124; in sado-masochism, 221; women in patriarchial society, 49

Suicide, 183, 214; in lesbian pulp novels, 142

Supreme Court, U.S., 187

Survivor, 137, 164

SWIP (Midwest Society of Women in Philosophy), 5, 72

Sybil (multiple personality), 137, 142

Szasz, Thomas, 18

Tailhook Association convention, 185

Tarn, Pauline, *see* Vivien, Renée

Teacher-student relations, *see* Student-teacher relations

Telfer, Elizabeth, 43; sharing, 102

Theseus, 24

Third ear, Reik's metaphor of, 146

Thomas, Ardel, 145

Thomas, M. Carey, 33

Thompson, Karen, 209

Thorne, Tracy, 178, 181

Threats: in battering and in punishing, 113; as mere assaults, 115

T'ien, Ju-K'ang, 86

Till Eulenspiegel Society, 220

Toklas, Alice, 44

Trebilcot, Joyce, 23, 72, 74

True friendship (friendship of excellence), 97–99, 103, 105

Uranianism, 63

Utilitarian goodness, 69

Veterans' Preference Act, 192

Vietnam War, 175

Violence, 75, 78, 115–16, 130, 191; and lesbian ethics, 122–29; *see also* Partner battering; Sadomasochism

Vivien, Renée, 27, 59; *A Woman Appeared to Me*, 59

Voluntarism, 17, 42–43, 47

Voyeurism, 135–36

Walker, Alice, 22, 90
Walker, Lenore, 114, 116
Warfare, 191; *see also* Military service
Washington, Booker T., 199
Watkins, Perry, 175, 177, 181
Weil, Simone, 103
What Color Is Your Handkerchief? (pamphlet), 220
Wight, Rebecca, 119, 164, 206
Williams, Pete, 195
Windows (film), 117
Winkte (Oglala Sioux), 16
Wisconsin, University of, 189; ROTC program, 170–74
Witches, 18–19, 138, 144
Withdrawal, 92, 123, 126, 129; partner battering, 111–12
Wittgenstein, Ludwig, 30–31, 45–46, 75, 97; *Philosophical Investigations*, 30

Wittig, Monique, 21–23, 39
Wollstonecraft, Mary, 59–60; *Vindication of the Rights of Woman*, 60
Woman, derived from *wifman*, 21
Womanist, 21–22
Women's ethics, 76–78
Woods, Marianne, 27
Woolf, Virginia, 59, 91, 159; *Orlando: A Biography*, 64–65; *A Room of One's Own*, 65; *Three Guineas*, 64–65
Woolley, Miss, 33
Worldlessness, 90–92
Worldliness, 91–92, 94
"World"-travel, Lugones' notion of, 95, 155
World War II, 171, 174–75, 191
Wyatt, Gail, 140

Zita, Jacqueline, 72
Zuniga, Joe, 187